COMMODORE 64 PROGRAMMER'S REFERENCE GUIDE

AF722861

Published by
Commodore Business Machines, Inc.
and
Howard W. Sams & Co., Inc.

FIRST EDITION
THIRD PRINTING—1983

Copyright © 1982 by Commodore Business Machines, Inc.
All rights reserved.

This manual is copyrighted and contains proprietary information. No part of this publication may be reproduced, stored in a retrieval system, or transmitted in any form or by any means, electronic, mechanical, photocopying, recording, or otherwise, without the prior written permission of COMMODORE BUSINESS MACHINES, Inc.

TABLE OF CONTENTS

3. PROGRAMMING GRAPHICS ON THE COMMODORE 64 99

INTRODUCTION

The **COMMODORE 64 PROGRAMMER'S REFERENCE GUIDE** has been developed as a working tool and reference source for those of you who want to maximize your use of the built-in capabilities of your **COMMODORE 64**. This manual contains the information you need for your programs, from the simplest example all the way to the most complex. The **PROGRAMMER'S REFERENCE GUIDE** is designed so that everyone from the beginning BASIC programmer to the professional experienced in 6502 machine language can get information to develop his or her own creative programs. At the same time this book shows you how clever your **COMMODORE 64** really is.

This **REFERENCE GUIDE** is not designed to teach the BASIC programming language or the 6502 machine language. There is, however, an extensive glossary of terms and a "semi-tutorial" approach to many of the sections in the book. If you don't already have a working knowledge of BASIC and how to use it to program, we suggest that you study the **COMMODORE 64 USER'S GUIDE** that came with your computer. The **USER'S GUIDE** gives you an easy to read introduction to the BASIC programming language. If you still have difficulty understanding how to use BASIC then turn to the back of this book (or Appendix N in the **USER'S GUIDE**) and check out the Bibliography.

The **COMMODORE 64 PROGRAMMER'S REFERENCE GUIDE** is just that; a reference. Like most reference books, your ability to apply the information creatively really depends on how much knowledge you have about the subject. In other words if you are a novice programmer you will not be able to use all the facts and figures in this book until you expand your current programming knowledge.

What you can do with this book is to find a considerable amount of valuable programming reference information written in easy to read, plain English with the programmer's jargon explained. On the other hand the programming professional will find all the information needed to use the capabilities of the **COMMODORE 64** effectively.

WHAT'S INCLUDED?

- Our complete "BASIC dictionary" includes Commodore BASIC language commands, statements and functions listed in alphabetical order. We've created a "quick list" which contains all the words and their abbreviations. This is followed by a section containing a more detailed definition of each word along with sample BASIC programs to illustrate how they work.
- If you need an introduction to using machine language with BASIC programs our layman's overview will get you started.
- A powerful feature of all Commodore computers is called the KERNAL. It helps insure that the programs you write today can also be used on your Commodore computer of tomorrow.
- The Input/Output Programming section gives you the opportunity to use your computer to the limit. It describes how to hook-up and use everything from lightpens and joysticks to disk drives, printers, and telecommunication devices called *modems*.
- You can explore the world of **SPRITES**, programmable characters, and high resolution graphics for the most detailed and advanced animated pictures in the microcomputer industry.
- You can also enter the world of music synthesis and create your own songs and sound effects with the best built-in synthesizer available in any personal computer.
- If you're an experienced programmer, the soft load language section gives you information about the **COMMODORE 64's** ability to run CP/M* and high level languages. This is in addition to BASIC.

Think of your **COMMODORE 64 PROGRAMMER'S REFERENCE GUIDE** as a useful tool to help you and you will enjoy the hours of programming ahead of you.

*CP/M is a registered trademark of Digital Research, Inc.

HOW TO USE THIS REFERENCE GUIDE

Throughout this manual certain conventional notations are used to describe the syntax (programming sentence structure) of BASIC commands or statements and to show both the required and optional parts of each BASIC keyword. The rules to use for interpreting statement syntax are as follows:

1. BASIC keywords are shown in capital letters. They must appear where shown in the statement, entered and spelled exactly as shown.
2. Items shown within quotation marks (" ") indicate variable data which you must put in. Both the quotation marks and the data inside the quotes must appear where shown in each statement.
3. Items inside the square brackets ([ ]) indicate an optional statement parameter. A parameter is a limitation or additional qualifier for your statements. If you use an optional parameter you must supply the data for that optional parameter. In addition, ellipses (. . .) show that an optional item can be repeated as many times as a programming line allows.
4. If an item in the square brackets ([ ]) is UNDERLINED, that means that you MUST use those certain characters in the optional parameters, and they also have to be spelled exactly as shown.
5. Items inside angle brackets (<>) indicate variable data which you provide. While the slash (/) indicates that you must make a choice between two mutually exclusive options.

EXAMPLE OF SYNTAX FORMAT:

OPEN<file-num>,<device> [,<address>], ["<drive>: <file-name>] [,<mode>]"

EXAMPLES OF ACTUAL STATEMENTS:

```
10 OPEN 2,8,6,"0:STOCK FOLIO,S,W"
20 OPEN 1,1,2,"CHECKBOOK"
30 OPEN 3,4
```

When you actually apply the syntax conventions in a practical situation, the sequence of parameters in your statements might not be exactly the same as the sequence shown in syntax examples. The examples are not meant to show every possible sequence. They are intended to present all required and optional parameters.

Programming examples in this book are shown with blanks separating words and operators for the sake of readability. Normally though, BASIC doesn't require blanks between words unless leaving them out would give you an ambiguous or incorrect syntax.

Shown below are some examples and descriptions of the symbols used for various statement parameters in the following chapters. The list is not meant to show every possibility, but to give you a better understanding as to how syntax examples are presented.

SYMBOL	EXAMPLE	DESCRIPTION
<file-num>	50	A logical file number
<device>	4	A hardware device number
<address>	15	A serial bus secondary device address number
<drive>	0	A physical disk drive number
<file-name>	"TEST.DATA"	The name of a data or program file
<constant>	"ABCDEFG"	Literal data supplied by the programmer
<variable>	X145	Any BASIC data variable name or constant
<string>	AB$	Use of a string type variable required
<number>	12345	Use of a numeric type variable required
<line-number>	1000	An actual program line number
<numeric>	1.5E4	An integer or floating-point variable

COMMODORE 64 APPLICATIONS GUIDE

When you first thought about buying a computer you probably asked yourself, "Now that I can afford to buy a computer, what can I do with it once I get one?"

The great thing about your **COMMODORE 64** is that you can make it do what YOU want it to do! You can make it calculate and keep track of home and business budget needs. You can use it for word processing. You can make it play arcade-style action games. You can make it sing. You can even create your own animated cartoons, and more. The best part of owning a **COMMODORE 64** is that even if it did only one of the things listed below it would be well worth the price you paid for it. But the **64** is a complete computer and it does do EVERYTHING listed and then some!

By the way, in addition to everything here you can pick up a lot of other creative and practical ideas by signing up with a local Commodore Users' Club, subscribing to the **COMMODORE** and **POWER/PLAY** magazines, and joining the **COMMODORE INFORMATION NETWORK** on CompuServe™ .

APPLICATION	COMMENTS/REQUIREMENTS
ACTION PACKED GAMES	You can get real Bally Midway arcade games like Omega Race, Gorf and Wizard of Wor, as well as "play and learn" games like Math Teacher I, Home Babysitter and Commodore Artist.
ADVERTISING & MERCHANDISING	Hook your **COMMODORE 64** to a TV, put it in a store window with a flashing, animated, and musical message and you've got a great point of purchase store display.
ANIMATION	Commodore's Sprite Graphics allow you to create real cartoons with 8 different levels so that shapes can move in front of or behind each other.
BABYSITTING	The **COMMODORE 64** HOME BABYSITTER cartridge can keep your youngest child occupied for hours and teach alphabet/ keyboard recognition at the same time. It also teaches special learning concepts and relationships.
BASIC PROGRAMMING	Your **COMMODORE 64 USER'S GUIDE** and the TEACH YOURSELF PROGRAMMING series of books and tapes offer an excellent starting point.
BUSINESS SPREADSHEET	The **COMMODORE 64** offers the "Easy" series of business aids including the most powerful word processor and largest spreadsheet available for any personal computer.
COMMUNICATION	Enter the fascinating world of computer "networking." If you hook a VICMODEM to your **COMMODORE 64** you can communicate with other computer owners all around the world.

Not only that, if you join the **COMMODORE INFORMATION NETWORK** on CompuServe™ you can get the latest news and updates on all Commodore products, financial information, shop at home services, you can even play games with the friends you make through the information systems you join.

COMPOSING SONGS

The **COMMODORE 64** is equipped with the most sophisticated built-in music synthesizer available on any computer. It has three completely programmable voices, nine full music octaves, and four controllable waveforms. Look for Commodore Music Cartridges and Commodore Music books to help you create or reproduce all kinds of music and sound effects.

CP/M*

Commodore offers a CP/M* add-on and access to software through an easy-to-load cartridge.

DEXTERITY TRAINING

Hand/Eye coordination and manual dexterity are aided by several Commodore games . . . including "Jupiter Lander" and night driving simulation.

EDUCATION

While working with a computer is an education in itself, The COMMODORE Educational Resource Book contains general information on the educational uses of computers. We also have a variety of learning cartridges designed to teach everything from music to math and art to astronomy.

FOREIGN LANGUAGE

The **COMMODORE 64** programmable character set lets you replace the standard character set with user defined foreign language characters.

GRAPHICS AND ART

In addition to the Sprite Graphics mentioned above, the **COMMODORE 64** offers high-resolution, multi-color graphics plotting, pro-

*CP/M is a Registered trademark of Digital Research, Inc.

grammable characters, and combinations of all the different graphics and character display modes.

INSTRUMENT CONTROL

Your **COMMODORE 64** has a serial port, RS-232 port and a user port for use with a variety of special industrial applications. An IEEE/488 cartridge is also available as an optional extra.

JOURNALS AND CREATIVE WRITING

The **COMMODORE 64** will soon offer an exceptional wordprocessing system that matches or exceeds the qualities and flexibilities of most "high-priced" wordprocessors available. Of course you can save the information on either a 1541 Disk Drive or a Datassette™ recorder and have it printed out using a VIC-PRINTER or PLOTTER.

LIGHTPEN CONTROL

Applications requiring the use of a lightpen can be performed by any lightpen that will fit the **COMMODORE 64** game port connector.

MACHINE CODE PROGRAMMING

Your **COMMODORE 64 PROGRAMMER'S REFERENCE GUIDE** includes a machine language section, as well as a BASIC to machine code interface section. There's even a bibliography available for more in-depth study.

PAYROLL & FORMS PRINTOUT

The **COMMODORE 64** can be programmed to handle a variety of entry-type business applications. Upper/lower case letters combined with **C64** "business form" graphics make it easy for you to design forms which can then be printed on your printer.

PRINTING

The **COMMODORE 64** interfaces with a variety of dot matrix and letter quality printers as well as plotters.

RECIPES

You can store your favorite recipes on your **COMMODORE 64** and its disk or cassette storage unit, and end the need for messy recipe cards that often get lost when you need them most.

SIMULATIONS — Computer simulations let you conduct dangerous or expensive experiments at minimum risk and cost.

SPORTS DATA — The Source™ and CompuServe™ both offer sports information which you can get using your **COMMODORE 64** and a VICMODEM.

STOCK QUOTES — With a VICMODEM and a subscription to any of the appropriate network services, your **COMMODORE 64** becomes your own private stock ticker.

These are just a few of the many applications for you and your **COMMODORE 64**. As you can see, for work or play, at home, in school or the office, your **COMMODORE 64** gives you a practical solution for just about any need.

Commodore wants you to know that our support for users only **STARTS** with your purchase of a Commodore computer. That's why we've created two publications with Commodore information from around the world, and a "two-way" computer information network with valuable input for users in the U.S. and Canada from coast to coast.

In addition, we wholeheartedly encourage and support the growth of Commodore Users' Clubs around the world. They are an excellent source of information for every Commodore computer owner from the beginner to the most advanced. The magazines and network, which are more fully described below, have the most up-to-date information about how to get involved with the Users' Club in your area.

Finally, your local Commodore dealer is a useful source of Commodore support and information.

POWER/PLAY
The Home Computer Magazine

When it comes to entertainment, learning at home and practical home applications, **POWER/PLAY** is THE prime source of information for Commodore home users. Find out where your nearest user clubs are and what they're doing, learn about software, games, programming techniques, telecommunications, and new products. **POWER/PLAY** is your personal connection to other Commodore users, outside software and hardware developers, and to Commodore itself. Published quarterly. Only $10.00 for a year of home computing excitement.

COMMODORE
The Microcomputer Magazine

Widely read by educators, businessmen and students, as well as home computerists, **COMMODORE Magazine** is our main vehicle for sharing exclusive information on the more technical use of Commodore systems. Regular departments cover business, science and education, programming tips, "excerpts from a technical notebook," and many other features of interest to anyone who uses or is thinking about purchasing Commodore equipment for business, scientific or educational applications. **COMMODORE** is the ideal complement to **POWER/ PLAY**. Published bi-monthly. Subscription price: $15.00 per year.

AND FOR EVEN MORE INFORMATION . . .
. . . DIAL UP OUR PAPERLESS USER MAGAZINE

COMMODORE INFORMATION NETWORK

The magazine of the future is here. To supplement and enhance your subscription to **POWER/PLAY** and **COMMODORE** magazines, the **COMMODORE INFORMATION NETWORK**—our "paperless magazine"—is available now over the telephone using your Commodore computer and modem.

Join our computer club, get help with a computing problem, "talk" to other Commodore friends, or get up-to-the-minute information on new products, software and educational resources. Soon you will even be able to save yourself the trouble of typing in the program listings you find in **POWER/PLAY** or **COMMODORE** by downloading direct from the Information Network (a new user service planned for early 1983). The best part is that most of the answers are there before you even ask the questions. (How's that for service?)

To call our electronic magazine you need only a modem and a subscription to CompuServe™, one of the nation's largest telecommunications networks. (To make it easy for you Commodore includes a FREE year's subscription to CompuServe™ in each VICMODEM package.)

Just dial your local number for the CompuServe™ data bank and connect your phone to the modem. When the CompuServe™ video text appears on your screen type G CBM on your computer keyboard. When the **COMMODORE INFORMATION NETWORK'S** table of contents, or "menu," appears on your screen choose from one of our sixteen departments, make yourself comfortable, and enjoy the paperless magazine other magazines are writing about.

For more information, visit your Commodore dealer or contact CompuServe™ customer service at 800-848-8990 (in Ohio, 614-457-8600).

COMMODORE INFORMATION NETWORK

Main Menu Description	Commodore Dealers
Direct Access Codes	Educational Resources
Special Commands	User Groups
User Questions	Descriptions
Public Bulletin Board	Questions and Answers
Magazines and Newsletters	Software Tips
Products Announced	Technical Tips
Commodore News Direct	Directory Descriptions

CHAPTER 1

BASIC PROGRAMMING RULES

- Introduction
- Screen Display Codes (BASIC Character Set)
- Programming Numbers and Variables
- Expressions and Operators
- Programming Techniques

INTRODUCTION

This chapter talks about how BASIC stores and manipulates data. The topics include:

1) A brief mention of the operating system components and functions as well as the character set used in the Commodore 64.
2) The formation of constants and variables. What types of variables there are. And how constants and variables are stored in memory.
3) The rules for arithmetic calculations, relationship tests, string handling, and logical operations. Also included are the rules for forming expressions, and the data conversions necessary when you're using BASIC with mixed data types.

SCREEN DISPLAY CODES (BASIC CHARACTER SET)

THE OPERATING SYSTEM (OS)

The Operating System is contained in the Read Only Memory (ROM) chips and is a combination of three separate, but interrelated, program modules.

1) The BASIC Interpreter
2) The KERNAL
3) The Screen Editor

1) The BASIC Interpreter is responsible for analyzing BASIC statement syntax and for performing the required calculations and/or data manipulation. The BASIC Interpreter has a vocabulary of 65 "keywords" which have special meanings. The upper and lower case alphabet and the digits 0–9 are used to make both keywords and variable names. Certain punctuation characters and special symbols also have meanings for the Interpreter. Table 1-1 lists the special characters and their uses.

2) The KERNAL handles most of the interrupt level processing in the system (for details on interrupt level processing, see Chapter 5). The KERNAL also does the actual input and output of data.

3) The Screen Editor controls the output to the video screen (television set) and the editing of BASIC program text. In addition, the Screen Editor intercepts keyboard input so that it can decide whether the

Table 1-1. CBM BASIC Character Set

CHARACTER	NAME and DESCRIPTION
	BLANK—separates keywords and variable names
;	SEMI-COLON—used in variable lists to format output
=	EQUAL SIGN—value assignment and relationship testing
+	PLUS SIGN—arithmetic addition or string concatenation (*concatenation:* linking together in a chain)
–	MINUS SIGN—arithmetic subtraction, unary minus (–1)
*	ASTERISK—arithmetic multiplication
/	SLASH—arithmetic division
↑	UP ARROW—arithmetic exponentiation
(	LEFT PARENTHESIS—expression evaluation and functions
)	RIGHT PARENTHESIS—expression evaluation and functions
%	PERCENT—declares variable name as an integer
#	NUMBER—comes before logical file number in input/output statements
$	DOLLAR SIGN—declares variable name as a string
,	COMMA—used in variable lists to format output; also separates command parameters
.	PERIOD—decimal point in floating point constants
"	QUOTATION MARK—encloses string constants
:	COLON—separates multiple BASIC statements in a line
?	QUESTION MARK—abbreviation for the keyword PRINT
<	LESS THAN—used in relationship tests
>	GREATER THAN—used in relationship tests
π	PI—the numeric constant 3.141592654

characters put in should be acted upon immediately, or passed on to the BASIC Interpreter.

The Operating System gives you two modes of BASIC operation:

1) DIRECT Mode
2) PROGRAM Mode

1) When you're using the DIRECT mode, BASIC statements don't have line numbers in front of the statement. They are executed whenever the RETURN key is pressed.
2) The PROGRAM mode is the one you use for running programs.

When using the PROGRAM mode, all of your BASIC statements must have line numbers in front of them. You can have more than one BASIC statement in a line of your program, but the number of statements is limited by the fact that you can only put 80 characters on a logical screen line. This means that if you are going to go over the 80 character limit you have to put the entire BASIC statement that doesn't fit on a new line with a new line number.

NOTE: Always type NEW and hit RETURN before starting a new program.

The Commodore 64 has two complete character sets that you can use either from the keyboard or in your programs.

In SET 1, the upper case alphabet and the numbers 0–9 are available without pressing the SHIFT key. If you hold down the SHIFT key while typing, the graphics characters on the RIGHT side of the front of the keys are used. If you hold down the C= key while typing, the graphics characters on the LEFT side of the front of the key are used. Holding down the SHIFT key while typing any character that doesn't have graphic symbols on the front of the key gives you the symbol on the top most part of the key.

In SET 2, the lower case alphabet and the numbers 0–9 are available without pressing the SHIFT key. The upper case alphabet is available when you hold down the SHIFT key while typing. Again, the graphic symbols on the LEFT side of the front of the keys are displayed by pressing the C= key, while the symbols on the top most part of any key without graphics characters are selected when you hold down the SHIFT key while typing.

To switch from one character set to the other press the C= and the SHIFT keys together.

PROGRAMMING NUMBERS AND VARIABLES

INTEGER, FLOATING-POINT AND STRING CONSTANTS

Constants are the data values that you put in your BASIC statements. BASIC uses these values to represent data during statement execution. CBM BASIC can recognize and manipulate three types of constants:

1) INTEGER NUMBERS
2) FLOATING-POINT NUMBERS
3) STRINGS

Integer constants are whole numbers (numbers without decimal points). Integer constants must be between −32768 and +32767. *Integer constants do not have decimal points or commas between digits.* If the plus (+) sign is left out, the constant is assumed to be a positive number. Zeros coming before a constant are ignored and shouldn't be used since they waste memory and slow down your program. However, they won't cause an error. Integers are stored in memory as two-byte binary numbers. Some examples of integer constants are:

−12
8765
−32768
+44
0
−32767

> **NOTE:** Do NOT put commas inside any number. For example, always type 32,000 as 32000. If you put a comma in the middle of a number you will get the BASIC error message **?SYNTAX ERROR.**

Floating-point constants are positive or negative numbers and can contain fractions. Fractional parts of a number may be shown using a decimal point. Once again remember that commas are NOT used between numbers. If the plus sign (+) is left off the front of a number, the Commodore 64 assumes that the number is positive. If you leave off the decimal point the computer will assume that it follows the last digit of the number. And as with integers, zeros that come before a constant are ignored. Floating-point constants can be used in two ways:

1) SIMPLE NUMBER
2) SCIENTIFIC NOTATION

Floating-point constants will show you up to nine digits on your screen. These digits can represent values between −999999999. and +999999999. If you enter more than nine digits the number will be rounded based on the tenth digit. If the tenth digit is greater than or equal to 5 the number will be rounded upward. Less than 5 the number will be rounded downward. This could be important to the final totals of some numbers you may want to work with.

Floating-point numbers are stored (using five bytes of memory) and are manipulated in calculations with ten places of accuracy. However, the numbers are rounded to nine digits when results are printed. Some examples of simple floating-point numbers are:

1.23
−.998877
+3.1459
.7777777
−333.
.01

Numbers smaller than .01 or larger than 999999999. will be printed in *scientific notation*. In scientific notation a floating-point constant is made up of three parts:

1) THE MANTISSA
2) THE LETTER E
3) THE EXPONENT

The *mantissa* is a simple floating-point number. The letter *E* is used to tell you that you're seeing the number in exponential form. In other words *E* represents *10 (eg., 3E3=3*10↑3=3000). And the *exponent* is what multiplication power of 10 the number is raised to.

Both the mantissa and the exponent are signed (+ or −) numbers. The exponent's range is from −39 to +38 and it indicates the number of places that the actual decimal point in the mantissa would be moved to the left (−) or right (+) if the value of the constant were represented as a simple number.

There is a limit to the size of floating-point numbers that BASIC can handle, even in scientific notation: the largest number is +1.70141183E+38 and calculations which would result in a larger number will display the BASIC error message **?OVERFLOW ERROR**. The smallest floating-point number is +2.93873588E−39 and calculations which result in a smaller value give you zero as an answer and NO error message. Some examples of floating-point numbers in scientific notation (and their decimal values) are:

235.988E−3	(.235988)
2359E6	(2359000000.)
−7.09E−12	(−.00000000000709)
−3.14159E+5	(−314159.)

String constants are groups of alphanumeric information like letters, numbers and symbols. When you enter a string from the keyboard, it can have any length up to the space available in an 80-character line (that is, any character spaces NOT taken up by the line number and other required parts of the statement).

A string constant can contain blanks, letters, numbers, punctuation and color or cursor control characters in any combination. You can even put commas between numbers. *The only character which cannot be included in a string is the double quote mark (").* This is because the double quote mark is used to define the beginning and end of the string. A string can also have a null value—which means that it can contain no character data. You can leave the ending quote mark off of a string if it's the last item on a line or if it's followed by a colon (:). Some examples of string constants are:

```
""              ( a null string)
"HELLO"
"$25,000.00"
"NUMBER OF EMPLOYEES"
```

> **NOTE:** Use CHR$(34) to include quotes (") in strings.

INTEGER, FLOATING-POINT AND STRING VARIABLES

Variables are names that represent data values used in your BASIC statements. The value represented by a variable can be assigned by setting it equal to a constant, or it can be the result of calculations in the program. Variable data, like constants, can be integers, floating-point numbers, or strings. If you refer to a variable name in a program before a value has been assigned, the BASIC Interpreter will automatically create the variable with a value of zero if it's an integer or floating-point number. Or it will create a variable with a null value if you're using strings.

Variable names can be any length but only the first two characters are considered significant in CBM BASIC. This means that all names used for variables must NOT have the same first two characters. *Variable names may NOT be the same as BASIC keywords and they may NOT contain keywords in the middle of variable names.* Keywords include all BASIC commands, statements, function names and logical operator names. If you accidentally use a keyword in the middle of a variable name, the BASIC error message **?SYNTAX ERROR** will show up on your screen.

The characters used to form variable names are the alphabet and the numbers 0–9. The first character of the name must be a letter. Data type declaration characters (%) and ($) can be used as the last character of the name. The percent sign (%) declares the variable to be an integer and the dollar sign ($) declares a string variable. If no type declaration character is used the Interpreter will assume that the variable is a floating-point. Some examples of variable names, value assignments and data types are:

```
A$="GROSS SALES"      (string variable)
MTH$="JAN"+A$         (string variable)
K%=5                  (integer variable)
CNT%=CNT%+1           (integer variable)
FP=12.5               (floating-point variable)
SUM=FP*CNT%           (floating-point variable)
```

INTEGER, FLOATING-POINT AND STRING ARRAYS

An *array* is a table (or list) of associated data items referred to by a single variable name. In other words, an array is a sequence of related variables. A table of numbers can be seen as an array, for example. The individual numbers within the table become "elements" of the array.

Arrays are a useful shorthand way of describing a large number of related variables. Take a table of numbers for instance. Let's say that the table has 10 rows of numbers with 20 numbers in each row. That makes a total of 200 numbers in the table. Without a single array name to call on you would have to assign a unique name to each value in the table. But because you can use arrays you only need one name for the array and all the elements in the array are identified by their individual locations within the array.

Array names can be integers, floating-points or string data types and all elements in the array have the same data type as the array name. Arrays can have a single dimension (as in a simple list) or they can have multiple dimensions (imagine a grid marked in rows and columns or a Rubik's Cube®). Each element of an array is uniquely identified and referred to by a subscript (or index variable) following the array name, enclosed within parentheses ( ).

The maximum number of dimensions an array can have in theory is 255 and the number of elements in each dimension is limited to 32767. But for practical purposes array sizes are limited by the memory space available to hold their data and/or the 80 character logical screen line. If an array has only one dimension and its subscript value will never exceed 10 (11 items: 0 thru 10) then the array will be created by the Interpreter and filled with zeros (or nulls if string type) the first time any element of the array is referred to, otherwise the BASIC DIM statement must be used to define the shape and size of the array. The amount of memory required to store an array can be determined as follows:

		5 bytes for the array name
	+	2 bytes for each dimension of the array
	+	2 bytes per element for integers
OR	+	5 bytes per element for floating-point
OR	+	3 bytes per element for strings
AND	+	1 byte per character in each string element

Subscripts can be integer constants, variables, or an arithmetic expression which gives an integer result. Separate subscripts, with commas between them, are required for each dimension of an array. Subscripts can have values from zero up to the number of elements in the respective dimensions of the array. Values outside that range will cause the BASIC error message **?BAD SUBSCRIPT.** Some examples of array names, value assignments and data types are:

A$(0)="GROSS SALES"	(string array)
MTH$(K%)="JAN"	(string array)
G2%(X)=5	(integer array)
CNT%(G2%(X))=CNT%(1)−2	(integer array)
FP(12*K%)=24.8	(floating-point array)
SUM(CNT%(1))=FP↑K%	(floating-point array)

A(5)=0	(sets the 5th element in the 1 dimensional array called "A" equal to 0)
B(5,6)=0	(sets the element in row position 5 and column position 6 in the 2 dimensional array called "B" equal to 0)
C(1,2,3)=0	(sets the element in row position 1, column position 2, and depth position 3 in the 3 dimensional array called "C" equal to 0)

EXPRESSIONS AND OPERATORS

Expressions are formed using constants, variables and/or arrays. An expression can be a single constant, simple variable, or an array variable of any type. It can also be a combination of constants and variables with arithmetic, relational or logical operators designed to produce a single value. How operators work is explained below. Expressions can be separated into two classes:

1) ARITHMETIC
2) STRING

Expressions are normally thought of as having two or more data items called *operands*. Each operand is separated by a single *operator* to produce the desired result. This is usually done by assigning the value of the expression to a variable name. All of the examples of constants and variables that you've seen so far, were also examples of expressions.

An operator is a special symbol the BASIC Interpreter in your Commodore 64 recognizes as representing an operation to be performed on the variables or constant data. One or more operators, combined with one or more variables and/or constants form an expression. Arithmetic, relational and logical operators are recognized by Commodore 64 BASIC.

ARITHMETIC EXPRESSIONS

Arithmetic expressions, when solved, will give an integer or floating-point value. The arithmetic operators (+, −, *, /, ↑) are used to perform addition, subtraction, multiplication, division and exponentiation operations respectively.

ARITHMETIC OPERATIONS

An arithmetic operator defines an arithmetic operation which is performed on the two operands on either side of the operator. Arithmetic operations are performed using floating-point numbers. Integers are converted to floating-point numbers before an arithmetic operation is performed. The result is converted back to an integer if it is assigned to an integer variable name.

ADDITION (+): The plus sign (+) specifies that the operand on the right is added to the operand on the left.

EXAMPLES:

```
2+2
A+B+C
X%+1
BR+10E−2
```

SUBTRACTION (−): The minus sign (−) specifies that the operand on the right is subtracted from the operand on the left.

EXAMPLES:

```
4−1
100−64
A−B
55−142
```

The minus can also be used as a unary minus. That means that it is the minus sign in front of a negative number. This is equal to subtracting the number from zero (0).

EXAMPLES:

```
−5
−9E4
−B
4− (−2) same as 4+2
```

MULTIPLICATION (*): An asterisk (*) specifies that the operand on the left is multiplied by the operand on the right.

EXAMPLES:

```
100*2
50*0
A*X1
R%*14
```

DIVISION (/): The slash (/) specifies that the operand on the left is divided by the operand on the right.

EXAMPLES:

```
10/2
6400/4
A/B
4E2/XR
```

EXPONENTIATION (↑): The up arrow (↑) specifies that the operand on the left is raised to the power specified by the operand on the right (the exponent). If the operand on the right is a 2, the number on the left is squared; if the exponent is a 3, the number on the left is cubed, etc. The exponent can be any number so long as the result of the operation gives a valid floating-point number.

EXAMPLES:

2↑2	Equivalent to: 2*2
3↑3	Equivalent to: 3*3*3
4↑4	Equivalent to: 4*4*4*4
AB↑CD	
3↑−2	Equivalent to: ⅓*⅓

RELATIONAL OPERATORS

The relational operators (<, =, >, <=, >=, <>) are primarily used to compare the values of two operands, but they also produce an arithmetic result. The relational operators and the logical operators (AND, OR, and NOT), when used in comparisons, actually produce an arithmetic true/false evaluation of an expression. If the relationship stated in the expression is true the result is assigned an integer value of −1 and if it's false a value of 0 is assigned. These are the relational operators:

<	LESS THAN
=	EQUAL TO
>	GREATER THAN
<=	LESS THAN OR EQUAL TO
>=	GREATER THAN OR EQUAL TO
<>	NOT EQUAL TO

EXAMPLES:

1=5−4	result true (−1)
14>66	result false (0)
15>=15	result true (−1)

Relational operators can be used to compare strings. For comparison purposes, the letters of the alphabet have the order A<B<C<D, etc. Strings are compared by evaluating the relationship between corresponding characters from left to right (see String Operations).

EXAMPLES:

```
"A" < "B"      result true (-1)
"X" = "YY"     result false (0)
BB$ <> CC$
```

Numeric data items can only be compared (or assigned) to other numeric items. The same is true when comparing strings, otherwise the BASIC error message **?TYPE MISMATCH** will occur. Numeric operands are compared by first converting the values of either or both operands from integer to floating-point form, as necessary. Then the relationship of the floating-point values is evaluated to give a true/false result.

At the end of all comparisons, you get an integer no matter what data type the operand is (even if both are strings). Because of this, a comparison of two operands can be used as an operand in performing calculations. The result will be −1 or 0 and can be used as anything but a divisor, since division by zero is illegal.

LOGICAL OPERATORS

The logical operators (AND, OR, NOT) can be used to modify the meanings of the relational operators or to produce an arithmetic result. Logical operators can produce results other than −1 and 0, though any nonzero result is considered true when testing for a true/false condition.

The logical operators (sometimes called *Boolean* operators) can also be used to perform logic operations on individual binary digits (bits) in two operands. But when you're using the NOT operator, the operation is performed only on the single operand to the right. The operands must be in the integer range of values (−32768 to +32767) (floating-point numbers are converted to integers) and logical operations give an integer result.

Logical operations are performed bit-by-corresponding-bit on the two operands. The logical AND produces a bit result of 1 only if both operand bits are 1. The logical OR produces a bit result of 1 if either operand bit is 1. The logical NOT is the opposite value of each bit as a single operand. In other words, it's really saying, "If it's NOT 1 then it is 0. If it's NOT 0 then it is 1."

The exclusive OR (XOR) doesn't have a logical operator but it is performed as part of the WAIT statement. Exclusive OR means that if the bits of two operands are equal then the result is 0 otherwise the result is 1.

Logical operations are defined by groups of statements which, taken together, constitute a Boolean "truth table" as shown in Table 1-2.

Table 1-2. Boolean Truth Table

The AND operation results in a 1 only if both bits are 1:

1 AND 1 = 1
0 AND 1 = 0
1 AND 0 = 0
0 AND 0 = 0

The OR operation results in a 1 if either bit is 1:

1 OR 1 = 1
0 OR 1 = 1
1 OR 0 = 1
0 OR 0 = 0

The NOT operation logically complements each bit:

NOT 1 = 0
NOT 0 = 1

The exclusive OR (XOR) is part of the WAIT statement:

1 XOR 1 = 0
1 XOR 0 = 1
0 XOR 1 = 1
0 XOR 0 = 0

The logical operators AND, OR and NOT specify a Boolean arithmetic operation to be performed on the two operand expressions on either side of the operator. In the case of NOT, ONLY the operand on the RIGHT is considered. Logical operations (or Boolean arithmetic) aren't performed until all arithmetic and relational operations in an expression have been completed.

EXAMPLES:

IF A=100 AND B=100 THEN 10	(if both A and B have a value of 100 then the result is true)
A=96 AND 32: PRINT A	(A = 32)

```
IF A=100 OR B=100 THEN 20     (if A or B is 100 then the
                               result is true)

A=64 OR 32: PRINT A           (A = 96)

IF NOT X<Y THEN 30            (if X>=Y the result is true)

X= NOT 96                     (result is −97 (two's complement))
```

HIERARCHY OF OPERATIONS

All expressions perform the different types of operations according to a fixed hierarchy. In other words, certain operations are performed before other operations. The normal order of operations can be modified by enclosing two or more operands within parentheses ( ), creating a "subexpression." The parts of an expression enclosed in parentheses will be reduced to a single value before working on parts outside the parentheses.

When you use parentheses in expressions, they must be paired so that you always have an equal number of left and right parentheses. Otherwise, the BASIC error message **?SYNTAX ERROR** will appear.

Expressions which have operands inside parentheses may themselves be enclosed in parentheses, forming complex expressions of multiple levels. This is called *nesting*. Parentheses can be nested in expressions to a maximum depth of ten levels—ten matching sets of parentheses. The inner-most expression has its operations performed first. Some examples of expressions are:

```
A+B
C↑(D+E)/2
((X−C↑(D+E)/2)*10)+1
GG$>HH$
JJ$+"MORE"
K%=1 AND M<>X
K%=2 OR (A=B AND M<X)
NOT (D=E)
```

The BASIC Interpreter will normally perform operations on expressions by performing arithmetic operations first, then relational operations, and logical operations last. Both arithmetic and logical operators have an order of precedence (or hierarchy of operations) within themselves. On the other hand, relational operators do not have an order of precedence and will be performed as the expression is evaluated from left to right.

If all remaining operators in an expression have the same level of precedence then operations happen from left to right. When performing operations on expressions within parentheses, the normal order of precedence is maintained. The hierarchy of arithmetic and logical operations is shown in Table 1-3 from first to last in order of precedence.

Table 1-3. Hierarchy of Operations Performed on Expressions

OPERATOR	DESCRIPTION	EXAMPLE
↑	Exponentiation	BASE ↑ EXP
−	Negation (Unary Minus)	−A
* /	Multiplication Division	AB * CD EF / GH
+ −	Addition Subtraction	CNT + 2 JK − PQ
> = <	Relational Operations	A <= B
NOT	Logical NOT (Integer Two's Complement)	NOT K%
AND	Logical AND	JK AND 128
OR	Logical OR	PQ OR 15

STRING OPERATIONS

Strings are compared using the same relational operators (=, <>, <=, >=, <, >) that are used for comparing numbers. String comparisons are made by taking one character at a time (left-to-right) from each string and evaluating each character code position from the PET/CBM character set. If the character codes are the same, the characters are equal. If the character codes differ, the character with the lower code number is lower in the character set. The comparison stops when the end of either string is reached. All other things being equal, the shorter string is considered less than the longer string. *Leading or trailing blanks ARE significant.*

Regardless of the data types, at the end of all comparisons you get an integer result. This is true even if both operands are strings. Because of this a comparison of two string operands can be used as an operand in performing calculations. The result will be −1 or 0 (true or false) and can be used as anything but a divisor since division by zero is illegal.

STRING EXPRESSIONS

Expressions are treated as if an implied "<>0" follows them. This means that if an expression is true then the next BASIC statements on the same program line are executed. If the expression is false the rest of the line is ignored and the next line in the program is executed.

Just as with numbers, you can also perform operations on string variables. The only string arithmetic operator recognized by CBM BASIC is the plus sign (+) which is used to perform concatenation of strings. When strings are concatenated, the string on the right of the plus sign is appended to the string on the left, forming a third string as a result. The result can be printed immediately, used in a comparison, or assigned to a variable name. If a string data item is compared with (or set equal to) a numeric item, or vice-versa, the BASIC error message **?TYPE MISMATCH** will occur. Some examples of string expressions and concatenation are:

```
10 A$="FILE" : B$="NAME"
20 NAM$ = A$ + B$                (gives the string: FILENAME)
30 RES$ = "NEW " + A$ + B$ (gives the string: NEW FILENAME)
```

Note space here.

PROGRAMMING TECHNIQUES

DATA CONVERSIONS

When necessary, the CBM BASIC Interpreter will convert a numeric data item from an integer to floating-point, or vice-versa, according to the following rules:

- All arithmetic and relational operations are performed in floating-point format. Integers are converted to floating-point form for evaluation of the expression, and the result is converted back to integer. Logical operations convert their operands to integers and return an integer result.
- If a numeric variable name of one type is set equal to a numeric data item of a different type, the number will be converted and stored as the data type declared in the variable name.
- When a floating-point value is converted to an integer, the fractional portion is truncated (eliminated) and the integer result is less than or equal to the floating-point value. If the result is outside the range of +32767 thru −32768, the BASIC error message **?ILLEGAL QUANTITY** will occur.

USING THE INPUT STATEMENT

Now that you know what variables are, let's take that information and put it together with the INPUT statement for some practical programming applications.

In our first example, you can think of a variable as a "storage compartment" where the Commodore 64 stores the user's response to your prompt question. To write a program which asks the user to type in a name, you might assign the variable N$ to the name typed in. Now every time you PRINT N$ in your program, the Commodore 64 will automatically PRINT the name that the user typed in.

Type the word NEW on your Commodore 64. Hit the RETURN key, and try this example:

```
10 PRINT "YOUR NAME":INPUT N$
20 PRINT "HELLO," N$
```

In this example you used N to remind yourself that this variable stands for "NAME." The dollar sign ($) is used to tell the computer that you're using a string variable. It is important to differentiate between the two types of variables:

1) NUMERIC
2) STRING

You probably remember from the earlier sections that numeric variables are used to store number values such as 1, 100, 4000, etc. A numeric variable can be a single letter (A), any two letters (AB), a letter and a number (A1), or two letters and a number (AB1). You can save memory space by using shorter variables. Another helpful hint is to use letters and numbers for different categories in the same program (A1, A2, A3). Also, if you want whole numbers for an answer instead of numbers with decimal points, all you have to do is put a percent sign (%) at the end of your variable name (AB%, A1%, etc.)

Now let's look at a few examples that use different types of variables and expressions with the INPUT statement.

```
10 PRINT "ENTER A NUMBER":INPUT A
20 PRINT A
```

```
10 PRINT "ENTER A WORD":INPUT A$
20 PRINT A$
```

```
10 PRINT "ENTER A NUMBER":INPUT A
20 PRINT A "TIMES 5 EQUALS" A*5
```

> **NOTE:** Example 3 shows that MESSAGES or PROMPTS are inside the quotation marks (" ") while the variables are outside. Notice, too, that in line 20 the variable A was printed first, then the message "TIMES 5 EQUALS", and then the calculation, multiply variable A by 5 (A*5).

Calculations are important in most programs. You have a choice of using "actual numbers" or variables when doing calculations, but if you're working with numbers supplied by a user you must use numeric variables. Begin by asking the user to type in two numbers like this:

```
10 PRINT "TYPE 2 NUMBERS":INPUT A:INPUT B
```

INCOME/EXPENSE BUDGET EXAMPLE

```
5 PRINT "♥"   ← SHIFT CLR/HOME
10 PRINT"MONTHLY INCOME":INPUT IN
20 PRINT
30 PRINT"EXPENSE CATEGORY 1":INPUT E1$
40 PRINT"EXPENSE AMOUNT":INPUT E1
50 PRINT
60 PRINT"EXPENSE CATEGORY 2":INPUT E2$
70 PRINT"EXPENSE AMOUNT":INPUT E2
80 PRINT
90 PRINT"EXPENSE CATEGORY 3":INPUT E3$
100 PRINT"EXPENSE AMOUNT":INPUT E3
110 PRINT "♥"   ← SHIFT CLR/HOME
120 E=E1+E2+E3
130 EP=E/IN
140 PRINT"MONTHLY INCOME: $"IN
150 PRINT"TOTAL EXPENSES: $"E
160 PRINT"BALANCE EQUALS: $"IN-E
170 PRINT
180 PRINT E1$"="(E1/E)*100"% OF TOTAL EXPENSES"
190 PRINT E2$"="(E2/E)*100"% OF TOTAL EXPENSES"
200 PRINTE3$"="(E3/E)*100"% OF TOTAL EXPENSES"
210 PRINT
220 PRINT"YOUR EXPENSES="EP*100"% OF YOUR TOTAL
INCOME"
230 FOR X=1TO5000:NEXT:PRINT
240 PRINT"REPEAT? (Y OR N)":INPUT Y$:IF Y$="Y"THEN5
250 PRINT "♥":END
              ↖ SHIFT CLR/HOME
```

> **NOTE:** IN can NOT = 0, and E1, E2, E3 can NOT all be 0 at the same time.

LINE-BY-LINE EXPLANATION OF INCOME/EXPENSE BUDGET EXAMPLE

Line(s)	Description
5	Clears the screen.
10	PRINT/INPUT statement.
20	Inserts blank line.
30	Expense Category 1 = E1$.
40	Expense Amount = E1.
50	Inserts blank line.
60	Expense Category 2 = E2$.
70	Expense Amount 2 = E2.
80	Inserts blank line.
90	Expense Category 3 = E3$.
100	Expense Amount 3 = E3.
110	Clears the screen.
120	Add Expense Amounts = E.
130	Calculate Expense/Income%.
140	Display Income.
150	Display Total Expenses.
160	Display Income – Expenses.
170	Inserts blank line.
180–200	Lines 180–200 calculate % each expense amount is of total expenses.
210	Inserts blank line.
220	Display E/I %.
230	Time delay loop.

Now multiply those two numbers together to create a new variable C as shown in line 20 below:

```
20 C=A*B
```

To PRINT the result as a message type

```
30 PRINT A "TIMES" B "EQUALS" C
```

Enter these 3 lines and RUN the program. Notice that the messages are inside the quotes while the variables are not.

Now let's say that you wanted a dollar sign ($) in front of the number represented by variable C. The $ must be PRINTed inside quotes and in front of variable C. To add the $ to your program hit the **RUN/STOP** and **RESTORE** keys. Now type in line 40 as follows:

```
40 PRINT "$" C
```

Now hit **RETURN**, type RUN and hit **RETURN** again.

The dollar sign goes in quotes because the variable C only represents a number and can't contain a $. If the number represented by C was 100 then the Commodore 64 screen would display $ 100. But, if you tried to PRINT $C without using the quotes, you would get a **?SYNTAX ERROR** message.

One last tip about $$$: You can create a variable that represents a dollar sign which you can then substitute for the $ when you want to use it with numeric variables. For example:

```
10 Z$="$"
```

Now whenever you need a dollar sign you can use the string variable Z$. Try this:

```
10 Z$="$":INPUT A
20 PRINT Z$A
```

Line 10 defines the $ as a string variable called Z$, and then INPUTs a number called A. Line 20 PRINTs Z$ ($) next to A (number).

You'll probably find that it's easier to assign certain characters, like dollar signs, to a string variable than to type "$" every time you want to calculate dollars or other items which require " " like %.

USING THE GET STATEMENT

Most simple programs use the INPUT statement to get data from the person operating the computer. When you're dealing with more complex needs, like protection from typing errors, the GET statement gives you more flexibility and your program more "intelligence." This section shows you how to use the GET statement to add some special screen editing features to your programs.

The Commodore 64 has a keyboard buffer that holds up to 10 characters. This means that if the computer is busy doing some operation and it's not reading the keyboard, you can still type in up to 10 characters, which will be used as soon as the Commodore 64 finishes what it was doing. To demonstrate this, type in this program on your Commodore 64:

```
NEW
10 TI$="000000"
20 IF TI$ < "000015" THEN 20
```

Now type RUN, hit RETURN and while the program is RUNning type in the word HELLO.

Notice that nothing happened for about 15 seconds when the program started. Only then did the message HELLO appear on the screen.

Imagine standing in line for a movie. The first person in the line is the first to get a ticket and leave the line. The last person in line is last for a ticket. The GET statement acts like a ticket taker. First it looks to see if there are any characters "in line." In other words have any keys been typed. If the answer is yes then that character gets placed in the appropriate variable. If no key was pressed then an empty value is assigned to a variable.

At this point it's important to note that if you try to put more than 10 characters into the buffer at one time, all those over the 10th character will be lost.

Since the GET statement will keep going even when no character is typed, it is often necessary to put the GET statement into a loop so that it will have to wait until someone hits a key or until a character is received through your program.

Below is the recommended form for the GET statement. Type NEW to erase your previous program.

```
10 GET A$ : IF A$ = "" THEN 10
```

Notice that there is NO SPACE between the quote marks ("") on this line. This indicates an empty value and sends the program back to the GET statement in a continuous loop until someone hits a key on the computer. Once a key is hit the program will continue with the line following line 10. Add this line to your program:

```
100 PRINT A$;: GOTO 10
```

Now RUN the program. Notice that no cursor ■ appears on the screen, but any character you type will be printed in the screen. This 2-line program can be turned into part of a screen editor program as shown below.

There are many things you can do with a screen editor. You can have a flashing cursor. You can keep certain keys like CLR/HOME from accidentally erasing the whole screen. You might even want to be able to use your function keys to represent whole words or phrases. And speaking of function keys, the following program lines give each function key a special purpose. Remember this is only the beginning of a program that you can customize for your needs.

```
20 IF A$ = CHR$(133) THEN POKE 53280,8:GOTO 10
30 IF A$ = CHR$(134) THEN POKE 53281,4:GOTO 10
40 IF A$ = CHR$(135) THEN A$="DEAR SIR:"+CHR$(13)
50 IF A$ = CHR$(136) THEN A$="SINCERELY,"+CHR$(13)
```

The CHR$ numbers in parentheses come from the CHR$ code chart in Appendix C. The chart lists a different number for each character. The four function keys are set up to perform the tasks represented by the instructions that follow the word THEN in each line. By changing the CHR$ number inside each set of parentheses you can designate different keys. Different instructions would be performed if you changed the information after the THEN statement.

HOW TO CRUNCH BASIC PROGRAMS

You can pack more instructions—and power—into your BASIC programs by making each program as short as possible. This process of shortening programs is called "crunching."

Crunching programs lets you squeeze the maximum possible number of instructions into your program. It also helps you reduce the size of programs which might not otherwise run in a given size; and if you're writing a program which requires the input of data such as inventory items, numbers or text, a short program will leave more memory space free to hold data.

ABBREVIATING KEYWORDS

A list of keyword abbreviations is given in Appendix A. This is helpful when you program because you can actually crowd more information on each line using abbreviations. The most frequently used abbreviation is the question mark (?) which is the BASIC abbreviation for the PRINT command. However, if you LIST a program that has abbreviations, the Commodore 64 will automatically print out the listing with the full-length keywords. If any program line exceeds 80 characters (2 lines on the screen) with the keywords unabbreviated, and you want to change it, you will have to re-enter that line with the abbreviations before saving the program. SAVEing a program incorporates the keywords without inflating any lines because BASIC keywords are tokenized by the Commodore 64. Usually, abbreviations are added after a program is written and it isn't going to be LISTed any more before SAVEing.

SHORTENING PROGRAM LINE NUMBERS

Most programmers start their programs at line 100 and number each line at intervals of 10 (i.e., 100, 110, 120). This allows extra lines of instruction to be added (111, 112, etc.) as the program is developed. One means of crunching the program after it is completed is to *change the line numbers to the lowest numbers possible* (i.e., 1, 2, 3) because longer line numbers take more memory than shorter numbers when referenced by GOTO and GOSUB statements. For instance, the number 100 uses 3 bytes of memory (one for each number) while the number 1 uses only 1 byte.

PUTTING MULTIPLE INSTRUCTIONS ON EACH LINE

You can put more than one instruction on each numbered line in your program by separating them by a colon. The only limitation is that all the instructions on each line, including colons, should not exceed the standard 80-character line length. Here is an example of two programs, before and after crunching:

BEFORE CRUNCHING:

```
10 PRINT "HELLO. . .";
20 FOR T=1 TO 500:NEXT
30 PRINT "HELLO, AGAIN . . ."
40 GOTO 10
```

AFTER CRUNCHING:

```
10 PRINT "HELLO . . .";:FORT=1TO
   500:NEXT:PRINT"HELLO,
   AGAIN . . .":GOTO10
```

REMOVING REM STATEMENTS

REM statements are helpful in reminding yourself—or showing other programmers—what a particular section of a program is doing. However, when the program is completed and ready to use, you probably won't need those REM statements anymore and you can save quite a bit of space by removing the REM statements. If you plan to revise or study the program structure in the future, it's a good idea to keep a copy on file with the REM statements intact.

USING VARIABLES

If a number, word or sentence is used repeatedly in your program it's usually best to define those long words or numbers with a one or two letter variable. Numbers can be defined as single letters. Words and sentences can be defined as string variables using a letter and dollar sign. Here's one example:

BEFORE CRUNCHING:

```
10 POKE 54296,15
20 POKE 54276,33
30 POKE 54273,10
40 POKE 54273,40
50 POKE 54273,70
60 POKE 54296,0
```

AFTER CRUNCHING:

```
10 V=54296:F=54273
20 POKEV,15:POKE54276,33
30 POKEF,10:POKEF,40:POKEF,70
40 POKEV,0
```

USING READ AND DATA STATEMENTS

Large amounts of data can be typed in as one piece of data at a time, over and over again . . . or you can print the instructional part of the program ONCE and print all the data to be handled in a long running list called the DATA statement. This is especially good for crowding large lists of numbers into a program.

USING ARRAYS AND MATRICES

Arrays and matrices are similar to DATA statements in that long amounts of data can be handled as a list, with the data handling portion of the program drawing from that list, in sequence. Arrays differ in that the list can be multi-dimensional

ELIMINATING SPACES

One of the easiest ways to reduce the size of your program is to eliminate all the spaces. Although we often include spaces in sample programs to provide clarity, you actually don't need any spaces in your program and will save space if you eliminate them.

USING GOSUB ROUTINES

If you use a particular line or instruction over and over, it might be wise to GOSUB to the line from several places in your program, rather than write the whole line or instruction every time you use it.

USING TAB AND SPC

Instead of PRINTing several cursor commands to position a character on the screen, it is often more economical to use the TAB and SPC instructions to position words or characters on the screen.

CHAPTER 2

BASIC LANGUAGE VOCABULARY

- Introduction
- BASIC Keywords, Abbreviations, and Function Types
- Description of BASIC Keywords (Alphabetical)
- The COMMODORE 64 Keyboard and Features
- Screen Editor

INTRODUCTION

This chapter explains ***CBM BASIC Language keywords***. First we give you an easy to read list of keywords, their abbreviations and what each letter looks like on the screen. Then we explain how the syntax and operation of each keyword works in detail, and examples are shown to give you an idea as to how to use them in your programs.

As a convenience, Commodore 64 BASIC allows you to abbreviate most keywords. Abbreviations are entered by typing enough letters of the keyword to distinguish it from all other keywords, with the last letter or graphics entered holding down the SHIFT key.

Abbreviations do NOT save any memory when they're used in programs, because all keywords are reduced to single-character "tokens" by the BASIC Interpreter. When a program containing abbreviations is listed, all keywords appear in their fully spelled form. You can use abbreviations to put more statements onto a program line even if they won't fit onto the 80-character logical screen line. The Screen Editor works on an 80-character line. This means that if you use abbreviations on any line that goes over 80 characters, you will NOT be able to edit that line when LISTed. Instead, what you'll have to do is (1) retype the entire line including all abbreviations, or (2) break the single line of code into two lines, each with its own line number, etc.

A complete list of keywords, abbreviations, and their appearance on the screen is presented in Table 2-1. They are followed by an alphabetical description of all the statements, commands, and functions available on your Commodore 64.

This chapter also explains the BASIC functions built into the BASIC Language Interpreter. Built-in functions can be used in direct mode statements or in any program, without having to define the function further. This is NOT the case with user-defined functions. The results of built-in BASIC functions can be used as immediate output or they can be assigned to a variable name of an appropriate type. There are two types of BASIC functions:

1) NUMERIC
2) STRING

Arguments of built-in functions are always enclosed in parentheses ( ). The parentheses always come directly after the function keyword and NO SPACES between the last letter of the keyword and the left parenthesis (.

The type of argument needed is generally decided by the data type in the result. Functions which return a string value as their result are identified by having a dollar sign ($) as the last character of the keyword. In some cases string functions contain one or more numeric argument.

Numeric functions will convert between integer and floating-point format as needed. In the descriptions that follow, the data type of the value returned is shown with each function name. The types of arguments are also given with the statement format.

Table 2-1. COMMODORE 64 BASIC KEYWORDS

COMMAND	ABBREVIATION	SCREEN	FUNCTION TYPE
ABS	A SHIFT B	A │	NUMERIC
AND	A SHIFT N	A ╱	
ASC	A SHIFT S	A ♥	NUMERIC
ATN	A SHIFT T	A ▏	NUMERIC
CHR$	C SHIFT H	C ▕	STRING
CLOSE	CL SHIFT O	CL ┌	
CLR	C SHIFT L	C └	
CMD	C SHIFT M	C ╲	
CONT	C SHIFT O	C ┌	
COS	none	COS	NUMERIC
DATA	D SHIFT A	D ♠	
DEF	D SHIFT E	D ▔	
DIM	D SHIFT I	D ╮	

COMMAND	ABBREVIATION	SCREEN	FUNCTION TYPE
END	E SHIFT N	E ╱	
EXP	E SHIFT X	E ♣	NUMERIC
FN	none	FN	
FOR	F SHIFT O	F ┌	
FRE	F SHIFT R	F ▁	NUMERIC
GET	G SHIFT E	G ▔	
GET#	none	GET#	
GOSUB	GO SHIFT S	GO ♥	
GOTO	G SHIFT O	G ▏	
IF	none	IF	
INPUT	none	INPUT	
INPUT#	I SHIFT N	I ╱	
INT	none	INT	NUMERIC
LEFT$	LE SHIFT F	LE ▁	STRING
LEN	none	LEN	NUMERIC
LET	L SHIFT E	L ▔	
LIST	L SHIFT I	L ╮	
LOAD	L SHIFT O	L ▏	
LOG	none	LOG	NUMERIC

COMMAND	ABBREVIATION	SCREEN	FUNCTION TYPE
MID$	M SHIFT I	M 	STRING
NEW	none	NEW	
NEXT	N SHIFT E	N 	
NOT	N SHIFT O	N 	
ON	none	ON	
OPEN	O SHIFT P	O 	
OR	none	OR	
PEEK	P SHIFT E	P 	NUMERIC
POKE	P SHIFT O	P 	
POS	none	POS	NUMERIC
PRINT	?	?	
PRINT#	P SHIFT R	P 	
READ	R SHIFT E	R 	
REM	none	REM	
RESTORE	RE SHIFT S	RE 	
RETURN	RE SHIFT T	RE 	
RIGHT$	R SHIFT I	R 	STRING
RND	R SHIFT N	R 	NUMERIC
RUN	R SHIFT U	R 	

COMMAND	ABBREVIATION	SCREEN	FUNCTION TYPE
SAVE	S SHIFT A	S ♠	
SGN	S SHIFT G	S ▏	NUMERIC
SIN	S SHIFT I	S ╮	NUMERIC
SPC(	S SHIFT P	S ┐	SPECIAL
SQR	S SHIFT Q	S ●	NUMERIC
STATUS	ST	ST	NUMERIC
STEP	ST SHIFT E	ST ▔	
STOP	S SHIFT T	S ▏	
STR$	ST SHIFT R	ST ▁	STRING
SYS	S SHIFT Y	S ▕	
TAB(	T SHIFT A	T ♠	SPECIAL
TAN	none	TAN	NUMERIC
THEN	T SHIFT H	T ▕	
TIME	TI	TI	NUMERIC
TIME$	TI$	TI$	STRING
TO	none	TO	
USR	U SHIFT S	U ♥	NUMERIC
VAL	V SHIFT A	V ♠	NUMERIC
VERIFY	V SHIFT E	V ▔	
WAIT	W SHIFT A	W ♠	

DESCRIPTION OF BASIC KEYWORDS

ABS

TYPE: Function-Numeric
FORMAT: ABS(<expression>)

Action: Returns the absolute value of the number, which is its value without any signs. The absolute value of a negative number is that number multiplied by −1.

EXAMPLES of ABS Function:

```
10 X = ABS ( Y )
10 PRINT ABS ( X * J )
10 IF X = ABS (X) THEN PRINT "POSITIVE"
```

AND

TYPE: Operator
FORMAT: <expression> AND <expression>

Action: AND is used in Boolean operations to test bits. It is also used in operations to check the truth of both operands.

In Boolean algebra, the result of an AND operation is 1 only if both numbers being ANDed are 1. The result is 0 if either or both is 0 (false).

EXAMPLES of 1-Bit AND Operation:

```
      0          1          0          1
  AND 0      AND 0      AND 1      AND 1
  -----      -----      -----      -----
      0          0          0          1
```

The Commodore 64 performs the AND operation on numbers in the range from −32768 to +32767. Any fractional values are not used, and numbers beyond the range will cause an **?ILLEGAL QUANTITY** error message. When converted to binary format, the range allowed yields 16 bits for each number. Corresponding bits are ANDed together, forming a 16-bit result in the same range.

EXAMPLES of 16-Bit AND Operation:

```
                          17
                     AND 194
                ------------
            0000000000010001
        AND 0000000011000010
----------------------------
   (BINARY) 0000000000000000
----------------------------
(DECIMAL)                  0


                       32007
                   AND 28761
                ------------
            0111110100000111
        AND 0111000001011001
----------------------------
   (BINARY) 0111000000000001
----------------------------
(DECIMAL)              28673


                        —241
                   AND 15359
                ------------
            1111111100001111
        AND 0011101111111111
----------------------------
   (BINARY) 0011101100001111
----------------------------
(DECIMAL)              15119
```

When evaluating a number for truth or falsehood, the computer assumes the number is true as long as its value isn't 0. When evaluating a comparison, it assigns a value of −1 if the result is true, while false has a value of 0. In binary format, −1 is all 1's and 0 is all 0's. Therefore, when ANDing true/false evaluations, the result will be true if any bits in the result are true.

EXAMPLES of Using AND with True/False Evaluations:

```
50 IF X=7 AND W=3 THEN GOTO 10: REM ONLY TRUE IF BOTH X=7
   AND W=3 ARE TRUE
60 IF A AND Q=7 THEN GOTO 10: REM TRUE IF A IS NON-ZERO
   AND Q=7 IS TRUE
```

ASC

TYPE: Function-Numeric
FORMAT: ASC (<string>)

Action: ASC will return a number from 0 to 255 which corresponds to the Commodore ASCII value of the first character in the string. The table of Commodore ASCII values is shown in Appendix C.

EXAMPLES OF ASC Function:

```
10 PRINT ASC("Z")
20 X = ASC("ZEBRA")
30 J = ASC(J$)
```

If there are no characters in the string, an **?ILLEGAL QUANTITY** error results. In the third example above, if J$="", the ASC function will not work. The GET and GET# statement read a CHR$(0) as a null string. To eliminate this problem, you should add a CHR$(0) to the end of the string as shown below.

EXAMPLE of ASC Function Avoiding ILLEGAL QUANTITY ERROR:

```
30 J = ASC(J$ + CHR$(0))
```

ATN

TYPE: Function-Numeric
FORMAT: ATN (<number>)

Action: This mathematical function returns the arctangent of the number. The result is the angle (in radians) whose tangent is the number given. The result is always in the range $-\pi/2$ to $+\pi/2$.

EXAMPLES of ATN Function:

```
10 PRINT ATN ( 0 )
20 X = ATN ( J ) * 180 / π : REM CONVERT TO DEGREES
```

CHR$

TYPE: Function-String
FORMAT: CHR$ (<number>)

Action: This function converts a Commodore ASCII code to its character equivalent. See Appendix C for a list of characters and their codes. The number must have a value between 0 and 255, or an **?ILLEGAL QUANTITY** error message results.

EXAMPLES of CHR$ Function:

```
10 PRINT CHR$(65) : REM 65 = UPPER CASE A
20 A$ = CHR$(13) : REM 13 = RETURN KEY
50 A = ASC(A$) : A$ = CHR$(A): REM CONVERTS TO C64 ASCII
    CODE AND BACK
```

CLOSE

TYPE: I/O Statement
FORMAT: CLOSE <file number>

Action: This statement shuts off any data file or channel to a device. The file number is the same as when the file or device was OPENed (see OPEN statement and the section on INPUT/OUTPUT programming).

When working with storage devices like cassette tape and disks, the CLOSE operation stores any incomplete buffers to the device. When this is not performed, the file will be incomplete on the tape and unreadable on the disk. The CLOSE operation isn't as necessary with other devices, but it does free up memory for other files. See your external device manual for more details.

EXAMPLES of CLOSE Statement:

```
10 CLOSE 1
20 CLOSE X
30 CLOSE 9 * ( 1 + J )
```

CLR

TYPE: Statement
FORMAT: CLR

Action: This statement makes available RAM memory that had been used but is no longer needed. Any BASIC program in memory is untouched, but all variables, arrays, GOSUB addresses, FOR. . . NEXT loops, user-defined functions, and files are erased from memory, and their space is made available to new variables, etc.

In the case of files to the disk and cassette tape, they are *not* properly CLOSEd by the CLR statement. The information about the files is lost to the computer, including any incomplete buffers. The disk drive will still think the file is OPEN. See the CLOSE statement for more information on this.

EXAMPLE of CLR Statement:

```
10 X=25
20 CLR
30 PRINT X

RUN
0

READY
```

CMD

TYPE: I/O Statement
FORMAT: CMD <file number> [, string]

Action: This statement switches the primary output device from the TV screen to the file specified. This file could be on disk, tape, printer, or an I/O device like the modem. The file number must be specified in a prior OPEN statement. The string, when specified, is sent to the file. This is handy for titling printouts, etc.

When this command is in effect, any PRINT statements and LIST commands will not display on the screen, but will send the text in the same format to the file.

To re-direct the output back to the screen, the PRINT# command should send a blank line to the CMD device before CLOSEing, so it will stop expecting data (called "un-listening" the device).

Any system error (like **?SYNTAX ERROR**) will cause output to return to the screen. Devices aren't un-listened by this, so you should send a blank line after an error condition. (See your printer or disk manual for more details.)

EXAMPLES of CMD Statement:

```
OPEN 4, 4: CMD 4, "TITLE" : LIST: REM LISTS PROGRAM ON PRINTER
PRINT# 4: CLOSE 4: REM UN-LISTENS AND CLOSES PRINTER

10 OPEN 1, 1, 1, "TEST": REM CREATE SEQ FILE
20 CMD 1: REM OUTPUT TO TAPE FILE, NOT SCREEN
30 FOR L = 1 TO 100
40 PRINT L: REM PUTS NUMBER IN TAPE BUFFER
50 NEXT
60 PRINT# 1: REM UNLISTEN
70 CLOSE 1: REM WRITE UNFINISHED BUFFER, PROPERLY FINISH
```

CONT

TYPE: Command
FORMAT: CONT

Action: This command re-starts the execution of a program which was halted by a STOP or END statement or the RUN/STOP key being pressed. The program will re-start at the exact place from which it left off.

While the program is stopped, the user can inspect or change any variables or look at the program. When de-bugging or examining a program, STOP statements can be placed at strategic locations to allow examination of variables and to check the flow of the program.

The error message **CAN'T CONTINUE** will result from editing the program (even just hitting RETURN with the cursor on an unchanged line), or if the program halted due to an error, or if you caused an error before typing CONT to re-start the program.

EXAMPLE of CONT Command:

```
10 PI=0:C=1
20 PI=PI+4/C-4/(C+2)
30 PRINT PI
40 C=C+4:GOTO 20
```

This program calculates the value of PI. RUN this program, and after a short while hit the **RUN/STOP** key. You will see the display:

BREAK IN 20 | **NOTE:** Might be different number.

Type the command PRINT C to see how far the Commodore 64 has gotten. Then use CONT to resume from where the Commodore 64 left off.

COS

TYPE: Function
FORMAT: COS (<number>)

Action: This mathematical function calculates the cosine of the number, where the number is an angle in radians.

EXAMPLES of COS Function:

```
10 PRINT COS ( 0 )
20 X = COS ( Y * π / 180 ) : REM CONVERT DEGREES TO RADIANS
```

DATA

TYPE: Statement
FORMAT: DATA <list of constants>

Action: DATA statements store information within a program. The program uses the information by means of the READ statement, which pulls successive constants from the DATA statements.

The DATA statements don't have to be executed by the program, they only have to be present. Therefore, they are usually placed at the end of the program.

All data statements in a program are treated as a continuous list. Data is READ from left to right, from the lowest numbered line to the highest. If the READ statement encounters data that doesn't fit the type requested (if it needs a number and finds a string) an error message occurs.

Any characters can be included as data, but if certain ones are used the data item must be enclosed by quote marks (" "). These include punctuation like comma (,), colon (:), blank spaces, and shifted letters, graphics, and cursor control characters.

EXAMPLES of DATA Statement:

```
10 DATA 1, 10, 5, 8
20 DATA JOHN, PAUL, GEORGE, RINGO
30 DATA "DEAR MARY, HOW ARE YOU, LOVE, BILL"
40 DATA −1.7E−9, 3.33
```

DEF FN

TYPE: Statement
FORMAT: DEF FN <name> (<variable>) = <expression>

Action: This sets up a user-defined function that can be used later in the program. The function can consist of any mathematical formula. Usec-defined functions save space in programs where a long formula is used in several places. The formula need only be specified once, in the definition statement, and then it is abbreviated as a function name. It must be executed once, but any subsequent executions are ignored.

The function name is the letters FN followed by any variable name. This can be 1 or 2 characters, the first being a letter and the second a letter or digit.

EXAMPLES of DEF FN Statement:

```
10 DEF FN A (X) = X + 7
20 DEF FN AA (X) = Y * Z
30 DEF FNA9 (Q) = INT( RND( 1)* Q+ 1)
```

The function is called later in the program by using the function name with a variable in parentheses. This function name is used like any other variable, and its value is automatically calculated.

EXAMPLES of FN Use:

```
40 PRINT FN A (9)
50 R = FNAA (9)
60 G = G + FN A9 (10)
```

In line 50 above, the number 9 inside the parentheses does not affect the outcome of the function, because the function definition in line 20 doesn't use the variable in the parentheses. The result is Y times Z, regardless of the value of X. In the other two functions, the value in parentheses does affect the result.

DIM

TYPE: Statement
FORMAT: DIM <variable> (<subscripts>) [, <variable> (<subscripts>) . . .]

Action: This statement defines an array or matrix of variables. This allows you to use the variable name with a subscript. The subscript points to the element being used. The lowest element number in an array is zero, and the highest is the number given in the DIM statement, which has a maximum of 32767.

The DIM statement must be executed once *and only* once for each array. A **REDIM'D ARRAY** error occurs if this line is re-executed. Therefore, most programs perform all DIM operations at the very beginning.

There may be any number of dimensions and 255 subscripts in an array, limited only by the amount of RAM memory which is available to hold the variables. The array may be made up of normal numeric variables, as shown above, or of strings or integer numbers. If the variables are other than normal numeric, use the $ or % signs after the variable name to indicate string or integer variables,

If an array referenced in a program was never DIMensioned, it is automatically dimensioned to 11 elements in each dimension used in the first reference.

EXAMPLES of DIM Statement:

```
10 DIM A ( 100 )
20 DIM Z ( 5, 7), Y ( 3, 4, 5)
30 DIM Y7% ( Q )
40 DIM PH$ (1000)
50 F (4) =9: REM AUTOMATICALLY PERFORMS DIM F (10)
```

EXAMPLE of FOOTBALL SCORE-KEEPING Using DIM:

```
 10 DIM S(1,5), T$(1)
 20 INPUT "TEAM NAMES"; T$(0), T$(1)
 30 FOR Q=1 TO 5: FOR T=0 TO 1
 40 PRINT T$(T), "SCORE IN QUARTER" Q
 50 INPUT S(T,Q): S(T,0)= S(T,0)+ S(T,Q)
 60 NEXT T,Q
 70 PRINT CHR$(147) "SCOREBOARD"
 80 PRINT "QUARTER"
 90 FOR Q=1 TO 5
100 PRINT TAB( Q*2 +9) Q;
110 NEXT: PRINT TAB(15) "TOTAL"
120 FOR T=0 TO 1: PRINT T$(T);
130 FOR Q=1 TO 5
140 PRINT TAB(Q*2 +9) S(T,Q);
150 NEXT: PRINT TAB(15) S(T,0)
160 NEXT
```

CALCULATING MEMORY USED BY DIM:

5 bytes for the array name
2 bytes for each dimension
2 bytes/element for integer variables
5 bytes/element for normal numeric variables
3 bytes/element for string variables
1 byte for each character in each string element

END

TYPE: Statement
FORMAT: END

Action: This finishes a program's execution and displays the READY message, returning control to the person operating the computer. There may be any number of END statements within a program. While it is not necessary to include any END statements at all, it is recommended that a program does conclude with one, rather than just running out of lines.

The END statement is similar to the STOP statement. The only difference is that STOP causes the computer to display the message **BREAK IN LINE XX** and END just displays READY. Both statements allow the computer to resume execution by typing the CONT command.

EXAMPLES of END Statement:

```
10 PRINT "DO YOU REALLY WANT TO RUN THIS PROGRAM"
20 INPUT A$
30 IF A$ = "NO" THEN END
40 REM REST OF PROGRAM . . .
999 END
```

EXP

TYPE: Function-Numeric
FORMAT: EXP (<number>)

Action: This mathematical function calculates the constant e (2.71828183) raised to the power of the number given. A value greater than 88.0296919 causes an **?OVERFLOW** error to occur.

EXAMPLES of EXP Function:

```
10 PRINT EXP (1)
20 X = Y * EXP (Z * Q)
```

FN

TYPE: Function-Numeric
FORMAT: FN <name> (<number>)

Action: This function references the previously DEFined formula specified by name. The number is substituted into its place (if any) and the formula is calculated. The result will be a numeric value.

This function can be used in direct mode, as long as the statement DEFining it has been executed.

If an FN is executed before the DEF statement which defines it, an **UNDEF'D FUNCTION** error occurs.

EXAMPLES of FN (User-Defined) Function:

```
PRINT FN A ( Q )
1100 J = FN J (7) + FN J (9)
9990 IF FN B7 (I+1)= 6 THEN END
```

FOR . . . TO . . . [STEP . . .]

TYPE: Statement
FORMAT: FOR <variable> = <start> TO <limit> [STEP <increment>]

Action: This is a special BASIC statement that lets you easily use a variable as a counter. You must specify certain parameters: the floating-point variable name, its starting value, the limit of the count, and how much to add during each cycle.

Here is a simple BASIC program that counts from 1 to 10, PRINTing each number and ENDing when complete, and using no FOR statements:

```
100 L = 1
110 PRINT L
120 L = L + 1
130 IF L <= 10 THEN 110
140 END
```

Using the FOR statement, here is the same program:

```
100 FOR L = 1 TO 10
110 PRINT L
120 NEXT L
130 END
```

As you can see, the program is shorter and easier to understand using the FOR statement.

When the FOR statement is executed, several operations take place. The <start> value is placed in the <variable> being used in the counter. In the example above, a 1 is placed in L.

When the NEXT statement is reached, the <increment> value is added to the <variable>. If a STEP was not included, the <increment> is set to +1. The first time the program above hits line 120, 1 is added to L, so the new value of L is 2.

Now the value in the <variable> is compared to the <limit>. If the <limit> has not been reached yet, the program GOes TO the line after the original FOR statement. In this case, the value of 2 in L is less than the limit of 10, so it GOes TO line 110.

Eventually, the value of <limit> is exceeded by the <variable>. At that time, the loop is concluded and the program continues with the line following the NEXT statement. In our example, the value of L reaches 11, which exceeds the limit of 10, and the program goes on with line 130.

When the value of <increment> is positive, the <variable> must exceed the <limit>, and when it is negative it must become less than the <limit>.

> **NOTE:** A loop always executes at least once.

EXAMPLES of FOR. . .TO. . .STEP. . .Statement:

```
100 FOR L = 100 TO 0 STEP -1
100 FOR L = PI TO 6*π STEP .01
100 FOR AA = 3 TO 3
```

FRE

TYPE: Function
FORMAT: FRE (<variable>)

Action: This function tells you how much RAM is available for your program and its variables. If a program tries to use more space than is available, the **OUT OF MEMORY** error results.

The number in parentheses can have any value, and it is not used in the calculation.

> **NOTE:** If the result of FRE is negative, add 65536 to the FRE number to get the number of bytes available in memory.

EXAMPLES of FRE Function:

```
PRINT FRE ( 0 )
10 X = ( FRE ( K ) - 1000 ) / 7
950 IF FRE ( 0 ) < 100 THEN PRINT "NOT ENOUGH ROOM"
```

> **NOTE:** The following always tells you the current available RAM:
>
> PRINT FRE(0) − (FRE(0) < 0)* 65536

GET

TYPE: Statement
FORMAT: GET <variable list>

Action: This statement reads each key typed by the user. As the user is typing, the characters are stored in the Commodore 64's keyboard buffer. Up to 10 characters are stored here, and any keys struck after the 10th are lost. Reading one of the characters with the GET statement makes room for another character.

If the GET statement specifies numeric data, and the user types a key other than a number, the message **?SYNTAX ERROR** appears. To be safe, read the keys as strings and convert them to numbers later.

The GET statement can be used to avoid some of the limitations of the INPUT statement. For more on this, see the section on Using the GET Statement in the Programming Techniques section.

EXAMPLES of GET Statement:

```
10 GET A$: IF A$ = "" THEN 10: REM LOOPS IN 10 UNTIL ANY KEY
   HIT
20 GET A$, B$, C$, D$, E$: REM READS 5 KEYS
30 GET A, A$
```

GET#

TYPE: I/O Statement
FORMAT: GET# <file number>, <variable list>

Action: This statement reads characters one-at-a-time from the device or file specified. It works the same as the GET statement, except that the data comes from a different place than the keyboard. If no character is received, the variable is set to an empty string (equal to "") or to 0 for numeric variables. Characters used to separate data in files, like the comma (,) or RETURN key code (ASC code of 13), are received like any other character.

When used with device #3 (TV screen), this statement will read characters one by one from the screen. Each use of GET# moves the cursor 1 position to the right. The character at the end of the logical line is changed to a CHR$ (13), the RETURN key code.

EXAMPLES of GET# Statement:

```
5 GET# 1, A$
10 OPEN 1, 3: GET# 1, Z7$
20 GET# 1, A, B, C$, D$
```

GOSUB

TYPE: Statement
FORMAT: GOSUB <line number>

Action: This is a specialized form of the GOTO statement, with one important difference: GOSUB remembers where it came from. When the RETURN statement (different from the RETURN key on the keyboard) is reached in the program, the program jumps back to the statement immediately following the original GOSUB statement.

The major use of a subroutine (GOSUB really means GO to a SUB-routine) is when a small section of program is used by different sections of the program. By using subroutines rather than repeating the same lines over and over at different places in the program, you can save lots of program space. In this way, GOSUB is similar to DEF FN. DEF FN lets you save space when using a formula, while GOSUB saves space when using a several-line routine. Here is an inefficient program that doesn't use GOSUB:

```
100 PRINT "THIS PROGRAM PRINTS"
110 FOR L = 1 TO 500 : NEXT
120 PRINT "SLOWLY ON THE SCREEN"
130 FOR L = 1 TO 500 : NEXT
140 PRINT "USING A SIMPLE LOOP"
150 FOR L = 1 TO 500 : NEXT
160 PRINT "AS A TIME DELAY."
170 FOR L = 1 TO 500 : NEXT
```

Here is the same program using GOSUB:

```
100 PRINT "THIS PROGRAM PRINTS"
110 GOSUB 200
120 PRINT "SLOWLY ON THE SCREEN"
130 GOSUB 200
140 PRINT "USING A SIMPLE LOOP"
150 GOSUB 200
160 PRINT "AS A TIME DELAY."
170 GOSUB 200
180 END
200 FOR L = 1 TO 500 : NEXT
210 RETURN
```

Each time the program executes a GOSUB, the line number and position in the program line are saved in a special area called the "stack," which takes up 256 bytes of your memory. This limits the amount of data that can be stored in the stack. Therefore, the number of subroutine return addresses that can be stored is limited, and care should be taken to make sure every GOSUB hits the corresponding RETURN, or else you'll run out of memory even though you have plenty of bytes free.

GOTO

TYPE: Statement
FORMAT: GOTO <line number>
or GO TO <line number>

Action: This statement allows the BASIC program to execute lines out of numerical order. The word GOTO followed by a number will make the program jump to the line with that number. GOTO NOT followed by a number equals GOTO 0. It must have the line number after the word GOTO.

It is possible to create loops with GOTO that will never end. The simplest example of this is a line that GOes TO itself, like 10 GOTO 10. These loops can be stopped using the RUN/STOP key on the keyboard.

EXAMPLES of GOTO Statement:

```
GOTO 100
10 GO TO 50
20 GOTO 999
```

IF . . . THEN . . .

TYPE: Statement
FORMAT: IF <expression> THEN <line number>
IF <expression> GOTO <line number>
IF <expression> THEN <statements>

Action: This is the statement that gives BASIC most of its "intelligence," the ability to evaluate conditions and take different actions depending on the outcome.

The word IF is followed by an expression, which can include variables, strings, numbers, comparisons, and logical operators. The word THEN appears *on the same line* and is followed by either a line number or one or more BASIC statements. When the expression is false, everything after the word THEN on that line is ignored, and execution continues with the next line number in the program. A true result makes the program either branch to the line number after the word THEN or execute whatever other BASIC statements are found on that line.

EXAMPLE of IF. . .GOTO. . .Statement:

```
100 INPUT "TYPE A NUMBER"; N
110 IF N <= 0 GOTO 200
120 PRINT "SQUARE ROOT=" SQR(N)
130 GOTO 100
200 PRINT "NUMBER MUST BE >0"
210 GOTO 100
```

This program prints out the square root of any positive number. The IF statement here is used to validate the result of the INPUT. When the result of N <= 0 is true, the program skips to line 200, and when the result is false the next line to be executed is 120. Note that THEN GOTO is not needed with IF. . .THEN, as in line 110 where GOTO 200 actually means THEN GOTO 200.

EXAMPLE OF IF. . . THEN. . . Statement:

```
100 FOR L = 1 TO 100
110 IF RND(1) < .5 THEN X = X+ 1 : GOTO 130
120 Y = Y+ 1
130 NEXT L
140 PRINT "HEADS= " X
150 PRINT "TAILS= " Y
```

The IF in line 110 tests a random number to see if it is less than .5. When the result is true, the whole series of statements following the word THEN are executed: first X is incremented by 1, then the program skips to line 130. When the result is false, the program drops to the next statement, line 120.

INPUT

TYPE: Statement
FORMAT: INPUT ["<prompt>" ;] <variable list>

Action: This is a statement that lets the person RUNning the program "feed" information into the computer. When executed, this statement PRINTs a question mark (?) on the screen, and positions the cursor 1 space to the right of the question mark. Now the computer waits, cursor blinking, for the operator to type in the answer and press the RETURN key.

The word INPUT may be followed by any text contained in quote marks (" "). This text is PRINTed on the screen, followed by the question mark.

After the text comes a semicolon (;) and the name of one or more variables separated by commas. This variable is where the computer stores the information that the operator types. The variable can be any legal variable name, and you can have several different variable names, each for a different input.

EXAMPLES of INPUT Statement:

```
100 INPUT A
110 INPUT B, C, D
120 INPUT "PROMPT"; E
```

When this program RUNs,the question mark appears to prompt the operator that the Commodore 64 is expecting an input for line 100. Any number typed in goes into A, for later use in the program. If the answer typed was not a number, the **?REDO FROM START** message appears, which means that a string was received when a number was expected. If the operator just hits RETURN without typing anything, the variable's value doesn't change.

Now the next question mark, for line 110, appears. If we type only one number and hit RETURN , the Commodore 64 will now display 2 question marks (??), which means that more input is required. You can just type as many inputs as you need separated by commas, which prevents the double question mark from appearing. If you type more data than the INPUT statement requested, the **?EXTRA IGNORED** message appears, which means that the extra items you typed were not put into any variables.

Line 120 displays the word PROMPT before the question mark appears. The semicolon is required between the prompt and any list of variables.

The INPUT statement can *never* be used outside a program. The Commodore 64 needs space for a buffer for the INPUT variables, the same space that is used for commands.

INPUT#

TYPE: I/O Statement
FORMAT: INPUT# <file number> , <variable list>

Action: This is usually the fastest and easiest way to retrieve data stored in a file on disk or tape. The data is in the form of whole variables of up to 80 characters in length, as opposed to the one-at-a-time method of GET#. First, the file must have been OPENed, then INPUT# can fill the variables.

The INPUT# command assumes a variable is finished when it reads a RETURN code (CHR$ (13)), a comma (,), semicolon (;), or colon (:). Quote marks can be used to enclose these characters when writing if they are needed (see PRINT# statement).

If the variable type used is numeric, and non-numeric characters are received, a **BAD DATA** error results. INPUT# can read strings up to 80 characters long, beyond which a **STRING TOO LONG** error results.

When used with device #3 (the screen), this statement will read an entire logical line and move the cursor down to the next line.

EXAMPLES of INPUT# Statement:

```
10 INPUT# 1, A
20 INPUT# 2, A$, B$
```

INT

TYPE: Integer Function
FORMAT: INT (<numeric>)

Action: Returns the integer value of the expression. If the expression is positive, the fractional part is left off. If the expression is negative, any fraction causes the next lower integer to be returned.

EXAMPLES of INT Function:

```
120 PRINT INT(99.4343), INT(-12.34)

 99        -13
```

LEFT$

TYPE: String Function
FORMAT: LEFT$ (<string>, <integer>)

Action: Returns a string comprised of the leftmost <integer> characters of the <string>. The integer argument value must be in the range 0 to 255. If the integer is greater than the length of the string, the entire string will be returned. If an <integer> value of zero is used, then a null string (of zero length) is returned.

EXAMPLES of LEFT$ Function:

```
10 A$ = "COMMODORE COMPUTERS"
20 B$ = LEFT$(A$,9): PRINT B$
RUN

COMMODORE
```

LEN

TYPE: Integer Function
Format: LEN (<string>)

Action: Returns the number of characters in the string expression. Non-printed characters and blanks are counted.

EXAMPLE of LEN Function:

```
CC$ = "COMMODORE COMPUTER": PRINT LEN(CC$)

 18
```

LET

TYPE: Statement
FORMAT: [LET] <variable> = <expression>

Action: The LET statement can be used to assign a value to a variable. But the word LET is optional and therefore most advanced programmers leave LET out because it's always understood and wastes valuable memory. The equal sign (=) alone is sufficient when assigning the value of an expression to a variable name.

EXAMPLES of LET Statement:

```
10 LET D= 12            (This is the same as D = 12)
20 LET E$ = "ABC"
30 F$ = "WORDS"
40 SUM$ = E$ + F$       (SUM$ would equal ABCWORDS)
```

LIST

TYPE: Command
FORMAT: LIST [[<first-line>]–[<last-line>]]

Action: The LIST command allows you to look at lines of the BASIC program currently in the memory of your Commodore 64. This lets you use your computer's powerful screen editor to edit programs which you've LISTed both quickly and easily.

The LIST system command displays all or part of the program that is currently in memory on the default output device. The LIST will normally be directed to the screen and the CMD statement can be used to switch output to an external device such as a printer or a disk. The LIST command can appear in a program, but BASIC always returns to the system READY message after a LIST is executed.

When you bring the program LIST onto the screen, the "scrolling" of the display from the bottom of the screen to the top can be slowed by holding down the ConTRoL CTRL key. LIST is aborted by typing the RUN/STOP key.

If no line-numbers are given the entire program is listed. If only the first-line number is specified, and followed by a hyphen (-), that line and all higher-numbered lines are listed. If only the last line-number is specified, and it is preceded by a hyphen, then all lines from the beginning of the program through that line are listed. If both numbers are specified, the entire range, including the line-numbers LISTed, is displayed.

EXAMPLES of LIST Command:

LIST	(Lists the program currently in memory.)
LIST 500	(Lists line 500 only.)
LIST 150-	(Lists all lines from 150 to the end.)
LIST -1000	(Lists all lines from the lowest through 1000.)
LIST 150-1000	(Lists lines 150 through 1000, inclusive.)

```
10 PRINT "THIS IS LINE 10"
20 LIST               (LIST used in Program Mode)
30 PRINT "THIS IS LINE 30"
```

LOAD

TYPE: Command
FORMAT: LOAD ["<file-name>"] [,<device>] [,<address>]

Action: The LOAD statement reads the contents of a program file from tape or disk into memory. That way you can use the information LOADed or change the information in some way. The device number is optional, but when it is left out the computer will automatically default to 1, the cassette unit. The disk unit is normally device number 8. The LOAD closes all open files and, if it is used in direct mode, it performs a CLR (clear) before reading the program. If LOAD is executed from within a program, the program is RUN. This means that you can use LOAD to "chain" several programs together. None of the variables are cleared during a chain operation.

If you are using file-name pattern matching, the first file which matches the pattern is loaded. The asterisk in quotes by itself ("*") causes the first file-name in the disk directory to be loaded. if the file-name used does not exist or if it is not a program file, the BASIC error message **?FILE NOT FOUND** occurs.

When LOADing programs from tape, the <file-name> can be left out, and the next program file on the tape will be read. The Commodore 64 will blank the screen to the border color after the PLAY key is pressed. When the program is found, the screen clears to the background color and the "FOUND" message is displayed. When the C= key, CTRL key, ← key, or SPACE BAR is pressed, the file will be loaded. Programs will LOAD starting at memory location 2048 unless a secondary <address> of 1 is used. If you use the secondary address of 1 this will cause the program to LOAD to the memory location from which it was saved.

EXAMPLES of LOAD Command:

LOAD	(Reads the next program on tape)
LOAD A$	(Uses the name in A$ to search)
LOAD "*",8	(LOADs first program from disk)
LOAD "",1,1	(Looks for the first program on tape, and LOADs it into the same part of memory that it came from)
LOAD "STAR TREK" PRESS PLAY ON TAPE FOUND STAR TREK LOADING READY.	(LOAD a file from tape)
LOAD "FUN",8 SEARCHING FOR FUN LOADING READY.	(LOAD a file from disk)
LOAD "GAME ONE",8,1 SEARCHING FOR GAME ONE LOADING READY.	(LOAD a file to the specific memory location from which the program was saved on the disk)

LOG

TYPE: Floating-Point Function
FORMAT: LOG (<numeric>)

Action: Returns the natural logarithm (log to the base of e) of the argument. If the value of the argument is zero or negative the BASIC error message **?ILLEGAL QUANTITY** will occur.

EXAMPLES of LOG Function:

```
25 PRINT LOG(45/7)
 1.86075234

10 NUM = LOG(ARG) / LOG(10) (Calculates the LOG of ARG to the
                            base 10)
```

MID$

TYPE: String Function
FORMAT: MID$ (<string>, <numeric-1> [,<numeric-2>])

Action: The MID$ function returns a sub-string which is taken from within a larger <string> argument. The starting position of the sub-string is defined by the <numeric-1> argument and the length of the sub-string by the <numeric-2> argument. Both of the numeric arguments can have values ranging from 0 to 255.

If the <numeric-1> value is greater than the length of the <string>, or if the <numeric-2> value is zero, then MID$ gives a null string value. If the <numeric-2> argument is left out, then the computer will assume that a length of the rest of the string is to be used. And if the source string has fewer characters than <numeric-2>, from the starting position to the end of the string argument, then the whole rest of the string is used.

EXAMPLE of MID$ Function:

```
10 A$="GOOD"
20 B$="MORNING EVENING AFTERNOON"
30 PRINT A$ + MID$(B$, 8, 8)

GOOD EVENING
```

NEW

TYPE: Command
FORMAT: NEW

Action: The NEW command is used to delete the program currently in memory and clear all variables. Before typing in a new program, NEW should be used in direct mode to clear memory. NEW can also be used in a program, but you should be aware of the fact that it will erase everything that has gone before and is still in the computer's memory. This can be particularly troublesome when you're trying to debug your program.

> **BE CAREFUL:** Not clearing out an old program before typing a new one can result in a confusing mix of the two programs.

EXAMPLES of NEW Command:

NEW	(Clears the program and all variables)
10 NEW	(Performs a NEW operation and STOPs the program.)

NEXT

TYPE: Statement
FORMAT: NEXT [<counter>] [,<counter>] . . . .

Action: The NEXT statement is used with FOR to establish the end of a FOR. . . NEXT loop. The NEXT need not be physically the last statement in the loop, but it is always the last statement executed in a loop. The <counter> is the loop index's variable name used with FOR to start the loop. A single NEXT can stop several nested loops when it is followed by each FOR's <counter> variable name(s). To do this each name must appear in the order of inner-most nested loop first, to outer-most nested loop last. When using a single NEXT to increment and stop several variable names, each variable name must be separated by commas. Loops can be nested to 9 levels. If the counter variable(s) are omitted, the counter associated with the FOR of the current level (of the nested loops) is incremented.

When the NEXT is reached, the counter value is incremented by 1 or by an optional STEP value. It is then tested against an end-value to see if it's time to stop the loop. A loop will be stopped when a NEXT is found which has its counter value greater than the end-value.

EXAMPLES of NEXT Statement:

```
10 FOR J=1 TO 5: FOR K = 10 TO 20: FOR N = 5 TO -5 STEP -1

20 NEXT N, K, J              (Stopping Nested Loops)

10 FOR L = 1 TO 100
20 FOR M = 1 TO 10
30 NEXT M
400 NEXT L                   (Note how the loops do NOT cross each
                             other)

10 FOR A = 1 TO 10
20 FOR B = 1 TO 20
30 NEXT
40 NEXT                      (Notice that no variable names are
                             needed)
```

NOT

TYPE: Logical Operator
FORMAT: NOT <expression>

Action: The NOT logical operator "complements" the value of each bit in its single operand, producing an integer "twos-complement" result. In other words, the NOT is really saying, "if it isn't. . . ". When working with a floating-point number, the operands are converted to integers and any fractions are lost. The NOT operator can also be used in a comparison to reverse the true/false value which was the result of a relationship test and therefore it will reverse the meaning of the comparison. In the first example below, if the "twos-complement" of "AA" is equal to "BB" and if "BB" is NOT equal to "CC" then the expression is true.

EXAMPLES of NOT Operator:

```
10 IF NOT AA = BB AND NOT(BB = CC) THEN . . . .
```

```
NN% = NOT 96: PRINT NN%
-97
```

> **NOTE:** To find the value of NOT use the expression X=(−(X+1)). (The two's complement of any integer is the bit complement plus one.)

ON

TYPE: Statement
FORMAT: ON <variable> GOTO / GOSUB <line-number> [,<line-number>] . . . .

Action: The ON statement is used to GOTO one of several given line-numbers, depending upon the value of a variable. The value of the variables can range from zero through the number of lines given. If the value is a non-integer, the fractional portion is left off. For example, if the variable value is 3, ON will GOTO the third line-number in the list.

If the value of the variable is negative, the BASIC error message **?ILLEGAL QUANTITY** occurs. If the number is zero, or greater than the number of items in the list, the program just "ignores" the statement and continues with the statement following the ON statement.

ON is really an underused variant of the IF. . .THEN. . . statement. Instead of using a whole lot of IF statements each of which sends the program to 1 specific line, 1 ON statement can replace a list of IF statements. When you look at the first example you should notice that the 1 ON statement replaces 4 IF. . .THEN. . . statements.

EXAMPLES of ON Statement:

```
ON -(A=7)-2*(A=3)- 3*(A<3)-4*(A>7)GOTO 400,900,1000,100

ON X GOTO 100,130,180,220

ON X+3 GOSUB 9000,20,9000

100 ON NUM GOTO 150, 300, 320, 390

500 ON SUM / 2 + 1 GOSUB 50, 80, 20
```

OPEN

TYPE: I/O Statement
FORMAT: OPEN <file-num>, [<device>] [,<address>] [,"<file-name> [,<type>] [,<mode>]"]

Action: This statement OPENs a channel for input and/or output to a peripheral device. However, you may NOT need all those parts for every OPEN statement. Some OPEN statements require only 2 codes:

1) LOGICAL FILE NUMBER
2) DEVICE NUMBER

The <file-num> is the logical file number, which relates the OPEN, CLOSE, CMD, GET#, INPUT#, and PRINT# statements to each other and associates them with the file-name and the piece of equipment being used. The logical file number can range from 1 to 255 and you can assign it any number you want in that range.

> **NOTE:** File numbers over 128 were really designed for other uses so it's good practice to use only numbers below 127 for file numbers.

Each peripheral device (printer, disk drive, cassette) in the system has its own number which it answers to. The <device> number is used with OPEN to specify on which device the data file exists. Peripherals like cassette decks, disk drives or printers also answer to several secondary addresses. Think of these as codes which tell each device what operation to perform. The device logical file number is used with every GET#, INPUT#, and PRINT#.

If the <device> number is left out the computer will automatically assume that you want your information to be sent to and received from the Datassette™, which is device number 1. The file-name can also be left out, but later on in your program, you can NOT call the file by name if you have not already given it one. When you are storing files on cassette tape, the computer will assume that the secondary <address> is zero (0) if you omit the secondary address (a READ operation).

A secondary address value of one (1) OPENs cassette tape files for writing. A secondary address value of two (2) causes an end-of-tape marker to be written when the file is later closed. The end-of-tape marker prevents accidentally reading past the end of data which results in the BASIC error message **?DEVICE NOT PRESENT.**

For disk files, the secondary addresses 2 thru 14 are available for data-files, but other numbers have special meanings in DOS commands. You must use a secondary address when using your disk drive(s). (See your disk drive manual for DOS command details.)

The <file-name> is a string of 1–16 characters and is optional for cassette or printer files. If the file <type> is left out the type of file will automatically default to the *Program* file unless the <mode> is given. *Sequential* files are OPENed for reading <mode>=R unless you specify that files should be OPENed for writing <mode>=W is specified. A file <type> can be used to OPEN an *existing* Relative file. Use REL for <type> with Relative files. Relative and Sequential files are for disk only.

If you try to access a file before it is OPENed the BASIC error message **?FILE NOT OPEN** will occur. If you try to OPEN a file for reading which does not exist the BASIC error message **?FILE NOT FOUND** will occur. If a file is OPENed to disk for writing and the file-name already exists, the DOS error message **FILE EXISTS** occurs. There is no check of this type available for tape files, so be sure that the tape is properly positioned or you might accidentally write over some data that had previously been SAVEd. If a file is OPENed that is already OPEN, the BASIC error message **FILE OPEN** occurs. (See Printer Manual for further details.)

EXAMPLES of OPEN Statements:

10 OPEN 2, 8, 4 "DISK-OUTPUT, SEQ,W"	(Opens sequential file on disk)
10 OPEN 1, 1, 2, "TAPE-WRITE"	(Write End-of-File on Close)
10 OPEN 50, 0	(Keyboard input)
10 OPEN 12, 3	(Screen output)
10 OPEN 130, 4	(Printer output)
10 OPEN 1,1,0, "NAME"	(Read from cassette)
10 OPEN 1,1,1, "NAME"	(Write to cassette)
10 OPEN 1,2,0, CHR$ (10)	(Open channel to RS-232 device)
10 OPEN 1,4,0, "STRING"	(Send upper case/graphics to the printer)
10 OPEN 1,4,7, "STRING"	(Send upper/lower case to printer)
10 OPEN 1,5,7, "STRING"	(Send upper/lower case to printer with device # 5)
10 OPEN 1,8,15, "COMMAND"	(Send a command to disk)

OR

TYPE: Logical Operator
FORMAT: <operand> OR <operand>

Action: Just as the relational operators can be used to make decisions egarding program flow, logical operators can connect two or more re- ations and return a true or false value which can then be used in a decision. When used in calculations, the logical OR gives you a bit result of 1 if the corresponding bit of either or both operands is 1. This will produce an integer as a result depending on the values of the operands. When used in comparisons the logical OR operator is also used to link two expressions into a single compound expression. If either of the expressions are true, the combined expression value is true (−1). In the first example below if AA is equal to BB OR if XX is 20, the expression is true.

Logical operators work by converting their operands to 16-bit, signed, two's complement integers in the range of −32768 to +32767. If the operands are not in the range an error message results. Each bit of the result is determined by the corresponding bits in the two operands.

EXAMPLES of OR Operator:

```
100 IF (AA = BB) OR (XX = 20) THEN . . . .
```

230 KK% = 64 OR 32: PRINT KK%	(You typed this with a bit value of 1000000 for 64 and 100000 for 32)
96	(The computer responded with bit value 1100000. 1100000=96.)

PEEK

TYPE: Integer Function
FORMAT: PEEK (<numeric>)

Action: Returns an integer in the range of 0 to 255, which is read from a memory location. The <numeric> expression is a memory location which must be in the range of 0 to 65535. If it isn't then the BASIC error message **?ILLEGAL QUANTITY** occurs.

EXAMPLES of PEEK Function:

10 PRINT PEEK(53280) AND 15	(Returns value of screen border color)
5 A%=PEEK(45)+PEEK(46)*256	(Returns address of BASIC variable table)

POKE

TYPE: Statement
FORMAT: POKE <location>, <value>

Action: The POKE statement is used to write a one-byte (8-bits) binary value into a given memory location or input/output register. The <location> is an arithmetic expression which must equal a value in the range of 0 to 65535. The <value> is an expression which can be reduced to an integer value of 0 to 255. If either value is out of its respective range, the BASIC error message **?ILLEGAL QUANTITY** occurs.

The POKE statement and PEEK statement (which is a built-in function that looks at a memory location) are useful for data storage, controlling graphics displays or sound generation, loading assembly language subroutines, and passing arguments and results to and from assembly language subroutines. In addition, Operating System parameters can be examined using PEEK statements or changed and manipulated using POKE statements. A complete memory map of useful locations is given in Appendix G.

EXAMPLES of POKE Statement:

```
POKE 1024, 1        (Puts an "A" at position 1 on the screen)
POKE 2040, PTR      (Updates Sprite #0 data pointer)
10 POKE RED, 32
20 POKE 36879, 8
2050 POKE A, B
```

POS

TYPE: Integer Function
FORMAT: POS (<dummy>)

Action: Tells you the current cursor position which, of course, is in the range of 0 (leftmost character) though position 79 on an 80-character logical screen line. Since the Commodore 64 has a 40-column screen, any position from 40 through 79 will refer to the second screen line. The dummy argument is ignored.

EXAMPLE of POS Function:

```
1000 IF POS(0) > 38 THEN PRINT CHR$(13)
```

PRINT

TYPE: Statement
FORMAT: PRINT [<variable>] [<,/;><variable>] . . . .

Action: The PRINT statement is normally used to write data items to the screen. However, the CMD statement may be used to re-direct that output to any other device in the system. The <variable(s)> in the output-list are expressions of any type. If no output-list is present, a blank line is printed. The position of each printed item is determined by the punctuation used to separate items in the output-list.

The punctuation characters that you can use are blanks, commas, or semicolons. The 80-character logical screen line is divided into 8 print zones of 10 spaces each. In the list of expressions, a comma causes the next value to be printed at the beginning of the next zone. A semicolon causes the next value to be printed immediately following the previous value. However, there are two exceptions to this rule:

1) Numeric items are followed by an added space.

2) Positive numbers have a space preceding them.

When you use blanks or no punctuation between string constants or variable names it has the same effect as a semicolon. However, blanks between a string and a numeric item or between two numeric items will stop output without printing the second item.

If a comma or a semicolon is at the end of the output-list, the next PRINT statement begins printing on the same line, and spaced accordingly. If no punctuation finishes the list, a carriage-return and a line-feed are printed at the end of the data. The next PRINT statement will begin on the next line. If your output is directed to the screen and the data printed is longer than 40 columns, the output is continued on the next screen line.

There is no statement in BASIC with more variety than the PRINT statement. There are so many symbols, functions, and parameters associated with this statement that it might almost be considered as a language of its own within BASIC; a language specially designed for writing on the screen.

EXAMPLES of PRINT Statement:

1)

```
 5 X = 5
10 PRINT −5*X, X−5, X+5, X ↑ 5

−25          0           10          3125
```

2)

```
 5 X=9
10 PRINT X;"SQUARED IS";X*X;"AND";
20 PRINT X "CUBED IS" X ↑ 3

 9 SQUARED IS 81 AND 9 CUBED IS 729
```

3)

```
 90 AA$="ALPHA":BB$="BAKER": CC$="CHARLIE":DD$="DOG":
    EE$="ECHO"
100 PRINT AA$BB$;CC$ DD$,EE$

ALPHABAKERCHARLIEDOG        ECHO
```

Quote Mode

Once the quote mark (SHIFT 2) is typed, the cursor controls stop operating and start displaying reversed characters which actually stand for the cursor control you are hitting. This allows you to program these cursor controls, because once the text inside the quotes is PRINTed they perform their functions. The INST/DEL key is the only cursor control not affected by "quote mode."

1. Cursor Movement

The cursor controls which can be "programmed" in quote mode are:

KEY	APPEARS AS
CLR/HOME	S
SHIFT CLR/HOME	♥
⇑ CRSR ⇓	Q
SHIFT ⇑ CRSR ⇓	●
⇐CRSR⇒	]
SHIFT ⇐CRSR⇒	|

If you wanted the word HELLO to PRINT diagonally from the upper left corner of the screen, you would type:

PRINT " CLR/HOME H ⇑ CRSR ⇓ E ⇑ CRSR ⇓ L ⇑ CRSR ⇓ L ⇑ CRSR ⇓ O"

which would appear as:

PRINT " S H Q E Q L Q L Q O"

2. Reverse Characters

Holding down the CTRL key and hitting 9 will cause R to appear inside the quotes. This will make all characters start printing in ***reverse video*** (like a negative of a picture). To end the reverse printing hit CTRL Ø , which prints a ▁ or else PRINT a RETURN (CHR$(13)). (Just ending the PRINT statement without a semicolon or comma will take care of this.)

3. Color Controls

Holding down the CTRL key or C= key with any of the 8 color keys will make a special reversed character appear in the quotes. When the character is PRINTed, then the color change will occur.

KEY	COLOR
CTRL 1	Black
CTRL 2	White
CTRL 3	Red
CTRL 4	Cyan
CTRL 5	Purple
CTRL 6	Green
CTRL 7	Blue
CTRL 8	Yellow
C= 1	Orange
C= 2	Brown
C= 3	Light Red
C= 4	Grey 1
C= 5	Grey 2
C= 6	Light Green
C= 7	Light Blue
C= 8	Grey 3

APPEARS AS

If you wanted to PRINT the word HELLO in cyan and the word THERE in white, type:

PRINT " CTRL 4 HELLO CTRL 2 THERE"

which would appear as:

PRINT "  **HELLO E THERE"**

4. Insert Mode

The spaces created by using the INST/DEL key have some of the same characteristics as quote mode. The cursor controls and color controls show up as reversed characters. The only difference is in the INST and DEL , which performs its normal function even in quote mode, now creates the T . And INST , which created a special character in quote mode, inserts spaces normally.

Because of this, it is possible to create a PRINT statement containing DELetes, which cannot be PRINTed in quote mode. Here is an example of how this is done:

10 PRINT"HELLO" INST/DEL SHIFT INST/DEL SHIFT INST/DEL INST/DEL INST/DEL P"

which displays as

10 PRINT"HELLO T T P"

When the above line is RUN, the word displayed will be HELP, because the last two letters are deleted and the P is put in their place.

> **WARNING:** The DELetes will work when LISTing as well as PRINTing, so editing a line with these characters will be difficult.

The "insert mode" condition is ended when the RETURN (or SHIFT RETURN) key is hit, or when as many characters have been typed as spaces were inserted.

5. Other Special Characters

There are some other characters that can be PRINTed for special functions, although they are not easily available from the keyboard. In order to get these into quotes, you must leave empty spaces for them in the line, hit RETURN or SHIFT RETURN , and go back to the spaces with the cursor controls. Now you must hit CTRL RVS/ON , to start typing reversed characters, and type the keys shown below:

Function	Type	Appears As
SHIFT RETURN	SHIFT M	╲
switch to lower case	N	N
switch to upper case	SHIFT N	╱
disable case-switching keys	H	H
enable case-switching keys	I	I

The SHIFT RETURN will work in the LISTing as well as PRINTing, so editing will be almost impossible if this character is used. The LISTing will also look very strange.

PRINT#

TYPE: I/O Statement
FORMAT: PRINT#<file-number> [<variable>] [<,/;><variable>] . . . .

Actions: The PRINT# statement is used to write data items to a logical file. It must use the same number used to OPEN the file. Output goes to the device-number used in the OPEN statement. The <variable> expressions in the output-list can be of any type. The punctuation characters between items are the same as with the PRINT statement and they can be used in the same ways. The effects of punctuation are different in two significant respects.

When PRINT# is used with tape files, the comma, instead of spacing by print zones, has the same effect as a semicolon. Therefore, whether blanks, commas, semicolons or no punctuation characters are used between data items, the effect on spacing is the same. The data items are written as a continuous stream of characters. Numeric items are followed by a space and, if positive, are preceded by a space.

If no punctuation finishes the list, a carriage-return and a line-feed are written at the end of the data. If a comma or semicolon terminates the output-list, the carriage-return and line-feed are suppressed. Regardless of the punctuation, the next PRINT# statement begins output in the next available character position. The line-feed will act as a stop when using the INPUT# statement, leaving an empty variable when the next INPUT# is executed. The line-feed can be suppressed or compensated for as shown in the examples below.

The easiest way to write more than one variable to a file on tape or disk is to set a string variable to CHR$(13), and use that string in between all the other variables when writing the file.

EXAMPLES of PRINT# Statement:

1)

```
10 OPEN 1,1,1, "TAPE FILE"
20 R$ = CHR$(13)
30 PRINT# 1,1;R$;2;R$;3;R$;4;R$;5
40 PRINT# 1,6
50 PRINT# 1,7
```

(By Changing the CHR$(13) to CHR$(44) you put a "," between each variable. CHR$(59) would put a ";" between each variable.)

2)

```
10 CO$=CHR$(44): CR$=CHR$(13)
20 PRINT#1, "AAA"CO$"BBB",
   "CCC";"DDD";"EEE"CR$
   "FFF"CR$;
30 INPUT#1, A$,BCDE$,F$
```

AAA,BBB CCCDDDEEE
(carriage return)
FFF(carriage return)

3)

```
 5 CR$=CHR$(13)
10 PRINT#2, "AAA";CR$;"BBB"
20 PRINT#2, "CCC";

30 INPUT#2, A$,B$,DUMMY$,C$
```

(10 blanks) AAA
BBB
(10 blanks)CCC

READ

TYPE: Statement
FORMAT: READ <variable> [,<variable>] . . . .

Action: The READ statement is used to fill variable names from constants in DATA statements. The data actually read must agree with the variable types specified or the BASIC error message **?SYNTAX ERROR** will result. Variables in the DATA input-list must be separated by commas.

A single READ statement can access one or more DATA statements, which will be accessed in order (see DATA), or several READ statements can access the same DATA statement. If more READ statements are executed than the number of elements in DATA statements(s) in the program, the BASIC error message **?OUT OF DATA** is printed. If the number of variables specified is fewer than the number of elements in the DATA statement(s), subsequent READ statements will continue reading at the next data element. (See RESTORE.)

> *NOTE: The **?SYNTAX ERROR** will appear with the line number from the DATA statement, NOT the READ statement.

EXAMPLES of READ Statement:

```
110 READ A,B,C$
120 DATA 1,2,HELLO

100 FOR X=1 TO 10: READ A(X):NEXT

200 DATA 3.08, 5.19, 3.12, 3.98, 4.24
210 DATA 5.08, 5.55, 4.00, 3.16, 3.37
```

(Fills array items (line 1) in order of constants shown (line 5))

```
1 READ CITY$,STATE$,ZIP

5 DATA DENVER,COLORADO, 80211
```

REM

TYPE: Statement
FORMAT: REM [<remark>]

Action: The REM statement makes your programs more easily understood when LISTed. It's a reminder to yourself to tell you what you had in mind when you were writing each section of the program. For instance, you might want to remember what a variable is used for, or some other useful information. The REMark can be any text, word, or character including the colon (:) or BASIC keywords.

The REM statement and anything following it on the same line-number are ignored by BASIC, but REMarks are printed exactly as entered when the program is listed. A REM statement can be referred to by a GOTO or GOSUB statement, and the execution of the program will continue with the next higher program line having executable statements.

EXAMPLES of REM Statement:

```
10 REM CALCULATE AVERAGE VELOCITY
20 FOR X=1 TO 20 :REM LOOP FOR TWENTY VALUES
30 SUM=SUM + VEL(X): NEXT
40 AVG=SUM/20
```

RESTORE

TYPE: Statement
FORMAT: RESTORE

Action: BASIC maintains an internal pointer to the next DATA constant to be READ. This pointer can be reset to the first DATA constant in a program using the RESTORE statement. The RESTORE statement can be used anywhere in the program to begin re-READing DATA.

EXAMPLES of RESTORE Statement:

```
100 FOR X=1 TO 10: READ A(X): NEXT
200 RESTORE
300 FOR Y=1 TO 10: READ B(Y): NEXT

4000 DATA 3.08, 5.19, 3.12, 3.98, 4.24
4100 DATA 5.08, 5.55, 4.00, 3.16, 3.37
```

(Fills the two arrays with identical data)

```
10 DATA 1,2,3,4
20 DATA 5,6,7,8
30 FOR L=1 TO 8
40 READ A: PRINT A
50 NEXT
60 RESTORE
70 FOR L=1 TO 8
80 READ A: PRINT A
90 NEXT
```

RETURN

TYPE: Statement
FORMAT: RETURN

Action: The RETURN statement is used to exit from a subroutine called for by a GOSUB statement. RETURN restarts the rest of your program at the next executable statement following the GOSUB. If you are nesting subroutines, each GOSUB must be paired with at least one RETURN statement. A subroutine can contain any number of RETURN statements, but the first one encountered will exit the subroutine.

EXAMPLE of RETURN Statement:

```
10 PRINT "THIS IS THE PROGRAM"
20 GOSUB 1000
30 PRINT "PROGRAM CONTINUES"
40 GOSUB 1000
50 PRINT "MORE PROGRAM"
60 END
1000 PRINT "THIS IS THE GOSUB":RETURN
```

RIGHT$

TYPE: String Function
FORMAT: RIGHT$ (<string>, <numeric>)

Action: The RIGHT$ function returns a sub-string taken from the right-most end of the <string> argument. The length of the sub-string is defined by the <numeric> argument which can be any integer in the range of 0 to 255. If the value of the numeric expression is zero, then a null string ("") is returned. If the value you give in the <numeric> argument is greater than the length of the <string> then the entire string is returned.

EXAMPLE of RIGHT$ Function:

```
10 MSG$ = "COMMODORE COMPUTERS"
20 PRINT RIGHT$(MSG$,9)
RUN

COMPUTERS
```

RND

TYPE: Floating-Point Function
FORMAT: RND (<numeric>)

Action: RND creates a floating-point random from 0.0 to 1.0. The computer generates a sequence of random numbers by performing calculations on a starting number, which in computer jargon is called a *seed*. The RND function is seeded on system power-up. The <numeric> argument is a dummy, except for its sign (positive, zero, or negative).

If the <numeric> argument is positive, the same "pseudorandom" sequence of numbers is returned, starting from a given seed value. Different number sequences will result from different seeds, but any sequence is repeatable by starting from the same seed number. Having a known sequence of "random" numbers is useful in testing programs.

If you choose a <numeric> argument of zero, then RND generates a number directly from a free-running hardware clock (the system "jiffy clock"). Negative arguments cause the RND function to be re-seeded with each function call.

EXAMPLES of RND Function:

220 PRINT INT(RND(0)*50)	(Return random integers 0–49)
100 X=INT(RND(1)*6)+INT(RND(1)*6)+2	(Simulates 2 dice)
100 X=INT(RND(1)*1000)+1	(Random integers from 1–1000)
100 X=INT(RND(1)*150)+100	(Random numbers from 100–249)
100 X=RND(1)*(U−L)+L	(Random numbers between upper (U) and lower (L) limits)

RUN

TYPE: Command
FORMAT: RUN [<line-number>]

Action: The system command RUN is used to start the program currently in memory. The RUN command causes an implied CLR operation to be performed before starting the program. You can avoid the ClearR-ing operation by using CONT or GOTO to restart a program instead of RUN. If a <line-number> is specified, your program will start on that line. Otherwise, the RUN command starts at first line of the program. The RUN command can also be used within a program. If the <line-number> you specify doesn't exist, the BASIC error message **UNDEF'D STATEMENT** occurs.

A RUNning program stops and BASIC returns to direct mode when an END or STOP statement is reached, when the last line of the program is finished, or when a BASIC error occurs during execution.

EXAMPLES of RUN Command:

RUN	(Starts at first line of program)
RUN 500	(Starts at line-number 500)
RUN X	(Starts at line X, or UNDEF'D STATEMENT ERROR if there is no line X)

SAVE

TYPE: Command
FORMAT: SAVE ["<file-name>"] [,<device-number>] [,<address>]

Action: The SAVE command is used to store the program that is currently in memory onto a tape or diskette file. The program being SAVEd is only affected by the command while the SAVE is happening. The program remains in the current computer memory even after the SAVE operation is completed until you put something else there by using another command. The file type will be "prg" (program). If the <device-number> is left out, then the C64 will automatically assume that you want the program saved on cassette, device number 1. If the <device-number> is an <8>, then the program is written onto disk. The SAVE statement can be used in your programs and execution will continue with the next statement after the SAVE is completed.

Programs on tape are automatically stored twice, so that your Commodore 64 can check for errors when LOADing the program back in. When saving programs to tape, the <file-name> and secondary <address> are optional. But following a SAVE with a program name in quotes (" ") or by a string variable (---$) helps your Commodore 64 find each program more easily. If the file-name is left out it can NOT be LOADed by name later on.

A secondary address of 1 will tell the KERNAL to LOAD the tape at a later time, with the program currently in memory instead of the normal 2048 location. A secondary address of 2 will cause an end-of-tape marker to follow the program. A secondary address of 3 combines both functions.

When saving programs onto a disk, the <file-name> must be present.

EXAMPLES of SAVE Command:

SAVE	(Write to tape without a name)
SAVE "ALPHA", 1	(Store on tape as file-name "alpha")
SAVE "ALPHA", 1, 2	(Store "alpha" with end-of-tape marker)
SAVE "FUN.DISK",8	(SAVES on disk (device 8 is the disk))
SAVE A$	(Store on tape with the name A$)
10 SAVE "HI"	(SAVEs program and then move to next program line)
SAVE "ME",1,3	(Stores at same memory location and puts an end-of-tape marker on)

SGN

TYPE: Integer Function
FORMAT: SGN (<numeric>)

Action: SGN gives you an integer value depending upon the sign of the <numeric> argument. If the argument is positive the result is 1, if zero the result is also 0, if negative the result is −1.

EXAMPLE of SGN Function:

```
90 ON SGN(DV)+2 GOTO 100, 200, 300
(jump to 100 if DV=negative, 200 if DV=0, 300 if DV=positive)
```

SIN

TYPE: Floating-Point Function
FORMAT: SIN (<numeric>)

Action: SIN gives you the sine of the <numeric> argument, in radians. The value of COS(x) is equal to SIN(x+3.14159265/2).

EXAMPLE of SIN Function:

```
235 AA = SIN(1.5): PRINT AA
 .997494987
```

SPC

TYPE: Special Function
FORMAT: SPC (<numeric>)

Action: The SPC function is used to control the formatting of data, as either an output to the screen or into a logical file. The number of SPaCes given by the <numeric> argument are printed, starting at the first available position. For screen or tape files the value of the argument is in the range of 0 to 255 and for disk files up to 254. For printer files, an automatic carriage-return and line-feed will be performed by the printer if a SPaCe is printed in the last character position of a line. No SPaCes are printed on the following line.

EXAMPLE of SPC Function:

```
10 PRINT "RIGHT "; "HERE &";
20 PRINT SPC(5) "OVER" SPC(14) "THERE"
RUN

RIGHT HERE &     OVER              THERE
```

SQR

TYPE: Floating-Point Function
FORMAT: SQR (<numeric>)

Action: SQR gives you the value of the SQuare Root of the <numeric> argument. The value of the argument must not be negative, or the BASIC error message **?ILLEGAL QUANTITY** will happen.

EXAMPLE of SQR Function:

```
FOR J = 2 TO 5: PRINT J*5, SQR(J * 5): NEXT

10      3.16227766
15      3.87298335
20      4.47213595
25      5
        READY
```

STATUS

TYPE: Integer Function
FORMAT: STATUS

Action: Returns a completion STATUS for the last input/output operation which was performed on an open file. The STATUS can be read from any peripheral device. The STATUS (or simply ST) keyword is a system defined variable-name into which the KERNAL puts the STATUS of I/O operations. A table of STATUS code values for tape, printer, disk and RS-232 file operations is shown below:

ST Bit Position	ST Numeric Value	Cassette Read	Serial Bus R/W	Tape Verify + Load
0	1		time out write	
1	2		time out read	
2	4	short block		short block
3	8	long block		long block
4	16	unrecoverable read error		any mismatch
5	32	checksum error		checksum error
6	64	end of file	EOI	
7	−128	end of tape	device not present	end of tape

EXAMPLES of STATUS Function:

```
10 OPEN 1, 4: OPEN 2, 8, 4, "MASTER FILE,SEQ,W"
20 GOSUB 100: REM CHECK STATUS
30 INPUT#2, A$, B, C
40 IF STATUS AND 64 THEN 80: REM HANDLE END-OF-FILE
50 GOSUB 100: REM CHECK STATUS
60 PRINT#1, A$, B; C
70 GOTO 20
80 CLOSE1: CLOSE2
90 GOSUB 100: END
100 IF ST > 0 THEN 9000: REM HANDLE FILE I/O ERROR
110 RETURN
```

STEP

TYPE: Statement
FORMAT: [STEP <expression>]

Action: The optional STEP keyword follows the <end-value> expression in a FOR statement. It defines an increment value for the loop counter variable. Any value can be used as the STEP increment. Of course, a STEP value of zero will loop forever. If the STEP keyword is left out, the increment value will be +1. When the NEXT statement in a FOR loop is reached, the STEP increment happens. Then the counter is tested against the end-value to see if the loop is finished. (See FOR statement for more information.)

> **NOTE:** The STEP value can NOT be changed once it's in the loop.

EXAMPLES of STEP Statement:

```
25 FOR XX = 2 TO 20 STEP 2          (Loop repeats 10 times)

35 FOR ZZ = 0 TO −20 STEP −2        (Loop repeats 11 times)
```

STOP

TYPE: Statement
FORMAT: STOP

Action: The STOP statement is used to halt execution of the current program and return to *direct mode*. Typing the RUN/STOP key on the keyboard has the same effect as a STOP statement. The BASIC error message **?BREAK IN LINE nnnnn** is displayed on the screen, followed by **READY.** The "nnnnn" is the line-number where the STOP occurs. Any open files remain open and all variables are preserved and can be examined. The program can be restarted by using CONT or GOTO statements.

EXAMPLES of STOP Statement:

```
10 INPUT#1, AA, BB, CC
20 IF AA = BB AND BB = CC THEN STOP
30 STOP
```

(If the variable AA is −1 and BB is equal to CC then:)
BREAK IN LINE 20
BREAK IN LINE 30 (For any other data values)

STR$

TYPE: String Function
FORMAT: STR$ (<numeric>)

Action: STR$ gives you the STRing representation of the numeric value of the argument. When the STR$ value is converted to each variable represented in the <numeric> argument, any number shown is followed by a space and, if it's positive, it is also preceded by a space.

EXAMPLE of STR$ Function:

```
100 FLT = 1.5E4: ALPHA$ = STR$(FLT)
110 PRINT FLT, ALPHA$

 15000     15000
```

SYS

TYPE: Statement
FORMAT: SYS <memory-location>

Action: This is the most common way to mix a BASIC program with a machine language program. The machine language program begins at the location given in the SYS statement. The system command SYS is used in either direct or program mode to transfer control of the microprocessor to an existing machine language program in memory. The memory-location given is by numeric expression and can be anywhere in memory, RAM or ROM.

When you're using the SYS statement you must end that section of machine language code with an RTS (ReTurn from Subroutine) instruction so that when the machine language program is finished, the BASIC execution will resume with the statement following the SYS command.

EXAMPLES of SYS Statement:

SYS 64738	(Jump to System Cold Start in ROM)
10 POKE 4400,96: SYS 4400	(Goes to machine code location 4400 and returns immediately)

TAB

TYPE: Special Function
FORMAT: TAB (<numeric>)

Action: The TAB function moves the cursor to a relative SPC move position on the screen given by the <numeric> argument, starting with the left-most position of the current line. The value of the argument can range from 0 to 255. The TAB function should only be used with the PRINT statement, since it has no effect if used with PRINT# to a logical file.

EXAMPLE of TAB Function:

```
100 PRINT "NAME" TAB(25) "AMOUNT": PRINT
110 INPUT#1, NAM$, AMT$
120 PRINT NAM$ TAB(25) AMT$

NAME                    AMOUNT

G.T. JONES              25.
```

TAN

TYPE: Floating-Point Function
FORMAT: TAN (<numeric>)

Action: Returns the tangent of the value of the <numeric> expression in radians. If the TAN function overflows, the BASIC error message **?DIVISION BY ZERO** is displayed.

EXAMPLE of TAN Function:

```
10 XX = .785398163: YY = TAN(XX): PRINT YY
 1
```

TIME

TYPE: Numeric Function
FORMAT: TI

Action: The TI function reads the interval TImer. This type of "clock" is called a "jiffy clock." The "jiffy clock" value is set at zero (initialized) when you power-up the system. This 1/60 second interval timer is turned off during tape I/O.

EXAMPLE of TI Function:

```
10 PRINT TI/60 "SECONDS SINCE POWER UP"
```

TIME$

TYPE: String Function
FORMAT: TI$

Action: The TI$ timer looks and works like a *real clock* as long as your system is powered-on. The hardware interval timer (or jiffy clock) is read and used to update the value of TI$, which will give you a TIme $tring of six characters in hours, minutes and seconds. The TI$ timer can also be assigned an arbitrary starting point similar to the way you set your wristwatch. The value of TI$ is not accurate after tape I/O.

EXAMPLE of TI$ Function:

```
1 TI$ = "000000": FOR J=1 TO 10000: NEXT: PRINT TI$

000011
```

USR

TYPE: Floating-Point Function
FORMAT: USR (<numeric>)

Action: The USR function jumps to a User callable machine language SubRoutine which has its starting address pointed to by the contents of memory locations 785–786. The starting address is established before calling the USR function by using POKE statements to set up locations 785–786. Unless POKE statements are used, locations 785–786 will give you an **?ILLEGAL QUANTITY** error message.

The value of the <numeric> argument is stored in the floating-point accumulator starting at location 97, for access by the Assembler code, and the result of the USR function is the value which ends up there when the subroutine returns to BASIC.

EXAMPLES of USR Function:

```
10 B = T * SIN(Y)
20 C = USR (B/2)
30 D = USR (B/3)
```

VAL

TYPE: Numeric Function
FORMAT: VAL (<string>)

Action: Returns a numeric VALue representing the data in the <string> argument. If the first non-blank character of the string is not a plus sign (+), minus sign (–), or a digit the VALue returned is zero. String conversion is finished when the end of the string or any non-digit character is found (except decimal point or exponential e).

EXAMPLE of VAL Function:

```
10 INPUT#1, NAM$, ZIP$
20 IF VAL(ZIP$) < 19400 OR VAL(ZIP$) > 96699
   THEN PRINT NAM$ TAB(25) "GREATER PHILADELPHIA"
```

VERIFY

TYPE: Command
FORMAT: VERIFY ["<file-name>"] [,<device>]

Action: The VERIFY command is used, in direct or program mode, to compare the contents of a BASIC program file on tape or disk with the program currently in memory. VERIFY is normally used right after a SAVE, to make sure that the program was stored correctly on tape or disk.

If the <device> number is left out, the program is assumed to be on the Datassette™ which is device number 1. For tape files, if the <file-name> is left out, the next program found on the tape will be compared. For disk files (device number 8), the file-name must be present. If any differences in program text are found, the BASIC error message **?VERIFY ERROR** is displayed.

A program name can be given either in quotes (" ") or as a string variable. VERIFY is also used to position a tape just past the last program, so that a new program can be added to the tape without accidentally writing over another program.

EXAMPLES of VERIFY Command:

```
VERIFY                          (Checks 1st program on tape)
PRESS PLAY ON TAPE
OK
SEARCHING
FOUND <FILENAME>
VERIFYING

9000 SAVE "ME",8:
9010 VERIFY "ME",8              (Looks at device 8 for the program)
```

WAIT

TYPE: Statement
FORMAT: WAIT <location>, <mask-1> [,<mask-2>]

Action: The WAIT statement causes program execution to be suspended until a given memory address recognizes a specified bit pattern. In other words WAIT can be used to halt the program until some external event has occurred. This is done by monitoring the status of bits in the input/output registers. The data items used with WAIT can be any numeric expressions, but they will be converted to integer values.

For most programmers, this statement should never be used. It causes the program to halt until a specific memory location's bits change in a specific way. This is used for certain I/O operations and almost nothing else.

The WAIT statement takes the value in the memory location and performs a logical AND operation with the value in mask-1. If there is a mask-2 in the statement, the result of the first operation is exclusive-ORed with mask-2. In other words mask-1 "filters out" any bits that you don't want to test. Where the bit is 0 in mask-1, the corresponding bit in the result will always be 0. The mask-2 value flips any bits, so that you can test for an off condition as well as an on condition. Any bits being tested for a 0 should have a 1 in the corresponding position in mask-2.

If corresponding bits of the <mask-1> and <mask-2> operands differ, the exclusive-OR operation gives a bit result of 1. If corresponding bits get the same result the bit is 0. It is possible to enter an infinite pause with the WAIT statement, in which case the **RUN/STOP** and **RESTORE** keys can be used to recover. Hold down the **RUN/STOP** key and then press **RESTORE**. The first example below WAITs until a key is pressed on the tape unit to continue with the program. The second example will WAIT until a sprite collides with the screen background.

EXAMPLES of WAIT Statement:

WAIT 1, 32, 32	
WAIT 53273, 6, 6	
WAIT 36868, 144, 16	(144 & 16 are masks. 144=10010000 in binary and 16=10000 in binary. The WAIT statement will halt the program until the 128 bit is on or until the 16 bit is off)

THE COMMODORE 64 KEYBOARD AND FEATURES

The Operating System has a ten-character keyboard "buffer" that is used to hold incoming keystrokes until they can be processed. This buffer, or queue, holds keystrokes in the order in which they occur so that the first one put into the queue is the first one processed. For example, if a second keystroke occurs before the first can be processed, the second character is stored in the buffer, while processing of the first character continues. After the program has finished with the first character, the keyboard buffer is examined for more data, and the second keystroke processed. Without this buffer, rapid keyboard input would occasionally drop characters.

In other words, the keyboard buffer allows you to "type-ahead" of the system, which means it can anticipate responses to INPUT prompts or GET statements. As you type on the keys their character values are lined up, single-file (queued) into the buffer to wait for processing in the order the keys were struck. This type-ahead feature can give you an occasional problem where an accidental keystroke causes a program to fetch an incorrect character from the buffer.

Normally, incorrect keystrokes present no problem, since they can be corrected by the CuRSoR-Left **⇐CRSR** or DELete **INST/DEL** keys and then retyping the character, and the corrections will be processed before a following carriage-return. However, if you press the **RETURN** key, no corrective action is possible, since all characters in the buffer up to and including the carriage-return will be processed before any corrections. This situation can be avoided by using a loop to empty the keyboard buffer before reading an intended response:

```
10 GET JUNK$: IF JUNK$ <>"" THEN 10: REM EMPTY THE
KEYBOARD BUFFER
```

In addition to GET and INPUT, the keyboard can also be read using PEEK to fetch from memory location 197 ($00C5) the integer value of the key currently being pressed. If no key is being held when the PEEK is executed, a value of 64 is returned. The numeric keyboard values, keyboard symbols and character equivalents (CHR$) are shown in Appendix C. The following example loops until a key is pressed then converts the integer to a character value.

```
10 AA = PEEK(197): IF AA = 64 THEN 10
20 BB$ = CHR$(AA)
```

The keyboard is treated as a set of switches organized into a matrix of 8 columns by 8 rows. The keyboard matrix is scanned for key switch-closures by the KERNAL using the CIA #1 I/O chip (MOS 6526 Complex Interface Adapter). Two CIA registers are used to perform the scan: register #0 at location 56320 ($DC00) for keyboard columns and register #1 at location 56321 ($DC01) for keyboard rows.

Bits 0–7 of memory location 56320 correspond to the columns 0–7. Bits 0–7 of memory location 56321 correspond to rows 0–7. By writing column values in sequence, then reading row values, the KERNAL decodes the switch closures into the CHR$ (N) value of the key pressed.

Eight columns by eight rows yields 64 possible values. However, if you first strike the RVS, CTRL or C= keys or hold down the SHIFT key and type a second character, additional values are generated. This is because the KERNAL decodes these keys separately and "remembers" when one of the control keys was pressed. The result of the keyboard scan is then placed in location 197.

Characters can also be written directly to the keyboard buffer at locations 631–640 using a POKE statement. These characters will be processed when the POKE is used to set a character count into location 198. These facts can be used to cause a series of direct-mode commands to be executed automatically by printing the statements onto the screen, putting carriage-returns into the buffer, and then setting the character count. In the example below, the program will LIST itself to the printer and then resume execution.

```
10 PRINT CHR$(147)"PRINT#1: CLOSE 1: GOTO 50"
20 POKE 631,19: POKE 632,13: POKE 633,13: POKE 198,3
30 OPEN 1,4: CMD1: LIST
40 END
50 REM PROGRAM RE-STARTS HERE
```

SCREEN EDITOR

The SCREEN EDITOR provides you with powerful and convenient facilities for editing program text. Once a section of a program is listed to the screen, the cursor keys and other special keys are used to move around the screen so that you can make any appropriate changes. After making all the changes you want to a specific line-number of text, hitting the RETURN key anywhere on the line, causes the SCREEN EDITOR to read the entire 80-character logical screen line.

The text is then passed to the Interpreter to be tokenized and stored in the program. The edited line replaces the old version of that line in memory. An additional copy of any line of text can be created simply by changing the line-number and pressing **RETURN**.

If you use keyword abbreviations which cause a program line to exceed 80 characters, the excess characters will be lost when that line is edited, because the EDITOR will read only two physical screen lines. This is also why using INPUT for more than a total of 80 characters is not possible. Thus, for all practical purposes, the length of a line of BASIC text is limited to 80 characters as displayed on the screen.

Under certain conditions the SCREEN EDITOR treats the *cursor control* keys differently from their normal mode of handling. If the CuRSoR is positioned to the *right* of an *odd number* of double-quote marks (") the EDITOR operates in what is known as the QUOTE-MODE.

In *quote mode* data characters are entered normally but the cursor controls no longer move the CuRSoR, instead reversed characters are displayed which actually stand for the cursor control being entered. The same is true of the color control keys. This allows you to include cursor and color controls inside string data items in programs. You will find that this is a very important and powerful feature. That's because when the text inside the quotes is printed to the screen it performs the cursor positioning and color control functions automatically as part of the string. An example of using cursor controls in strings is:

You type →	**10 PRINT "A(R)(R)B(L)(L)(L)C(R)(R)D":REM(R)=CRSR RIGHT, (L)=CRSR LEFT**
Computer prints →	**AC BD**

The **DEL** key is the only cursor control NOT affected by quote mode. Therefore, if an error is made while keying in quote mode, the **⇐CRSR** key can't be used to back up and strike over the error—even the **INST** key produces a reverse video character. Instead, finish entering the line, and then, after hitting the **RETURN** key, you can edit the line normally. Another alternative, if no further cursor-controls are needed in the string, is to press the **RUN/STOP** and **RESTORE** keys which will cancel QUOTE MODE. The cursor control keys that you can use in strings are shown in Table 2-2.

Table 2–2. Cursor Control Characters in QUOTE MODE

Control Key		Appearance
CRSR up	**⇑ CRSR**	●
CRSR down	**CRSR ⇓**	Q
CRSR left	**⇐CRSR**	▌
CRSR right	**CRSR⇒**	]
CLR	**CLR/**	♥
HOME	**/HOME**	S
INST	**INST/DEL**	▐

When you are NOT in quote mode, holding down the **SHIFT** key and then pressing the INSerT **INST** key shifts data to the right of the cursor to open up space between two characters for entering data between them. The Editor then begins operating in *INSERT MODE* until all of the space opened up is filled.

The cursor controls and color controls again show as reversed characters in insert mode. The only difference occurs on the DELete and INSerT **INST/DEL** key. The **DEL** instead of operating normally as in the quote mode, now creates the reversed **T** . The **INST** key, which created a reverse character in quote mode, inserts spaces normally.

Ths means that a PRINT statement can be created, containing DELetes, which can't be done in quote mode. The insert mode is cancelled by pressing the **RETURN** , **SHIFT** and **RETURN** , or **RUN/STOP** and **RESTORE** keys. Or you can cancel the insert mode by filling all the inserted spaces. An example of using DEL characters in strings is:

10 PRINT "HELLO" DEL INST INST DEL DEL P"
(Keystroke sequence shown above, appearance when listed below)
10 PRINT"HELP"

When the example is RUN, the word displayed will be HELP, because the letters LO are deleted before the P is printed. The DELete character in strings will work with LIST as well as PRINT. You can use this to "hide" part or all of a line of text using this technique. However, trying to edit a line with these characters will be difficult if not impossible.

There are some other characters that can be printed for special functions, although they are not easily available from the keyboard. In order to get these into quotes, you must leave empty spaces for them in the line, press RETURN, and go back to edit the line. Now you hold down the CTRL (ConTRoL) key and type RVS/ON (ReVerSe-ON) to start typing reversed characters. Type the keys as shown below:

Key Function	Key Entered	Appearance
Shifted RETURN	SHIFT M	\
Switch to upper/lower case	N	N
Switch to upper/graphics	SHIFT N	/

Holding down the SHIFT key and hitting RETURN causes a carriage-return and line-feed on the screen but does not end the string. This works with LIST as well as PRINT, so editing will be almost impossible if this character is used. When output is switched to the printer via the CMD statement, the reverse "N" character shifts the printer into its upper-lower case character set and the SHIFT "N" shifts the printer into the upper-case/graphics character set.

Reverse video characters can be included in strings by holding down the ConTRoL CTRL key and pressing ReVerSe RVS, causing a reversed R to appear inside the quotes. This will make all characters print in reverse video (like a negative of a photograph). To end the reverse printing, press CTRL and RVS/OFF (ReVerSe OFF) by holding down the CTRL key and typing the RVS/OFF key, which prints a reverse R. Numeric data can be printed in reverse video by first printing a CHR$(18). Printing a CHR$(146) or a carriage-return will cancel reverse video output.

CHAPTER 3

PROGRAMMING GRAPHICS ON THE COMMODORE 64

- Graphics Overview
- Graphics Locations
- Standard Character Mode
- Programmable Characters
- Multi-Color Mode Graphics
- Extended Background Color Mode
- Bit Mapped Graphics
- Multi-Color Bit Map Mode
- Smooth Scrolling
- Sprites
- Other Graphics Features
- Programming Sprites—Another Look

GRAPHICS OVERVIEW

All of the graphics abilities of the Commodore 64 come from the 6567 Video Interface Chip (also known as the VIC-II chip). This chip gives a variety of graphics modes, including a 40 column by 25 line text display, a 320 by 200 dot high resolution display, and SPRITES, small movable objects which make writing games simple. And if this weren't enough, many of the graphics modes can be mixed on the same screen. It is possible, for example, to define the top half of the screen to be in high resolution mode, while the bottom half is in text mode. And SPRITES will combine with anything! More on sprites later. First the other graphics modes.

The VIC-II chip has the following graphics display modes:

A) CHARACTER DISPLAY MODES

1) Standard Character Mode
- a) ROM characters
- b) RAM programmable characters

2) Multi-Color Character Mode
- a) ROM characters
- b) RAM programmable characters

3) Extended Background Color Mode
- a) ROM characters
- b) RAM programmable characters

B) BIT MAP MODES

1) Standard Bit Map Mode
2) Multi-Color Bit Map Mode

C) SPRITES

1) Standard Sprites
2) Multi-Color Sprites

GRAPHICS LOCATIONS

Some general information first. There are 1000 possible locations on the Commodore 64 screen. Normally, the screen starts at location 1024 ($0400 in HEXadecimal notation) and goes to location 2023. Each of these locations is 8 bits wide. This means that it can hold any integer number from 0 to 255. Connected with screen memory is a group of 1000 locations called **COLOR MEMORY** or **COLOR RAM.** These start at location 55296 ($D800 in HEX) and go up to 56295. Each of the color RAM locations is 4 bits wide, which means that it can hold any integer number from 0 to 15. Since there are 16 possible colors that the Commodore 64 can use, this works out well.

In addition, there are 256 different characters that can be displayed at any time. For normal screen display, each of the 1000 locations in screen memory contains a code number which tells the VIC-II chip which character to display at that screen location.

The various graphics modes are selected by the 47 **CONTROL** registers in the VIC-II chip. Many of the graphics functions can be controlled by POKEing the correct value into one of the registers. The VIC-II chip is located starting at 53248 ($D000 in HEX) through 53294 ($D02E in HEX).

VIDEO BANK SELECTION

The VIC-II chip can access ("see") 16K of memory at a time. Since there is 64K of memory in the Commodore 64, you want to be able to have the VIC-II chip see all of it. There is a way. There are 4 possible **BANKS** (or sections) of 16K of memory. All that is needed is some means of controlling which 16K bank the VIC-II chip looks at. In that way, the chip can "see" the entire 64K of memory. The **BANK SELECT** bits that allow you access to all the different sections of memory are located in the **6526 COMPLEX INTERFACE ADAPTER CHIP #2 (CIA #2).** The POKE and PEEK BASIC statements (or their machine language versions) are used to select a bank by controlling bits 0 and 1 of PORT A of CIA#2 (location 56576 (or $DD00 HEX)). These 2 bits must be set to *outputs* by setting bits 0 and 1 of location 56578 ($DD02,HEX) to change banks. The following example shows this:

```
POKE 56578,PEEK(56578)OR 3 :REM MAKE SURE BITS 0 AND 1 ARE
SET TO OUTPUTS
POKE 56576,(PEEK(56576)AND 252)OR A:REM CHANGE BANKS
```

"A" should have one of the following values:

VALUE OF A	BITS	BANK	STARTING LOCATION	VIC-II CHIP RANGE
0	00	3	49152	($C000–$FFFF)*
1	01	2	32768	($8000–$BFFF)
2	10	1	16384	($4000–$7FFF)*
3	11	0	0	($0000–$3FFF) (DEFAULT VALUE)

This 16K bank concept is part of everything that the VIC-II chip does. You should always be aware of which bank the VIC-II chip is pointing at, since this will affect where character data patterns come from, where the screen is, where sprites come from, etc. When you turn on the power of your Commodore 64, bits 0 and 1 of location 56576 are automatically set to BANK 0 ($0000–$3FFF) for all display information.

***NOTE:** The Commodore 64 character set is not available to the VIC-II chip in BANKS 1 and 3. (See character memory section.)

SCREEN MEMORY

The location of screen memory can be changed easily by a POKE to control register 53272 ($D018 HEX). However, this register is also used to control which character set is used, so be careful to avoid disturbing that part of the control register. The **UPPER 4** bits control the location of screen memory. To move the screen, the following statement should be used:

```
POKE53272,(PEEK(53272)AND15)ORA
```

Where "A" has one of the following values:

A	BITS	LOCATION*	
		DECIMAL	HEX
0	0000XXXX	0	$0000
16	0001XXXX	1024	$0400 (DEFAULT)
32	0010XXXX	2048	$0800
48	0011XXXX	3072	$0C00
64	0100XXXX	4096	$1000
80	0101XXXX	5120	$1400
96	0110XXXX	6144	$1800
112	0111XXXX	7168	$1C00
128	1000XXXX	8192	$2000
144	1001XXXX	9216	$2400
160	1010XXXX	10240	$2800
176	1011XXXX	11264	$2C00
192	1100XXXX	12288	$3000
208	1101XXXX	13312	$3400
224	1110XXXX	14336	$3800
240	1111XXXX	15360	$3C00

*Remember that the BANK ADDRESS of the VIC-II chip must be added in.
You must also tell the KERNAL'S screen editor where the screen is as follows: POKE 648, page (where page = address/256, e.g., 1024/256= 4, so POKE 648,4).

COLOR MEMORY

Color memory can NOT move. It is always located at locations 55296 ($D800) through 56295 ($DBE7). Screen memory (the 1000 locations starting at 1024) and color memory are used differently in the different graphics modes. A picture created in one mode will often look completely different when displayed in another graphics mode.

CHARACTER MEMORY

Exactly where the VIC-II gets it character information is important to graphic programming. Normally, the chip gets the shapes of the characters you want to be displayed from the **CHARACTER GENERATOR ROM.** In this chip are stored the *patterns* which make up the various letters, numbers, punctuation symbols, and the other things that you see on the keyboard. One of the features of the Commodore 64 is the ability to use patterns located in RAM memory. These RAM patterns are created by you, and that means that you can have an almost infinite set of symbols for games, business applications, etc.

A normal character set contains 256 characters in which each character is defined by 8 bytes of data. Since each character takes up 8 bytes this means that a full character set is 256*8=2K bytes of memory. Since the VIC-II chip looks at 16K of memory at a time, there are 8 possible locations for a complete character set. Naturally, you are free to use less than a full character set. However, it must still start at one of the 8 possible starting locations.

The location of character memory is controlled by 3 bits of the VIC-II control register located at 53272 ($D018 in HEX notation). Bits 3,2, and 1 control where the characters' set is located in 2K blocks. Bit 0 is ignored. Remember that this is the same register that determines where screen memory is located so avoid disturbing the screen memory bits. To change the location of character memory, the following BASIC statement can be used:

```
POKE 53272,(PEEK(53272)AND240)OR A
```

Where A is one of the following values:

VALUE of A	BITS	LOCATION OF CHARACTER MEMORY*	
		DECIMAL	HEX
0	XXXX000X	0	$0000–$07FF
2	XXXX001X	2048	$0800–$0FFF
4	XXXX010X	4096	$1000–$17FF ROM IMAGE in BANK 0 & 2 (default)
6	XXXX011X	6144	$1800–$1FFF ROM IMAGE in BANK 0 & 2
8	XXXX100X	8192	$2000–$27FF
10	XXXX101X	10240	$2800–$2FFF
12	XXXX110X	12288	$3000–$37FF
14	XXXX111X	14336	$3800–$3FFF

***Remember** to add in the BANK address.*

The **ROM IMAGE** in the above table refers to the character generator ROM. It appears in place of RAM at the above locations in bank 0. It also appears in the corresponding RAM at locations 36864–40959 ($9000–$9FFF) in bank 2. Since the VIC-II chip can only access 16K of memory at a time, the ROM character patterns appear in the 16K block of memory the VIC-II chip looks at. Therefore, the system was designed to make the VIC-II chip think that the ROM characters are at 4096–8191 ($1000–$1FFF) when your data is in bank 0, and 36864–40959 ($9000–$9FFF) when your data is in bank 2, even though the character ROM is actually at location 53248–57343 ($D000–$DFFF). This imaging only applies to character data as seen by the VIC-II chip. It can be used for programs, other data, etc., just like any other RAM memory.

NOTE: If these ROM images get in the way of your own graphics, then set the **BANK SELECT BITS** to one of the BANKS *without* the images (BANKS 1 or 3). The ROM patterns won't be there.

The location and contents of the character set in ROM are as follows:

BLOCK	ADDRESS		VIC-II IMAGE	CONTENTS
	DECIMAL	HEX		
0	53248	D000–D1FF	1000–11FF	Upper case characters
	53760	D200–D3FF	1200–13FF	Graphics characters
	54272	D400–D5FF	1400–15FF	Reversed upper case characters
	54784	D600–D7FF	1600–17FF	Reversed graphics characters
1	55296	D800–D9FF	1800–19FF	Lower case characters
	55808	DA00–DBFF	1A00–1BFF	Upper case & graphics characters
	56320	DC00–DDFF	1C00–1DFF	Reversed lower case characters
	56832	DE00–DFFF	1E00–1FFF	Reversed upper case & graphics characters

Sharp-eyed readers will have just noticed something. The locations occupied by the character ROM are the same as the ones occupied by the VIC-II chip control registers. This is possible because they don't occupy the same locations at the same time. When the VIC-II chip needs to access character data the ROM is switched in. It becomes an image in the 16K bank of memory that the VIC-II chip is looking at. Otherwise, the area is occupied by the I/O control registers, and the character ROM is only available to the VIC-II chip.

However, you may need to get to the character ROM if you are going to use programmable characters and want to copy some of the character ROM for some of your character definitions. In this case you must switch out the I/O register, switch in the character ROM, and do your copying. When you're finished, you must switch the I/O registers back in again. During the copying process (when I/O is switched out) no interrupts can be allowed to take place. This is because the I/O registers are needed to service the interrupts. If you forget and perform an interrupt, really strange things happen. The keyboard should not be read during the copying process. To turn off the keyboard and other normal interrupts that occur with your Commodore 64, the following POKE should be used:

```
POKE 56334,PEEK(56334)AND254      (TURNS INTERRUPTS OFF)
```

After you are finished getting characters from the character ROM, and are ready to continue with your program, you must turn the keyboard scan back on by the following POKE:

```
POKE 56334,PEEK(56334)OR1      (TURNS INTERRUPTS ON)
```

The following POKE will switch out I/O and switch the CHARACTER ROM in:

```
POKE 1,PEEK(1)AND251
```

The character ROM is now in the locations from 53248 57343 ($D000–$DFFF).

To switch I/O back into $D000 for normal operation use the following POKE:

```
POKE 1,PEEK(1)OR 4
```

STANDARD CHARACTER MODE

Standard character mode is the mode the Commodore 64 is in when you first turn it on. It is the mode you will generally program in.

Characters can be taken from ROM or from RAM, but normally they are taken from ROM. When you want special graphics characters for a program, all you have to do is define the new character shapes in RAM, and tell the VIC-II chip to get its character information from there instead of the character ROM. This is covered in more detail in the next section.

In order to display characters on the screen in color, the VIC-II chip accesses the screen memory to determine the character code for that location on the screen. At the same time, it accesses the color memory to determine what color you want for the character displayed. The character code is translated by the VIC-II into the starting address of the 8-byte block holding your character pattern. The 8-byte block is located in character memory.

The translation isn't too complicated, but a number of items are combined to generate the desired address. First the character code you use to POKE screen memory is multiplied by 8. Next add the start of character memory (see CHARACTER MEMORY section). Then the Bank Select Bits are taken into account by adding in the base address (see VIDEO BANK SELECTION section). Below is a simple formula to illustrate what happens:

CHARACTER ADDRESS = SCREEN CODE*8+(CHARACTER SET*2048)+(BANK*16384)

CHARACTER DEFINITIONS

Each character is formed in an 8 by 8 grid of dots, where each dot may be either on or off. The Commodore 64 character images are stored in the Character Generator ROM chip. The characters are stored as a set of 8 bytes for each character, with each byte representing the dot pattern of a row in the character, and each bit representing a dot. A zero bit means that dot is off, and a one bit means the dot is on.

The character memory in ROM begins at location 53248 (when the I/O is switched off). The first 8 bytes from location 53248 ($D000) to 53255 ($D007) contain the pattern for the @ sign, which has a character code value of zero in the screen memory. The next 8 bytes, from location

53256 ($D008) to 53263 ($D00F), contain the information for forming the letter A.

IMAGE	BINARY	PEEK
`   **   `	00011000	24
`  ****  `	00111100	60
` **  ** `	01100110	102
` ****** `	01111110	126
` **  ** `	01100110	102
` **  ** `	01100110	102
` **  ** `	01100110	102
	00000000	0

Each complete character set takes up 2K (2048 bits) of memory, 8 bytes per character and 256 characters. Since there are two character sets, one for upper case and graphics and the other with upper and lower case, the character generator ROM takes up a total of 4K locations.

PROGRAMMABLE CHARACTERS

Since the characters are stored in ROM, it would seem that there is no way to change them for customizing characters. However, the memory location that tells the VIC-II chip where to find the characters is a programmable register which can be changed to point to many sections of memory. By changing the character memory pointer to point to RAM, the character set may be programmed for any need.

If you want your character set to be located in RAM, there are a few **VERY IMPORTANT** things to take into account when you decide to actually program your own character sets. In addition, there are two other important points you must know to create your own special characters:

1) It is an all or nothing process. Generally, if you use your own character set by telling the VIC-II chip to get the character information from the area you have prepared in RAM, the standard Commodore 64 characters are unavailable to you. To solve this, you must copy any letters, numbers, or standard Commodore 64 graphics you intend to use into your own character memory in RAM. You can pick and choose, take only the ones you want, and don't even have to keep them in order!

2) Your character set takes memory space away from your BASIC program. Of course, with 38K available for a BASIC program, most applications won't have problems.

WARNING: You must be careful to protect the character set from being overwritten by your BASIC program, which also uses the RAM.

There are two locations in the Commodore 64 to start your character set that **should NOT be used with BASIC: location 0 and location 2048.** The first should not be used because the system stores important data on page 0. The second can't be used because that is where your BASIC program starts! However, there are 6 other starting positions for your custom character set.

The best place to put your character set for use with BASIC while experimenting is beginning at 12288 ($3000 in HEX). This is done by POKEing the low 4 bits of location 53272 with 12. Try the POKE now, like this:

```
POKE 53272,(PEEK(53272)AND240)+12
```

Immediately, all the letters on the screen turn to garbage, This is because there are no characters set up at location 12288 right now . . . only random bytes. Set the Commodore 64 back to normal by hitting the **RUN/STOP** key and then the **RESTORE** key.

Now let's begin creating graphics characters. To protect your character set from BASIC, you should reduce the amount of memory BASIC thinks it has. The amount of memory in your computer stays the same. . . it's just that you've told BASIC not to use some of it. Type:

```
PRINT FRE(0)-(SGN(FRE(0))<0)*65535
```

The number displayed is the amount of memory space left unused. Now type the following:

```
POKE 52,48:POKE56,48:CLR
```

Now type:

```
PRINT FRE(0)-(SGN(FRE(0))<0)*65535
```

See the change? BASIC now thinks it has less memory to work with. The memory you just claimed from BASIC is where you are going to put your character set, safe from actions of BASIC.

The next step is to put your characters into RAM. When you begin, there is random data beginning at 12288 ($3000 HEX). You must put character patterns in RAM (in the same style as the ones in ROM) for the VIC-II chip to use.

The following program moves 64 characters from ROM to your character set RAM:

```
5 PRINTCHR$(142)                       :REM SWITCH TO
UPPER CASE
10 POKE52,48:POKE56,48:CLR             :REM RESERVE MEMORY
FOR CHARACTERS
20 POKE56334,PEEK(56334)AND254 :REM TURN OFF
KEYSCAN INTERRUPT TIMER
30 POKE1,PEEK(1)AND251                 :REM SWITCH IN
CHARACTER
40 FORI=0TO511:POKEI+12288,PEEK(I+53248):NEXT
50 POKE1,PEEK(1)OR4                    :REM SWITCH IN I/O
60 POKE56334,PEEK(56334)OR1     :REM RESTART
KEYSCAN INTERRUPT TIMER
70 END
```

Now POKE location 53272 with (PEEK(53272)AND240)+12. Nothing happens, right? Well, almost nothing. The Commodore 64 is now getting it's character information from your RAM, instead of from ROM. But since we copied the characters from ROM exactly, no difference can be seen. . . . yet.

You can easily change the characters now. Clear the screen and type an @ sign. Move the cursor down a couple of lines, then type:

FOR I = 12288 TO 12288+7:POKE I, 255 – PEEK(I) : NEXT

You just created a reversed @ sign!

> **TIP:** Reversed characters are just characters with their bit patterns in character memory reversed.

Now move the cursor up to the program again and hit **RETURN** again to re-reverse the character (bring it back to normal). By looking at the table of screen display codes, you can figure out where in RAM each character is. Just remember that each character takes eight memory locations to store. Here's a few examples just to get you started:

CHARACTER	DISPLAY CODE	CURRENT STARTING LOCATION IN RAM
@	0	12288
A	1	12296
!	33	12552
>	62	12784

Remember that we only took the first 64 characters. Something else will have to be done if you want one of the other characters.

What if you wanted character number 154, a reversed Z? Well, you could make it yourself, by reversing a Z, or you could copy the set of reversed characters from the ROM, or just take the one character you want from ROM and replace one of the characters you have in RAM that you don't need.

Suppose you decide that you won't need the > sign. Let's replace the > sign with the reversed Z. Type this:

```
FOR I=0 TO 7: POKE 12784 + I, 255-PEEK(I+12496): NEXT
```

Now type a > sign. It comes up as a reversed Z. No matter how many times you type the >, it comes out as a reversed Z. (This change is really an illusion. Though the > sign looks like a reversed Z, it still acts like a > in a program. Try something that needs a > sign. It will still work fine, only it will look strange.)

A quick review: You can now copy characters from ROM into RAM. You can even pick and choose only the ones you want. There's only one step left in programmable characters (the best step!) . . . making your own characters.

Remember how characters are stored in ROM? Each character is stored as a group of eight bytes. The bit patterns of the bytes directly control the character. If you arrange 8 bytes, one on top of another, and write out each byte as eight binary digits, it forms an eight by eight matrix, looking like the characters. When a bit is a one, there is a dot at that location. When a bit is a zero, there is a space at that location.

When creating your own characters, you set up the same kind of table in memory. Type NEW and then type this program:

```
10 FOR I = 12448 TO 12455 : READ A: POKE I,A: NEXT
20 DATA 60, 66, 165, 129, 165, 153, 66, 60
```

Now type RUN. The program will replace the letter T with a smile face character. Type a few T's to see the face. Each of the numbers in the DATA statement in line 20 is a row in the smile face character. The matrix for the face looks like this:

	7	6	5	4	3	2	1	0	BINARY	DECIMAL
ROW 0			*	*	*	*			00111100	60
1		*					*		01000010	66
2	*		*			*		*	10100101	165
3	*							*	10000001	129
4	*		*			*		*	10100101	165
5	*			*	*			*	10011001	153
6		*					*		01000010	66
ROW 7			*	*	*	*			00111100	60

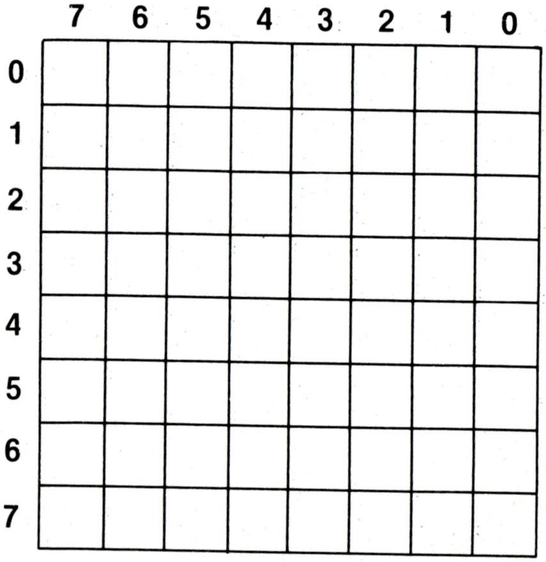

Figure 3-1. Programmable Character Worksheet.

The Programmable Character Worksheet (Figure 3-1) will help you design your own characters. There is an 8 by 8 matrix on the sheet, with row numbers, and numbers at the top of each column. (If you view each row as a binary word, the numbers are the value of that bit position. Each is a power of 2. The leftmost bit is equal to 128 or 2 to the 7th power, the next is equal to 64 or 2 to the 6th, and so on, until you reach the rightmost bit (bit 0) which is equal to 1 or 2 to the 0 power.)

Place an X on the matrix at every location where you want a dot to be in your character. When your character is ready you can create the DATA statement for your character.

Begin with the first row. Wherever you placed an X, take the number at the top of the column (the power-of-2 number, as explained above) and write it down. When you have the numbers for every column of the first row, add them together. Write this number down, next to the row. This is the number that you will put into the DATA statement to draw this row.

Do the same thing with all of the other rows (1–7). When you are finished you should have 8 numbers between 0 and 255. If any of your numbers are not within range, recheck your addition. The numbers must be in this range to be correct! If you have less than 8 numbers, you missed a row. It's OK if some are 0. The 0 rows are just as important as the other numbers.

Replace the numbers in the DATA statement in line 20 with the numbers you just calculated, and RUN the program. Then type a T. Every time you type it, you'll see your own character!

If you don't like the way the character turned out, just change the numbers in the DATA statement and re-RUN the program until you are happy with your character.

That's all there is to it!

HINT: For best results, always make any vertical lines in your characters at least 2 dots (bits) wide. This helps prevent CHROMA noise (color distortion) on your characters when they are displayed on a TV screen.

Here is an example of a program using standard programmable characters:

```
10 REM * EXAMPLE 1 *
20 REM CREATING PROGRAMMABLE CHARACTERS
31 POKE56334,PEEK(56334)AND254:POKE1,PEEK(1)AND251:
REM TURN OFF KB AND I/O
35 FORI=0TO63:REM CHARACTER RANGE TO BE COPIED
FROM ROM
36 FORJ=0TO7:REM COPY ALL 8 BYTES PER CHARACTER
37 POKE12288+I*8+J,PEEK(53248+I*8+J):REM COPY A
BYTE
38 NEXTJ:NEXTI:REM GOTO NEXT BYTE OR CHARACTER
39 POKE1,PEEK(1)OR4:POKE56334,PEEK(56334)OR1:REM
TURN ON I/O AND KB
40 POKE53272,(PEEK(53272)AND240)+12:REM SET CHAR
POINTER TO MEM. 12288
60 FORCHAR=60TO63:REM PROGRAM CHARACTERS 60 THRU 63
80 FORBYTE=0TO7:REM DO ALL 8 BYTES OF A CHARACTER
100 READ NUMBER:REM READ IN 1/8TH OF CHARACTER DATA
120 POKE12288+(8*CHAR)+BYTE,NUMBER:REM STORE THE
DATA IN MEMORY
140 NEXTBYTE:NEXTCHAR:REM ALSO COULD BE NEXT BYTE,
CHAR
150 PRINTCHR$(147)TAB(255)CHR$(60);
155 PRINTCHR$(61)TAB(55)CHR$(62)CHR$(63)
160 REM LINE 150 PUTS THE NEWLY DEFINED CHARACTERS
ON THE SCREEN
170 GETA$:REM WAIT FOR USER TO PRESS A KEY
180 IFA$=""THENGOTO170:REM IF NO KEYS WERE PRESSED,
 TRY AGAIN!
190 POKE53272,21:REM RETURN TO NORMAL CHARACTERS
200 DATA4,6,7,5,7,7,3,3:REM DATA FOR CHARACTER 60
210 DATA 32,96,224,160,224,224,192,192:REM DATA
FOR CHARACTER 61
220 DATA7,7,7,31,31,95,143,127:REM DATA FOR
CHARACTER 62
230 DATA 224,224,224,248,248,248,240,224:REM DATA
FOR CHARACTER 63
240 END
```

MULTI-COLOR MODE GRAPHICS

Standard high-resolution graphics give you control of very small dots on the screen. Each dot in character memory can have 2 possible values, 1 for on and 0 for off. When a dot is off, the color of the screen is used in the space reserved for that dot. If the dot is on, the dot is colored with the character color you have chosen for that screen position. When you're using standard high-resolution graphics, all the dots within each 8×8 character can either have background color or foreground color. In some ways this limits the color resolution within that space. For example, problems may occur when two different colored lines cross.

Multi-color mode gives you a solution to this problem. Each dot in multi-color mode can be one of 4 colors: screen color (background color register #0), the color in background register #1, the color in background color register #2, or character color. The only sacrifice is in the horizontal resolution, because each multi-color mode dot is twice as wide as a high-resolution dot. This minimal loss of resolution is more than compensated for by the extra abilities of multi-color mode.

MULTI-COLOR MODE BIT

To turn on multi-color character mode, set bit 4 of the VIC-II control register at 53270 ($D016) to a 1 by using the following POKE:

```
POKE 53270,PEEK(53270)OR 16
```

To turn off multi-color character mode, set bit 4 of location 53270 to a 0 by the following POKE:

```
POKE 53270,PEEK(53270)AND 239
```

Multi-color mode is set on or off for each space on the screen, so that multi-color graphics can be mixed with high-resolution (hi-res) graphics. This is controlled by bit 3 in color memory. Color memory begins at location 55296 ($D800 in HEX). If the number in color memory is less than 8 (0–7) the corresponding space on the video screen will be standard hi-res, in the color (0–7) you've chosen. If the number located in color memory is greater or equal to 8 (from 8 to 15), then that space will be displayed in multi-color mode.

By POKEing a number into color memory, you can change the color of the character in that position on the screen. POKEing a number from 0 to 7 gives the normal character colors. POKEing a number between 8 and 15 puts the space into multi-color mode. In other words, turning BIT 3 ON in color memory, sets MULTI-COLOR MODE. Turning BIT 3 OFF in color memory, sets the normal, HIGH-RESOLUTION mode.

Once multi-color mode is set in a space, the bits in the character determine which colors are displayed for the dots. For example, here is a picture of the letter A, and its bit pattern:

```
 IMAGE     BIT PATTERN
   **       00011000
  *****     00111100
 **   **    01100110
 ******     01111110
 **   **    01100110
 **   **    01100110
 **   **    01100110
            00000000
```

In normal or high-resolution mode, the screen color is displayed everywhere there is a 0 bit, and the character color is displayed where the bit is a 1. Multi-color mode uses the bits in pairs, like so:

```
 IMAGE      BIT PATTERN
   AABB     00 01 10 00
   CCCC     00 11 11 00
 AABBAABB   01 10 01 10
 AACCCCBB   01 11 11 10
 AABBAABB   01 10 01 10
 AABBAABB   01 10 01 10
 AABBAABB   01 10 01 10
            00 00 00 00
```

In the image area above, the spaces marked AA are drawn in the background #1 color, the spaces marked BB use the background #2 color, and the spaces marked CC use the character color. The bit pairs determine this, according to the following chart:

BIT PAIR	COLOR REGISTER	LOCATION
00	Background #0 color (screen color)	53281 ($D021)
01	Background #1 color	53282 ($D022)
10	Background #2 color	53283 ($D023)
11	Color specified by the lower 3 bits in color memory	color RAM

NOTE: The sprite foreground color is a 10. The character foreground color is a 11.

Type NEW and then type this demonstration program:

```
100 POKE53281,1:REM SET BACKGROUND COLOR #0 TO
WHITE
110 POKE53282,3:REM SET BACKGROUND COLOR #1 TO CYAN
120 POKE53283,8:REM SET BACKGROUND COLOR #2 TO
ORANGE
130 POKE53270,PEEK(53270)OR16:REM TURN ON
MULTICOLOR MODE
140 C=13*4096+8*256:REM SET C TO POINT TO COLOR
MEMORY
150 PRINTCHR$(147)"AAAAAAAAAA"
160 FORL=0TO9
170 POKEC+L,8:REM USE MULTI BLACK
180 NEXT
```

The screen color is white, the character color is black, one color register is cyan (greenish blue), the other is orange.

You're not really putting color codes in the space for character color, you're actually using references to the registers associated with those colors. This conserves memory, since 2 bits can be used to pick 16 colors (background) or 8 colors (character). This also makes some neat tricks possible. Simply changing one of the indirect registers will change every dot drawn in that color. Therefore everything drawn in the screen and background colors can be changed on the whole screen instantly. Here is an example of changing background color register #1:

```
100 POKE53270,PEEK(53270)OR16:REM TURN ON
MULTICOLOR MODE
110 PRINTCHR$(147)CHR$(18);
                  C= 1
120 PRINT"■";:REM TYPE C= & 1 FOR ORANGE OR
MULTICOLOR BLACK BACKGROUND
130 FORL=1TO22:PRINTCHR$(65);:NEXT
135 FORT=1TO500:NEXT
                  CTRL 7
140 PRINT"■";:REM TYPE CTRL & 7 FOR BLUE COLOR
CHANGE
145 FORT=1TO500:NEXT
                  CTRL 1
150 PRINT"■HIT A KEY"
160 GETA$:IFA$=""THEN160
170 X=INT(RND(1)*16)
180 POKE 53282,X
190 GOTO 160
```

By using the C= key and the COLOR keys the characters can be changed to any color, including multi-color characters. For example, type this command:

POKE 53270,PEEK(53270)OR 16:PRINT " £ ";: REM LT.RED/ MULTI-COLOR RED

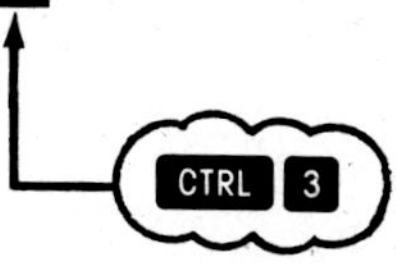

The word READY and anything else you type will be displayed in multi-color mode. Another color control can set you back to regular text.

Here is an example of a program using multi-color programmable characters:

```
10 REM * EXAMPLE 2 *
20 REM CREATING MULTI COLOR PROGRAMMABLE CHARACTERS
31 POKE56334,PEEK(56334)AND254:POKE1,PEEK(1)AND251
35 FORI=0TO63:REM CHARACTER RANGE TO BE COPIED
FROM ROM
36 FORJ=0TO7:REM COPY ALL 8 BYTES PER CHARACTER
37 POKE12288+I*8+J,PEEK(53248+I*8+J):REM COPY A
BYTE
38 NEXTJ,I:REM GOTO NEXT BYTE OR CHARACTER
39 POKE1,PEEK(1)OR4:POKE56334,PEEK(56334)OR1:REM
TURN ON I/O AND KB
40 POKE53272,(PEEK(53272)AND240)+12:REM SET CHAR
POINTER TO MEM. 12288
50 POKE53270,PEEK(53270)OR16
51 POKE53281,0:REM SET BACKGROUND COLOR #0 TO BLACK
52 POKE53282,2:REM SET BACKGROUND COLOR #1 TO RED
53 POKE53283,7:REM SET BACKGROUND COLOR #2 TO
YELLOW
60 FORCHAR=60TO63:REM PROGRAM CHARACTERS 60 THRU 63
80 FORBYTE=0TO7:REM DO ALL 8 BYTES OF A CHARACTER
100 READNUMBER:REM READ 1/8TH OF CHARACTER DATA
120 POKE12288+(8*CHAR)+BYTE,NUMBER:REM STORE THE
DATA IN MEMORY
140 NEXTBYTE,CHAR
150
          SHIFT CLR/HOME
PRINT"♥"TAB(255)CHR$(60)CHR$(61)TAB(55)CHR$(62)CHR$(63)
160 REM LINE 150 PUTS THE NEWLY DEFINED CHARACTERS
ON THE SCREEN
170 GETA$:REM WAIT FOR USER TO PRESS A KEY
180 IFA$=""THEN170:REM IF NO KEYS WERE PRESSED,
TRY AGAIN
190 POKE53272,21:POKE53270,PEEK(53270)AND239:REM
RETURN TO NORMAL CHARACTERS
200 DATA129,37,21,29,93,85,85,85:REM DATA FOR
CHARACTER 60
210 DATA66,72,84,116,117,85,85,85:REM DATA FOR
CHARACTER 61
220 DATA87,87,85,21,8,8,40,0:REM DATA FOR
CHARACTER 62
230 DATA213,213,85,84,32,32,40,0:REM DATA FOR
CHARACTER 63
240 END
```

EXTENDED BACKGROUND COLOR MODE

Extended background color mode gives you control over the background color of each individual character, as well as over the foreground color. For example, in this mode you could display a blue character with a yellow background on a white screen.

There are 4 registers available for extended background color mode. Each of the registers can be set to any of the 16 colors.

Color memory is used to hold the foreground color in extended background mode. It is used the same as in standard character mode.

Extended character mode places a limit on the number of different characters you can display, however. When extended color mode is on, only the first 64 characters in the character ROM (or the first 64 characters in your programmable character set) can be used. This is because two of the bits of the character code are used to select the background color. It might work something like this:

The character code (the number you would POKE to the screen) of the letter "A" is a 1. When extended color mode is on, if you POKEd a 1 to the screen, an "A" would appear. If you POKEd a 65 to the screen normally, you would expect the character with character code (CHR$) 129 to appear, which is a reversed "A." This does NOT happen in extended color mode. Instead you get the same unreversed "A" as before, but on a different background color. The following chart gives the codes:

CHARACTER CODE			BACKGROUND COLOR REGISTER	
RANGE	BIT 7	BIT 6	NUMBER	ADDRESS
0–63	0	0	0	53281 ($D021)
64–127	0	1	1	53282 ($D022)
128–191	1	0	2	53283 ($D023)
192–255	1	1	3	53284 ($D024)

Extended color mode is turned ON by setting bit 6 of the VIC-II register to a 1 at location 53265 ($D011 in HEX). The following POKE does it:

```
POKE 53265, PEEK(53265)OR 64
```

Extended color mode is turned OFF by setting bit 6 of the VIC-II register to a 0 at location 53265 ($D011). The following statement will do this:

```
POKE 53265, PEEK(53265)AND 191
```

BIT MAPPED GRAPHICS

When writing games, plotting charts for business applications, or other types of programs, sooner or later you get to the point where you want high-resolution displays.

The Commodore 64 has been designed to do just that: high resolution is available through bit mapping of the screen. Bit mapping is the method in which each possible dot (pixel) of resolution on the screen is assigned its own bit (location) in memory. If that memory bit is a one, the dot it is assigned to is on. If the bit is set to zero, the dot is off.

High-resolution graphic design has a couple of drawbacks, which is why it is not used all the time. First of all, it takes lots of memory to bit map the entire screen. This is because every pixel must have a memory bit to control it. You are going to need one bit of memory for each pixel (or one byte for 8 pixels). Since each character is 8 by 8, and there are 40 lines with 25 characters in each line, the resolution is 320 pixels (dots) by 200 pixels for the whole screen. That gives you 64000 separate dots, each of which requires a bit in memory. In other words, 8000 bytes of memory are needed to map the whole screen.

Generally, high-resolution operations are made of many short, simple, repetitive routines. Unfortunately, this kind of thing is usually rather slow if you are trying to write high-resolution routines in BASIC. However, short, simple, repetitive routines are exactly what machine language does best. The solution is to either write your programs entirely in machine language, or call machine language, high-resolution subroutines from your BASIC program using the SYS command from BASIC. That way you get both the ease of writing in BASIC, and the speed of machine language for graphics. The VSP cartridge is also available to add high-resolution commands to COMMODORE 64 BASIC.

All of the examples given in this section will be in BASIC to make them clear. Now to the technical details.

BIT MAPPING is one of the most popular graphics techniques in the computer world. It is used to create highly detailed pictures. Basically, when the Commodore 64 goes into bit map mode, it directly displays an

8K section of memory on the TV screen. When in bit map mode, you can *directly* control whether an individual dot on the screen is on or off.

There are two types of bit mapping available on the Commodore 64. They are:

1) Standard (high-resolution) bit mapped mode (320-dot by 200-dot resolution)
2) Multi-color bit mapped mode (160-dot by 200-dot resolution)

Each is very similar to the character type it is named for: standard has greater resolution, but fewer color selections. On the other hand, multi-color bit mapping trades horizontal resolution for a greater number of colors in an 8-dot by 8-dot square.

STANDARD HIGH-RESOLUTION BIT MAP MODE

Standard bit map mode gives you a 320 horizontal dot by 200 vertical dot resolution, with a choice of 2 colors in each 8-dot by 8-dot section. Bit map mode is selected (turned ON) by setting bit 5 of the VIC-II control register to a 1 at location 53265 ($D011 in HEX). The following POKE will do this:

```
POKE 53265,PEEK(53265)OR 32
```

Bit map mode is turned OFF by setting bit 5 of the VIC-II control register to 0 at location 53265 ($D011), like this:

```
POKE 53265,PEEK(53265)AND 223
```

Before we get into the details of the bit map mode, there is one more issue to tackle, and that is where to locate the bit map area.

HOW IT WORKS

If you remember the PROGRAMMABLE CHARACTERS section you will recall that you were able to set the bit pattern of a character stored in RAM to almost anything you wanted. If at the same time you change the character that is displayed on the screen, you would be able to change a single dot, and watch it happen. This is the basis of bit-mapping. The entire screen is filled with programmable characters, and you make your changes directly into the memory that the programmable characters get their patterns from.

Each of the locations in screen memory that were used to control what character was displayed, are now used for color information. For example, instead of POKEing a 1 in location 1024 to make an "A" appear in the top left hand corner of the screen, location 1024 now controls the colors of the bits in that top left space.

Colors of squares in bit map mode do not come from color memory, as they do in the character modes. Instead, colors are taken from screen memory. The upper 4 bits of screen memory become the color of any bit that is set to 1 in the 8 by 8 area controlled by that screen memory location. The lower 4 bits become the color of any bit that is set to a 0.

EXAMPLE: Type the following:

```
5 BASE=2*4096:POKE53272,PEEK(53272)OR8:REM PUT BIT
MAP AT 8192
10 POKE53265,PEEK(53265)OR32:REM ENTER BIT MAP MODE
```

Now RUN the program.

Garbage appears on the screen, right? Just like the normal screen mode, you have to clear the HIGH-RESOLUTION (HI-RES) screen before you use it. Unfortunately, printing a CLR won't work in this case. Instead you have to clear out the section of memory that you're using for your programmable characters. Hit the **RUN/STOP** and **RESTORE** keys, then add the following lines to your program to clear the HI-RES screen:

```
20 FORI=BASETOBASE+7999:POKEI,0:NEXT:REM CLEAR BIT
MAP
30 FORI=1024TO2023:POKEI,3:NEXT:REM SET COLOR TO
CYAN AND BLACK
```

Now RUN the program again. You should see the screen clearing, then the greenish blue color, cyan, should cover the whole screen. What we want to do now is to turn the dots on and off on the HI-RES screen.

To SET a dot (turn a dot ON) or UNSET a dot (turn a dot OFF) you must know how to find the correct bit in the character memory that you have to set to a 1. In other words, you have to find the character you need to change, the row of the character, and which bit of the row that you have to change. You need a formula to calculate this.

We will use X and Y to stand for the horizontal and vertical positions of a dot. The dot where X=0 and Y=0 is at the upper-left of the display. Dots to the right have higher X values, and the dots toward the bottom have higher Y values. The best way to use bit mapping is to arrange the bit map display something like this:

```
0-------------------------------------------X-------------------------------------319
.                                                                                   .
.                                                                                   .
.                                                                                   .
Y                                                                                   .
.                                                                                   .
.                                                                                   .
.                                                                                   .
199---------------------------------------------------------------------------------
```

Each dot will have an X and a Y coordinate. With this format it is easy to control any dot on the screen.

However, what you actually have is something like this:

TOP LINE (ROW 0)	BYTE 0	BYTE 8	BYTE 16	BYTE 24	....	BYTE 312
	BYTE 1	BYTE 9	.	.		BYTE 313
	BYTE 2	BYTE 10	.	.		BYTE 314
	BYTE 3	BYTE 11	.	.		BYTE 315
	BYTE 4	BYTE 12	.	.		BYTE 316
	BYTE 5	BYTE 13	.	.		BYTE 317
	BYTE 6	BYTE 14	.	.		BYTE 318
	BYTE 7	BYTE 15	.	.		BYTE 319
SECOND LINE (ROW 1)	BYTE 320	BYTE 328	BYTE 336	BYTE 344	....	BYTE 632
	BYTE 321	BYTE 329	.	.		BYTE 633
	BYTE 322	BYTE 330	.	.		BYTE 634
	BYTE 323	BYTE 331	.	.		BYTE 635
	BYTE 324	BYTE 332	.	.		BYTE 636
	BYTE 325	BYTE 333	.	.		BYTE 637
	BYTE 326	BYTE 334	.	.		BYTE 638
	BYTE 327	BYTE 335	.	.		BYTE 639

The programmable characters which make up the bit map are arranged in 25 rows of 40 columns each. While this is a good method of organization for text, it makes bit mapping somewhat difficult. (There is a good reason for this method. See the section on MIXED MODES.)

The following formula will make it easier to control a dot on the bit map screen:

The start of the display memory area is known as the BASE. The row number (from 0 to 24) of your dot is:

ROW = INT(Y/8) (There are 320 bytes per line.)

The character position on that line (from 0 to 39) is:

CHAR = INT(X/8) (There are 8 bytes per character.)

The line of that character position (from 0 to 7) is:

LINE = Y AND 7

The bit of that byte is:

BIT = 7−(X AND 7)

Now we put these formulas together. The byte in which character memory dot (X,Y) is located is calculated by:

BYTE = BASE + ROW*320+ CHAR*8 + LINE

To turn on any bit on the grid with coordinates (X,Y), use this line:

POKE BYTE, PEEK(BYTE) OR 2↑BIT

Let's add these calculations to the program. In the following example, the COMMODORE 64 will plot a sine curve:

```
50 FORX=0TO319STEP.5:REM WAVE WILL FILL THE SCREEN
60 Y=INT(90+80*SIN(X/10))
70 CH=INT(X/8)
80 RO=INT(Y/8)
85 LN=YAND7
90 BY=BASE+RO*320+8*CH+LN
100 BI=7-(XAND7)
110 POKEBY,PEEK(BY)OR(2↑BI)
120 NEXTX
125 POKE1024,16
130 GOTO130
```

The calculation in line 60 will change the values for the sine function from a range of +1 to −1 to a range of 10 to 170. Lines 70 to 100 calculate the character, row, byte, and bit being affected, using the formulae as shown above. Line 125 signals the program is finished by changing the color of the top left corner of the screen. Line 130 freezes the program by putting it into an infinite loop. When you have finished looking at the display, just hold down **RUN/STOP** and hit **RESTORE**.

As a further example, you can modify the sine curve program to display a semicircle. Here are the lines to type to make the changes:

```
50 FORX=0TO160:REM DO HALF THE SCREEN
55 Y1=100+SQR(160*X-X*X)
56 Y2=100-SQR(160*X-X*X)
60 FORY=Y1TOY2STEPY1-Y2
70 CH=INT(X/8)
80 RO=INT(Y/8)
85 LN=YAND7
90 BY=BASE+RO*320+8*CH+LN
100 BI=7-(XAND7)
110 POKEBY,PEEK(BY)OR(2↑BI)
114 NEXT
```

This will create a semicircle in the HI-RES area of the screen.

> **WARNING:** BASIC variables can overlay your high-resolution screen. If you need more memory space you must move the bottom of BASIC above the high-resolution screen area. Or, you must move your high-resolution screen area. This problem will NOT occur in machine language. It ONLY happens when you're writing programs in BASIC.

MULTI-COLOR BIT MAP MODE

Like multi-color mode characters, multi-color bit map mode allows you to display up to four different colors in each 8 by 8 section of bit map. And as in multi-character mode, there is a sacrifice of horizontal resolution (from 320 dots to 160 dots).

Multi-color bit map mode uses an 8K section of memory for the bit map. You select your colors for multi-color bit map mode from (1) the background color register 0, (the screen background color), (2) the video matrix (the upper 4 bits give one possible color, the lower 4 bits another), and (3) color memory.

Multi-color bit mapped mode is turned ON by setting bit 5 of 53265 ($D011) and bit 4 at location 53270 ($D016) to a 1. The following POKE does this:

POKE 53265,PEEK(53625)OR 32: POKE 53270,PEEK(53270)OR 16

Multi-color bit mapped mode is turned OFF by setting bit 5 of 53265 ($D011) and bit 4 at location 53270 ($D016) to a 0. The following POKE does this:

POKE 53265,PEEK(53265)AND 223: POKE 53270,PEEK(53270)AND 239

As in standard (HI-RES) bit mapped mode, there is a one to one correspondence between the 8K section of memory being used for the display, and what is shown on the screen. However, the horizontal dots are two bits wide. Each 2 bits in the display memory area form a dot, which can have one of 4 colors.

BITS	COLOR INFORMATION COMES FROM
00	Background color #0 (screen color)
01	Upper 4 bits of screen memory
10	Lower 4 bits of screen memory
11	Color nybble (nybble = 1/2 byte = 4 bits)

SMOOTH SCROLLING

The VIC-II chip supports smooth scrolling in both the horizontal and vertical directions. Smooth scrolling is a one pixel movement of the entire screen in one direction. It can move either up, or down, or left, or right. It is used to move new information smoothly onto the screen, while smoothly removing characters from the other side.

While the VIC-II chip does much of the task for you, the actual scrolling must be done by a machine language program. The VIC-II chip features the ability to place the video screen in any of 8 horizontal positions, and 8 vertical positions. Positioning is controlled by the VIC-II scrolling registers. The VIC-II chip also has a 38 column mode, and a 24 row mode. the smaller screen sizes are used to give you a place for your new data to scroll on from.

The following are the steps for SMOOTH SCROLLING:

1) Shrink the screen (the border will expand).
2) Set the scrolling register to maximum (or minimum value depending upon the direction of your scroll).
3) Place the new data on the proper (covered) portion of the screen.
4) Increment (or decrement) the scrolling register until it reaches the maximum (or minimum) value.
5) At this point, use your machine language routine to shift the entire screen one entire character in the direction of the scroll.
6) Go back to step 2.

To go into 38 column mode, bit 3 of location 53270 ($D016) must be set to a 0. The following POKE does this:

```
POKE 53270,PEEK(53270)AND 247
```

To return to 40 column mode, set bit 3 of location 53270 ($D016) to a 1. The following POKE does this:

```
POKE 53270,PEEK(53270)OR 8
```

To go into 24 row mode, bit 3 of location 53265 ($D011) must be set to a 0. The following POKE will do this:

```
POKE 53265,PEEK(53265)AND 247
```

To return to 25 row mode, set bit 3 of location 53265 ($D011) to a 1. The following POKE does this:

```
POKE 53265,PEEK(53265)OR 8
```

When scrolling in the X direction, it is necessary to place the VIC-II chip into 38 column mode. This gives new data a place to scroll from. When scrolling LEFT, the new data should be placed on the right. When scrolling RIGHT the new data should be placed on the left. Please note that there are still 40 columns to screen memory, but only 38 are visible.

When scrolling in the Y direction, it is necessary to place the VIC-II chip into 24 row mode. When scrolling UP, place the new data in the LAST row. When scrolling DOWN, place the new data on the FIRST row. Unlike X scrolling, where there are covered areas on each side of the screen, there is only one covered area in Y scrolling. When the Y scrolling register is set to 0, the first line is covered, ready for new data. When the Y scrolling register is set to 7 the last row is covered.

For scrolling in the X direction, the scroll register is located in bits 2 to 0 of the VIC-II control register at location 53270 ($D016 in HEX). As always, it is important to affect only those bits. The following POKE does this:

POKE 53270, (PEEK(53270)AND 248)+X

where X is the X position of the screen from 0 to 7.

For scrolling in the Y direction, the scroll register is located in bits 2 to 0 of the VIC-II control register at location 53265 ($D011 in HEX). As always, it is important to affect only those bits. The following POKE does this:

POKE 53265, (PEEK(53265)AND 248)+Y

where Y is the Y position of the screen from 0 to 7.

To scroll text onto the screen from the bottom, you would step the low-order 3 bits of location 53265 from 0–7, put more data on the covered line at the bottom of the screen, and then repeat the process. To scroll characters onto the screen from left to right, you would step the low-order 3 bits of location 53270 from 0 to 7, print or POKE another column of new data into column 0 of the screen, then repeat the process.

If you step the scroll bits by −1, your text will move in the opposite direction.

EXAMPLE: Text scrolling onto the bottom of the screen:

```
10 POKE53265,PEEK(53265)AND247             :REM GO
INTO 24 ROW MODE
20 PRINTCHR$(147)                          :REM
CLEAR THE SCREEN
30 FORX=1TO24:PRINTCHR$(17);:NEXT          :REM MOVE
THE CURSOR TO THE BOTTOM
40 POKE53265,(PEEK(53265)AND248)+7:PRINT  :REM
POSITION FOR 1ST SCROLL
50 PRINT"     HELLO";
60 FORP=6TO0STEP-1
70 POKE53265,(PEEK(53265)AND248)+P
80 FORX=1TO50:NEXT                         :REM
DELAY LOOP
90 NEXT:GOTO40
```

SPRITES

A SPRITE is a special type of user definable character which can be displayed anywhere on the screen. Sprites are maintained directly by the VIC-II chip. And all you have to do is tell a sprite "what to look like," "what color to be," and "where to appear." The VIC-II chip will do the rest! Sprites can be any of the 16 colors available.

Sprites can be used with ANY of the other graphics modes, bit mapped, character, multi-color, etc., and they'll keep their shape in all of them. The sprite carries its own color definition, its own mode (HI-RES or multi-colored), and its own shape.

Up to 8 sprites at a time can be maintained by the VIC-II chip automatically. More sprites can be displayed using RASTER INTERRUPT techniques.

The features of SPRITES include:

1) 24 horizontal dot by 21 vertical dot size.
2) Individual color control for each sprite.
3) Sprite multi-color mode.
4) Magnification (2×) in horizontal, vertical, or both directions.
5) Selectable sprite to background priority.
6) Fixed sprite to sprite priorities.
7) Sprite to sprite collision detection.
8) Sprite to background collision detection.

These special sprite abilities make it simple to program many arcade style games. Because the sprites are maintained by hardware, it is even possible to write a good quality game in BASIC!

There are 8 sprites supported directly by the VIC-II chip. They are numbered from 0 to 7. Each of the sprites has it own definition location, position registers and color register, and has its own bits for enable and collision detection.

DEFINING A SPRITE

Sprites are defined like programmable characters are defined. However, since the size of the sprite is larger, more bytes are needed. A sprite is 24 by 21 dots, or 504 dots. This works out to 63 bytes (504/8

COLUMN NUMBER	00	01	02	03	04	05	06	07	08	09	10	11	12	13	14	15	16	17	18	19	20	21	22	23
BIT	7	6	5	4	3	2	1	0	7	6	5	4	3	2	1	0	7	6	5	4	3	2	1	0
BIT DATA VALUES (ON = 1 × VAL)	128	64	32	16	8	4	2	1	128	64	32	16	8	4	2	1	128	64	32	16	8	4	2	1
ROW 0																								
ROW 1																								
ROW 2																								
ROW 3																								
ROW 4																								
ROW 5																								
ROW 6																								
ROW 7																								
ROW 8																								
ROW 9																								
ROW 10																								
ROW 11																								
ROW 12																								
ROW 13																								
ROW 14																								
ROW 15																								
ROW 16																								
ROW 17																								
ROW 18																								
ROW 19																								
ROW 20																								

Figure 3-2. Sprite Definition Block.

bits) needed to define a sprite. The 63 bytes are arranged in 21 rows of 3 bytes each. A sprite definition looks like this:

BYTE 0	BYTE 1	BYTE 2
BYTE 3	BYTE 4	BYTE 5
BYTE 6	BYTE 7	BYTE 8
..	..	..
..	..	..
..	..	..
BYTE 60	BYTE 61	BYTE 62

Another way to view how a sprite is created is to take a look at the sprite definition block on the bit level. It would look something like Figure 3-2.

In a standard (HI-RES) sprite, each bit set to 1 is displayed in that sprite's foreground color. Each bit set to 0 is transparent and will display whatever data is behind it. This is similar to a standard character.

Multi-color sprites are similar to multi-color characters. Horizontal resolution is traded for extra color resolution. The resolution of the sprite becomes 12 horizontal dots by 21 vertical dots. Each dot in the sprite becomes twice as wide, but the number of colors displayable in the sprite is increased to 4.

SPRITE POINTERS

Even though each sprite takes only 63 bytes to define, one more byte is needed as a place holder at the end of each sprite. Each sprite, then, takes up 64 bytes. This makes it easy to calculate where in memory your sprite definition is, since 64 bytes is an even number and in binary it's an even power.

Each of the 8 sprites has a byte associated with it called the **SPRITE POINTER.** The sprite pointers control where each sprite definition is located in memory. These 8 bytes are always located as the last 8 bytes of the 1K chunk of screen memory. Normally, on the Commodore 64, this means they begin at location 2040 ($07F8 in HEX). However, if you move the screen, the location of your sprite pointers will also move.

Each sprite pointer can hold a number from 0 to 255. This number points to the definition for that sprite. Since each sprite definition takes 64 bytes, that means that the pointer can "see" anywhere in the 16K block of memory that the VIC-II chip can access (since 256*64=16K).

If sprite pointer #0, at location 2040, contains the number 14, for example, this means that sprite 0 will be displayed using the 64 bytes beginning at location 14*64 = 896 which is in the cassette buffer. The following formula makes this clear:

LOCATION = (BANK * 16384) + (SPRITE POINTER VALUE * 64)

Where BANK is the 16K segment of memory that the VIC-II chip is looking at and is from 0 to 3.

The above formula gives the start of the 64 bytes of the sprite definition block.

When the VIC-II chip is looking at BANK 0 or BANK 2, there is a ROM IMAGE of the character set present in certain locations, as mentioned before. Sprite definitions can NOT be placed there. If for some reason you need more than 128 different sprite definitions, you should use one of the banks without the ROM IMAGE, 1 or 3.

TURNING SPRITES ON

The VIC-II control register at location 53269 ($D015 in HEX) is known as the **SPRITE ENABLE** register. Each of the sprites has a bit in this register which controls whether that sprite is ON or OFF. The register looks like this:

$D015 7 6 5 4 3 2 1 0

To turn on sprite 1, for example, it is necessary to turn that bit to a 1. The following POKE does this:

```
POKE 53269,PEEK(53269)OR 2
```

A more general statement would be the following:

```
POKE 53269,PEEK(53269)OR (2↑SN)
```

where SN is the sprite number, from 0 to 7.

> **NOTE:** A sprite must be turned ON before it can be seen.

TURNING SPRITES OFF

A sprite is turned off by setting its bit in the VIC-II control register at 53269 ($D015 in HEX) to a 0. The following POKE will do this:

POKE 53269, PEEK(53269)AND (255−2↑SN)

where SN is the sprite number from 0 to 7.

COLORS

A sprite can be any of the 16 colors generated by the VIC-II chip. Each of the sprites has its own sprite color register. These are the memory locations of the color registers:

ADDRESS		DESCRIPTION
53287	($D027)	SPRITE 0 COLOR REGISTER
53288	($D028)	SPRITE 1 COLOR REGISTER
53289	($D029)	SPRITE 2 COLOR REGISTER
53290	($D02A)	SPRITE 3 COLOR REGISTER
53291	($D02B)	SPRITE 4 COLOR REGISTER
53292	($D02C)	SPRITE 5 COLOR REGISTER
53293	($D02D)	SPRITE 6 COLOR REGISTER
53294	($D02E)	SPRITE 7 COLOR REGISTER

All dots in the sprite will be displayed in the color contained in the sprite color register. The rest of the sprite will be transparent, and will show whatever is behind the sprite.

MULTI-COLOR MODE

Multi-color mode allows you to have up to 4 different colors in each sprite. However, just like other multi-color modes, horizontal resolution is cut in half. In other words, when you're working with sprite multi-color mode (like in multi-color character mode), instead of 24 dots across the sprite, there are 12 pairs of dots. Each pair of dots is called a BIT PAIR. Think of each bit pair (pair of dots) as a single dot in your overall sprite when it comes to choosing colors for the dots in your sprites. The table below gives you the bit pair values needed to turn ON each of the four colors you've chosen for your sprite:

BIT PAIR	DESCRIPTION
00	TRANSPARENT, SCREEN COLOR
01	SPRITE MULTI-COLOR REGISTER #0 (53285) ($D025)
10	SPRITE COLOR REGISTER
11	SPRITE MULTI-COLOR REGISTER #1 (53286) ($D026)

NOTE: The sprite foreground color is a 10. The character foreground is a 11.

SETTING A SPRITE TO MULTI-COLOR MODE

To switch a sprite into multi-color mode you must turn ON the VIC-II control register at location 53276 ($D01C). The following POKE does this:

```
POKE 53276,PEEK(53276) OR (2↑SN)
```

where SN is the sprite number (0 to 7).

To switch a sprite out of multi-color mode you must turn OFF the VIC-II control register at location 53276 ($D01C). The following POKE does this:

```
POKE 53276,PEEK(53276) AND (255−2↑SN)
```

where SN is the sprite number (0 to 7).

EXPANDED SPRITES

The VIC-II chip has the ability to expand a sprite in the vertical direction, the horizontal direction, or both at once. When expanded, each dot in the sprite is twice as wide or twice as tall. Resolution doesn't actually increase . . . the sprite just gets bigger.

To expand a sprite in the horizontal direction, the corresponding bit in the VIC-II control register at location 53277 ($D01D in HEX) must be turned ON (set to a 1). The following POKE expands a sprite in the X direction:

```
POKE 53277,PEEK(53277)OR (2↑SN)
```

where SN is the sprite number from 0 to 7.

To unexpand a sprite in the horizontal direction, the corresponding bit in the VIC-II control register at location 53277 ($D01D in HEX) must be turned OFF (set to a 0). The following POKE "unexpands" a sprite in the X direction:

```
POKE 53277,PEEK(53277)AND (255−2↑SN)
```

where SN is the sprite number from 0 to 7.

To expand a sprite in the vertical direction, the corresponding bit in the VIC-II control register at location 53271 ($D017 in HEX) must be turned ON (set to a 1). The following POKE expands a sprite in the Y direction:

```
POKE 53271,PEEK(53271)OR (2↑SN)
```

where SN is the sprite number from 0 to 7.

To unexpand a sprite in the vertical direction, the corresponding bit in the VIC-II control register at location 53271 ($D017 in HEX) must be turned OFF (set to a 0). The following POKE "unexpands" a sprite in the Y direction:

```
POKE 53271,PEEK(53271)AND (255−2↑SN)
```

where SN is the sprite number from 0 to 7.

SPRITE POSITIONING

Once you've made a sprite you want to be able to move it around the screen. To do this, your Commodore 64 uses three positioning registers:

1) SPRITE X POSITION REGISTER
2) SPRITE Y POSITION REGISTER
3) MOST SIGNIFICANT BIT X POSITION REGISTER

Each sprite has an X position register, a Y position register, and a bit in the X most significant bit register. This lets you position your sprites very accurately. You can place your sprite in 512 possible X positions and 256 possible Y positions.

The X and Y position registers work together, in pairs, as a team. The locations of the X and Y registers appear in the memory map as follows: First is the X register for sprite 0, then the Y register for sprite 0. Next comes the X register for sprite 1, the Y register for sprite 1, and so on. After all 16 X and Y registers comes the most significant bit in the X position (X MSB) located in its own register.

The chart below lists the locations of each sprite position register. You use the locations at their appropriate time through POKE statements:

LOCATION		DESCRIPTION
DECIMAL	HEX	
53248	($D000)	SPRITE 0 X POSITION REGISTER
53249	($D001)	SPRITE 0 Y POSITION REGISTER
53250	($D002)	SPRITE 1 X POSITION REGISTER
53251	($D003)	SPRITE 1 Y POSITION REGISTER
53252	($D004)	SPRITE 2 X POSITION REGISTER
53253	($D005)	SPRITE 2 Y POSITION REGISTER
53254	($D006)	SPRITE 3 X POSITION REGISTER
53255	($D007)	SPRITE 3 Y POSITION REGISTER
53256	($D008)	SPRITE 4 X POSITION REGISTER
53257	($D009)	SPRITE 4 Y POSITION REGISTER
53258	($D00A)	SPRITE 5 X POSITION REGISTER
53259	($D00B)	SPRITE 5 Y POSITION REGISTER
53260	($D00C)	SPRITE 6 X POSITION REGISTER
53261	($D00D)	SPRITE 6 Y POSITION REGISTER
53262	($D00E)	SPRITE 7 X POSITION REGISTER
53263	($D00F)	SPRITE 7 Y POSITION REGISTER
53264	($D010)	SPRITE X MSB REGISTER

The position of a sprite is calculated from the TOP LEFT corner of the 24 dot by 21 dot area that your sprite can be designed in. It does NOT matter how many or how few dots you use to make up a sprite. Even if only one dot is used as a sprite, and you happen to want it in the middle of the screen, you must still calculate the exact positioning by starting at the top left corner location.

VERTICAL POSITIONING

Setting up positions in the horizontal direction is a little more difficult than vertical positioning, so we'll discuss vertical (Y) positioning first.

There are 200 different dot positions that can be individually programmed onto your TV screen in the Y direction. The sprite Y position registers can handle numbers up to 255. This means that you have more than enough register locations to handle moving a sprite up and down. You also want to be able to smoothly move a sprite on and off the screen. More than 200 values are needed for this.

The first on-screen value from the top of the screen, and in the Y direction for an unexpanded sprite is 30. For a sprite expanded in the Y direction it would be 9. (Since each dot is twice as tall, this makes a certain amount of sense, as the initial position is STILL calculated from the top left corner of the sprite.)

The first Y value in which a sprite (expanded or not) is fully on the screen (all 21 possible lines displayed) is 50.

The last Y value in which an unexpanded sprite is fully on the screen is 229. The last Y value in which an expanded sprite is fully on the screen is 208.

The first Y value in which a sprite is fully off the screen is 250.

EXAMPLE:

SHIFT CLR/HOME

```
10 PRINT"♥"                             :REM CLEAR SCREEN
20 POKE2040,13                          :REM GET SPRITE 0
DATA FROM BLOCK 13
30 FORI=0TO62:POKE832+I,129:NEXT:REM POKE SPRITE
DATA INTO BLOCK 13 (13*64=832)
40 V=53248                              :REM SET BEGINNING
OF VIDEO CHIP
50 POKEV+21,1                           :REM ENABLE SPRITE
1
60 POKEV+39,1                           :REM SET SPRITE 0
COLOR
70 POKEV+1,100                          :REM SET SPRITE 0
Y POSITION
80 POKEV+16,0:POKEV,100                 :REM SET SPRITE 0
X POSITION
```

HORIZONTAL POSITIONING

Positioning in the horizontal direction is more complicated because there are more than 256 positions. This means that an extra bit, or 9th bit is used to control the X position. By adding the extra bit when necessary a sprite now has 512 possible positions in the left/right, X, direction. This makes more possible combinations than can be seen on the visible part of the screen. Each sprite can have a position from 0 to 511. However, only those values between 24 and 343 are visible on the screen. If the X position of a sprite is greater than 255 (on the right side of the screen), the bit in the X MOST SIGNIFICANT BIT POSITION register must be set to a 1 (turned ON). If the X position of a sprite is less than

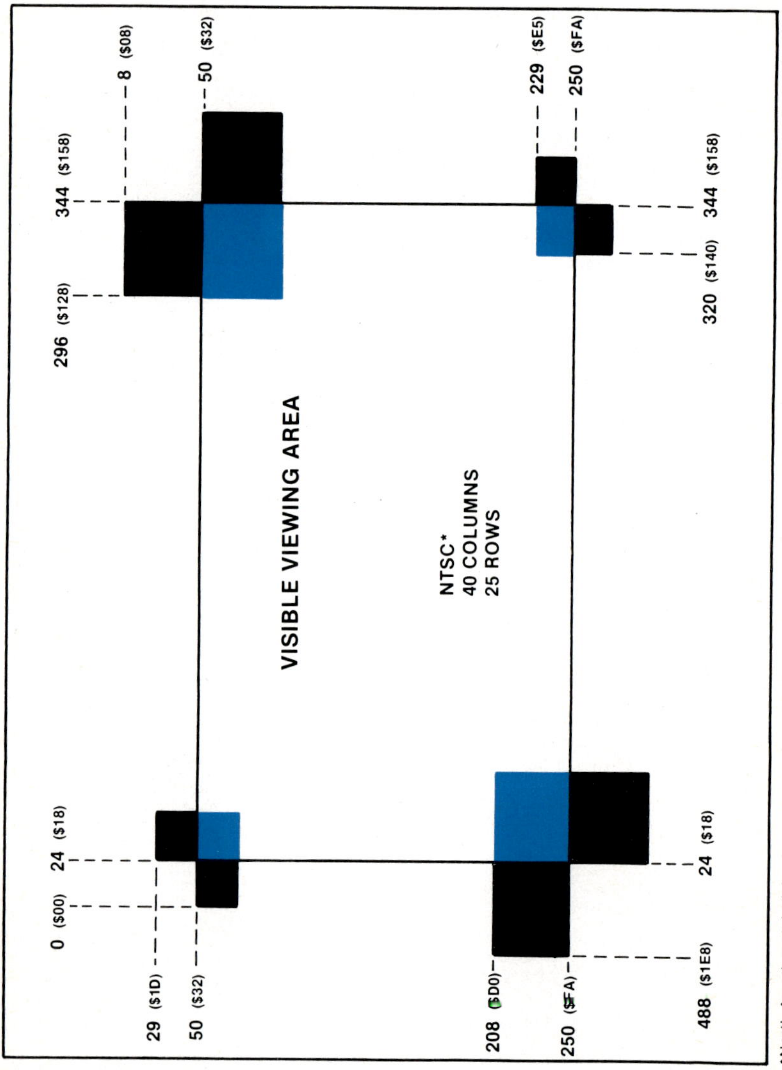

*North American television transmission standards for your home TV.

Figure 3-3. Sprite

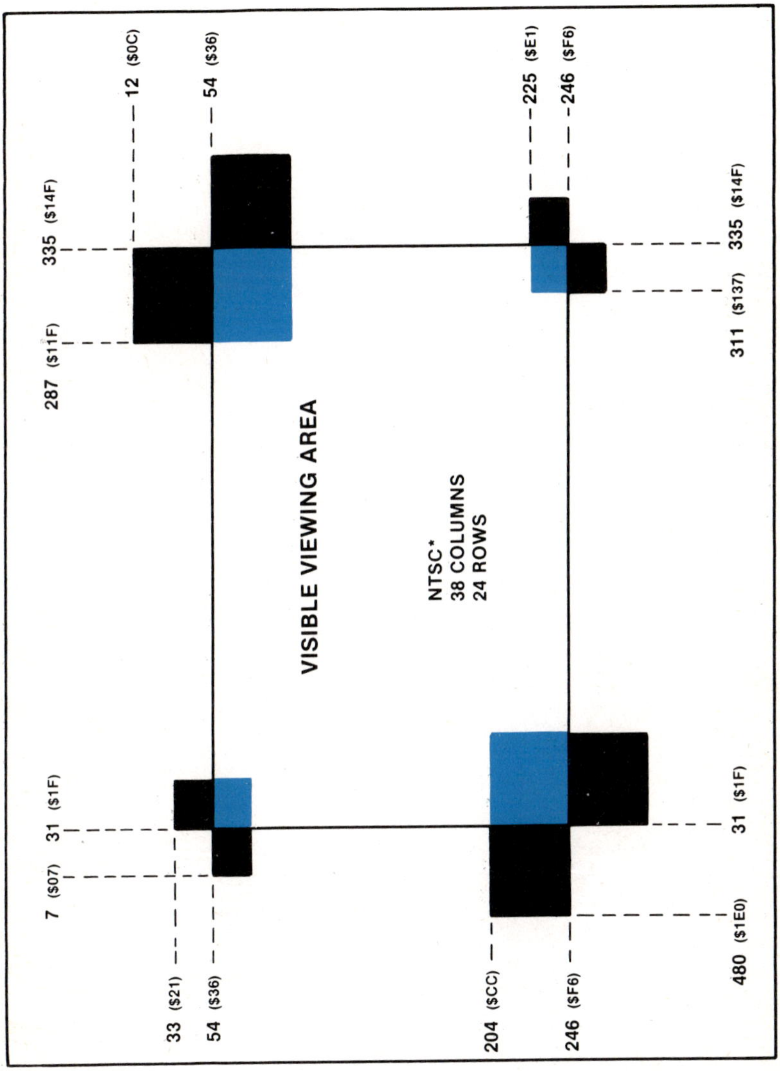

*North American television transmission standards for your home TV.

Positioning Charts.

256 (on the left side of the screen), then the X MSB of that sprite must be 0 (turned OFF). Bits 0 to 7 of the X MSB register correspond to sprites 0 to 7, respectively.

The following program moves a sprite across the screen:

EXAMPLE:

SHIFT CLR/HOME

```
10 PRINT"♥"
20 POKE2040,13
30 FORI=0TO62:POKE832+I,129:NEXT
40 V=53248
50 POKEV+21,1
60 POKEV+39,1
70 POKEV+1,100
80 FORJ=0TO347
90 HX=INT(J/256):LX=J-256*HX
100 POKEV,LX:POKEV+16,HX:NEXT
```

When moving expanded sprites onto the left side of the screen in the X direction, you have to start the sprite OFF SCREEN on the RIGHT SIDE. This is because an expanded sprite is larger than the amount of space available on the left side of the screen.

EXAMPLE:

SHIFT CLR/HOME

```
10 PRINT"♥"
20 POKE2040,13
30 FORI=0TO62:POKE832+I,129:NEXT
40 V=53248
50 POKEV+21,1
60 POKEV+39,1:POKEV+23,1:POKEV+29,1
70 POKEV+1,100
80 J=488
90 HX=INT(J/256):LX=J-256*HX
100 POKEV,LX:POKEV+16,HX
110 J=J+1:IFJ>511THENJ=0
120 IFJ>488ORJ<348GOTO90
```

The charts in Figure 3-3 explain sprite positioning.

By using these values, you can position each sprite anywhere. By moving the sprite a single dot position at a time, very smooth movement is easy to achieve.

SPRITE POSITIONING SUMMARY

Unexpanded sprites are at least partially visible in the 40 column, by 25 row mode within the following parameters:

$$1 < = X < = 343$$

$$30 < = Y < = 249$$

In the 38 column mode, the X parameters change to the following:

$$8 < = X < = 334$$

In the 24 row mode, the Y parameters change to the following:

$$34 < = Y < = 245$$

Expanded sprites are at least partially visible in the 40 column, by 25 row mode within the following parameters:

$$489 > = X < = 343$$

$$9 > = Y < = 249$$

In the 38 column mode, the X parameters change to the following:

$$496 > = X < = 334$$

In the 24 row mode, the Y parameters change to the following:

$$13 < = Y < = 245$$

SPRITE DISPLAY PRIORITIES

Sprites have the ability to cross each other's paths, as well as cross in front of, or behind other objects on the screen. This can give you a truly three dimensional effect for games.

Sprite to sprite priority is fixed. That means that sprite 0 has the highest priority, sprite 1 has the next priority, and so on, until we get to sprite 7, which has the lowest priority. In other words, if sprite 1 and sprite 6 are positioned so that they cross each other, sprite 1 will be in front of sprite 6.

So when you're planning which sprites will appear to be in the foreground of the picture, they must be assigned lower sprite numbers than those sprites you want to put towards the back of the scene. Those sprites will be given higher sprite numbers.

> **NOTE:** A "window" effect is possible. If a sprite with higher priority has "holes" in it (areas where the dots are not set to 1 and thus turned ON), the sprite with the lower priority will show through. This also happens with sprite and background data.

Sprite to background priority is controllable by the SPRITE-BACKGROUND priority register located at 53275 ($D01B). Each sprite has a bit in this register. If that bit is 0, that sprite has a higher priority than the background on the screen. In other words, the sprite appears in front of background data. If that bit is a 1, that sprite has a lower priority than the background. Then the sprite appears behind the background data.

COLLISION DETECTS

One of the more interesting aspects of the VIC-II chip is its collision detection abilities. Collisions can be detected between sprites, or between sprites and background data. A collision occurs when a non-zero part of a sprite overlaps a non-zero portion of another sprite or characters on the screen.

SPRITE TO SPRITE COLLISIONS

Sprite to sprite collisions are recognized by the computer, or flagged, in the spite to sprite collision register at location 53278 ($D01E in HEX) in the VIC-II chip control register. Each sprite has a bit in this register. If that bit is a 1, then that sprite is involved in a collision. The bits in this register will remain set until read (PEEKed). Once read, the register is automatically cleared, so it is a good idea to save the value in a variable until you are finished with it.

> **NOTE:** Collisions can take place even when the sprites are off screen.

SPRITE TO DATA COLLISIONS

Sprite to data collisions are detected in the sprite to data collision register at location 53279 ($D01F in HEX) of the VIC-II chip control register.

Each sprite has a bit in this register. If that bit is a 1, then that sprite is involved in a collision. The bits in this register remain set until read (PEEKed). Once read, the register is automatically cleared, so it is a good idea to save the value in a variable until you are finished with it.

> **NOTE:** MULTI-COLOR data **01** is considered transparent for collisions, even though it shows up on the screen. When setting up a background screen, it is a good idea to make everything that should not cause a collision 01 in multi-color mode.

```
10 REM SPRITE EXAMPLE 1...
20 REM THE HOT AIR BALLOON
30 VIC=13*4096:REM THIS IS WHERE THE VIC REGISTERS
BEGIN
35 POKEVIC+21,1:REM ENABLE SPRITE 0
36 POKEVIC+33,14:REM SET BACKGROUND COLOR TO LIGHT
BLUE
37 POKEVIC+23,1:REM EXPAND SPRITE 0 IN Y
38 POKEVIC+29,1:REM EXPAND SPRITE 0 IN X
40 POKE2040,192:REM SET SPRITE 0'S POINTER
180 POKEVIC+0,100:REM SET SPRITE 0'S X POSITION
190 POKEVIC+1,100:REM SET SPRITE 0'S Y POSITION
220 POKEVIC+39,1:REM SET SPRITE 0'S COLOR
250 FORY=0TO63:REM BYTE COUNTER WITH SPRITE LOOP
300 READA:REM READ IN A BYTE
310 POKE192*64+Y,A:REM STORE THE DATA IN SPRITE
AREA
320 NEXTY:REM CLOSE LOOP
330 DX=1:DY=1
340 X=PEEK(VIC):REM LOOK AT SPRITE 0'S X POSITION
350 Y=PEEK(VIC+1):REM LOOK AT SPRITE 0'S Y POSITION
360 IFY=50ORY=208THENDY=-DY:REM IF Y IS ON THE
EDGE OF THE....
370 REM SCREEN, THEN REVERSE DELTA Y
380 IFX=24AND(PEEK(VIC+16)AND1)=0THENDX=-DX:REM IF
SPRITE IS....
390 REM TOUCHING THE LEFT EDGE (X=24 AND THE MSB
FOR SPRITE 0 IS 0), REVERSE IT
400 IFX=40AND(PEEK(VIC+16)AND1)=1THENDX=-DX:REM IF
SPRITE IS....
410 REM TOUCHING THE RIGHT EDGE (X=40 AND THE MSB
FOR SPRITE 0 IS 1), REVERSE IT
420 IFX=255ANDDX=1THENX=-1:SIDE=1
430 REM SWITCH TO OTHER SIDE OF THE SCREEN
440 IFX=0ANDDX=-1THENX=256:SIDE=0
450 REM SWITCH TO OTHER SIDE OF THE SCREEN
460 X=X+DX:REM ADD DELTA X TO X
470 X=XAND255:REM MAKE SURE X IS IN ALLOWED RANGE
480 Y=Y+DY:REM ADD DELTA Y TO Y
485 POKEVIC+16,SIDE
490 POKEVIC,X:REM PUT NEW X VALUE INTO SPRITE 0'S
X POSITION
510 POKEVIC+1,Y:REM PUT NEW Y VALUE INTO SPRITE
0'S Y POSITION
530 GOTO340
600 REM ***** SPRITE DATA *****
610 DATA0,127,0,1,255,192,3,255,224,3,231,224
620 DATA7,217,240,7,223,240,7,217,240,3,231,224
630 DATA3,255,224,3,255,224,2,255,160,1,127,64
640 DATA1,62,64,0,156,128,0,156,128,0,73,0,0,73,0
650 DATA0,62,0,0,62,0,0,62,0,0,28,0,0
```

```
10 REM SPRITE EXAMPLE 2...
20 REM THE HOT AIR BALLOON AGAIN
30 VIC=13*4096:REM THIS IS WHERE THE VIC REGISTERS
BEGIN
35 POKEVIC+21,63:REM ENABLE SPRITES 0 THRU 5
36 POKEVIC+33,14:REM SET BACKGROUND COLOR TO LIGHT
BLUE
37 POKEVIC+23,3:REM EXPAND SPRITES 0 AND 1 IN Y
38 POKEVIC+29,3:REM EXPAND SPRITES 0 AND 1 IN X
40 POKE2040,192:REM SET SPRITE 0'S POINTER
50 POKE2041,193:REM SET SPRITE 1'S POINTER
60 POKE2042,192:REM SET SPRITE 2'S POINTER
70 POKE2043,193:REM SET SPRITE 3'S POINTER
80 POKE2044,192:REM SET SPRITE 4'S POINTER
90 POKE2045,193:REM SET SPRITE 5'S POINTER
100 POKEVIC+4,30:REM SET SPRITE 2'S X POSITION
110 POKEVIC+5,58:REM SET SPRITE 2'S Y POSITION
120 POKEVIC+6,65:REM SET SPRITE 3'S X POSITION
130 POKEVIC+7,58:REM SET SPRITE 3'S Y POSITION
140 POKEVIC+8,100:REM SET SPRITE 4'S X POSITION
150 POKEVIC+9,58:REM SET SPRITE 4'S Y POSITION
160 POKEVIC+10,100:REM SET SPRITE 5'S X POSITION
170 POKEVIC+11,58:REM SET SPRITE 5'S Y POSITION
       CTRL 2
175 PRINT"♥■"TAB(15)"THIS IS TWO HIRES SPRITES";
       SHIFT CLR/HOME
176 PRINTTAB(55)"ON TOP OF EACH OTHER"
180 POKEVIC+0,100:REM SET SPRITE 0'S X POSITION
190 POKEVIC+1,100:REM SET SPRITE 0'S Y POSITION
200 POKEVIC+2,100:REM SET SPRITE 1'S X POSITION
210 POKEVIC+3,100:REM SET SPRITE 1'S Y POSITION
220 POKEVIC+39,1:REM SET SPRITE 0'S COLOR
230 POKEVIC+41,1:REM SET SPRITE 2'S COLOR
240 POKEVIC+43,1:REM SET SPRITE 4'S COLOR
250 POKEVIC+40,6:REM SET SPRITE 1'S COLOR
260 POKEVIC+42,6:REM SET SPRITE 3'S COLOR
270 POKEVIC+44,6:REM SET SPRITE 5'S COLOR
280 FORX=192TO193:REM THE START OF THE LOOP THAT
DEFINES THE SPRITES
290 FORY=0TO63:REM BYTE COUNTER WITH SPRITE LOOP
300 READA:REM READ IN A BYTE
310 POKEX*64+Y,A:REM STORE THE DATA IN SPRITE AREA
320 NEXTY,X:REM CLOSE LOOPS
330 DX=1:DY=1
340 X=PEEK(VIC):REM LOOK AT SPRITE 0'S X POSITION
350 Y=PEEK(VIC+1):REM LOOK AT SPRITE 0'S Y POSITION
360 IFY=50ORY=208THENDY=-DY:REM IF Y IS ON THE
EDGE OF THE...
370 REM SCREEN, THEN REVERSE DELTA Y
380 IFX=24AND(PEEK(VIC+16)AND1)=0THENDX=-DX:REM IF
SPRITE IS...
390 REM TOUCHING THE LEFT EDGE, THEN REVERSE IT
```

```
400 IFX=40AND(PEEK(VIC+16)AND1)=1THENDX=-DX:REM IF
SPRITE IS...
410 REM TOUCHING THE RIGHT EDGE, THEN REVERSE IT
420 IFX=255ANDDX=1THENX=-1:SIDE=3
430 REM SWITCH TO OTHER SIDE OF THE SCREEN
440 IFX=0ANDDX=-1THENX=256:SIDE=0
450 REM SWITCH TO OTHER SIDE OF THE SCREEN
460 X=X+DX:REM ADD DELTA X TO X
470 X=XAND255:REM MAKE SURE X IS IN ALLOWED RANGE
480 Y=Y+DY:REM ADD DELTA Y TO Y
485 POKEVIC+16,SIDE
490 POKEVIC,X:REM PUT NEW X VALUE INTO SPRITE 0'S
X POSITION
500 POKEVIC+2,X:REM PUT NEW X VALUE INTO SPRITE
1'S X POSITION
510 POKEVIC+1,Y:REM PUT NEW Y VALUE INTO SPRITE
0'S Y POSITION
520 POKEVIC+3,Y:REM PUT NEW Y VALUE INTO SPRITE
1'S Y POSITION
530 GOTO340
600 REM ***** SPRITE DATA *****
610 DATA0,255,0,3,153,192,7,24,224,7,56,224,14,126,
112,14,126,112,14,126,112
620 DATA6,126,96,7,56,224,7,56,224,1,56,128,0,153,
0,0,90,0,0,56,0
630 DATA0,56,0,0,0,0,0,0,0,0,126,0,0,42,0,0,84,0,0,
40,0,0
640 DATA0,0,0,0,102,0,0,231,0,0,195,0,1,129,128,1,
129,128,1,129,128
650 DATA1,129,128,0,195,0,0,195,0,4,195,32,2,102,
64,2,36,64,1,0,128
660 DATA1,0,128,0,153,0,0,153,0,0,0,0,0,84,0,0,42,
0,0,20,0,0
```

```
10 REM SPRITE EXAMPLE 3...
20 REM THE HOT AIR GORF
30 VIC=53248:REM THIS IS WHERE THE VIC REGISTERS
BEGIN
35 POKEVIC+21,1:REM ENABLE SPRITE 0
```

```
36 POKEVIC+33,14:REM SET BACKGROUND COLOR TO LIGHT
BLUE
37 POKEVIC+23,1:REM EXPAND SPRITE 0 IN Y
38 POKEVIC+29,1:REM EXPAND SPRITE 0 IN X
40 POKE2040,192:REM SET SPRITE 0'S POINTER
50 POKEVIC+28,1:REM TURN ON MULTICOLOR
60 POKEVIC+37,7:REM SET MULTICOLOR 0
70 POKEVIC+38,4:REM SET MULTICOLOR 1
180 POKEVIC+0,100:REM SET SPRITE 0'S X POSITION
190 POKEVIC+1,100:REM SET SPRITE 0'S Y POSITION
220 POKEVIC+39,2:REM SET SPRITE 0'S COLOR
290 FORY=0TO63:REM BYTE COUNTER WITH SPRITE LOOP
300 READA:REM READ IN A BYTE
310 POKE12288+Y,A:REM STORE THE DATA IN SPRITE AREA
320 NEXT Y:REM CLOSE LOOP
330 DX=1:DY=1
340 X=PEEK(VIC):REM LOOK AT SPRITE 0'S X POSITION
350 Y=PEEK(VIC+1):REM LOOK AT SPRITE 0'S Y POSITION
360 IFY=50ORY=208THENDY=-DY:REM IF Y IS ON THE
EDGE OF THE...
370 REM SCREEN, THEN REVERSE DELTA Y
380 IF X=24AND(PEEK(VIC+16)AND1)=0THENDX=-DX:REM
IF SPRITE IS...
390 REM TOUCHING THE LEFT EDGE, THEN REVERSE IT
400 IFX=40AND(PEEK(VIC+16)AND1)=1THENDX=-DX:REM IF
SPRITE IS...
410 REM TOUCHING THE RIGHT EDGE, THEN REVERSE IT
420 IFX=255ANDDX=1THENX=-1:SIDE=1
430 REM SWITCH TO OTHER SIDE OF THE SCREEN
440 IFX=0ANDDX=-1THENX=256:SIDE=0
450 REM SWITCH TO OTHER SIDE OF THE SCREEN
460 X=X+DX:REM ADD DELTA X TO X
470 X=XAND255:REM MAKE SURE X IS IN ALLOWED RANGE
480 Y=Y+DY:REM ADD DELTA Y TO Y
485 POKEVIC+16,SIDE
490 POKEVIC,X:REM PUT NEW X VALUE INTO SPRITE 0'S
X POSITION
510 POKEVIC+1,Y:REM PUT NEW Y VALUE INTO SPRITE
0'S Y POSITION
520 GETA$:REM GET A KEY FROM THE KEYBOARD
521 IFA$="M"THENPOKEVIC+28,1:REM USER SELECTED
MULTICOLOR
522 IFA$="H"THENPOKEVIC+28,0:REM USER SELECTED
HIGH RESOLUTION
530 GOTO340
600 REM ***** SPRITE DATA *****
610 DATA64,0,1,16,170,4,6,170,144,10,170,160,42,
170,168,41,105,104,169,235,106
620 DATA169,235,106,169,235,106,170,170,170,170,
170,170,170,170,170,170,170,170
630 DATA166,170,154,169,85,106,170,85,170,42,170,
168,10,170,160,1,0,64,1,0,64
640 DATA5,0,80,0
```

OTHER GRAPHICS FEATURES

SCREEN BLANKING

Bit 4 of the VIC-II control register controls the screen blanking function. It is found in the control register at location 53265 ($D011). When it is turned ON (in other words, set to a 1) the screen is normal. When bit 4 is set to 0 (turned OFF), the entire screen changes to border color.

The following POKE blanks the screen. No data is lost, it just isn't displayed.

```
POKE 53265,PEEK(53265)AND 239
```

To bring back the screen, use the POKE shown below:

```
POKE 53265,PEEK(53265)OR 16
```

> **NOTE:** Turning off the screen will speed up the processor slightly. This means that program RUNning is also sped up.

RASTER REGISTER

The raster register is found in the VIC-II chip at location 53266 ($D012). The raster register is a dual purpose register. When you read this register it returns the lower 8 bits of the current raster position. The raster position of the most significant bit is in register location 53265 ($D011). You use the raster register to set up timing changes in your display so that you can get rid of screen flicker. The changes on your screen should be made when the raster is not in the visible display area, which is when your dot positions fall between 51 and 251.

When the raster register is written to (including the MSB) the number written to is saved for use with the raster compare function. When the actual raster value becomes the same as the number written to the raster register, a bit in the VIC-II chip interrupt register 53273 ($D019) is turned ON by setting it to 1.

> **NOTE:** If the proper interrupt bit is enabled (turned on), an interrupt (IRQ) will occur.

INTERRUPT STATUS REGISTER

The interrupt status register shows the current status of any interrupt source. The current status of bit 2 of the interrupt register will be a 1 when two sprites hit each other. The same is true, in a corresponding 1 to 1 relationship, for bits 0–3 listed in the chart below. Bit 7 is also set with a 1, whenever an interrupt occurs.

The interrupt status register is located at 53273 ($D019) and is as follows:

LATCH	BIT #	DESCRIPTION
IRST	0	Set when current raster count = stored raster count
IMDC	1	Set by SPRITE-DATA collision (1st one only, until reset)
IMMC	2	Set by SPRITE-SPRITE collision (1st one only, until reset)
ILP	3	Set by negative transition of light pen (1 per frame)
IRQ	7	Set by latch set and enabled

Once an interrupt bit has been set, it's "latched" in and must be cleared by writing a 1 to that bit in the interrupt register when you're ready to handle it. This allows selective interrupt handling, without having to store the other interrupt bits.

The **INTERRUPT ENABLE REGISTER** is located at 53274 ($D01A). It has the same format as the interrupt status register. Unless the corresponding bit in the interrupt enable register is set to a 1, no interrupt from that source will take place. The interrupt status register can still be polled for information, but no interrupts will be generated.

To enable an interrupt request the corresponding interrupt enable bit (as shown in the chart above) must be set to a 1.

This powerful interrupt structure lets you use split screen modes. For instance you can have half of the screen bit mapped, half text, more than 8 sprites at a time, etc. The secret is to use interrupts properly. For example, if you want the top half of the screen to be bit mapped and the bottom to be text, just set the raster compare register (as explained previously) for halfway down the screen. When the interrupt occurs, tell the VIC-II chip to get characters from ROM, then set the raster compare register to interrupt at the top of the screen. When the interrupt occurs at the top of the screen, tell the VIC-II chip to get characters from RAM (bit map mode).

You can also display more than 8 sprites in the same way. Unfortunately BASIC isn't fast enough to do this very well. So if you want to start using display interrupts, you should work in machine language.

SUGGESTED SCREEN AND CHARACTER COLOR COMBINATIONS

Color TV sets are limited in their ability to place certain colors next to each other on the same line. Certain combinations of screen and character colors produce blurred images. This chart shows which color combinations to avoid, and which work especially well together.

SCREEN COLOR \ CHARACTER COLOR	0	1	2	3	4	5	6	7	8	9	10	11	12	13	14	15
0	X	●	X	●	●	•	X	●	●	X	●	●	●	●	●	●
1	●	X	●	X	●	●	●	X	•	●	•	●	●	X	●	●
2	X	●	X	X	•	X	X	●	●	X	●	X	X	X	X	•
3	●	X	X	X	X	•	●	X	X	X	X	•	X	X	•	X
4	●	•	X	X	X	X	X	X	X	X	X	X	X	X	X	•
5	●	•	X	•	X	X	X	X	X	X	X	•	X	●	X	•
6	•	●	X	●	X	X	X	X	X	X	X	X	X	•	●	●
7	●	X	●	X	X	X	•	X	•	●	•	●	●	X	X	X
8	•	●	●	X	X	X	X	●	X	●	X	X	X	X	X	•
9	X	●	X	X	X	X	X	●	●	X	●	X	X	X	X	●
10	•	•	●	X	X	X	X	•	X	●	X	X	X	X	X	•
11	●	●	X	•	X	X	X	●	X	X	X	X	●	●	•	●
12	●	●	•	X	X	X	•	X	X	•	X	●	X	X	X	●
13	●	X	X	X	X	●	•	X	X	X	X	●	X	X	X	X
14	●	●	X	●	X	X	●	X	X	X	X	•	X	X	X	•
15	●	●	●	X	•	•	●	X	X	•	•	●	●	X	•	X

● = EXCELLENT
• = FAIR
X = POOR

PROGRAMMING SPRITES—ANOTHER LOOK

For those of you having trouble with graphics, this section has been designed as a more elementary tutorial approach to sprites.

MAKING SPRITES IN BASIC—A SHORT PROGRAM

There are at least three different BASIC programming techniques which let you create graphic images and cartoon animations on the Commodore 64. You can use the computer's built-in graphics character set (see Page 376). You can program your own characters (see Page 108) or . . . best of all . . . you can use the computer's built-in "sprite graphics." To illustrate how easy it is, here's one of the shortest spritemaking programs you can write in BASIC:

SHIFT CLR/HOME

```
10 PRINT"♥"
20 POKE2040,13
30 FORS=832TO832+62:POKES,255:NEXT
40 V=53248
50 POKEV+21,1
60 POKEV+39,1
70 POKEV,24
80 POKEV+1,100
```

This program includes the key "ingredients" you need to create any sprite. The POKE numbers come from the SPRITEMAKING CHART on Page 176. This program defines the first sprite . . . sprite 0 . . . as a solid white square on the screen. Here's a line-by-line explanation of the program:

LINE 10 clears the screen.

LINE 20 sets the "sprite pointer" to where the Commodore 64 will read its sprite data from. Sprite 0 is set at 2040, sprite 1 at 2041, sprite 2 at 2042, and so on up to sprite 7 at 2047. You can set all 8 sprite pointers to 13 by using this line in place of line 20:

```
20 FOR SP=2040TO2047:POKE SP,13:NEXT SP
```

LINE 30 puts the first sprite (sprite 0) into 63 bytes of the Commodore 64's RAM memory starting at location 832 (each sprite requires 63 bytes of memory). The first sprite (sprite 0) is "addressed" at memory locations 832 to 894.

LINE 40 sets the variable "V" equal to 53248, the starting address of the VIDEO CHIP. This entry lets us use the form (V+number) for sprite settings. We're using the form (V+number) when POKEing sprite settings because this format conserves memory and lets us work with smaller numbers. For example, in line 50 we typed POKE V+21. This is the same as typing POKE 53248+21 or POKE 53269 . . . but V+21 requires less space than 53269, and is easier to remember.

LINE 50 enables or "turns on" sprite 0. There are 8 sprites, numbered from 0 to 7. To turn on an individual sprite, or a combination of sprites, all you have to do is POKE V+21 followed by a number from 0 (turn all sprites off) to 255 (turn all 8 sprites on). You can turn on one or more sprites by POKEing the following numbers:

ALL ON	SPRITE0	SPRITE1	SPRITE2	SPRITE3	SPRITE4	SPRITE5	SPRITE6	SPRITE7	ALL OFF
V+21,255	V+21,1	V+21,2	V+21,4	V+21,8	V+21,16	V+21,32	V+21,64	V+21,128	V+21,0

POKE V+21,1 turns on sprite 0. POKE V+21,128 turns on sprite 7. You can also turn on combinations of sprites. For example, POKE V+21,129 turns on *both* sprite 0 and sprite 7 by adding the two "turn on" numbers (1+128) together. (See SPRITEMAKING CHART, Page 176.)

LINE 60 sets the COLOR of sprite 0. There are 16 possible sprite colors, numbered from 0 (black) to 15 (grey). Each sprite requires a different POKE to set its color, from V+39 to V+46. POKE V+39,1 colors sprite 0 white. POKE V+46,15 colors sprite 7 grey. (See the SPRITEMAKING CHART for more information.)

When you create a sprite, as you just did, the sprite will STAY IN MEMORY until you POKE it off, redefine it, or turn off your computer. This lets you change the color, position and even shape of the sprite in DIRECT or IMMEDIATE mode, which is useful for editing purposes. As an example, RUN the program above, then type this line in DIRECT mode (without a line number) and hit the RETURN key:

POKE V+39,8

The sprite on the screen is now ORANGE. Try POKEing some other numbers from 0 to 15 to see the other sprite colors. Because you did this in DIRECT mode, if you RUN your program the sprite will return to its original color (white).

LINE 70 determines the HORIZONTAL or "X" POSITION of the sprite on the screen. This number represents the location of the UPPER LEFT CORNER of the sprite. The farthest left horizontal (X) position which you can see on your television screen is position number 24, although you can move the sprite OFF THE SCREEN to position number 0.

LINE 80 determines the VERTICAL or "Y" POSITION of the sprite. In this program, we placed the sprite at X (horizontal) position 24, and Y (vertical) position 100. To try another location, type this POKE in DIRECT mode and hit RETURN:

POKE V,24:POKE V+1,50

This places the sprite at the upper left corner of the screen. To move the sprite to the lower left corner, type this:

POKE V,24:POKE V+1,229

Each number from 832 to 895 in our sprite 0 address represents one block of 8 pixels, with three 8-pixel blocks in each horizontal row of the sprite. The loop in line 80 tells the computer to POKE 832,255 which makes the first 8 pixels solid . . . then POKE 833,255 to make the second 8 pixels solid, and so on to location 894 which is the last group of 8 pixels in the bottom right corner of the sprite. To better see how this works, try typing the following in DIRECT mode, and notice that the second group of 8 pixels is erased:

POKE 833,0 (to put it back type POKE 833,255 or RUN your program)

The following line, which you can add to your program, erases the blocks in the MIDDLE of the sprite you created:

```
90 FOR A=836 TO 891 STEP 3:POKE A,0:NEXT A
```

Remember, the pixels that make up the sprite are grouped in blocks of eight. This line erases the 5th group of eight pixels (block 836) and every third block up to block 890. Try POKEing any of the other numbers from 832 to 894 with either a 255 to make them solid or 0 to make them blank.

CRUNCHING YOUR SPRITE PROGRAMS

Here's a helpful "crunching" tip: The program described above is already short, but it can be made even shorter by "crunching" it smaller. In our example we list the key sprite settings on separate program lines so you can see what's happening in the program. In actual practice, a good programmer would probably write this program as a TWO LINE PROGRAM . . . by "crunching" it as follows:

```
10PRINTCHR$(147):V=53248:POKEV+21,1:POKE2040,13:
  POKEV+39,1
20FORS=832TO894:POKES,255:NEXT:POKEV,24:POKEV+1,100
```

For more tips on how to crunch your programs so they fit in less memory and run more efficiently, see the "crunching guide" on Page 24.

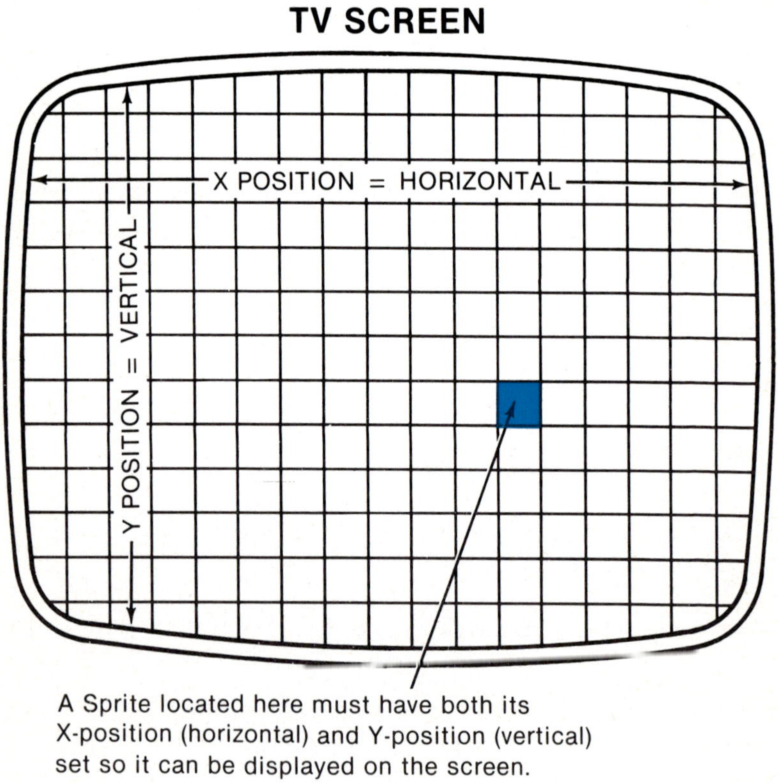

Figure 3-4. The display screen is divided into a grid of X and Y coordinates.

POSITIONING SPRITES ON THE SCREEN

The entire display screen is divided into a grid of X and Y coordinates, like a graph. The X COORDINATE is the HORIZONTAL position across the screen and the Y COORDINATE is the VERTICAL position up and down (see Figure 3-4).

To position any sprite on the screen, you must POKE TWO SETTINGS . . . the X position and the Y position . . . these tell the computer where to display the UPPER LEFT HAND CORNER of the sprite. Remember that a sprite consists of 504 individual pixels, 24 across by 21 down . . . so if you POKE a sprite onto the upper left corner of your screen, the sprite will be displayed as a graphic image 24 pixels ACROSS and 21 pixels DOWN starting at the X-Y position you defined. The sprite will be displayed based on the upper left corner of the entire sprite, even if you define the sprite using only a small part of the 24×21-pixel sprite area.

To understand how X-Y positioning works, study the following diagram (Figure 3-5), which shows the X and Y numbers in relation to your display screen. Note that the GREY AREA in the diagram shows your television viewing area . . . the white area represents positions which are OFF your viewing screen . . .

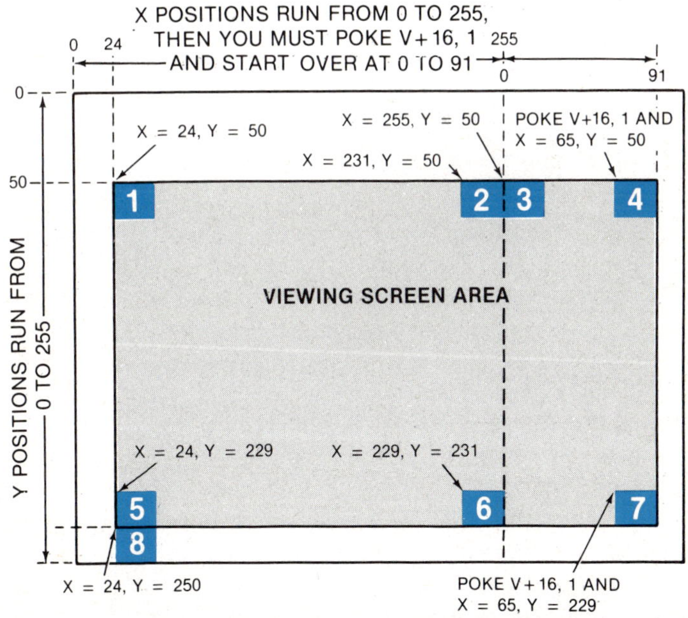

Figure 3-5. Determining X-Y sprite positions.

To display a sprite in a given location, you must POKE the X and Y settings for each SPRITE . . . remembering that every sprite has its own unique X POKE and Y POKE. The X and Y settings for all 8 sprites are shown here:

POKE THESE VALUES TO SET X-Y SPRITE POSITIONS

	SPRITE0	SPRITE1	SPRITE2	SPRITE3	SPRITE4	SPRITE5	SPRITE6	SPRITE7
SET X	V,X	V+2,X	V+4,X	V+6,X	V+8,X	V+10,X	V+12,X	V+14,X
SET Y	V+1,Y	V+3,Y	V+5,Y	V+7,Y	V+9,Y	V+11,Y	V+13,Y	V+15,Y
RIGHTX	V+16,1	V+16,2	V+16,4	V+16,8	V+16,16	V+16,32	V+16,64	V+16,128

POKEING AN X POSITION: The possible values of X are 0 to 255, counting from left to right. Values 0 to 23 place all or part of the sprite OUT OF THE VIEWING AREA off the left side of the screen . . . values 24 to 255 place the sprite IN THE VIEWING AREA up to the 255th position (see next paragraph for settings beyond the 255th X position). To place the sprite at one of these positions, just type the X-POSITION POKE for the sprite you're using. For example, to POKE sprite 1 at the farthest left X position IN THE VIEWING AREA, type: POKE V+2,24.

X VALUES BEYOND THE 255TH POSITION: To get beyond the 255th position across the screen, you need to make a SECOND POKE using the numbers in the "RIGHT X" row of the chart (Figure 3-5). Normally, the horizontal (X) numbering would continue past the 255th position to 256, 257, etc., but because registers only contain 8 bits we must use a "second register" to access the RIGHT SIDE of the screen and start our X numbering over again at 0. So to get beyond X position 255, you must POKE V+16 and a number (depending on the sprite). This gives you 65 additional X positions (renumbered from 0 to 65) in the viewing area on the RIGHT side of the viewing screen. (You can actually POKE the right side X value as high as 255, which takes you off the right edge of the viewing screen.)

POKEING A Y POSITION: The possible values of Y are 0 to 255, counting from top to bottom. Values 0 to 49 place all or part of the sprite OUT OF THE VIEWING AREA off the TOP of the screen. Values 50 to 229 place the sprite IN THE VIEWING AREA. Values 230 to 255 place all or part of the sprite OUT OF THE VIEWING AREA off the BOTTOM of the screen.

Let's see how this X-Y positioning works, using sprite 1. Type this program:

```
              SHIFT CLR/HOME
10 PRINT"♥":V=53248:POKEV+21,2:POKE2041,13:
FORS=832TO895:POKES,255:NEXT
20 POKEV+40,7
30 POKEV+2,24
40 POKEV+3,50
```

This simple program establishes sprite 1 as a solid box and positions it at the upper left corner of the screen. Now change line 40 to read:

40 POKE V+3,229

This moves the sprite to the bottom left corner of the screen. Now let's test the RIGHT X LIMIT of the sprite. Change line 30 as shown:

30 POKE V+2,255

This moves the sprite to the RIGHT but reaches the RIGHT X LIMIT, which is 255. At this point, the "most significant bit" in register 16 must be SET. In other words, you must type POKE V+16 and the number shown in the "RIGHT X" column in the X-Y POKE CHART above to RESTART the X position counter at the 256th pixel/position on the screen. Change line 30 as follows:

30 POKE V+16, PEEK(V+16)OR 2:POKE V+2,0

POKE V+16,2 sets the most significant bit of the X position for sprite 1 and restarts it at the 256th pixel/position on the screen. **POKE V+2,0** displays the sprite at the NEW POSITION ZERO, which is now reset to the 256th pixel.

To get back to the left side of the screen, you must reset the most significant bit of the X position counter to 0 by typing (for sprite 1):

POKE V+16, PEEK(V+16)AND 253

TO SUMMARIZE how the X positioning works . . . POKE the X POSITION for any sprite with a number from 0 to 255. To access a position beyond the 255th position/pixel across the screen, you must use an additional POKE (V+16) which sets the most significant bit of the X position and start counting from 0 again at the 256th pixel across the screen.

This POKE starts the X numbering over again from 0 at the 256th position (**Example: POKE V+16, PEEK(V+16)OR 1** and **POKE V,1** must be included to place sprite 0 at the 257th pixel across the screen.) To get back to the left side X positions you have to TURN OFF the control setting by typing **POKE V+16, PEEK(V+16)AND 254.**

POSITIONING MULTIPLE SPRITES ON THE SCREEN

Here's a program which defines THREE DIFFERENT SPRITES (0, 1, and 2) in different colors and places them in different positions on the screen:

SHIFT CLR/HOME

```
10 PRINT"♥":V=53248:FORS=832TO895:POKES,255:NEXT
20 FORM=2040TO2042:POKEM,13:NEXT
30 POKEV+21,7
40 POKEV+39,1:POKEV+40,7:POKEV+41,8
50 POKEV,24:POKEV+1,50
60 POKEV+2,12:POKEV+3,229
70 POKEV+4,255:POKEV+5,50
```

For convenience, all 3 sprites have been defined as solid squares, getting their data from the same place. The important lesson here is how the 3 sprites are positioned. The white sprite 0 is at the top lefthand corner. The yellow sprite 1 is at the bottom lefthand corner but HALF the sprite is OFF THE SCREEN (remember, 24 is the leftmost X position in the viewing area . . . an X position less than 24 puts all or part of the sprite off the screen and we used an X position 12 here which put the sprite halfway off the screen). Finally, the orange sprite 2 is at the RIGHT X LIMIT (position 255) . . . but what if you want to display a sprite in the area to the RIGHT of X position 255?

DISPLAYING A SPRITE BEYOND THE 255TH X-POSITION

Displaying a sprite beyond the 255th X position requires a special POKE which SETS the most significant bit of the X position and starts over at the 256th pixel position across the screen. Here's how it works . . .

First, you POKE V+16 with the number for the sprite you're using (check the "RIGHT X" row in the X-Y chart . . . we'll use sprite 0). Now we assign an X position, keeping in mind that the X counter starts over from 0 at the 256th position on the screen. Change line 50 to read as follows:

```
50 POKE V+16,1:POKE V,24:POKE V+1,75
```

This line POKEs V+16 with the number required to "open up" the right side of the screen. . .the new X position 24 for sprite 0 now begins 24 pixels to the RIGHT of position 255. To check the right edge of the screen, change line 60 to:

60 POKE V+16,1:POKE V,65:POKE V+1,75

Some experimentation with the settings in the sprite chart will give you the settings you need to position and move sprites on the left and right sides of the screen. The section on "moving sprites" will also increase your understanding of how sprite positioning works.

SPRITE PRIORITIES

You can actually make different sprites seem to move IN FRONT OF or BEHIND each other on the screen. This incredible three dimensional illusion is achieved by the built-in SPRITE PRIORITIES which determine which sprites have priority over the others when 2 or more sprites OVERLAP on the screen.

The rule is "first come, first served" which means lower-numbered sprites AUTOMATICALLY have priority over higher-numbered sprites. For example, if you display sprite 0 and sprite 1 so they overlap on the screen, sprite 0 will appear to be IN FRONT OF sprite 1. Actually, sprite 0 always supersedes all the other sprites because it's the lowest numbered sprite. In comparison, sprite 1 has priority over sprites 2–7; sprite 2 has priority over sprites 3–7, etc. Sprite 7 (the last sprite) has LESS PRIORITY than any of the other sprites, and will always appear to be displayed "BEHIND" any other sprites which overlap its position.

To illustrate how priorities work, change lines 50, 60, and 70 in the program above to the following:

SHIFT CLR/HOME

```
10 PRINT"♥":V=53248:FORS=832TO895:POKES,255:NEXT
20 FORM=2040TO2042:POKEM,13:NEXT
30 POKEV+21,7
40 POKEV+39,1:POKEV+40,7:POKEV+41,8
50 POKEV,24:POKEV+1,50:POKEV+16,0
60 POKEV+2,34:POKEV+3,60
70 POKEV+4,44:POKEV+5,70
```

You should see a white sprite on top of a yellow sprite on top of an orange sprite. Of course, now that you see how priorities work, you can also MOVE SPRITES and take advantage of these priorities in your animation.

DRAWING A SPRITE

Drawing a Commodore sprite is like coloring the empty spaces in a coloring book. Every sprite consists of tiny dots called *pixels*. To draw a sprite, all you have to do is "color in" some of the pixels.

Look at the spritemaking grid in Figure 3-6. This is what a blank sprite looks like:

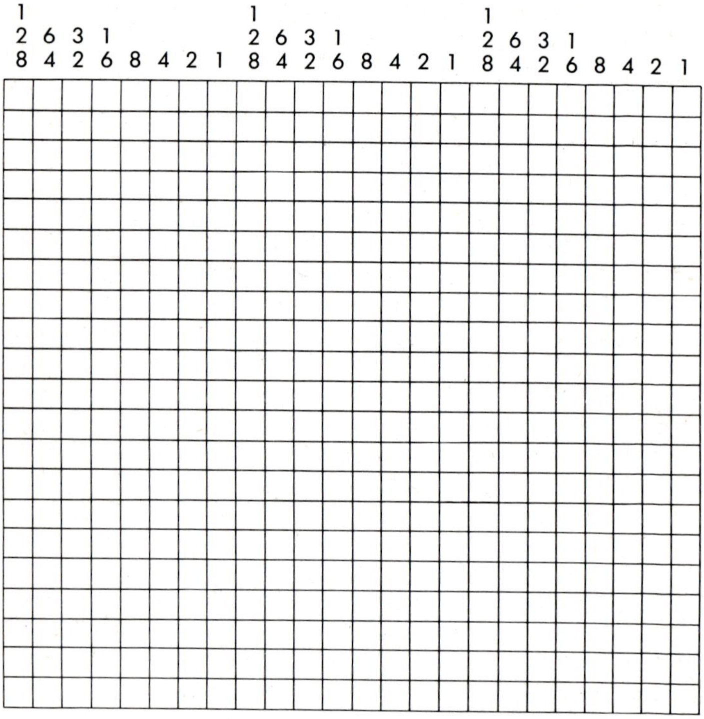

Figure 3-6. Spritemaking grid.

Each little "square" represents one pixel in the sprite. There are 24 pixels across and 21 pixels up and down, or 504 pixels in the entire sprite. To make the sprite look like something, you have to color in these pixels using a special PROGRAM . . . but how can you control over 500 individual pixels? That's where computer programming can help you. Instead of typing 504 separate numbers, you only have to type 63 numbers for each sprite. Here's how it works . . .

CREATING A SPRITE . . . STEP BY STEP

To make this as easy as possible for you, we've put together this simple step by step guide to help you draw your own sprites.

STEP 1:

Write the spritemaking program shown here ON A PIECE OF PAPER . . . note that line 100 starts a special DATA section of your program which will contain the 63 numbers you need to create your sprite.

SHIFT CLR/HOME

```
10 PRINT"♥":POKE53280,5:POKE53281,6
20 V=53248:POKEV+34,3
30 POKE53269,4:POKE2042,13
40 FORN=0TO62:READQ:POKE832+N,Q:NEXT
100 DATA255,255,255
101 DATA128,0,1
102 DATA128,0,1
103 DATA128,0,1
104 DATA144,0,1
105 DATA144,0,1
106 DATA144,0,1
107 DATA144,0,1
108 DATA144,0,1
109 DATA144,0,1
110 DATA144,0,1
111 DATA144,0,1
112 DATA144,0,1
113 DATA144,0,1
114 DATA128,0,1
115 DATA128,0,1
116 DATA128,0,1
117 DATA128,0,1
118 DATA128,0,1
119 DATA128,0,1
120 DATA255,255,255
200 X=200:Y=100:POKE53252,X:POKE53253,Y
```

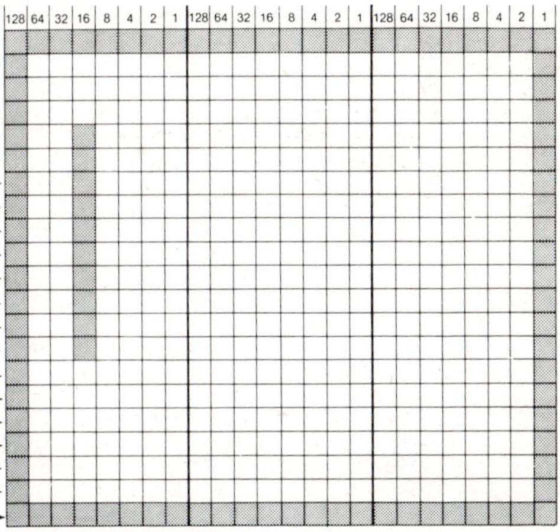

STEP 2:

Color in the pixels on the spritemaking grid on Page 162 (or use a piece of graph paper . . . remember, a sprite has 24 squares across and 21 squares down). We suggest you use a pencil and draw lightly so you can reuse this grid. You can create any image you like, but for our example we'll draw a simple box.

STEP 3:

Look at the first EIGHT pixels. Each column of pixels has a number (128, 64, 32, 16, 8, 4, 2, 1). The special type of addition we are going to show you is a type of BINARY ARITHMETIC which is used by most computers as a special way of counting. Here's a close-up view of the first eight pixels in the top left hand corner of the sprite:

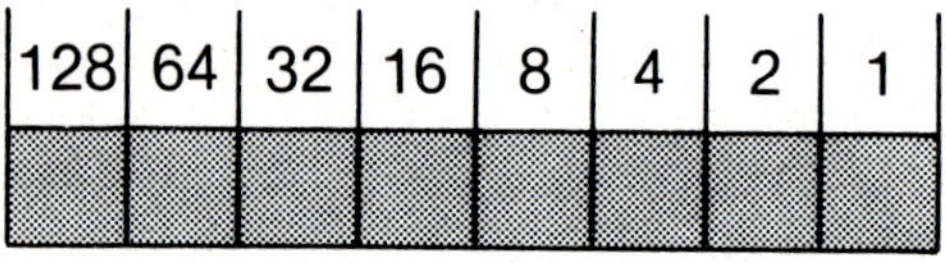

STEP 4:

Add up the numbers of the SOLID pixels. This first group of eight pixels is completely solid, so the total number is 255.

STEP 5:

Enter that number as the FIRST DATA STATEMENT in line 100 of the Spritemaking Program below. Enter 255 for the second and third groups of eight.

STEP 6:

Look at the FIRST EIGHT PIXELS IN THE SECOND ROW of the sprite. Add up the values of the solid pixels. Since only one of these pixels is solid, the total value is 128. Enter this as the first DATA number in line 101.

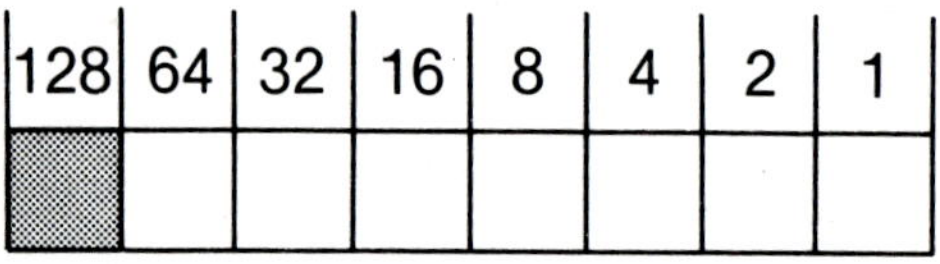

STEP 7:

Add up the values of the next group of eight pixels (which is 0 because they're all BLANK) and enter in line 101. Now move to the next group of pixels and repeat the process for each GROUP OF EIGHT PIXELS (there are 3 groups across each row, and 21 rows). This will give you a total of 63 numbers. Each number represents ONE group of 8 pixels, and 63 groups of eight equals 504 total individual pixels. Perhaps a better way of looking at the program is like this . . . each line in the program represents ONE ROW in the sprite. Each of the 3 numbers in each row represents ONE GROUP OF EIGHT PIXELS. And each number tells the computer which pixels to make SOLID and which pixels to leave blank.

STEP 8:

CRUNCH YOUR PROGRAM INTO A SMALLER SPACE BY RUNNING TOGETHER ALL THE DATA STATEMENTS, AS SHOWN IN THE SAMPLE PROGRAM BELOW. Note that we asked you to write your sprite program on a piece of paper. We did this for a good reason. The DATA STATEMENT LINES 100–120 in the program in STEP 1 are only there to help you see which numbers relate to which groups of pixels in your sprite. Your final program should be "crunched" like this:

SHIFT CLR/HOME

```
10 PRINT"⌐":POKE53280,5:POKE53281,6
20 V=53248:POKEV+34,3
30 POKE53269,4:POKE2042,13
40 FORN=0TO62:READQ:POKE832+N,Q:NEXT
100 DATA255,255,255,128,0,1,128,0,1,128,0,1,144,0,
1,144,0,1,144,0,1,144,0,1
101 DATA144,0,1,144,0,1,144,0,1,144,0,1,144,0,1,
144,0,1,128,0,1,128,0,1
102 DATA128,0,1,128,0,1,128,0,1,128,0,1,255,255,255
200 X=200:Y=100:POKE53252,X:POKE53253,Y
```

MOVING YOUR SPRITE ON THE SCREEN

Now that you've created your sprite, let's do some interesting things with it. To move your sprite smoothly across the screen, add these two lines to your program:

```
50 POKE V+5,100:FOR X=24TO255:POKE V+4,X:NEXT:POKE
   V+16,4
55 FOR X=0TO65:POKE V+4,X:NEXT X:POKE V+16,0:GOTO 50
```

LINE 50 POKEs the Y POSITION at 100 (try 50 or 229 instead for variety). Then it sets up a FOR . . . NEXT loop which POKEs the sprite into X position 0 to X position 255, in order. When it reaches the 255th position, it POKEs the RIGHT X POSITION (POKE V+16,4) which is required to cross to the right side of the screen.

LINE 55 has a FOR . . . NEXT loop which continues to POKE the sprite in the last 65 positions on the screen. Note that the X value was reset to zero but because you used the RIGHT X setting (POKE V+16,2) X starts over on the right side of the screen.

This line keeps going back to itself (GOTO 50). If you just want the sprite to move ONCE across the screen and disappear, then take out GOTO50.

Here's a line which moves the sprite BACK AND FORTH:

```
50 POKE V+5,100:FOR X=24TO255:POKE V+4,X:NEXT: POKE
   V+16,4:FOR X=0TO65: POKE V+4,X: NEXT X
55 FOR X=65TO0 STEP-1:POKE V+4,X:NEXT:POKE V+16,0: FOR
   X=255TO24 STEP-1: POKE V+4,X:NEXT
60 GOTO 50
```

Do you see how these programs work? This program is the same as the previous one, except when it reaches the end of the right side of the screen, it REVERSES ITSELF and goes back in the other direction. That is what the STEP−1 accomplishes . . . it tells the program to POKE the sprite into X values from 65 to 0 on the right side of the screen, then from 255 to 0 on the left side of the screen, STEPping backwards minus−1 position at a time.

VERTICAL SCROLLING

This type of sprite movement is called "scrolling." To scroll your sprite up or down in the Y position, you only have to use ONE LINE. ERASE LINES 50 and 55 by typing the line numbers by themselves and hitting RETURN like this:

```
50 ( RETURN )
55 ( RETURN )
```

Now enter LINE 50 again as follows:

```
50 POKE V+4,24:FOR Y=0TO255:POKE V+5,Y:NEXT
```

THE DANCING MOUSE—A SPRITE PROGRAM EXAMPLE

Sometimes the techniques described in a programmer's reference manual are difficult to understand, so we've put together a fun sprite program called "Michael's Dancing Mouse." This program uses three different sprites in a cute animation with sound effects—and to help you understand how it works we've included an explanation of EACH COMMAND so you can see exactly how the program is constructed:

```
5 S=54272:POKES+24,15:POKES,220:POKES+1,68:POKES+5,
15:POKES+6,215
10 POKES+7,120:POKES+8,100:POKES+12,15:POKES+13,215
          SHIFT CLR/HOME
15 PRINT"♥":V=53248:POKEV+21,1
20 FORS1=12288TO12350:READQ1:POKES1,Q1:NEXT
25 FORS2=12352TO12414:READQ2:POKES2,Q2:NEXT
30 FORS3=12416TO12478:READQ3:POKES3,Q3:NEXT
35 POKEV+39,15:POKEV+1,68
                   CTRL 2                    C= 7
40 PRINTTAB(160)"■I AM THE DANCING MOUSE!■"
45 P=192
50 FORX=0TO347STEP3
55 RX=INT(X/256):LX=X-RX*256
60 POKEV,LX:POKEV+16,RX
70 IFP=192THENGOSUB200
75 IFP=193THENGOSUB300
80 POKE2040,P:FORT=1TO60:NEXT
85 P=P+1:IFP>194THENP=192
90 NEXT
95 END
100 DATA30,0,120,63,0,252,127,129,254,127,129,254,
127,189,254,127,255,254
101 DATA63,255,252,31,187,248,3,187,192,1,255,128,
3,189,192,1,231,128,1,255,0
102 DATA31,255,0,0,124,0,0,254,0,1,199,32,3,131,
224,7,1,192,1,192,0,3,192,0
103 DATA30,0,120,63,0,252,127,129,254,127,129,254,
127,189,254,127,255,254
104 DATA63,255,252,31,221,248,3,221,192,1,255,128,
3,255,192,1,195,128,1,231,3
105 DATA31,255,255,0,124,0,0,254,0,1,199,0,7,1,128,
7,0,204,1,128,124,7,128,56
106 DATA30,0,120,63,0,252,127,129,254,127,129,254,
127,189,254,127,255,254
107 DATA63,255,252,31,221,248,3,221,192,1,255,134,
3,189,204,1,199,152,1,255,48
108 DATA1,255,224,1,252,0,3,254,0
109 DATA7,14,0,204,14,0,248,56,0,112,112,0,0,60,0,
-1
200 POKES+4,129:POKES+4,128:RETURN
300 POKES+11,129:POKES+11,128:RETURN
```

LINE 5:

S=54272	Sets the variable S equal to 54272, which is the beginning memory location of the SOUND CHIP. From now on, instead of poking a direct memory location, we will POKE S plus a value.
POKES+24,15	Same as POKE 54296,15 which sets VOLUME to highest level.
POKES,220	Same as POKE 54272,220 which sets Low Frequency in Voice 1 for a note which approximates high C in Octave 6.
POKES+1,68	Same as POKE 54273,68 which sets High Frequency in Voice 1 for a note which approximates high C in Octave 6.
POKES+5,15	Same as POKE 54277,15 which sets Attack/Decay for Voice 1 and in this case consists of the maximum DECAY level with no attack, which produces the "echo" effect.
POKES+6,215	Same as POKE 54278,215 which sets Sustain/ Release for Voice 1 (215 represents a combination of sustain and release values).

LINE 10:

POKES+7,120	Same as POKE 54279,120 which sets the Low Frequency for Voice 2.
POKES+8,100	Same as POKE 54280,100 which sets the High Frequency for Voice 2.
POKES+12,15	Same as POKE 54284,15 which sets Attack/Decay for Voice 2 to same level as Voice 1 above.
POKES+13,215	Same as POKE 54285,215 which sets Sustain/ Release for Voice 2 to same level as Voice 1 above.

LINE 15:

PRINT" SHIFT CLR/HOME "	Clears the screen when the program begins.
V=53248	Defines the variable "V" as the starting location of the VIC chip which controls sprites. From now on we will define sprite locations as V plus a value.
POKEV+21,1	Turns on (enables) sprite number 1.

LINE 20:

FORS1=12288 TO 12350	We are going to use ONE SPRITE (sprite 0) in this animation, but we are going to use THREE sets of sprite data to define three separate shapes. To get our animation, we will switch the POINTERS for sprite 0 to the three places in memory where we have stored the data which defines our three different shapes. The same sprite will be redefined rapidly over and over again as 3 different shapes to produce the dancing mouse animation. You can define dozens of sprite shapes in DATA STATEMENTS, and rotate those shapes through one or more sprites. So you see, you don't have to limit one sprite to one shape or vice-versa. One sprite can have many different shapes, simply by changing the POINTER SETTING FOR THAT SPRITE to different places in memory where the sprite data for different shapes is stored. This line means we have put the DATA for "sprite shape 1" at memory locations 12288 to 12350.
READ Q1	Reads 63 numbers in order from the DATA statements which begin at line 100. Q1 is an arbitrary variable name. It could just as easily be A, Z1 or another numeric variable.
POKES1,Q1	Pokes the first number from the DATA statements (the first "Q1" is 30) into the first memory location (the first memory location is 12288). This is the same as POKE12288,30.
NEXT	This tells the computer to look BETWEEN the FOR and NEXT parts of the loop and perform those in-between commands (READQ1 and POKES1,Q1 using the NEXT numbers in order). In other words, the NEXT statement makes the computer READ the NEXT Q1 from the DATA STATEMENTS, which is 0, and also increments S1 by 1 to the next value, which is 12289. The result is POKE12289,0 . . . the NEXT command makes the loop keep going back until the last values in the series, which are POKE 12350,0.

LINE 25:

FORS2=12352 TO 12414	The second shape of sprite zero is defined by the DATA which is located at locations 12352 to 12414. NOTE that location 12351 is SKIPPED . . . this is the 64th location which is used in the definition of the first sprite group but does not contain any of the sprite data numbers. Just remember when defining sprites in consecutive locations that you will use 64 locations, but only POKE sprite data into the first 63 locations.
READQ2	Reads the 63 numbers which follow the numbers we used for the first sprite shape. This READ simply looks for the very next number in the DATA area and starts reading 63 numbers, one at a time.
POKES2,Q2	Pokes the data (Q2) into the memory locations (S2) for our second sprite shape, which begins at location 12352.
NEXT	Same use as line 20 above.

LINE 30:

FORS3=12416 TO 12478	The third shape of sprite zero is defined by the DATA to be located at locations 12416 to 12478.
READQ3	Reads last 63 numbers in order as Q3.
POKES3,Q3	Pokes those numbers into locations 12416 to 12478.
NEXT	Same as lines 20 and 25.

LINE 35:

POKEV+39,15	Sets color for sprite 0 to light grey.
POKEV+1,68	Sets the upper right hand corner of the sprite square to vertical (Y) position 68. For the sake of comparison, position 50 is the top lefthand corner Y position on the viewing screen.

LINE 40:

PRINTTAB(160)	Tabs 160 spaces from the top lefthand CHARACTER SPACE on the screen, which is the same as 4 rows beneath the clear command . . . this starts your PRINT message on the 6th line down on the screen.
"[CTRL] [WHT]	Hold down the [CTRL] key and press the key marked [WHT] at the same time. If you do this inside quotation marks, a "reversed E" will appear. This sets the color to everything PRINTed from then on to WHITE.
I AM THE DANCING MOUSE!	This is a simple PRINT statement.
[C=] [7]"	This sets the color back to light blue when the PRINT statement ends. Holding down [C=] and [7] at the same time inside quotation marks causes a "reversed diamond symbol" to appear.

LINE 45:

P=192	Sets the variable P equal to 192. This number 192 is the pointer you must use, in this case to "point" sprite 0 to the memory locations that begin at location 12288. Changing this pointer to the locations of the other two sprite shapes is the secret of using one sprite to create an animation that is actually three different shapes.

LINE 50:

FORX=0TO347 STEP3	Steps the movement of your sprite 3 X positions at a time (to provide fast movement) from position 0 to position 347.

LINE 55:

RX=INT(X/256)	RX is the integer of X/256 which means that RX is rounded off to 0 when X is less than 256, and RX becomes 1 when X reaches position 256. We will use RX in a moment to POKE V+16 with a 0 or 1 to turn on the "RIGHT SIDE" of the screen.
LX=X−RX*256	When the sprite is at X position 0, the formula looks like this: LX = 0 − (0 times 256) or 0. When the sprite is at X position 1 the formula looks like this: LX = 1 − (0 times 256) or 1. When the sprite is at X position 256 the formula looks like this: LX = 256 − (1 times 256) or 0 which resets X back to 0 which must be done when you start over on the RIGHT SIDE of the screen (POKEV+16,1).

LINE 60:

POKEV,LX	You POKE V by itself with a value to set the Horizontal (X) Position of sprite 0 on the screen. (See SPRITEMAKING CHART on Page 176). As shown above, the value of LX, which is the horizontal position of the sprite, changes from 0 to 255 and when it reaches 255 it automatically resets back to zero because of the LX equation set up in line 55.
POKEV+16,RX	POKEV+16 always turns on the "right side" of the screen beyond position 256, and resets the horizontal positioning coordinates to zero. RX is either a 0 or a 1 based on the position of the sprite as determined by the RX formula in line 55.

LINE 70:

IFP=192THEN GOSUB200	If the sprite pointer is set to 192 (the first sprite shape) the waveform control for the first sound effect is set to 129 and 128 per line 200.

LINE 75:

IFP=193THEN GOSUB300	If the sprite pointer is set to 193 (the second sprite shape) the waveform control for the second sound effect (Voice 2) is set to 129 and 128 per line 300.

LINE 80:

POKE2040,P	Sets the SPRITE POINTER to location 192 (remember P=192 in line 45? Here's where we use the P).
FORT=1TO60: NEXT	A simple time delay loop which sets the speed at which the mouse dances. (Try a faster or slower speed by increasing/decreasing the number 60.)

LINE 85:

P=P+1	Now we increase the value of the pointer by adding 1 to the original value of P.
IFP>194THEN P=192	We only want to point the sprite to 3 memory locations. 192 points to locations 12288 to 12350, 193 points to locations 12352 to 12414, and 194 points to locations 12416 to 12478. This line tells the computer to reset P back to 192 as soon as P becomes 195 so P never really becomes 195. P is 192, 193, 194 and then resets back to 192 and the pointer winds up pointing consecutively to the three sprite shapes in the three 64-byte groups of memory locations containing the DATA.

LINE 90:

NEXTX

After the sprite has become one of the 3 different shapes defined by the DATA, only then is it allowed to move across the screen. It will jump 3 X positions at a time (instead of scrolling smoothly one position at a time, which is also possible). STEPping 3 positions at a time makes the mouse "dance" faster across the screen. NEXT X matches the FOR. . . X position loop in line 50.

LINE 95

END

ENDs the program, which occurs when the sprite moves off the screen.

LINES 100–109

DATA

The sprite shapes are read from the data numbers, in order. First the 63 numbers which comprise sprite shape 1 are read, then the 63 numbers for sprite shape 2, and then sprite shape 3. This data is permanently read into the 3 memory locations and after it is read into these locations, all the program has to do is point sprite 0 at the 3 memory locations and the sprite automatically takes the shape of the data in those locations. We are pointing the sprite at 3 locations one at a time which produces the "animation" effect. If you want to see how these numbers affect each sprite, try changing the first 3 numbers in LINE 100 to 255, 255, 255. See the section on defining sprite shapes for more information.

LINE 200:

POKES+4,129	Waveform control set to 129 turns on the sound effect.
POKES+4,128	Waveform control set to 128 turns off the sound effect.
RETURN	Sends program back to end of line 70 after waveform control settings are changed, to resume program.

LINE 300:

POKES+11,129	Waveform control set to 129 turns on the sound effect.
POKES+11,128	Waveform control set to 128 turns off the sound effect.
RETURN	Sends program back to end of line 75 to resume.

EASY SPRITEMAKING CHART

	SPRITE 0	SPRITE 1	SPRITE 2	SPRITE 3	SPRITE 4	SPRITE 5	SPRITE 6	SPRITE 7
Turn on Sprite	V+21,1	V+21,2	V+21,4	V+21,8	V+21,16	V+21,32	V+21,64	V+21,128
Put in Memory (Set Pointers)	2040, 192	2041, 193	2042, 194	2043, 195	2044, 196	2045, 197	2046, 198	2047, 199
Locations for Sprite Pixel (12288–12798)	12288 to 12350	12352 to 12414	12416 to 12478	12480 to 12542	12544 to 12606	12608 to 12670	12672 to 12734	12736 to 12798
Sprite Color	V+39,C	V+40,C	V+41,C	V+42,C	V+43,C	V+44,C	V+45,C	V+46,C
Set LEFT X Position (0–255)	V+0,X	V+2,X	V+4,X	V+6,X	V+8,X	V+10,X	V+12,X	V+14,X
Set RIGHT X Position (0–255)	V+16,1 V+0,X	V+16,2 V+2,X	V+16,4 V+4,X	V+16,8 V+6,X	V+16,16 V+8,X	V+16,32 V+10,X	V+16,64 V+12,X	V+16,128 V+14,X
Set Y Position	V+1,Y	V+3,Y	V+5,Y	V+7,Y	V+9,Y	V+11,Y	V+13,Y	V+15,Y
Expand Sprite Horizontally/X	V+29,1	V+29,2	V+29,4	V+29,8	V+29,16	V+29,32	V+29,64	V+29,128
Expand Sprite Vertically/Y	V+23,1	V+23,2	V+23,4	V+23,8	V+23,16	V+23,32	V+23,64	V+23,128
Turn On (Set) Multi-Color Mode	V+28,1	V+28,2	V+28,4	V+28,8	V+28,16	V+28,32	V+28,64	V+28,128
Multi-Color 1 (First Color)	V+37,C	V+37,C	V+37,C	V+37,C	V+37,C	V+37,C	V+37,C	V+37,C
Multi-Color 2 (Second Color)	V+38,C	V+38,C	V+38,C	V+38,C	V+38,C	V+38,C	V+38,C	V+38,C
Set Priority of Sprites	The rule is that lower numbered sprites always have display priority over higher numbered sprites. For example, sprite 0 has priority over ALL other sprites, sprite 7 has last priority. This means lower numbered sprites always appear to move IN FRONT OF or ON TOP OF higher numbered sprites.							
Collision (Sprite to Sprite)	V+30 IF PEEK(V+30)ANDX=X THEN [action]							
Collision (Sprite to Background)	V+31 IF PEEK(V+31)ANDX=X THEN [action]							

SPRITEMAKING NOTES

Alternative Sprite Memory Pointers and Memory Locations Using Cassette Buffer

Put in Memory (Set pointers)	SPRITE 0 2040,13	SPRITE 1 2041,14	SPRITE 2 2042,15	If you're using 1 to 3 sprites you can use these memory locations in the cassette buffer (832 to 1023) but for more than 3 sprites we suggest using locations from 12288 to 12798 (see chart).
Sprite Pixel Locations for Blocks 13–15	832 to 894	896 to 958	960 to 1022	

TURNING ON SPRITES:

You can turn on any individual sprite by using POKE V+21 and the number from the chart . . . BUT . . . turning on just ONE sprite will turn OFF any others. To turn on TWO OR MORE sprites, ADD TOGETHER the numbers of the sprites you want to turn on (Example: POKE V+21, 6 turns on sprites 1 and 2). Here is a method you can use to turn one sprite off and on without affecting any of the others (useful for animation).

EXAMPLE:

To turn off just sprite 0 type: POKE V+21,PEEK V+21AND(255–1). Change the number 1 in (255–1) to 1,2,4,8,16,32,64, or 128 (for sprites 0–7). To re-enable the sprite and not affect the other sprites currently turned on, POKE V+21, PEEK(V+21)OR 1 and change the OR 1 to OR 2 (sprite 2), OR 4 (sprite 3), etc.

X POSITION VALUES BEYOND 255:

X positions run from 0 to 255 . . . and then START OVER from 0 to 255. To put a sprite beyond X position 255 on the far right side of the screen, you must first POKE V+16 as shown, THEN POKE a new X value from 0 to 63, which will place the sprite in one of the X positions at the right side of the screen. To get back to positions 0–255, POKE V+16,0 and POKE in an X value from 0 to 255.

Y POSITION VALUES:

Y positions run from 0 to 255, including 0 to 49 off the TOP of the viewing area, 50 to 229 IN the viewing area, and 230 to 255 off the BOTTOM of the viewing area.

SPRITE COLORS:

To make sprite 0 WHITE, type: POKE V+39,1 (use COLOR POKE SETTING shown in chart, and INDIVIDUAL COLOR CODES shown below):

0—BLACK	4—PURPLE	8—ORANGE	12—MED. GREY
1—WHITE	5—GREEN	9—BROWN	13—LT. GREEN
2—RED	6—BLUE	10—LT. RED	14—LT. BLUE
3—CYAN	7—YELLOW	11—DARK GREY	15—LT. GREY

MEMORY LOCATION:

You must "reserve" a separate 64-BYTE BLOCK of numbers in the computer's memory for each sprite of which 63 BYTES will be used for sprite data. The memory settings shown below are recommended for the "sprite pointer" settings in the chart above. Each sprite will be unique and you'll have to define it as you wish. To make all sprites exactly the same, point the sprites you want to look the same to the same register for sprites.

DIFFERENT SPRITE POINTER SETTINGS:

These sprite pointer settings are RECOMMENDATIONS ONLY.

Caution: you can set your sprite pointers anywhere in RAM memory but if you set them too "low" in memory a long BASIC program may overwrite your sprite data, or vice versa. To protect an especially LONG BASIC PROGRAM from overwriting sprite data, you may want to set the sprites at a higher area of memory (for example, 2040,192 for sprite 0 at locations 12288 to 12350 . . . 2041,193 at locations 12352 to 12414 for sprite 1 and so on . . . by adjusting the memory locations from which sprites get their "data," you can define as many as 64 different sprites plus a sizable BASIC program. To do this, define several sprite "shapes" in your DATA statements and then redefine a particular sprite by changing the "pointer" so the sprite you are using is "pointed" at different areas of memory containing different sprite picture data. See the "Dancing Mouse" to see how this works. If you want two or more sprites to have THE SAME SHAPE (you can still change position and color of each sprite), use the same sprite pointer and memory location for the sprites you want to match (for example, you can point sprites 0 and 1 to the same location by using POKE 2040,192 and POKE 2041, 192).

PRIORITY:

Priority means one sprite will appear to move "in front of" or "behind" another sprite on the display screen. Sprites with more priority always appear to move "in front of" or "on top of" sprites with less priority. The rule is that lower numbered sprites have priority over higher numbered sprites. Sprite 0 has priority over all other sprites. Sprite 7 has no priority in relation to the other sprites. Sprite 1 has priority over sprites 2–7, etc. If you put two sprites in the same position, the sprite with the higher priority will appear IN FRONT OF the sprite with the lower priority. The sprite with lower priority will either be obscured, or will "show through" (from "behind") the sprite with higher priority.

USING MULTI-COLOR:

You can create multi-colored sprites although using multi-color mode requires that you use PAIRS of pixels instead of individual pixels in your sprite picture (in other words each colored "dot" or "block" in the sprite will consist of two pixels side by side). You have 4 colors to choose from: Sprite Color (chart above), Multi-Color 1, Multi-Color 2 and "Background Color" (background is achieved by using zero settings which let the background color "show through"). Consider one horizontal 8-pixel block in a sprite picture. The color of each PAIR of pixels is determined according to whether the left, right, or both pixels are solid, like this:

BACKGROUND (Making BOTH PIXELS BLANK (zero) lets the INNER SCREEN COLOR (background) show through.)

MULTI-COLOR 1 (Making the RIGHT PIXEL SOLID in a pair of pixels sets BOTH PIXELS to Multi-Color 1.)

SPRITE COLOR (Making the LEFT PIXEL SOLID in a pair of pixels sets BOTH PIXELS to Sprite Color.)

MULTI-COLOR 2 (Making BOTH PIXELS SOLID in a pair of pixels sets BOTH PIXELS to Multi-Color 2.)

Look at the horizontal 8-pixel row shown below. This block sets the first two pixels to background color, the second two pixels to Multi-Color 1, the third two pixels to Sprite Color and the fourth two pixels to Multi-Color 2. The color of each PAIR of pixels depends on which bits in each pair are solid and which are blank, according to the illustration above. After you determine which colors you want in each pair of pixels, the next step is to add the values of the solid pixels in the 8-pixel block, and POKE that number into the proper memory location. For example, if the 8-pixel row shown below is the first block in a sprite which begins at memory location 832, the value of the solid pixels is 16+8+2+1 = 27, so you would POKE 832,27.

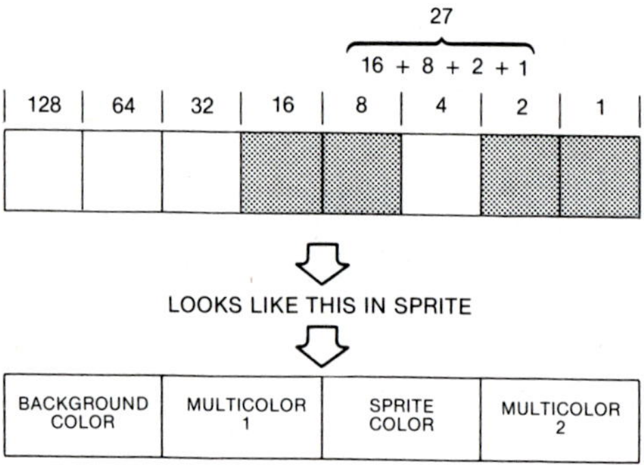

COLLISION:

You can detect whether a sprite has collided with another sprite by using this line: IF PEEK(V+30)ANDX=XTHEN [insert action here]. This line checks to see if a particular sprite has collided with ANY OTHER SPRITE, where X equals 1 for sprite 0, 2 for sprite 1, 4 for sprite 2, 8 for sprite 3, 16 for sprite 4, 32 for sprite 5, 64 for sprite 6, and 128 for sprite 7. To check to see if the sprite has collided with a "BACKGROUND CHARACTER" use this line: IF PEEK(V+31)ANDX=XTHEN [insert action here].

USING GRAPHIC CHARACTERS IN DATA STATEMENTS

The following program allows you to create a sprite using blanks and solid circles (SHIFT Q) in DATA statements. The sprite and the numbers POKEd into the sprite data registers are displayed.

SHIFT CLR/HOME

```
10 PRINT"♥":FORI=0TO63:POKE832+I,0:NEXT
20 GOSUB60000
999 END
60000 DATA"         ●●●●●●●        "
60001 DATA"       ●●●●●●●●●●●      "
60002 DATA"      ●●●●●●●●●●●●●     "
60003 DATA"      ●●●●●   ●●●●●     "
60004 DATA"     ●●●●● ●●●  ●●●●    "
60005 DATA"     ●●●●● ●●● ●●●●●    "
60006 DATA"     ●●●●● ●●●  ●●●●    "
60007 DATA"      ●●●●●   ●●●●●     "
60008 DATA"      ●●●●●●●●●●●●●     "
60009 DATA"      ●●●●●●●●●●●●●     "
60010 DATA"      ● ●●●●●●●●● ●     "
60011 DATA"       ● ●●●●●●● ●      "
60012 DATA"       ●  ●●●●●  ●      "
60013 DATA"        ●  ●●●  ●       "
60014 DATA"        ●  ●●●  ●       "
60015 DATA"         ●  ●  ●        "
60016 DATA"         ●  ●  ●        "
60017 DATA"          ●●●●●         "
60018 DATA"          ●●●●●         "
60019 DATA"          ●●●●●         "
60020 DATA"           ●●●          "
60100 V=53248:POKEV,200:POKEV+1,100:POKEV+21,1:
POKEV+39,14:POKE2040,13
60105 POKEV+23,1:POKEV+29,1
60110 FORI=0TO20:READA$:FORK=0TO2:T=0:FORJ=0TO7:B=0
60140 IFMID$(A$,J+K*8+1,1)="●"THENB=1
60150 T=T+B*2↑(7-J):NEXT:PRINTT;:POKE832+I*3+K,T:
NEXT:PRINT:NEXT
60200 RETURN
```

CHAPTER 4

PROGRAMMING SOUND AND MUSIC ON YOUR COMMODORE 64

- Introduction
  - Volume Control
  - Frequencies of Sound Waves
- Using Multiple Voices
- Changing Waveforms
- The Envelope Generator
- Filtering
- Advanced Techniques
- Synchronization and Ring Modulation

INTRODUCTION

Your Commodore computer is equipped with one of the most sophisticated electronic music synthesizers available on any computer. It comes complete with three voices, totally addressable, **ATTACK/DECAY/SUSTAIN/RELEASE (ADSR)**, filtering, modulation, and "white noise." All of these capabilities are directly available for you through a few easy to use BASIC and/or assembly language statements and functions. This means that you can make very complex sounds and songs using programs that are relatively simple to design.

This section of your Programmer's Reference Guide has been created to help you explore all the capabilities of the 6581 "SID" chip, the sound and music synthesizer inside your Commodore computer. We'll explain both the theory behind musical ideas and the practical aspects of turning those ideas into real finished songs on your Commodore computer.

You need not be an experienced programmer nor a music expert to achieve exciting results from the music synthesizer. This section is full of programming examples with complete explanations to get you started.

You get to the sound generator by POKEing into specified memory locations. A full list of the locations used is provided in Appendix O. We will go through each concept, step by step. By the end you should be able to create an almost infinite variety of sounds, and be ready to perform experiments with sound on your own.

Each section of this chapter begins by giving you an example and a full line-by-line description of each program, which will show you how to use the characteristic being discussed. The technical explanation is for you to read whenever you are curious about what is actually going on.

The workhorse of your sound programs is the POKE statement. POKE sets the indicated memory location (MEM) equal to a specified value (NUM).

POKE MEM,NUM

The memory locations (MEM) used for music synthesis start at 54272 ($D400) in the Commodore 64. The memory locations 54272 to 54296 inclusive are the POKE locations you need to remember when you're using the 6581 (SID) chip register map. Another way to use the locations above is to remember only location 54272 and then add a number from 0 through 24 to it. By doing this you can POKE all the locations from 54272 to 54296 that you need from the SID chip. The numbers (NUM) that you use in your POKE statement must be between 0 and 255, inclusive.

When you've had a little more practice with making music, then you can get a little more involved, by using the PEEK function. PEEK is a function that is equal to the value currently in the indicated memory location.

X=PEEK(MEM)

The value of the variable X is set equal to the current contents of memory location MEM.

Of course, your programs include other BASIC commands, but for a full explanation of them, refer to the BASIC Statements section of this manual.

Let's jump right in and try a simple program using only one of the three voices. Computer ready? Type NEW, then type in this program, and save it on your Commodore DATASSETTE™ or disk. Then, RUN it.

EXAMPLE PROGRAM 1:

```
5 S=54272
10 FORL=STOS+24:POKEL,0:NEXT:REM CLEAR SOUND CHIP
20 POKES+5,9:POKES+6,0
30 POKES+24,15                    :REM SET VOLUME TO
MAXIMUM
40 READHF,LF,DR
50 IFHF<0THENEND
60 POKES+1,HF:POKES,LF
70 POKES+4,33
80 FORT=1TODR:NEXT
90 POKES+4,32:FORT=1TO50:NEXT
100 GOTO40
110 DATA25,177,250,28,214,250
120 DATA25,177,250,25,177,250
130 DATA25,177,125,28,214,125
140 DATA32,94,750,25,177,250
150 DATA28,214,250,19,63,250
160 DATA19,63,250,19,63,250
170 DATA21,154,63,24,63,63
180 DATA25,177,250,24,63,125
190 DATA19,63,250,-1,-1,-1
```

Here's a line-by-line description of the program you've just typed in. Refer to it whenever you feel the need to investigate parts of the program that you don't understand completely.

LINE-BY-LINE EXPLANATION OF EXAMPLE PROGRAM 1:

Line(s)	Description
5	Set S to start of sound chip.
10	Clear all sound chip registers.
20	Set Attack/Decay for voice 1 (A=0,D=9). Set Sustain/Release for voice 1 (S=0,R=0).
30	Set volume at maximum.
40	Read high frequency, low frequency, duration of note.
50	When high frequency less than zero, song is over.
60	Poke high and low frequency of voice 1.
70	Gate sawtooth waveform for voice 1.
80	Timing loop for duration of note.
90	Release sawtooth waveform for voice 1.
100	Return for next note.
110–180	Data for song: high frequency, low frequency, duration (number of counts) for each note.
190	Last note of song and negative 1s signaling end of song.

VOLUME CONTROL

Chip register 24 contains the overall volume control. The volume can be set anywhere between 0 and 15. The other four bits are used for purposes we'll get into later. For now it is enough to know volume is 0 to 15. Look at line 30 to see how it's set in Example Program 1.

FREQUENCIES OF SOUND WAVES

Sound is created by the movement of air in waves. Think of throwing a stone into a pool and seeing the waves radiate outward. When similar waves are created in air, we hear it. If we measure the time between one peak of a wave and the next, we find the number of seconds for one cycle of the wave (n = number of seconds). The reciprocal of this number (1/n) gives you the cycles per second. Cycles per second are more commonly known as the frequency. The highness or lowness of a sound (pitch) is determined by the frequency of the sound waves produced.

The sound generator in your Commodore computer uses two locations to determine the frequency. Appendix E gives you the frequency values you need to reproduce a full eight octaves of musical notes. To create a frequency other than the ones listed in the note table use "F_{out}" (frequency output) and the following formula to represent the frequency (F_n) of the sound you want to create. Remember that each note requires both a high and a low frequency number.

$$F_n = F_{out}/.06097$$

Once you've figured out what F_n is for your "new" note the next step is to create the high and low frequency values for that note. To do this you must first round off F_n so that any numbers to the right of the decimal point are left off. You are now left with an integer value. Now you can set the high frequency location (F_{hi}) by using the formula $F_{hi}=INT(F_n/256)$ and the low frequency location (F_{lo}) should be $F_{lo}=F_n-(256*F_{hi})$.

At this point you have already played with one voice of your computer. If you wanted to stop here you could find a copy of your favorite tune and become the maestro conducting your own computer orchestra in your "at home" concert hall.

USING MULTIPLE VOICES

Your Commodore computer has three independently controlled voices (oscillators). Our first example program used only one of them. Later on, you'll learn how to change the quality of the sound made by the voices. But right now, let's get all three voices singing.

This example program shows you one way to translate sheet music for your computer orchestra. Try typing it in, and then SAVE it on your DATASSETTE™ or disk. Don't forget to type NEW before typing in this program.

EXAMPLE PROGRAM 2:

```
10 S=54272:FORL=STOS+24:POKEL,0:NEXT
20 DIMH(2,200),L(2,200),C(2,200)
30 DIMFQ(11)
40 V(0)=17:V(1)=65:V(2)=33
50 POKES+10,8:POKES+22,128:POKES+23,244
60 FORI=0TO11:READFQ(I):NEXT
100 FORK=0TO2
110 I=0
120 READNM
130 IFNM=0THEN250
140 WA=V(K):WB=WA-1:IFNM<0THENNM=-NM:WA=0:WB=0
150 DR%=NM/128:OC%=(NM-128*DR%)/16
160 NT=NM-128*DR%-16*OC%
170 FR=FQ(NT)
```

```
180 IFOC%=7THEN200
190 FORJ=6TOOC%STEP-1:FR=FR/2:NEXT
200 HF%=FR/256:LF%=FR-256*HF%
210 IFDR%=1THENH(K,I)=HF%:L(K,I)=LF%:C(K,I)=WA:
I=I+1:GOTO120
220 FORJ=1TODR%-1:H(K,I)=HF%:L(K,I)=LF%:C(K,I)=WA:
I=I+1:NEXT
230 H(K,I)=HF%:L(K,I)=LF%:C(K,I)=WB
240 I=I+1:GOTO120
250 IFI>IMTHENIM=I
260 NEXT
500 POKES+5,0:POKES+6,240
510 POKES+12,85:POKES+13,133
520 POKES+19,10:POKES+20,197
530 POKES+24,31
540 FORI=0TOIM
550 POKES,L(0,I):POKES+7,L(1,I):POKES+14,L(2,I)
560 POKES+1,H(0,I):POKES+8,H(1,I):POKES+15,H(2,I)
570 POKES+4,C(0,I):POKES+11,C(1,I):POKES+18,C(2,I)
580 FORT=1TO80:NEXT:NEXT
590 FORT=1TO200:NEXT:POKES+24,0
600 DATA34334,36376,38539,40830
610 DATA43258,45830,48556,51443
620 DATA54502,57743,61176,64814
1000 DATA594,594,594,596,596
1010 DATA1618,587,592,587,585,331,336
1020 DATA1097,583,585,585,585,587,587
1030 DATA1609,585,331,337,594,594,593
1040 DATA1618,594,596,594,592,587
1050 DATA1616,587,585,331,336,841,327
1060 DATA1607
1999 DATA0
2000 DATA583,585,583,583,327,329
2010 DATA1611,583,585,578,578,578
2020 DATA196,198,583,326,578
2030 DATA326,327,329,327,329,326,578,583
2040 DATA1606,582,322,324,582,587
2050 DATA329,327,1606,583
2060 DATA327,329,587,331,329
2070 DATA329,328,1609,578,834
2080 DATA324,322,327,585,1602
2999 DATA0
3000 DATA567,566,567,304,306,308,310
3010 DATA1591,567,311,310,567
3020 DATA306,304,299,308
3030 DATA304,171,176,306,291,551,306,308
3040 DATA310,308,310,306,295,297,299,304
3050 DATA1506,562,567,310,315,311
3060 DATA308,313,297
3070 DATA1586,567,560,311,309
3080 DATA308,309,306,308
3090 DATA1577,299,295,306,310,311,304
3100 DATA562,546,1575
3999 DATA0
```

Here is a line-by-line explanation of Example Program 2. For now, we are interested in how the three voices are controlled.

LINE-BY-LINE EXPLANATION OF EXAMPLE PROGRAM 2:

Line(s)	Description
10	Set S equal to start of sound chip and clear all sound chip registers.
20	Dimension arrays to contain activity of song, 1/16th of a measure per location.
30	Dimension array to contain base frequency for each note.
40	Store waveform control byte for each voice.
50	Set high pulse width for voice 2. Set high frequency for filter cutoff. Set resonance for filter and filter voice 3.
60	Read in base frequency for each note.
100	Begin decoding loop for each voice.
110	Initialize pointer to activity array.
120	Read coded note.
130	If coded note is zero, then next voice.
140	Set waveform controls to proper voice. If silence, set waveform controls to 0.
150	Decode duration and octave.
160	Decode note.
170	Get base frequency for this note.
180	If highest octave, skip division loop.
190	Divide base frequency by 2 appropriate number of times.
200	Get high and low frequency bytes.
210	If sixteenth note, set activity array: high frequency, low frequency, and waveform control (voice on).
220	For all but last beat of note, set activity array: high frequency, low frequency, waveform control (voice on).
230	For last beat of note, set activity array: high frequency, low frequency, waveform control (voice off).
240	Increment pointer to activity array. Get next note.
250	If longer than before, reset number of activities.
260	Go back for next voice.
500	Set Attack/Decay for voice 1 (A=0, D=0). Set Sustain/Release for voice 1 (S=15, R=0).

Line(s)	Description
510	Set Attack/Decay for voice 2 (A=5, D=5). Set Sustain/Release for voice 2 (S=8, R=5).
520	Set Attack/Decay for voice 3 (A=0, D=10). Set Sustain/Release for voice 3 (S=12, R=5).
530	Set volume 15, low-pass filtering.
540	Start loop for every 1/16th of a measure.
550	POKE low frequency from activity array for all voices.
560	POKE high frequency from activity array for all voices.
570	POKE waveform control from activity array for all voices.
580	Timing loop for 1/16th of a measure and back for next 1/16th measure.
590	Pause, then turn off volume.
600–620	Base frequency data.
1000–1999	Voice 1 data.
2000–2999	Voice 2 data.
3000–3999	Voice 3 data.

The values used in the data statements were found by using the note table in Appendix E and the chart below:

NOTE TYPE	DURATION
1/16	128
1/8	256
DOTTED 1/8	384
1/4	512
1/4+1/16	640
DOTTED 1/4	768
1/2	1024
1/2+1/16	1152
1/2+1/8	1280
DOTTED 1/2	1536
WHOLE	2048

The note number from the note table is added to the duration above. Then each note can be entered using only one number which is decoded by your program. This is only one method of coding note values. You may be able to come up with one with which you are more comfortable. The formula used here for encoding a note is as follows:

1) The duration (number of 1/16ths of a measure) is multiplied by 8.
2) The result of step 1 is added to the octave you've chosen (0–7).
3) The result of step 2 is then multiplied by 16.
4) Add your note choice (0–11) to the result of the operation in step 3.

In other words:

$$((((D*8)+O)\ *16)+N)$$

Where D = duration, O = octave, and N = note

A silence is obtained by using the negative of the duration number (number of 1/16ths of a measure * 128).

CONTROLLING MULTIPLE VOICES

Once you have gotten used to using more than one voice, you will find that the timing of the three voices needs to be coordinated. This is accomplished in this program by:

1) Divide each musical measure into 16 parts.
2) Store the events that occur in each 1/16th measure interval in three separate arrays.

The high and low frequency bytes are calculated by dividing the frequencies of the highest octave by two (lines 180 and 190). The waveform control byte is a start signal for beginning a note or continuing a note that is already playing. It is a stop signal to end a note. The waveform choice is made once for each voice in line 40.

Again, this is only one way to control multiple voices. You may come up with your own methods. However, you should now be able to take any piece of sheet music and figure out the notes for all three voices.

CHANGING WAVEFORMS

The tonal quality of a sound is called the *timbre*. The timbre of a sound is determined primarily by its "waveform." If you remember the example of throwing a pebble into the water you know that the waves ripple evenly across the pond. These waves almost look like the first sound wave we're going to talk about, the sinusoidal wave, or sine wave for short (shown below).

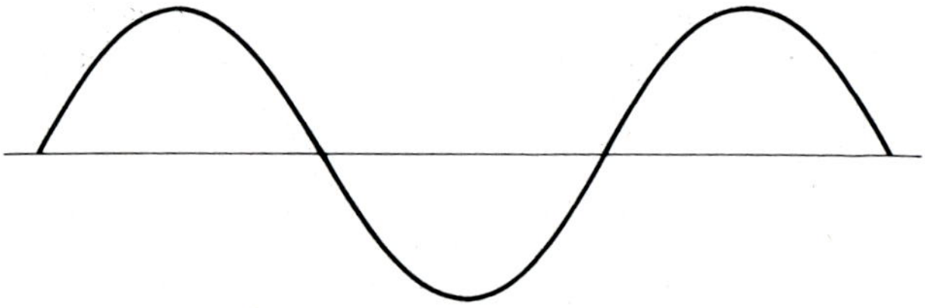

To make what we're talking about a bit more practical, let's go back to the first example program to investigate different waveforms. The reason for this is that you can hear the changes more easily using only one voice. LOAD the first music program that you typed in earlier, from your DATASSETTE™ or disk, and RUN it again. That program is using the sawtooth waveform (shown here)

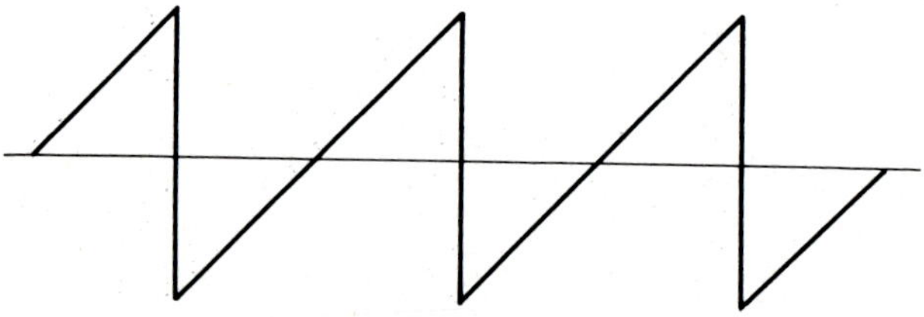

from the 6581 SID chip's sound generating device. Try changing the note start number in line 70 from 33 to 17 and the note stop number in line 90 from 32 to 16. Your program should now look like this:

EXAMPLE PROGRAM 3 (EXAMPLE 1 MODIFIED):

```
5 S=54272
10 FORL=STOS+24:POKEL,0:NEXT
20 POKES+5,9:POKES+6,0
30 POKES+24,15
40 READHF,LF,DR
50 IFHF<0THENEND
60 POKES+1,HF:POKES,LF
70 POKES+4,17
80 FORT=1TODR:NEXT
90 POKES+4,16:FORT=1TO50:NEXT
100 GOTO40
110 DATA25,177,250,28,214,250
120 DATA25,177,250,25,177,250
130 DATA25,177,125,28,214,125
140 DATA32,94,750,25,177,250
150 DATA28,214,250,19,63,250
160 DATA19,63,250,19,63,250
170 DATA21,154,63,24,63,63
180 DATA25,177,250,24,63,125
190 DATA19,63,250,-1,-1,-1
```

Now RUN the program.

Notice how the sound quality is different, less twangy, more hollow. That's because we changed the sawtooth waveform into a triangular waveform (show below).

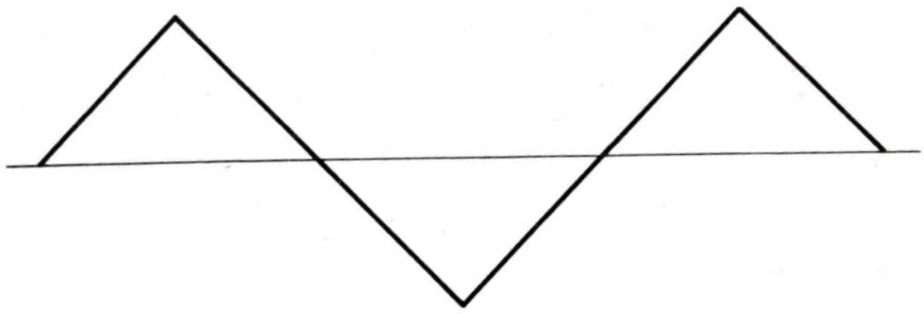

The third musical waveform is called a variable pulse wave (shown below).

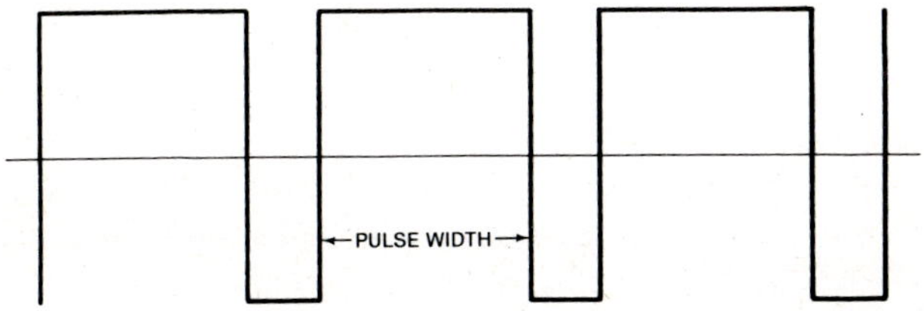

It is a rectangular wave and you determine the length of the pulse cycle by defining the proportion of the wave which will be high. This is accomplished for voice 1 by using registers 2 and 3: Register 2 is the low byte of the pulse width (L_{pw} = 0 through 255). Register 3 is the high 4 bits (H_{pw} = 0 through 15).

Together these registers specify a 12-bit number for your pulse width, which you can determine by using the following formula:

$$PW_n = H_{pw} * 256 + L_{pw}$$

The pulse width is determined by the following equation:

$$PW_{out} = (PW_n/40.95)\ \%$$

When PW_n has a value of 2048, it will give you a square wave. That means that register 2 (L_{pw}) = 0 and register 3 (H_{pw}) = 8.

Now try adding this line to your program:

15 POKES+3,8:POKES+2,0

Then change the start number in line 70 to 65 and the stop number in line 90 to 64, and RUN the program. Now change the high pulse width (register 3 in line 15) from an 8 to a 1. Notice how dramatic the difference in sound quality is?

The last waveform available to you is white noise (shown here).

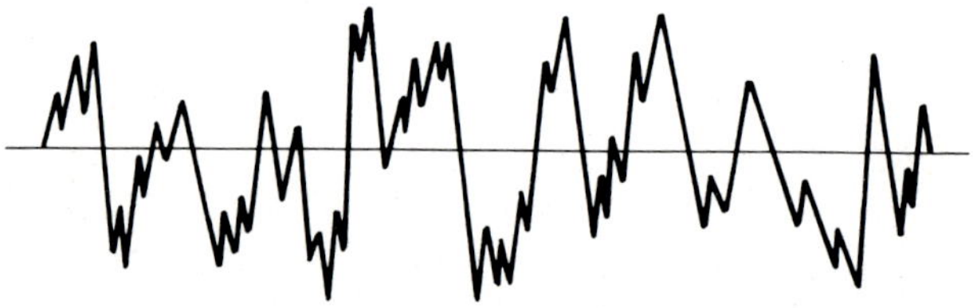

It is used mostly for sound effects and such. To hear how it sounds, try changing the start number in line 70 to 129 and the stop number in line 90 to 128.

UNDERSTANDING WAVEFORMS

When a note is played, it consists of a sine wave oscillating at the fundamental frequency and the harmonics of that wave.

The fundamental frequency defines the overall pitch of the note. Harmonics are sine waves having frequencies which are integer multiples of the fundamental frequency. A sound wave is the fundamental frequency and all of the harmonics it takes to make up that sound.

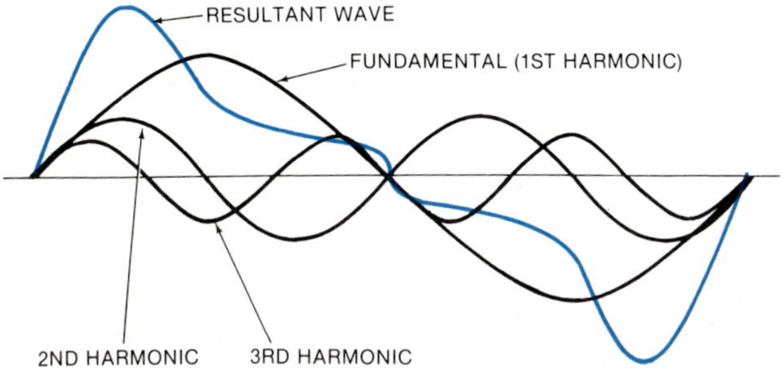

In musical theory let's say that the fundamental frequency is harmonic number 1. The second harmonic has a frequency twice the fundamental frequency, the third harmonic is three times the fundamental frequency, and so on. The amounts of each harmonic present in a note give it its timbre.

An acoustic instrument, like a guitar or a violin, has a very complicated harmonic structure. In fact, the harmonic structure may vary as a single note is played. You have already played with the waveforms available in your Commodore music synthesizer. Now let's talk about how the harmonics work with the triangular, sawtooth, and rectangular waves.

A triangular wave contains only odd harmonics. The amount of each harmonic present is proportional to the reciprocal of the square of the harmonic number. In other words harmonic number 3 is 1/9 quieter than harmonic number 1, because the harmonic 3 squared is 9 (3 × 3) and the reciprocal of 9 is 1/9.

As you can see, there is a similarity in shape of a triangular wave to a sine wave oscillating at the fundamental frequency.

Sawtooth waves contain all the harmonics. The amount of each harmonic present is proportional to the reciprocal of the harmonic number. For example, harmonic number 2 is 1/2 as loud as harmonic number 1.

The square wave contains odd harmonics in proportion to the reciprocal of the harmonic number. Other rectangular waves have varying harmonic content. By changing the pulse width, the timbre of the sound of a rectangular wave can be varied tremendously.

By choosing carefully the waveform used, you can start with a harmonic structure that looks somewhat like the sound you want. To refine the sound, you can add another aspect of sound quality available on your Commodore 64 called *filtering,* which we'll discuss later in this section.

THE ENVELOPE GENERATOR

The volume of a musical tone changes from the moment you first hear it, all the way through until it dies out and you can't hear it anymore. When a note is first struck, it rises from zero volume to its peak volume. The rate at which this happens is called the **ATTACK**. Then, it falls from the peak to some middle-ranged volume. The rate at which the fall of the note occurs is called the **DECAY**. The mid-ranged volume itself is called the **SUSTAIN** level. And finally, when the note stops playing, it falls from the **SUSTAIN** level to zero volume. The rate at which it falls is called the **RELEASE**. Here is a sketch of the four phases of a note:

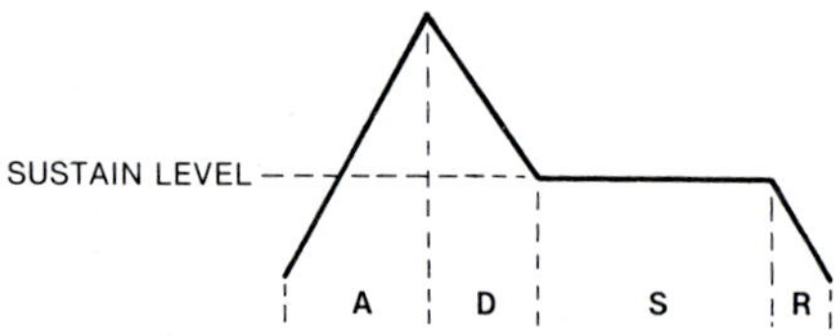

Each of the items mentioned above give certain qualities and restrictions to a note. The bounds are called parameters.

The parameters **ATTACK/DECAY/SUSTAIN/RELEASE** and collectively called **ADSR**, can be controlled by your use of another set of locations in the sound generator chip. LOAD your first example program again. RUN it again and remember how it sounds. Then, try changing line 20 so the program is like this:

EXAMPLE PROGRAM 4 (EXAMPLE 1 MODIFIED):

```
5 S=54272
10 FORL=STOS+24:POKEL,0:NEXT
20 POKES+5,88:POKES+6,195
30 POKES+24,15
40 READHF,LF,DR
50 IFHF<0THENEND
60 POKES+1,HF:POKES,LF
70 POKES+4,33
80 FORT=1TODR:NEXT
90 POKES+4,32:FORT=1TO50:NEXT
100 GOTO40
110 DATA25,177,250,28,214,250
120 DATA25,177,250,25,177,250
130 DATA25,177,125,28,214,125
140 DATA32,94,750,25,177,250
150 DATA28,214,250,19,63,250
160 DATA19,63,250,19,63,250
170 DATA21,154,63,24,63,63
180 DATA25,177,250,24,63,125
190 DATA19,63,250,-1,-1,-1
```

Registers 5 and 6 define the ADSR for voice 1. The **ATTACK** is the high nybble of register 5. Nybble is half a byte, in other words the lower 4 or higher 4 on/off locations (bits) in each register. **DECAY** is the low nybble. You can pick any number 0 through 15 for **ATTACK**, multiply it by 16 and add to any number 0 through 15 for **DECAY**. The values that correspond to these numbers are listed below.

SUSTAIN level is the high nybble of register 6. It can be 0 through 15. It defines the proportion of the peak volume that the **SUSTAIN** level will be. **RELEASE** rate is the low nybble of register 6.

Here are the meanings of the values for ATTACK, DECAY, and RELEASE:

VALUE	ATTACK RATE (TIME/CYCLE)	DECAY/RELEASE RATE (TIME/CYCLE)
0	2 ms	6 ms
1	8 ms	24 ms
2	16 ms	48 ms
3	24 ms	72 ms
4	38 ms	114 ms
5	56 ms	168 ms
6	68 ms	204 ms
7	80 ms	240 ms
8	100 ms	300 ms
9	250 ms	750 ms
10	500 ms	1.5 s
11	800 ms	2.4 s
12	1 s	3 s
13	3 s	9 s
14	5 s	15 s
15	8 s	24 s

Here are a few sample settings to try in your example program. Try these and a few of your own. The variety of sounds you can produce is astounding! For a violin type sound, try changing line 20 to read:

```
20 POKES+5,88:POKES+6,89:REM A=5;D=8;S=5;R=9
```

Change the waveform to triangle and get a xylophone type sound by using these lines:

```
20 POKES+5,9:POKES+6,9:REM A=0;D=9;S=0;R=9
70 POKES+4,17
90 POKES+4,16: FORT=1TO50:NEXT
```

Change the waveform to square and try a piano type sound with these lines:

```
15 POKES+3,8:POKES+2,0
20 POKES+5,9:POKES+6,0: REM A=0;D=9;S=0;R=0
70 POKES+4,65
90 POKES+4,64:FORT=1TO50:NEXT
```

The most exciting sounds are those unique to the music synthesizer itself, ones that do not attempt to mimic acoustic instruments. For example try:

```
20 POKES+5,144:POKES+6,243:REM A=9;D=0; S=15;R=3
```

FILTERING

The harmonic content of a waveform can be changed by using a filter. The SID chip is equipped with *three* types of filtering. They can be used separately or in combination with one another. Let's go back to the sample program you've been using to play with a simple example that uses a filter. There are several filter controls to set.

You add line 15 in the program to set the *cutoff frequency* of the filter. The cutoff frequency is the reference point for the filter. You SET the high and low frequency cutoff points in registers 21 and 22. To turn ON the filter for voice 1, POKE register 23.

Next change line 30 to show that a high-pass filter will be used (see the SID register map).

EXAMPLE PROGRAM 5 (EXAMPLE 1 MODIFIED):

```
5 S=54272
10 FORL=STOS+24:POKEL,0:NEXT
15 POKES+22,128:POKES+21,0:POKES+23,1
20 POKES+5,9:POKES+6,0
30 POKES+24,79
40 READHF,LF,DR
50 IFHF<0THENEND
60 POKES+1,HF:POKES,LF
70 POKES+4,33
80 FORT=1TODR:NEXT
90 POKES+4,32:FORT=1TO50:NEXT
100 GOTO40
110 DATA25,177,250,28,214,250
120 DATA25,177,250,25,177,250
130 DATA25,177,125,28,214,125
140 DATA32,94,750,25,177,250
150 DATA28,214,250,19,63,250
160 DATA19,63,250,19,63,250
170 DATA21,154,63,24,63,63
180 DATA25,177,250,24,63,125
190 DATA19,63,250,-1,-1,-1
```

Try RUNning the program now. Notice the lower tones have had their volume cut down. It makes the overall quality of the note sound tinny. This is because you are using a high-pass filter which attenuates (cuts down the level of) frequencies below the specified cutoff frequency.

There are three types of filters in your Commodore computer's SID chip. We have been using the *high-pass filter*. It will pass all the frequencies at or above the cutoff, while attenuating the frequencies below the cutoff.

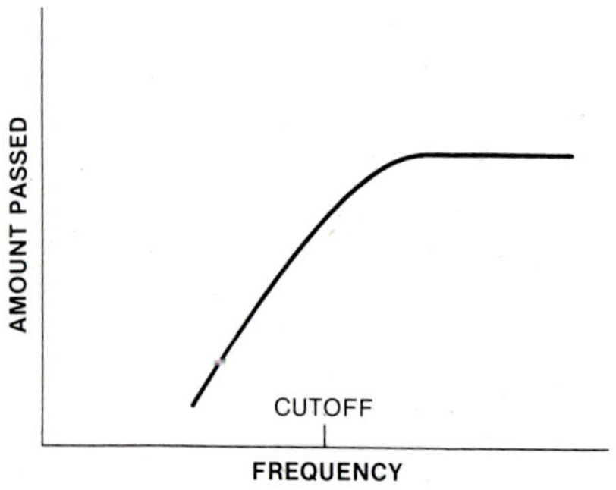

The SID chip also has a *low-pass filter*. As its name implies, this filter will pass the frequencies below cutoff and attenuate those above.

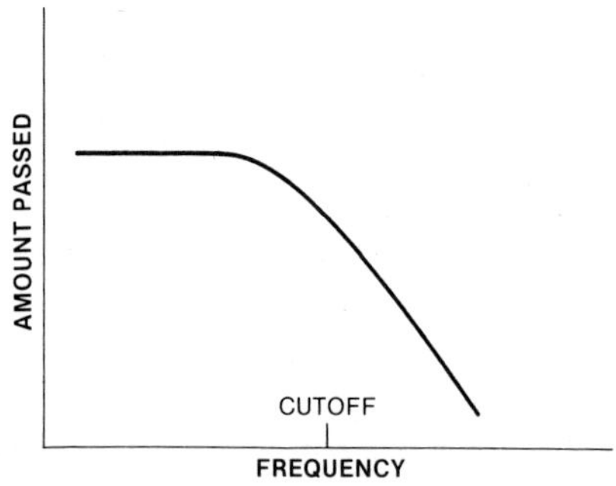

Finally, the chip is equipped with a *bandpass* filter, which passes a narrow band of frequencies around the cutoff, and attenuates all others.

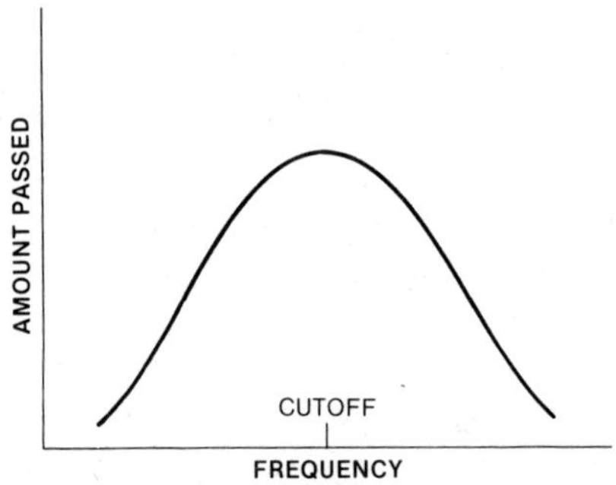

The high- and low-pass filters can be combined to form a *notch reject filter* which passes frequencies away from the cutoff while attenuating at the cutoff frequency.

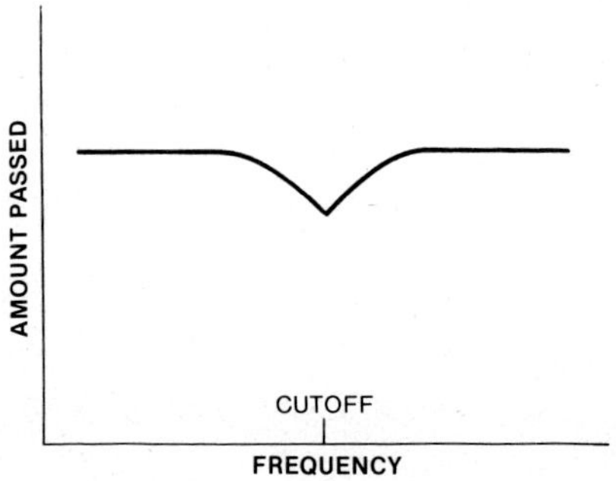

Register 24 determines which type filter you want to use. This is in addition to register 24's function as the overall volume control. Bit 6 controls the high-pass filter (0 = off, 1 = on), bit 5 is the bandpass filter, and bit 4 is the low-pass filter. The low 3 bits of the cutoff frequency are determined by register 21 (L_{cf}) (L_{cf} = 0 through 7). While the 8 bits of the high cutoff frequency are determined by register 22 (H_{cf}) (H_{cf} = 0 through 255).

Through careful use of filtering, you can change the harmonic structure of any waveform to get just the sound you want. In addition, changing the filtering of a sound as it goes through the ADSR phases of its life can produce interesting effects.

ADVANCED TECHNIQUES

The SID chip's parameters can be changed dynamically during a note or sound to create many interesting and fun effects. In order to make this easy to do, digitized outputs from *oscillator three* and *envelope generator three* are available for you in registers 27 and 28, respectively.

The output of oscillator 3 (register 27) is directly related to the waveform selected. If you choose the sawtooth waveform of oscillator 3, this register will present a series of numbers incremented (increased step by step) from 0 to 255 at a rate determined by the frequency of oscillator 3. If you choose the triangle waveform, the output will increment from 0 up to 255, then decrement (decrease step by step) back down to 0. If you choose the pulse wave, the output will jump back-and-forth between 0 and 255. Finally, choosing the noise waveform will give you a series of random numbers. When oscillator 3 is used for modulation, you usually do NOT want to hear its output. Setting bit 7 of register 24 turns the audio output of voice 3 off. Register 27 always reflects the changing output of the oscillator and is not affected in any way by the envelope (ADSR) generator.

Register 25 gives you access to the output of the envelope generator of oscillator 3. It functions in much the same fashion that the output of oscillator 3 does. The oscillator must be turned on to produce any output from this register.

Vibrato (a rapid variation in frequency) can be achieved by adding the output of oscillator 3 to the frequency of another oscillator. Example Program 6 illustrates this idea.

EXAMPLE PROGRAM 6:

```
10 S=54272
20 FORL=0TO24:POKES+L,0:NEXT
30 POKES+3,8
40 POKES+5,41:POKES+6,89
50 POKES+14,117
60 POKES+18,16
70 POKES+24,143
80 READFR,DR
90 IFFR=0THENEND
100 POKES+4,65
110 FORT=1TODR*2
120 FQ=FR+PEEK(S+27)/2
130 HF=INT(FQ/256):LF=FQAND255
140 POKES+0,LF:POKES+1,HF
150 NEXT
160 POKES+4,64
170 GOTO80
500 DATA4817,2,5103,2,5407,2
510 DATA8583,4,5407,2,8583,4
520 DATA5407,4,8583,12,9634,2
530 DATA10207,2,10814,2,8583,2
540 DATA9634,4,10814,2,8583,2
550 DATA9634,4,8583,12
560 DATA0,0
```

Here is a line-by-line explanation of Example Program 6:

LINE-BY-LINE EXPLANATION OF EXAMPLE PROGRAM 6:

Lines(s)	Description
10	Set S to beginning of sound chip.
20	Clear all sound chip locations.
30	Set high pulse width for voice 1.
40	Set Attack/Decay for voice 1 (A=2, D=9).
	Set Sustain/Release for voice 1 (S=5, R=9).
50	Set low frequency for voice 3.
60	Set triangle waveform for voice 3.
70	Set volume 15, turn off audio output of voice 3.
80	Read frequency and duration of note.
90	If frequency equals zero, stop.
100	POKE start pulse waveform control voice 1.
110	Start timing loop for duration.
120	Get new frequency using oscillator 3 output.
130	Get high and low frequency.
140	POKE high and low frequency for voice 1.
150	End of timing loop.
160	POKE stop pulse waveform control voice 1.
170	Go back for next note.
500–550	Frequencies and durations for song.
560	Zeros signal end of song.

A wide variety of sound effects can also be achieved using dynamic effects. For example, the following siren program dynamically changes the frequency output of oscillator 1 when it's based on the output of oscillator 3's triangular wave:

EXAMPLE PROGRAM 7:

```
10 S=54272
20 FORL=0TO24:POKES+L,0:NEXT
30 POKES+14,5
40 POKES+18,16
50 POKES+3,1
60 POKES+24,143
70 POKES+6,240
80 POKES+4,65
90 FR=5389
100 FORT=1TO200
110 FQ=FR+PEEK(S+27)*3.5
120 HF=INT(FQ/256):LF=FQ-HF*256
130 POKES+0,LF:POKES+1,HF
140 NEXT
150 POKES+24,0
```

Here is a line-by-line explanation of Example Program 7:

LINE-BY-LINE EXPLANATION OF EXAMPLE PROGRAM 7:

Line(s)	Description
10	Set S to start of sound chip.
20	Clear sound chip registers.
30	Set low frequency of voice 3.
40	Set triangular waveform voice 3.
50	Set high pulse width for voice 1.
60	Set volume 15, turn off audio output of voice 3.
70	Set Sustain/Release for voice 1 (S=15, R=0).
80	POKE start pulse waveform control voice 1.
90	Set lowest frequency for siren.
100	Begin timing loop.
110	Get new frequency using output of oscillator 3.
120	Get high and low frequencies.
130	POKE high and low frequencies for voice 1.
140	End timing loop.
150	Turn off volume.

The noise waveform can be used to provide a wide range of sound effects. This example mimics a hand clap using a filtered noise waveform:

EXAMPLE PROGRAM 8:

```
10 S=54272
20 FORL=0TO24:POKES+L,0:NEXT
30 POKES+0,240:POKES+1,33
40 POKES+5,8
50 POKES+22,104
60 POKES+23,1
70 POKES+24,79
80 FORN=1TO15
90 POKES+4,129
100 FORT=1TO250:NEXT:POKES+4,128
110 FORT=1TO30:NEXT:NEXT
120 POKES+24,0
```

Here is a line-by-line explanation of Example Program 8:

LINE-BY-LINE EXPLANATION OF EXAMPLE PROGRAM 8:

Line(s)	Description
10	Set S to start of sound chip.
20	Clear all sound chip registers.
30	Set high and low frequencies for voice 1.
40	Set Attack/Decay for voice 1 (A=0, D=8).
50	Set high cutoff frequency for filter.
60	Turn on filter for voice 1.
70	Set volume 15, high-pass filter.
80	Count 15 claps.
90	Set start noise waveform control.
100	Wait, then set stop noise waveform control.
110	Wait, then start next clap.
120	Turn off volume.

SYNCHRONIZATION AND RING MODULATION

The 6581 SID chip lets you create more complex harmonic structures through synchronization or ring modulation of two voices.

The process of synchronization is basically a logical ANDing of two wave forms. When either is zero, the output is zero. The following example uses this process to create an imitation of a mosquito:

EXAMPLE PROGRAM 9:

```
10 S=54272
20 FORL=0TO24:POKES+L,0:NEXT
30 POKES+1,100
40 POKES+5,219
50 POKES+15,28
60 POKES+24,15
70 POKES+4,19
80 FORT=1TO5000:NEXT
90 POKES+4,18
100 FORT=1TO1000:NEXT:POKES+24,0
```

Here is a line-by-line explanation of Example Program 9:

LINE-BY-LINE EXPLANATION OF EXAMPLE PROGRAM 9:

Line(s)	Description
10	Set S to start of sound chip.
20	Clear sound chip registers.
30	Set high frequency voice 1.
40	Set Attack/Decay for voice 1 (A=13, D=11).
50	Set high frequency voice 3.
60	Set volume 15.
70	Set start triangle, sync waveform control for voice 1.
80	Timing loop.
90	Set stop triangle, sync waveform control for voice 1.
100	Wait, then turn off volume.

The synchronization feature is enabled (turned on) in line 70, where bits 0,1, and 4 of register 4 are set. Bit 1 enables the syncing function between voice 1 and voice 3. Bits 0 and 4 have their usual functions of gating voice 1 and setting the triangular waveform.

Ring modulation (accomplished for voice 1 by setting bit 3 of register 4 in line 70 of the program below) replaces the triangular output of oscillator 1 with a "ring modulated" combination of oscillators 1 and 3. This produces non-harmonic overtone structures for use in mimicking bell or gong sounds. This program produces a clock chime imitation:

EXAMPLE PROGRAM 10:

```
10 S=54272
20 FORL=0TO24:POKES+L,0:NEXT
30 POKES+1,130
40 POKES+5,9
50 POKES+15,30
60 POKES+24,15
70 FORL=1TO12:POKES+4,21
80 FORT=1TO1000:NEXT:POKES+4,20
90 FORT=1TO1000:NEXT:NEXT
```

Here is a line-by-line explanation of Example Program 10:

LINE-BY-LINE EXPLANATION OF EXAMPLE PROGRAM 10:

Line(s)	Description
10	Set S to start of sound chip.
20	Clear sound chip registers.
30	Set high frequency for voice 1.
40	Set Attack/Decay for voice 1 (A=0, D=9).
50	Set high frequency for voice 3.
60	Set volume 15.
70	Count number of dings, set start triangle, ring mod waveform control voice 1.
80	Timing loop, set stop triangle, ring mod.
90	Timing loop, next ding.

The effects available through the use of the parameters of your Commodore 64's SID chip are numerous and varied. Only through experimentation on your own will you fully appreciate the capabilities of your machine. The examples in this section of the Programmer's Reference Guide merely scratch the surface.

Watch for the book **MAKING MUSIC ON YOUR COMMODORE COMPUTER** for everything from simple fun and games to professional-type musical instruction.

CHAPTER 5

BASIC TO MACHINE LANGUAGE

WHAT IS MACHINE LANGUAGE?

At the heart of every microcomputer, is a central microprocessor. It's a very special microchip which is the "brain" of the computer. The Commodore 64 is no exception. Every microprocessor understands its own language of instructions. These instructions are called machine language instructions. To put it more precisely, machine language is the ONLY programming language that your Commodore 64 understands. It is the NATIVE language of the machine.

If machine language is the only language that the Commodore 64 understands, then how does it understand the CBM BASIC programming language? CBM BASIC is NOT the machine language of the Commodore 64. What, then, makes the Commodore 64 understand CBM BASIC instructions like PRINT and GOTO?

To answer this question, you must first see what happens inside your Commodore 64. Apart from the microprocessor which is the brain of the Commodore 64, there is a machine language program which is stored in a special type of memory so that it can't be changed. And, more importantly, it does not disappear when the Commodore 64 is turned off, unlike a program that you may have written. This machine language program is called the OPERATING SYSTEM of the Commodore 64. Your Commodore 64 knows what to do when it's turned on because its OPERATING SYSTEM (program) is automatically "RUN."

The OPERATING SYSTEM is in charge of "organizing" all the memory in your machine for various tasks. It also looks at what characters you type on the keyboard and puts them onto the screen, plus a whole number of other functions. The OPERATING SYSTEM can be thought of as the "intelligence and personality" of the Commodore 64 (or any computer for that matter). So when you turn on your Commodore 64, the OPERATING SYSTEM takes control of your machine, and after it has done its housework, it then says:

```
READY.
■
```

The OPERATING SYSTEM of the Commodore 64 then allows you to type on the keyboard, and use the built-in SCREEN EDITOR on the Commodore 64. The SCREEN EDITOR allows you to move the cursor, DELete, INSert, etc., and is, in fact, only one part of the operating system that is built in for your convenience.

All of the commands that are available in CBM BASIC are simply recognized by another huge machine language program built into your Commodore 64. This huge program "RUNs" the appropriate piece of machine language depending on which CBM BASIC command is being executed. This program is called the BASIC INTERPRETER, because it interprets each command, one by one, unless it encounters a command it does not understand, and then the familiar message appears:

```
?SYNTAX ERROR

READY.
■
```

WHAT DOES MACHINE CODE LOOK LIKE?

You should be familiar with the PEEK and POKE commands in the CBM BASIC language for changing memory locations. You've probably used them for graphics on the screen, and for sound effects. Each memory location has its own number which identifies it. This number is known as the "address" of a memory location. If you imagine the memory in the Commodore 64 as a street of buildings, then the number on each door is, of course, the address. Now let's look at which parts of the street are used for what purposes.

SIMPLE MEMORY MAP OF THE COMMODORE 64

ADDRESS	DESCRIPTION
0 & 1	—6510 Registers.
2	—Start of memory.
up to: 1023	—Memory used by the operating system.
1024 up to: 2039	—Screen memory.
2040 up to: 2047	—SPRITE pointers.
2048 up to: 40959	—This is YOUR memory. This is where your BASIC or machine language programs, or both, are stored.
40960 up to: 49151	—8K CBM BASIC Interpreter.
49152 up to: 53247	—Special programs RAM area.
53248 up to: 53294	—VIC-II.
54272 up to: 55295	—SID Registers.
55296 up to: 56296	—Color RAM.
56320 up to: 57343	—I/O Registers. (6526's)
57344 up to: 65535	—8K CBM KERNAL Operating System.

If you don't understand what the description of each part of memory means right now, this will become clear from other parts of this manual.

Machine language programs consist of instructions which may or may not have operands (parameters) associated with them. Each instruction takes up one memory location, and any operand is contained in one or two locations following the instruction.

In your BASIC programs, words like PRINT and GOTO do, in fact, only take up one memory location, rather than one for each character of the word. The contents of the location that represents a particular BASIC keyword is called a *token*. In machine language, there are different tokens for different instructions, which also take up just one byte (memory location=byte).

Machine language instructions are very simple. Therefore, each individual instruction cannot achieve a great deal. Machine language instructions either change the contents of a memory location, or change one of the internal registers (special storage locations) inside the microprocessor. The internal registers form the very basis of machine language.

THE REGISTERS INSIDE THE 6510 MICROPROCESSOR

THE ACCUMULATOR

This is THE most important register in the microprocessor. Various machine language instructions allow you to copy the contents of a memory location into the accumulator, copy the contents of the accumulator into a memory location, modify the contents of the accumulator or some other register directly, without affecting any memory. And the accumulator is the only register that has instructions for performing math.

THE X INDEX REGISTER

This is a very important register. There are instructions for nearly all of the transformations you can make to the accumulator. But there are other instructions for things that only the X register can do. Various machine language instructions allow you to copy the contents of a memory location into the X register, copy the contents of the X register into a memory location, and modify the contents of the X, or some other register directly.

THE Y INDEX REGISTER

This is a very important register. There are instructions for nearly all of the transformations you can make to the accumulator, and the X register. But there are other instructions for things that only the Y register can do. Various machine language instructions allow you to copy the contents of a memory location into the Y register, copy the contents of the Y register into a memory location, and modify the contents of the Y, or some other register directly.

THE STATUS REGISTER

This register consists of eight "flags" (a flag = something that indicates whether something has, or has not occurred).

THE PROGRAM COUNTER

This contains the address of the current machine language instruction being executed. Since the operating system is always "RUN"ning in the Commodore 64 (or, for that matter, any computer), the program counter is always changing. It could only be stopped by halting the microprocessor in some way.

THE STACK POINTER

This register contains the location of the first empty place on the stack. The stack is used for temporary storage by machine language programs, and by the computer.

THE INPUT/OUTPUT PORT

This register appears at memory locations 0 (for the DATA DIRECTION REGISTER) and 1 (for the actual PORT). It is an 8-bit input/output port. On the Commodore 64 this register is used for memory management, to allow the chip to control more than 64K of RAM and ROM memory.

The details of these registers are not given here. They are explained as the principles needed to explain them are explained.

HOW DO YOU WRITE MACHINE LANGUAGE PROGRAMS?

Since machine language programs reside in memory, and there is no facility in your Commodore 64 for writing and editing machine language programs, you must use either a program to do this, or write for yourself a BASIC program that "allows" you to write machine language.

The most common methods used to write machine language programs are *assembler* progams. These packages allow you to write machine language instructions in a standardized *mnemonic* format, which makes the machine language program a lot more readable than a stream of numbers! Let's review: A program that allows you to write machine language programs in mnemonic format is called an *assembler*. Incidentally, a program that displays a machine language program in mnemonic format is called a *disassembler*. Available for your Commodore 64 is a machine language monitor cartridge (with assembler/ disassembler, etc.) made by Commodore:

64MON

The 64MON cartridge available from your local dealer, is a program that allows you to escape from the world of CBM BASIC, into the land of machine language. It can display the contents of the internal registers in the 6510 microprocessor, and it allows you to display portions of memory, and change them on the screen, using the screen editor. It also has a built-in assembler and disassembler, as well as many other features that allow you to write and edit machine language programs easily. You don't HAVE to use an assembler to write machine language, but the task is considerably easier with it. If you wish to write machine language programs, it is strongly suggested that you purchase an assembler of some sort. Without an assembler you will probably have to "POKE" the machine language program into memory, which is totally unadvisable. This manual will give its examples in the format that 64MON uses, from now on. Nearly all assembler formats are the same, therefore the machine language examples shown will almost certainly be compatible with any assembler. But before explaining any of the other features of 64MON, the hexadecimal numbering system must be explained.

HEXADECIMAL NOTATION

Hexadecimal notation is used by most machine language programmers when they talk about a number or address in a machine language program.

Some assemblers let you refer to addresses and numbers in decimal (base 10), binary (base 2), or even octal (base 8) as well as hexadecimal (base 16) (or just "hex" as most people say). These assemblers do the conversions for you.

Hexadecimal probably seems a little hard to grasp at first, but like most things, it won't take long to master with practice.

By looking at decimal (base 10) numbers, you can see that each digit falls somewhere in the range between zero and a number equal to the base less one (e.g., 9). THIS IS TRUE OF ALL NUMBER BASES. Binary (base 2) numbers have digits ranging from zero to one (which is one less than the base). Similarly, hexadecimal numbers should have digits ranging from zero to fifteen, but we do not have any single digit figures for the numbers ten to fifteen, so the first six letters of the alphabet are used instead:

DECIMAL	HEXADECIMAL	BINARY
0	0	00000000
1	1	00000001
2	2	00000010
3	3	00000011
4	4	00000100
5	5	00000101
6	6	00000110
7	7	00000111
8	8	00001000
9	9	00001001
10	A	00001010
11	B	00001011
12	C	00001100
13	D	00001101
14	E	00001110
15	F	00001111
16	10	00010000

Let's look at it another way; here's an example of how a base 10 (decimal number) is constructed:

Base raised by increasing powers: . . .	10^3	10^2	10^1	10^0
Equals:	1000	100	10	1
Consider 4569 (base 10)	4	5	6	9

$$=(4\times1000)+(5\times100)+(6\times10)+9$$

Now look at an example of how a base 16 (hexadecimal number) is constructed:

Base raised by increasing powers: . . .	16^3	16^2	16^1	16^0
Equals:	4096	256	16	1
Consider 11D9 (base 16)	1	1	D	9

$$=1\times4096+1\times256+13\times16+9$$

Therefore, 4569 (base 10) = 11D9 (base 16)

The range for addressable memory locations is 0–65535 (as was stated earlier). This range is therefore 0–FFFF in hexadecimal notation.

Usually hexadecimal numbers are prefixed with a dollar sign ($). This is to distinguish them from decimal numbers. Let's look at some "hex" numbers, using 64MON, by displaying the contents of some memory by typing:

```
SYS 8*4096          (or SYS 12*4096)
B*
    PC SR AC XR YR SP
.; 0401 32 04 5E 00 F6 (these may be different)
```

Then if you type in:

.M 0000 0020 (and press RETURN).

you will see rows of 9 hex numbers. The first 4-digit number is the address of the first byte of memory being shown in that row, and the other eight numbers are the actual contents of the memory locations beginning at that start address.

You should really try to learn to "think" in hexadecimal. It's not too difficult, because you don't have to think about converting it back into decimal. For example, if you said that a particular value is stored at $14ED instead of 5357, it shouldn't make any difference.

YOUR FIRST MACHINE LANGUAGE INSTRUCTION

LDA — LOAD THE ACCUMULATOR

In 6510 assembly language, mnemonics are always three characters. LDA represents "load accumulator with . . . ," and what the accumulator should be loaded with is decided by the parameter(s) associated with that instruction. The assembler knows which token is represented by each mnemonic, and when it "assembles" an instruction, it simply puts into memory (at whatever address has been specified), the token, and what parameters, are given. Some assemblers give error messages, or warnings when you try to assemble something that either the assembler, or the 6510 microprocessor, cannot do.

If you put a "#" symbol in front of the parameter associated with the instruction, this means that you want the register specified in the instruction to be loaded with the "value" after the "#." For example:

```
LDA #$05
```

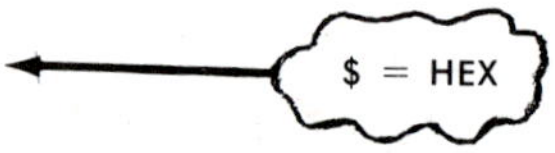

This instruction will put $05 (decimal 5) into the accumulator register. The assembler will put into the specified address for this instruction, $A9 (which is the token for this particular instruction, in this mode), and it will put $05 into the next location after the location containing the instruction ($A9).

If the parameter to be used by an instruction has "#" before it; i.e., the parameter is a "value," rather than the contents of a memory location, or another register, the instruction is said to be in the "immediate" mode. To put this into perspective, let's compare this with another mode:

If you want to put the contents of memory location $102E into the accumulator, you're using the "absolute" mode of instruction:

```
LDA $102E
```

The assembler can distinguish between the two different modes because the latter does not have a "#" before the parameter. The 6510 microprocessor can distinguish between the immediate mode, and the absolute mode of the LDA instruction, because they have slightly different tokens. LDA (immediate) has $A9 as its token, and LDA (absolute), has $AD as its token.

The mnemonic representing an instruction usually implies what it does. For instance, if we consider another instruction, LDX, what do you think this does?

If you said "load the X register with . . . ," go to the top of the class. If you didn't, then don't worry, learning machine language does take patience, and cannot be learned in a day.

The various internal registers can be thought of as special memory locations, because they too can hold one byte of information. It is not necessary for us to explain the binary numbering system (base 2) since it follows the same rules as outlined for hexadecimal and decimal outlined previously, but one "bit" is one binary digit and eight bits make up one byte! This means that the maximum number that can be contained in a byte is the largest number that an eight digit binary number can be. This number is 11111111 (binary), which equals $FF (hexadecimal), which equals 255 (decimal). You have probably wondered why only numbers from zero to 255 could be put into a memory location. If you try POKE 7680,260 (which is a BASIC statement that "says": "Put the number two hundred and sixty, into memory location seven thousand, six hundred and eighty," the BASIC interpreter knows that only numbers 0 – 255 can be put in a memory location, and your Commodore 64 will reply with:

```
?ILLEGAL QUANTITY ERROR

READY.
■
```

If the limit of one byte is $FF (hex), how is the address parameter in the absolute instruction "LDA $102E" expressed in memory? It's expressed in two bytes (it won't fit into one, of course). The lower (rightmost) two digits of the hexadecimal address form the "low byte" of the address, and the upper (leftmost) two digits form the "high byte."

The 6510 requires any address to be specified with its low byte first, and then the high byte. This means that the instruction "LDA $102E" is represented in memory by the three consecutive values:

```
$AD, $2E, $10
```

Now all you need to know is one more instruction and then you can write your first program. That instruction is BRK. For a full explanation of this instruction, refer to *M.O.S. 6502 Programming Manual*. But right now, you can think of it as the END instruction in machine language.

If we write a program with 64MON and put the BRK instruction at the end, then when the program is executed, it will return to 64MON when it is finished. This might not happen if there is a mistake in your program, or the BRK instruction is never reached (just like an END statement in BASIC may never get executed). This means that if the Commodore 64 didn't have a STOP key, you wouldn't be able to abort your BASIC programs!

WRITING YOUR FIRST PROGRAM

If you've used the POKE statement in BASIC to put characters onto the screen, you're aware that the character codes for POKEing are different from CBM ASCII character values. For example, if you enter:

PRINT ASC("A") (and press RETURN)

the Commodore 64 will respond with:

65

READY.
■

However, to put an "A" onto the screen by POKEing, the code is 1, enter:

SHIFT CLR/HOME to clear the screen

POKE 1024,1:POKE 55296,14 (and RETURN) (1024 is the start of screen memory)

The "P" in the POKE statement should now be an "A."

Now let's try this in machine language. Type the following in 64MON: (Your cursor should be flashing alongside a "." right now.)

.A 1400 LDA #$01 (and press RETURN)

The Commodore 64 will prompt you with:

```
.A 1400 A9 01      LDA #$01
.A 1402 ■
```

Type:

```
.A 1402 STA $0400
```

(The STA instruction stores the contents of the accumulator in a specified memory location.)
The Commodore 64 will prompt you with:

```
.A 1405 ■
```

Now type in:

```
.A 1405 LDA #$0E
.A 1407 STA $D800
.A 140A BRK
```

Clear the screen, and type:

```
G 1400
```

The G should turn into an "A" if you've done everything correctly.

You have now written your first machine language program. Its purpose is to store one character ("A") at the first location in the screen memory. Having achieved this, we must now explore some of the other instructions, and principles.

ADDRESSING MODES

ZERO PAGE

As shown earlier, absolute addresses are expressed in terms of a high and a low order byte. The high order byte is often referred to as the *page* of memory. For example, the address $1637 is in page $16 (22), and $0277 is in page $02 (2). There is, however, a special mode of addressing known as *zero page* addressing and is, as the name implies, associated with the addressing of memory locations in page zero. These addresses, therefore, ALWAYS have a high order byte of zero. The zero page mode of addressing only expects one byte to describe the address, rather than two when using an absolute address. The zero page addressing mode tells the microprocessor to assume that the high order address is zero. Therefore zero page addressing can reference memory locations whose addresses are between $0000 and $00FF. This may not seem too important at the moment, but you'll need the principles of zero page addressing soon.

THE STACK

The 6510 microprocessor has what is known as a *stack*. This is used by both the programmer and the microprocessor to temporarily remember things, and to remember, for example, an order of events. The GOSUB statement in BASIC, which allows the programmer to call a *subroutine*, must remember where it is being called from, so that when the RETURN statement is executed in the subroutine, the BASIC interpreter "knows" where to go back to continue executing. When a GOSUB statement is encountered in a program by the BASIC interpreter, the BASIC interpreter "pushes" its current position onto the stack before going to do the subroutine, and when a RETURN is executed, the interpreter "pulls" off the stack the information that tells it where it was before the subroutine call was made. The interpreter uses instructions like **PHA**, which pushes the contents of the accumulator onto the stack, and **PLA** (the reverse) which pulls a value off the stack and into the accumulator. The status register can also be pushed and pulled with the **PHP** and **PLP**, respectively.

The stack is 256 bytes long, and is located in page one of memory. It is therefore from $0100 to $01FF. It is organized backwards in memory. In other words, the first position in the stack is at $01FF, and the last is at $0100. Another register in the 6510 microprocessor is called the *stack pointer,* and it always points to the next available location in the stack. When something is pushed onto the stack, it is placed where the stack pointer points to, and the stack pointer is moved down to the next position (decremented). When something is pulled off the stack, the stack pointer is incremented, and the byte pointed to by the stack pointer is placed into the specified register.

Up to this point, we have covered immediate, zero page, and absolute mode instructions. We have also covered, but have not really talked about, the "implied" mode. The implied mode means that information is implied by an instruction itself. In other words, what registers, flags, and memory the instruction is referring to. The examples we have seen are PHA, PLA, PHP, and PLP, which refer to stack processing and the accumulator and status registers, respectively.

NOTE: The X register will be referred to as X from now on, and similarly A (accumulator), Y (Y index register), S (stack pointer), and P (processor status).

INDEXING

Indexing plays an extremely important part in the running of the 6510 microprocessor. It can be defined as "creating an actual address from a base address plus the contents of either the X or Y index registers."

For example, if X contains $05, and the microprocessor executes an LDA instruction in the "absolute X indexed mode" with base address (e.g., $9000), then the actual location that is loaded into the A register is $9000 + $05 = $9005. The mnemonic format of an absolute indexed instruction is the same as an absolute instruction except a ",X" or ",Y" denoting the index is added to the address.

EXAMPLE:

```
LDA $9000,X
```

There are absolute indexed, zero page indexed, indirect indexed, and indexed indirect modes of addressing available on the 6510 microprocessor.

INDIRECT INDEXED

This only allows usage of the Y register as the index. The actual address can only be in zero page, and the mode of instruction is called indirect because the zero page address specified in the instruction contains the low byte of the actual address, and the next byte to it contains the high order byte.

EXAMPLE:

Let us suppose that location $02 contains $45, and location $03 contains $1E. If the instruction to load the accumulator in the indirect indexed mode is executed and the specified zero page address is $02, then the actual address will be:

Low order = contents of $02
High order = contents of $03
Y register =$00

Thus the actual address = $1E45 + Y = $1E45.

The title of this mode does in fact imply an indirect principle, although this may be difficult to grasp at first sight. Let's look at it another way:

"I am going to deliver this letter to the post office at address $02,MEMORY ST., and the address on the letter is $05 houses past $1600, MEMORY street." This is equivalent to the code:

```
LDA #$00      — load low order actual base address
STA $02       — set the low byte of the indirect address
LDA #$16      — load high order indirect address
STA $03       — set the high byte of the indirect address
LDY #$05      — set the indirect index (Y)
LDA ($02),Y   — load indirectly indexed by Y
```

INDEXED INDIRECT

Indexed indirect only allows usage of the X register as the index. This is the same as indirect indexed, except it is the zero page address of the *pointer* that is indexed, rather than the actual base address. Therefore, the actual base address IS the actual address because the index has already been used for the indirect. Index indirect would also be used if a *table* of indirect pointers were located in zero page memory, and the X register could then specify which indirect pointer to use.

EXAMPLE:

Let us suppose that location $02 contains $45, and location $03 contains $10. If the instruction to load the accumulator in the indexed indirect mode is executed and the specified zero page address is $02, then the actual address will be:

Low order = contents of ($02+X)
High order = contents of ($03+X)
X register = $00

Thus the actual pointer is in = $02 + X = $02.

Therefore, the actual address is the indirect address contained in $02 which is again $1045.

The title of this mode does in fact imply the principle, although it may be difficult to grasp at first sight. Look at it this way:

"I am going to deliver this letter to the fourth post office at address $01,MEMORY ST., and the address on the letter will then be delivered to $1600, MEMORY street." This is equivalent to the code:

```
LDA #$00      — load low order actual base address
STA $06       — set the low byte of the indirect address
LDA #$16      — load high order indirect address
STA $07       — set the high byte of the indirect address
LDX #$05      — set the indirect index (X)
LDA ($02,X)   —load indirectly indexed by X
```

NOTE: Of the two indirect methods of addressing, the first (indirect indexed) is far more widely used.

BRANCHES AND TESTING

Another very important principle in machine language is the ability to test, and detect certain conditions, in a smiliar fashion to the "IF . . . THEN, IF . . . GOTO" structure in CBM BASIC.

The various *flags* in the status register are affected by different instructions in different ways. For example, there is a flag that is set when an instruction has caused a zero result, and is reset when a result is not zero. The instruction:

LDA #$00

will cause *the zero result flag* to be set, because the instruction has resulted in the accumulator containing a zero.

There are a set of instructions that will, given a particular condition, *branch* to another part of the program. An example of a branch instruction is **BEQ**, which means *Branch if result EQual to zero*. The branch instructions *branch if the condition is true,* and if not, the program continues onto the next instruction, as if nothing had occurred. The branch instructions branch not by the result of the previous instruction(s), but by internally examining the status register. As was just mentioned, there is a *zero result flag* in the status register. The BEQ instruction branches if the zero result flag (known as **Z**) is set. Every branch instruction has an opposite branch instruction. The BEQ instruction has an opposite instruction **BNE**, which means *Branch on result Not Equal to zero* (i.e., *Z* not set).

The index registers have a number of associated instructions which modify their contents. For example, the **INX** instruction *INcrements the X index register*. If the X register contained $FF before it was incremented (the maximum number the X register can contain), it will "wrap around" back to zero. If you wanted a program to continue to do something until you had performed the increment of the X index that pushed it around to zero, you could use the BNE instruction to continue "looping" around, until X became zero.

The reverse of INX, is **DEX**, which is *DEcrement the X index register*. If the X index register is zero, DEX wraps around to $FF. Similarly, there are **INY** and **DEY** for the *Y index register*.

But what if a program didn't want to wait until X or Y had reached (or not reached) zero? Well there are *comparison instructions,* **CPX** and **CPY**, which allow the machine language programmer to test the index registers with specific values, or even the contents of memory locations. If you wanted to see if the X register contained $40, you would use the instruction:

CPX #$40 — **compare X with the "value" $40.**
BEQ — **branch to somewhere else in the**
(some other part of the program) **program, if this condition is "true."**

The compare, and branch instructions play a major part in any machine language program.

The operand specified in a branch instruction when using 64MON is the address of the part of the program that the branch goes to when the proper conditions are met. However, the operand is only an *offset*, which gets you from where the program currently is to the address specified. This offset is just one byte, and therefore the range that a branch instruction can branch to is limited. It can branch from 128 bytes backward, to 127 bytes forward.

NOTE: This is a total range of 255 bytes which is, of course, the maximum range of values one byte can contain.

64MON will tell you if you "branch out of range" by refusing to "assemble" that particular instruction. But don't worry about that now because it's unlikely that you will have such branches for quite a while. The branch is a "quick" instruction by machine language standards because of the "offset" principle as opposed to an absolute address. 64MON allows you to type in an absolute address, and it calculates the correct offset. This is just one of the "comforts" of using an assembler.

NOTE: It is NOT possible to cover every single branch instruction. For further information, refer to the Bibliography section in Appendix F.

SUBROUTINES

In machine language (in the same way as using BASIC), you can call subroutines. The instruction to call a subroutine is **JSR** (Jump to Sub-Routine), followed by the specified absolute address.

Incorporated in the operating system, there is a machine language subroutine that will PRINT a character to the screen. The CBM ASCII code of the character should be in the accumulator before calling the subroutine. The address of this subroutine is $FFD2.

Therefore, to print "HI" to the screen, the following program should be entered:

```
.A 1400 LDA #$48     — load the CBM ASCII code of "H"
.A 1402 JSR $FFD2    — print it
.A 1405 LDA #$49     — load the CBM ASCII code of "I"
.A 1407 JSR $FFD2    — print that too
.A 140A LDA #$0D     — print a carriage return as well
.A 140C JSR $FFD2
.A 140F BRK          — return to 64MON
.G 1400              — will print "HI" and return to 64MON
```

The "PRINT a character" routine we have just used is part of the KERNAL *jump table*. The instruction similar to GOTO in BASIC is **JMP**, which means *JuMP to the specified absolute address*. The KERNAL is a long list of "standardized" subroutines that control ALL input and output of the Commodore 64. Each entry in the KERNAL JMPs to a subroutine in the operating system. This "jump table" is found between memory locations $FF84 to $FFF5 in the operating system. A full explanation of the KERNAL is available in the "KERNAL Reference Section" of this manual. However, certain routines are used here to show how easy and effective the KERNAL is.

Let's now use the new principles you've just learned in another program. It will help you to put the instructions into context:

This program will display the alphabet using a KERNAL routine. The only new instruction introduced here is **TXA** *Transfer the contents of the X index register, into the Accumulator*.

```
.A 1400 LDX #$41      — X = CBM ASCII of "A"
.A 1402 TXA           — A = X
.A 1403 JSR $FFD2     — print character
.A 1406 INX           — bump count
.A 1407 CPX #$5B      — have we gone past "Z" ?
.A 1409 BNE $1402     — no, go back and do more
.A 140B BRK           — yes, return to 64MON
```

To see the Commodore 64 print the alphabet, type the familiar command:

```
.G 1400
```

The comments that are beside the program, explain the program flow and logic. If you are writing a program, write it on paper first, and then test it in small parts if possible.

USEFUL TIPS FOR THE BEGINNER

One of the best ways to learn machine language is to look at other peoples' machine language programs. These are published all the time in magazines and newsletters. Look at them even if the article is for a different computer, which also uses the 6510 (or 6502) microprocessor. You should make sure that you thoroughly understand the code that you look at. This will require perseverence, especially when you see a new technique that you have never come across before. This can be infuriating, but if patience prevails, you will be the victor.

Having looked at other machine language programs, you MUST write your own. These may be utilities for your BASIC programs, or they may be an all machine language program.

You should also use the utilities that are available, either IN your computer, or in a program, that aid you in writing, editing, or tracking down errors in a machine language program. An example would be the KERNAL, which allows you to check the keyboard, print text, control peripheral devices like disk drives, printers, modems, etc., manage memory and the screen. It is extremely powerful and it is advised strongly that it is used (refer to KERNAL section, Page 268).

Advantages of writing programs in machine language:

1. Speed—Machine language is hundreds, and in some cases thousands of times faster than a high level language such as BASIC.
2. Tightness—A machine language program can be made totally "watertight," i.e., the user can be made to do ONLY what the program allows, and no more. With a high level language, you are relying on the user not "crashing" the BASIC interpreter by entering, for example, a zero which later causes a:

```
?DIVISION BY ZERO ERROR IN LINE 830

READY.
■
```

In essence, the computer can only be maximized by the machine language programmer.

APPROACHING A LARGE TASK

When approaching a large task in machine language, a certain amount of subconscious thought has usually taken place. You think about how certain processes are carried out in machine language. When the task is started, it is usually a good idea to write it out on paper. Use block diagrams of memory usage, functional modules of code required, and a program flow. Let's say that you wanted to write a roulette game in machine language. You could outline it something like this:

- Display title
- Ask if player requires instructions
- YES—display them—Go to START
- NO—Go to START
- START Initialize everything
- MAIN display roulette table
- Take in bets
- Spin wheel
- Slow wheel to stop
- Check bets with result
- Inform player
- Player any money left?
- YES—Go to MAIN
- NO—Inform user!, and go to START

This is the main outline. As each module is approached, you can break it down further. If you look at a large indigestable problem as something that can be broken down into small enough pieces to be eaten, then you'll be able to approach something that seems impossible, and have it all fall into place.

This process only improves with practice, so KEEP TRYING.

MCS6510 MICROPROCESSOR

ADC	Add Memory to Accumulator with Carry
AND	"AND" Memory with Accumulator
ASL	Shift Left One Bit (Memory or Accumulator)
BCC	Branch on Carry Clear
BCS	Branch on Carry Set
BEQ	Branch on Result Zero
BIT	Test Bits in Memory with Accumulator
BMI	Branch on Result Minus
BNE	Branch on Result not Zero
BPL	Branch on Result Plus
BRK	Force Break
BVC	Branch on Overflow Clear
BVS	Branch on Overflow Set
CLC	Clear Carry Flag
CLD	Clear Decimal Mode
CLI	Clear Interrupt Disable Bit
CLV	Clear Overflow Flag
CMP	Compare Memory and Accumulator
CPX	Compare Memory and Index X
CPY	Compare Memory and Index Y
DEC	Decrement Memory by One
DEX	Decrement Index X by One
DEY	Decrement Index Y by One
EOR	"Exclusive-Or" Memory with Accumulator
INC	Increment Memory by One
INX	Increment Index X by One
INY	Increment Index Y by One
JMP	Jump to New Location

INSTRUCTION SET—ALPHABETIC SEQUENCE

JSR	Jump to New Location Saving Return Address
LDA	Load Accumulator with Memory
LDX	Load Index X with Memory
LDY	Load Index Y with Memory
LSR	Shift Right One Bit (Memory or Accumulator)
NOP	No Operation
ORA	"OR" Memory with Accumulator
PHA	Push Accumulator on Stack
PHP	Push Processor Status on Stack
PLA	Pull Accumulator from Stack
PLP	Pull Processor Status from Stack
ROL	Rotate One Bit Left (Memory or Accumulator)
ROR	Rotate One Bit Right (Memory or Accumulator)
RTI	Return from Interrupt
RTS	Return from Subroutine
SBC	Subtract Memory from Accumulator with Borrow
SEC	Set Carry Flag
SED	Set Decimal Mode
SEI	Set Interrupt Disable Status
STA	Store Accumulator in Memory
STX	Store Index X in Memory
STY	Store Index Y in Memory
TAX	Transfer Accumulator to Index X
TAY	Transfer Accumulator to Index Y
TSX	Transfer Stack Pointer to Index X
TXA	Transfer Index X to Accumulator
TXS	Transfer Index X to Stack Pointer
TYA	Transfer Index Y to Accumulator

The following notation applies to this summary:

A	Accumulator
X, Y	Index Registers
M	Memory
P	Processor Status Register
S	Stack Pointer
✓	Change
_	No Change
+	Add
∧	Logical AND
-	Subtract
⊻	Logical Exclusive Or
↑	Transfer from Stack
↓	Transfer to Stack
→	Transfer to
←	Transfer from
V	Logical OR
PC	Program Counter
PCH	Program Counter High
PCL	Program Counter Low
OPER	OPERAND
#	IMMEDIATE ADDRESSING MODE

Note: At the top of each table is located in parentheses a reference number (Ref: XX) which directs the user to that Section in the MCS6500 Microcomputer Family Programming Manual in which the instruction is defined and discussed.

ADC — Add memory to accumulator with carry — ADC

Operation: A + M + C → A, C

N Z C I D V
✓ ✓ ✓ — — ✓

(Ref: 2.2.1)

Addressing Mode	Assembly Language Form	OP CODE	No. Bytes	No. Cycles
Immediate	ADC # Oper	69	2	2
Zero Page	ADC Oper	65	2	3
Zero Page, X	ADC Oper, X	75	2	4
Absolute	ADC Oper	6D	3	4
Absolute, X	ADC Oper, X	7D	3	4*
Absolute, Y	ADC Oper, Y	79	3	4*
(Indirect, X)	ADC (Oper, X)	61	2	6
(Indirect), Y	ADC (Oper), Y	71	2	5*

* Add 1 if page boundary is crossed.

AND — "AND" memory with accumulator — AND

Logical AND to the accumulator

Operation: A ∧ M → A

N Z C I D V
✓ ✓ — — — —

(Ref: 2.2.3.0)

Addressing Mode	Assembly Language Form	OP CODE	No. Bytes	No. Cycles
Immediate	AND # Oper	29	2	2
Zero Page	AND Oper	25	2	3
Zero Page, X	AND Oper, X	35	2	4
Absolute	AND Oper	2D	3	4
Absolute, X	AND Oper, X	3D	3	4*
Absolute, Y	AND Oper, Y	39	3	4*
(Indirect, X)	AND (Oper, X)	21	2	6
(Indirect), Y	AND (Oper), Y	31	2	5

* Add 1 if page boundary is crossed.

ASL — ASL *Shift Left One Bit (Memory or Accumulator)* — ASL

Operation: C ← [7|6|5|4|3|2|1|Ø] ← Ø

N Ƶ C I D V
✓ ✓ ✓ — — —

(Ref: 10.2)

Addressing Mode	Assembly Language Form	OP CODE	No. Bytes	No. Cycles
Accumulator	ASL A	ØA	1	2
Zero Page	ASL Oper	Ø6	2	5
Zero Page, X	ASL Oper, X	16	2	6
Absolute	ASL Oper	ØE	3	6
Absolute, X	ASL Oper, X	1E	3	7

BCC — BCC *Branch on Carry Clear* — BCC

Operation: Branch on C = Ø

N Ƶ C I D V
— — — — — —

(Ref: 4.1.1.3)

Addressing Mode	Assembly Language Form	OP CODE	No. Bytes	No. Cycles
Relative	BCC Oper	9Ø	2	2*

* Add 1 if branch occurs to same page.

* Add 2 if branch occurs to different page.

BCS — BCS *Branch on carry set* — BCS

Operation: Branch on C = 1

N Ƶ C I D V
— — — — — —

(Ref: 4.1.1.4)

Addressing Mode	Assembly Language Form	OP CODE	No. Bytes	No. Cycles
Relative	BCS Oper	BØ	2	2*

* Add 1 if branch occurs to same page.

* Add 2 if branch occurs to next page.

BEQ

BEQ *Branch on result zero*

Operation: Branch on Z = 1

N Z C I D V

(Ref: 4.1.1.5)

_ _ _ _ _ _

Addressing Mode	Assembly Language Form	OP CODE	No. Bytes	No. Cycles
Relative	BEQ Oper	FØ	2	2*

* Add 1 if branch occurs to same page.

* Add 2 if branch occurs to next page.

BIT

BIT *Test bits in memory with accumulator*

Operation: $A \wedge M$, $M_7 \rightarrow N$, $M_6 \rightarrow V$

Bit 6 and 7 are transferred to the status register. If the result of $A \wedge M$ is zero then Z = 1, otherwise Z = Ø

N Z C I D V

M_7 ✓ — — — M_6

(Ref: 4.2.1.1)

Addressing Mode	Assembly Language Form	OP CODE	No. Bytes	No. Cycles
Zero Page	BIT Oper	24	2	3
Absolute	BIT Oper	2C	3	4

BMI

BMI *Branch on result minus*

Operation: Branch on N = 1

N Z C I D V

(Ref: 4.1.1.1)

_ _ _ _ _ _

Addressing Mode	Assembly Language Form	OP CODE	No. Bytes	No. Cycles
Relative	BMI Oper	3Ø	2	2*

* Add 1 if branch occurs to same page.

* Add 2 if branch occurs to different page.

BNE

BNE *Branch on result not zero*

BNE

Operation: Branch on Z = 0

N Ƶ C I D V

_ _ _ _ _ _

(Ref: 4.1.1.6)

Addressing Mode	Assembly Language Form	OP CODE	No. Bytes	No. Cycles
Relative	BNE Oper	DØ	2	2*

* Add 1 if branch occurs to same page.

* Add 2 if branch occurs to different page.

BPL

BPL *Branch on result plus*

BPL

Operation: Branch on N = Ø

N Ƶ C I D V

_ _ _ _ _ _

(Ref: 4.1.1.2)

Addressing Mode	Assembly Language Form	OP CODE	No. Bytes	No. Cycles
Relative	BPL Oper	1Ø	2	2*

* Add 1 if branch occurs to same page.

* Add 2 if branch occurs to different page.

BRK

BRK *Force Break*

BRK

Operation: Forced Interrupt PC + 2 ↓ P ↓

N Ƶ C I D V

_ _ _ 1 _ _

(Ref: 9.11)

Addressing Mode	Assembly Language Form	OP CODE	No. Bytes	No. Cycles
Implied	BRK	ØØ	1	7

1. A BRK command cannot be masked by setting I.

BVC

BVC *Branch on overflow clear*

Operation: Branch on V = 0

N Ƶ C I D V

_ _ _ _ _ _

(Ref: 4.1.1.8)

Addressing Mode	Assembly Language Form	OP CODE	No. Bytes	No. Cycles
Relative	BVC Oper	5Ø	2	2*

* Add 1 if branch occurs to same page.

* Add 2 if branch occurs to different page.

BVS

BVS *Branch on overflow set*

Operation: Branch on V = 1

N Ƶ C I D V

_ _ _ _ _ _

(Ref: 4.1.1.7)

Addressing Mode	Assembly Language Form	OP CODE	No. Bytes	No. Cycles
Relative	BVS Oper	7Ø	2	2*

* Add 1 if branch occurs to same page.

* Add 2 if branch occurs to different page.

CLC

CLC *Clear carry flag*

Operation: Ø → C

N Ƶ C I D V

_ _ Ø _ _ _

(Ref: 3.0.2)

Addressing Mode	Assembly Language Form	OP CODE	No. Bytes	No. Cycles
Implied	CLC	18	1	2

CLD

CLD *Clear decimal mode*

Operation: Ø → D

N Z C I D V
— — — — Ø —

(Ref: 3.3.2)

Addressing Mode	Assembly Language Form	OP CODE	No. Bytes	No. Cycles
Implied	CLD	D8	1	2

CLI

CLI *Clear interrupt disable bit*

Operation: Ø → I

N Z C I D V
— — — Ø — —

(Ref: 3.2.2)

Addressing Mode	Assembly Language Form	OP CODE	No. Bytes	No. Cycles
Implied	CLI	58	1	2

CLV

CLV *Clear overflow flag*

Operation: Ø → V

N Z C I D V
— — — — — Ø

(Ref: 3.6.1)

Addressing Mode	Assembly Language Form	OP CODE	No. Bytes	No. Cycles
Implied	CLV	B8	1	2

CMP — CMP *Compare memory and accumulator* — CMP

Operation: A - M

N Ƶ C I D V
✓ ✓ ✓ — — —

(Ref: 4.2.1)

Addressing Mode	Assembly Language Form	OP CODE	No. Bytes	No. Cycles
Immediate	CMP #Oper	C9	2	2
Zero Page	CMP Oper	C5	2	3
Zero Page, X	CMP Oper, X	D5	2	4
Absolute	CMP Oper	CD	3	4
Absolute, X	CMP Oper, X	DD	3	4*
Absolute, Y	CMP Oper, Y	D9	3	4*
(Indirect, X)	CMP (Oper, X)	C1	2	6
(Indirect), Y	CMP (Oper), Y	D1	2	5*

* Add 1 if page boundary is crossed.

CPX — CPX *Compare Memory and Index X* — CPX

Operation: X - M

N Ƶ C I D V
✓ ✓ ✓ — — —

(Ref: 7.8)

Addressing Mode	Assembly Language Form	OP CODE	No. Bytes	No. Cycles
Immediate	CPX #Oper	EØ	2	2
Zero Page	CPX Oper	E4	2	3
Absolute	CPX Oper	EC	3	4

CPY — CPY *Compare memory and index Y* — CPY

Operation: Y - M

N Ƶ C I D V
✓ ✓ ✓ — — —

(Ref: 7.9)

Addressing Mode	Assembly Language Form	OP CODE	No. Bytes	No. Cycles
Immediate	CPY #Oper	CØ	2	2
Zero Page	CPY Oper	C4	2	3
Absolute	CPY Oper	CC	3	4

DEC

DEC *Decrement memory by one*

Operation: M - 1 → M

N Z C I D V
✓ ✓ — — — —

(Ref: 10.7)

Addressing Mode	Assembly Language Form	OP CODE	No. Bytes	No. Cycles
Zero Page	DEC Oper	C6	2	5
Zero Page, X	DEC Oper, X	D6	2	6
Absolute	DEC Oper	CE	3	6
Absolute, X	DEC Oper, X	DE	3	7

DEX

DEX *Decrement index X by one*

Operation: X - 1 → X

N Z C I D V
✓ ✓ — — — —

(Ref: 7.6)

Addressing Mode	Assembly Language Form	OP CODE	No. Bytes	No. Cycles
Implied	DEX	CA	1	2

DEY

DEY *Decrement index Y by one*

Operation: Y - 1 → Y

N Z C I D V
✓ ✓ — — — —

(Ref: 7.7)

Addressing Mode	Assembly Language Form	OP CODE	No. Bytes	No. Cycles
Implied	DEY	88	1	2

EOR

EOR *"Exclusive–Or" memory with accumulator* **EOR**

Operation: A ⊻ M → A

N	Z	C	I	D	V
✓	✓	–	–	–	–

(Ref: 2.2.3.2)

Addressing Mode	Assembly Language Form	OP CODE	No. Bytes	No. Cycles
Immediate	EOR #Oper	49	2	2
Zero Page	EOR Oper	45	2	3
Zero Page, X	EOR Oper, X	55	2	4
Absolute	EOR Oper	4D	3	4
Absolute, X	EOR Oper, X	5D	3	4*
Absolute, Y	EOR Oper, Y	59	3	4*
(Indirect, X)	EOR (Oper, X)	41	2	6
(Indirect),Y	EOR (Oper), Y	51	2	5*

* Add 1 if page boundary is crossed.

INC

INC *Increment memory by one* **INC**

Operation: M + 1 → M

N	Z	C	I	D	V
✓	✓	–	–	–	–

(Ref: 10.6)

Addressing Mode	Assembly Language Form	CP CODE	No. Bytes	No. Cycles
Zero Page	INC Oper	E6	2	5
Zero Page, X	INC Oper, X	F6	2	6
Absolute	INC Oper	EE	3	6
Absolute, X	INC Oper, X	FE	3	7

INX

INX *Increment Index X by one* **INX**

Operation: X + 1 → X

N	Z	C	I	D	V
✓	✓	–	–	–	–

(Ref: 7.4)

Addressing Mode	Assembly Language Form	OP CODE	No. Bytes	No. Cycles
Implied	INX	E8	1	2

INY

INY *Increment Index Y by one*

Operation: Y + 1 → Y

N Ƶ C I D V
✓ ✓ — — — —

(Ref: 7.5)

Addressing Mode	Assembly Language Form	OP CODE	No. Bytes	No. Cycles
Implied	INY	C8	1	2

JMP

JMP *Jump to new location*

Operation: (PC + 1) → PCL
(PC + 2) → PCH

(Ref: 4.0.2)
(Ref: 9.8.1)

N Ƶ C I D V
— — — — — —

Addressing Mode	Assembly Language Form	OP CODE	No. Bytes	No. Cycles
Absolute	JMP Oper	4C	3	3
Indirect	JMP (Oper)	6C	3	5

JSR

JSR *Jump to new location saving return address*

Operation: PC + 2 ↓, (PC + 1) → PCL
(PC + 2) → PCH

(Ref: 8.1)

N Ƶ C I D V
— — — — — —

Addressing Mode	Assembly Language Form	OP CODE	No. Bytes	No. Cycles
Absolute	JSR Oper	20	3	6

LDA — LDA *Load accumulator with memory* — LDA

Operation: M → A

N Z C I D V
✓ ✓ — — — —

(Ref: 2.1.1)

Addressing Mode	Assembly Language Form	OP CODE	No. Bytes	No. Cycles
Immediate	LDA # Oper	A9	2	2
Zero Page	LDA Oper	A5	2	3
Zero Page, X	LDA Oper, X	B5	2	4
Absolute	LDA Oper	AD	3	4
Absolute, X	LDA Oper, X	BD	3	4*
Absolute, Y	LDA Oper, Y	B9	3	4*
(Indirect, X)	LDA (Oper, X)	A1	2	6
(Indirect), Y	LDA (Oper), Y	B1	2	5*

* Add 1 if page boundary is crossed.

LDX — LDX *Load index X with memory* — LDX

Operation: M → X

N Z C I D V
✓ ✓ — — — —

(Ref: 7.0)

Addressing Mode	Assembly Language Form	OP CODE	No. Bytes	No. Cycles
Immediate	LDX # Oper	A2	2	2
Zero Page	LDX Oper	A6	2	3
Zero Page, Y	LDX Oper, Y	B6	2	4
Absolute	LDX Oper	AE	3	4
Absolute, Y	LDX Oper, Y	BE	3	4*

* Add 1 when page boundary is crossed.

LDY

LDY *Load index Y with memory*

LDY

Operation: M → Y

N	Z	C	I	D	V
✓	✓	—	—	—	—

(Ref: 7.1)

Addressing Mode	Assembly Language Form	OP CODE	No. Bytes	No. Cycles
Immediate	LDY #Oper	AØ	2	2
Zero Page	LDY Oper	A4	2	3
Zero Page, X	LDY Oper, X	B4	2	4
Absolute	LDY Oper	AC	3	4
Absolute, X	LDY Oper, X	BC	3	4*

* Add 1 when page boundary is crossed.

LSR

LSR *Shift right one bit (memory or accumulator)*

LSR

Operation: Ø → | 7 | 6 | 5 | 4 | 3 | 2 | 1 | 0 | → C

N	Z	C	I	D	V
Ø	✓	✓	—	—	—

(Ref: 10.1)

Addressing Mode	Assembly Language Form	OP CODE	No. Bytes	No. Cycles
Accumulator	LSR A	4A	1	2
Zero Page	LSR Oper	46	2	5
Zero Page, X	LSR Oper, X	56	2	6
Absolute	LSR Oper	4E	3	6
Absolute, X	LSR Oper, X	5E	3	7

NOP

NOP *No operation*

NOP

Operation: No Operation (2 cycles)

N	Z	C	I	D	V
—	—	—	—	—	—

Addressing Mode	Assembly Language Form	OP CODE	No. Bytes	No. Cycles
Implied	NOP	EA	1	2

ORA

ORA *"OR" memory with accumulator* **ORA**

Operation: A V M → A

N Ƶ C I D V

✓ ✓ – – – –

(Ref: 2.2.3.1)

Addressing Mode	Assembly Language Form	OP CODE	No. Bytes	No. Cycles
Immediate	ORA #Oper	Ø9	2	2
Zero Page	ORA Oper	Ø5	2	3
Zero Page, X	ORA Oper, X	15	2	4
Absolute	ORA Oper	ØD	3	4
Absolute, X	ORA Oper, X	1D	3	4*
Absolute, Y	ORA Oper, Y	19	3	4*
(Indirect, X)	ORA (Oper, X)	Ø1	2	6
(Indirect), Y	ORA (Oper), Y	11	2	5

* Add 1 on page crossing

PHA

PHA *Push accumulator on stack* **PHA**

Operation: A ↓

N Ƶ C I D V

– – – – – –

(Ref: 8.5)

Addressing Mode	Assembly Language Form	OP CODE	No. Bytes	No. Cycles
Implied	PHA	48	1	3

PHP

PHP *Push processor status on stack* **PHP**

Operation: P↓

N Ƶ C I D V

– – – – – –

(Ref: 8.11)

Addressing Mode	Assembly Language Form	OP CODE	No. Bytes	No. Cycles
Implied	PHP	Ø8	1	3

PLA

PLA *Pull accumulator from stack*

Operation: A ↑

N Z C I D V
✓ ✓ — — — —

(Ref: 8.6)

Addressing Mode	Assembly Language Form	OP CODE	No. Bytes	No. Cycles
Implied	PLA	68	1	4

PLP

PLP *Pull processor status from stack*

Operation: P ↑

N Z C I D V
From Stack

(Ref: 8.12)

Addressing Mode	Assembly Language Form	OP CODE	No. Bytes	No. Cycles
Implied	PLP	28	1	4

ROL

ROL *Rotate one bit left (memory or accumulator)*

Operation:

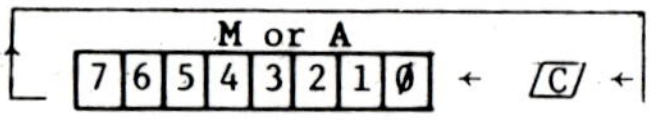

N Z C I D V
✓ ✓ ✓ — — —

(Ref: 10.3)

Addressing Mode	Assembly Language Form	OP CODE	No. Bytes	No. Cycles
Accumulator	ROL A	2A	1	2
Zero Page	ROL Oper	26	2	5
Zero Page, X	ROL Oper, X	36	2	6
Absolute	ROL Oper	2E	3	6
Absolute, X	ROL Oper, X	3E	3	7

ROR

ROR *Rotate one bit right (memory or accumulator)*

Operation:

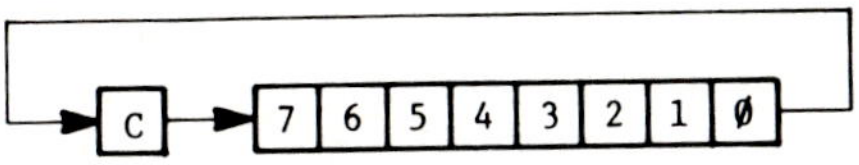

N Z C I D V

✓ ✓ ✓ - - -

(Ref: 10.4)

Addressing Mode	Assembly Language Form	OP CODE	No. Bytes	No. Cycles
Accumulator	ROR A	6A	1	2
Zero Page	ROR Oper	66	2	5
Zero Page,X	ROR Oper,X	76	2	6
Absolute	ROR Oper	6E	3	6
Absolute,X	ROR Oper,X	7E	3	7

Note: ROR instruction is available on MCS650X microprocessors after June, 1976.

RTI

RTI *Return from interrupt*

Operation: P↑ PC↑

N Z C I D V

From Stack

(Ref: 9.6)

Addressing Mode	Assembly Language Form	OP CODE	No. Bytes	No. Cycles
Implied	RTI	40	1	6

RTS

RTS *Return from subroutine*

Operation: PC↑, PC + 1 → PC

N Z C I D V

\- - - - - -

(Ref: 8.2)

Addressing Mode	Assembly Language Form	OP CODE	No. Bytes	No. Cycles
Implied	RTS	60	1	6

SBC — SBC *Subtract memory from accumulator with borrow* — SBC

Operation: A - M - $\overline{C}$ → A

Note: $\overline{C}$ = Borrow (Ref: 2.2.2)

N	Z	C	I	D	V
✓	✓	✓	—	—	✓

Addressing Mode	Assembly Language Form	OP CODE	No. Bytes	No. Cycles
Immediate	SBC #Oper	E9	2	2
Zero Page	SBC Oper	E5	2	3
Zero Page, X	SBC Oper, X	F5	2	4
Absolute	SBC Oper	ED	3	4
Absolute, X	SBC Oper, X	FD	3	4*
Absolute, Y	SBC Oper, Y	F9	3	4*
(Indirect, X)	SBC (Oper, X)	E1	2	6
(Indirect), Y	SBC (Oper), Y	F1	2	5*

* Add 1 when page boundary is crossed.

SEC — SEC *Set carry flag* — SEC

Operation: 1 → C

(Ref: 3.0.1)

N	Z	C	I	D	V
—	—	1	—	—	—

Addressing Mode	Assembly Language Form	OP CODE	No. Bytes	No. Cycles
Implied	SEC	38	1	2

SED — SED *Set decimal mode* — SED

Operation: 1 → D

(Ref: 3.3.1)

N	Z	C	I	D	V
—	—	—	—	1	—

Addressing Mode	Assembly Language Form	OP CODE	No. Bytes	No. Cycles
Implied	SED	F8	1	2

SEI

SEI *Set interrupt disable status*

Operation: 1 → I

N Ƶ C I D V

— — — 1 — —

(Ref: 3.2.1)

Addressing Mode	Assembly Language Form	OP CODE	No. Bytes	No. Cycles
Implied	SEI	78	1	2

STA

STA *Store accumulator in memory*

Operation: A → M

N Ƶ C I D V

— — — — — —

(Ref: 2.1.2)

Addressing Mode	Assembly Language Form	OP CODE	No. Bytes	No. Cycles
Zero Page	STA Oper	85	2	3
Zero Page, X	STA Oper, X	95	2	4
Absolute	STA Oper	8D	3	4
Absolute, X	STA Oper, X	9D	3	5
Absolute, Y	STA Oper, Y	99	3	5
(Indirect, X)	STA (Oper, X)	81	2	6
(Indirect), Y	STA (Oper), Y	91	2	6

STX

STX *Store index X in memory*

Operation: X → M

N Ƶ C I D V

— — — — — —

(Ref: 7.2)

Addressing Mode	Assembly Language Form	OP CODE	No. Bytes	No. Cycles
Zero Page	STX Oper	86	2	3
Zero Page, Y	STX Oper, Y	96	2	4
Absolute	STX Oper	8E	3	4

STY — STY *Store index Y in memory* — STY

Operation: Y → M

N Z C I D V
– – – – – –

(Ref: 7.3)

Addressing Mode	Assembly Language Form	OP CODE	No. Bytes	No. Cycles
Zero Page	STY Oper	84	2	3
Zero Page, X	STY Oper, X	94	2	4
Absolute	STY Oper	8C	3	4

TAX — TAX *Transfer accumulator to index X* — TAX

Operation: A → X

N Z C I D V
✓ ✓ – – – –

(Ref: 7.11)

Addressing Mode	Assembly Language Form	OP CODE	No. Bytes	No. Cycles
Implied	TAX	AA	1	2

TAY — TAY *Transfer accumulator to index Y* — TAY

Operation: A → Y

N Z C I D V
✓ ✓ – – – –

(Ref: 7.13)

Addressing Mode	Assembly Language Form	OP CODE	No. Bytes	No. Cycles
Implied	TAY	A8	1	2

TSX **TSX** *Transfer stack pointer to index X* TSX

Operation: S → X

N Z C I D V
✓ ✓ – – – –

(Ref: 8.9)

Addressing Mode	Assembly Language Form	OP CODE	No. Bytes	No. Cycles
Implied	TSX	BA	1	2

TXA **TXA** *Transfer index X to accumulator* TXA

Operation: X → A

N Z C I D V
✓ ✓ – – – –

(Ref: 7.12)

Addressing Mode	Assembly Language Form	OP CODE	No. Bytes	No. Cycles
Implied	TXA	8A	1	2

TXS **TXS** *Transfer index X to stack pointer* TXS

Operation: X → S

N Z C I D V
– – – – – –

(Ref: 8.8)

Addressing Mode	Assembly Language Form	OP CODE	No. Bytes	No. Cycles
Implied	TXS	9A	1	2

TYA **TYA** *Transfer index Y to accumulator* TYA

Operation: Y → A

N Z C I D V
✓ ✓ – – – –

(Ref: 7.14)

Addressing Mode	Assembly Language Form	OP CODE	No. Bytes	No. Cycles
Implied	TYA	98	1	2

INSTRUCTION ADDRESSING MODES AND

	Accumulator	Immediate	Zero Page	Zero Page, X	Zero Page, Y	Absolute	Absolute, X	Absolute, Y	Implied	Relative	(Indirect, X)	(Indirect), Y	Absolute Indirect
ADC	.	2	3	4	.	4	4*	4*	.	.	6	5*	.
AND	.	2	3	4	.	4	4*	4*	.	.	6	5*	.
ASL	2	.	5	6	.	6	7	.	.	.	.	.	.
BCC	.	.	.	.	.	.	.	.	.	2**	.	.	.
BCS	.	.	.	.	.	.	.	.	.	2**	.	.	.
BEQ	.	.	.	.	.	.	.	.	.	2**	.	.	.
BIT	.	.	3	.	.	4	.	.	.	.	.	.	.
BMI	.	.	.	.	.	.	.	.	.	2**	.	.	.
BNE	.	.	.	.	.	.	.	.	.	2**	.	.	.
BPL	.	.	.	.	.	.	.	.	.	2**	.	.	.
BRK	.	.	.	.	.	.	.	.	.	.	.	.	.
BVC	.	.	.	.	.	.	.	.	.	2**	.	.	.
BVS	.	.	.	.	.	.	.	.	.	2**	.	.	.
CLC	.	.	.	.	.	.	.	.	2	.	.	.	.
CLD	.	.	.	.	.	.	.	.	2	.	.	.	.
CLI	.	.	.	.	.	.	.	.	2	.	.	.	.
CLV	.	.	.	.	.	.	.	.	2	.	.	.	.
CMP	.	2	3	4	.	4	4*	4*	.	.	6	5*	.
CPX	.	2	3	.	.	4	.	.	.	.	.	.	.
CPY	.	2	3	.	.	4	.	.	.	.	.	.	.
DEC	.	.	5	6	.	6	7	.	.	.	.	.	.
DEX	.	.	.	.	.	.	.	.	2	.	.	.	.
DEY	.	.	.	.	.	.	.	.	2	.	.	.	.
EOR	.	2	3	4	.	4	4*	4*	.	.	6	5*	.
INC	.	.	5	6	.	6	7	.	.	.	.	.	.
INX	.	.	.	.	.	.	.	.	2	.	.	.	.
INY	.	.	.	.	.	.	.	.	2	.	.	.	.
JMP	.	.	.	.	.	3	.	.	.	.	.	.	5

* Add one cycle if indexing across page boundary
** Add one cycle if branch is taken, Add one additional

RELATED EXECUTION TIMES (in clock cycles)

	Accumulator	Immediate	Zero Page	Zero Page, X	Zero Page, Y	Absolute	Absolute, X	Absolute, Y	Implied	Relative	(Indirect, X)	(Indirect), Y	Absolute Indirect
JSR	.	.	.	.	.	6	.	.	.	.	.	.	.
LDA	.	2	3	4	.	4	4*	4*	.	.	6	5*	.
LDX	.	2	3	.	4	4	.	4*	.	.	.	.	.
LDY	.	2	3	4	.	4	4*	.	.	.	.	.	.
LSR	2	.	5	6	.	6	7	.	.	.	.	.	.
NOP	.	.	.	.	.	.	.	.	2	.	.	.	.
ORA	.	2	3	4	.	4	4*	4*	.	.	6	5*	.
PHA	.	.	.	.	.	.	.	.	3	.	.	.	.
PHP	.	.	.	.	.	.	.	.	3	.	.	.	.
PLA	.	.	.	.	.	.	.	.	4	.	.	.	.
PLP	.	.	.	.	.	.	.	.	4	.	.	.	.
ROL	2	.	5	6	.	6	7	.	.	.	.	.	.
ROR	2	.	5	6	.	6	7	.	.	.	.	.	.
RTI	.	.	.	.	.	.	.	.	6	.	.	.	.
RTS	.	.	.	.	.	.	.	.	6	.	.	.	.
SBC	.	2	3	4	.	4	4*	4*	.	.	6	5*	.
SEC	.	.	.	.	.	.	.	.	2	.	.	.	.
SED	.	.	.	.	.	.	.	.	2	.	.	.	.
SEI	.	.	.	.	.	.	.	.	2	.	.	.	.
STA	.	.	3	4	.	4	5	5	.	.	6	6	.
STX	.	.	3	.	4	4	.	.	.	.	.	.	.
STY	.	.	3	4	.	4	.	.	.	.	.	.	.
TAX	.	.	.	.	.	.	.	.	2	.	.	.	.
TAY	.	.	.	.	.	.	.	.	2	.	.	.	.
TSX	.	.	.	.	.	.	.	.	2	.	.	.	.
TXA	.	.	.	.	.	.	.	.	2	.	.	.	.
TXS	.	.	.	.	.	.	.	.	2	.	.	.	.
TYA	.	.	.	.	.	.	.	.	2	.	.	.	.

if branching operation crosses page boundary

ØØ - BRK

Ø1 - ORA - (Indirect,X)

Ø2 - Future Expansion

Ø3 - Future Expansion

Ø4 - Future Expansion

Ø5 - ORA - Zero Page

Ø6 - ASL - Zero Page

Ø7 - Future Expansion

Ø8 - PHP

Ø9 - ORA - Immediate

ØA - ASL - Accumulator

ØB - Future Expansion

ØC - Future Expansion

ØD - ORA - Absolute

ØE - ASL - Absolute

ØF - Future Expansion

1Ø - BPL

11 - ORA - (Indirect),Y

12 - Future Expansion

13 - Future Expansion

14 - Future Expansion

15 - ORA - Zero Page,X

16 - ASL - Zero Page,X

17 - Future Expansion

18 - CLC

19 - ORA - Absolute,Y

1A - Future Expansion

1B - Future Expansion

1C - Future Expansion

1D - ORA - Absolute,X

1E - ASL - Absolute,X

1F - Future Expansion

2Ø - JSR

21 - AND - (Indirect,X)

22 - Future Expansion

23 - Future Expansion

24 - BIT - Zero Page

25 - AND - Zero Page

26 - ROL - Zero Page

27 - Future Expansion

28 - PLP

29 - AND - Immediate

2A - ROL - Accumulator

2B - Future Expansion

2C - BIT - Absolute

2D - AND - Absolute

2E - ROL - Absolute

2F - Future Expansion

3Ø - BMI

31 - AND - (Indirect),Y

32 - Future Expansion

33 - Future Expansion

34 - Future Expansion

35 - AND - Zero Page,X

36 - ROL - Zero Page,X

37 - Future Expansion

38 - SEC

39 - AND - Absolute,Y

3A - Future Expansion

3B - Future Expansion

3C - Future Expansion

3D - AND - Absolute,X

3E - ROL - Absolute,X

3F - Future Expansion

4Ø - RTI
41 - EOR - (Indirect,X)
42 - Future Expansion
43 - Future Expansion
44 - Future Expansion
45 - EOR - Zero Page
46 - LSR - Zero Page
47 - Future Expansion
48 - PHA
49 - EOR - Immediate
4A - LSR - Accumulator
4B - Future Expansion
4C - JMP - Absolute
4D - EOR - Absolute
4E - LSR - Absolute
4F - Future Expansion
5Ø - BVC
51 - EOR - (Indirect),Y
52 - Future Expansion
53 - Future Expansion
54 - Future Expansion
55 - EOR - Zero Page,X
56 - LSR - Zero Page,X
57 - Future Expansion
58 - CLI
59 - EOR - Absolute,Y
5A - Future Expansion
5B - Future Expansion
5C - Future Expansion
5D - EOR - Absolute,X
5E - LSR - Absolute,X
5F - Future Expansion

6Ø - RTS
61 - ADC - (Indirect,X)
62 - Future Expansion
63 - Future Expansion
64 - Future Expansion
65 - ADC - Zero Page
66 - ROR - Zero Page
67 - Future Expansion
68 - PLA
69 - ADC - Immediate
6A - ROR - Accumulator
6B - Future Expansion
6C - JMP - Indirect
6D - ADC - Absolute
6E - ROR - Absolute
6F - Future Expansion
7Ø - BVS
71 - ADC - (Indirect),Y
72 - Future Expansion
73 - Future Expansion
74 - Future Expansion
75 - ADC - Zero Page,X
76 - ROR - Zero Page,X
77 - Future Expansion
78 - SEI
79 - ADC - Absolute,Y
7A - Future Expansion
7B - Future Expansion
7C - Future Expansion
7D - ADC - Absolute,X
7E - ROR - Absolute,X
7F - Future Expansion

8Ø - Future Expansion
81 - STA - (Indirect,X)
82 - Future Expansion
83 - Future Expansion
84 - STY - Zero Page
85 - STA - Zero Page
86 - STX - Zero Page
87 - Future Expansion
88 - DEY
89 - Future Expansion
8A - TXA
8B - Future Expansion
8C - STY - Absolute
8D - STA - Absolute
8E - STX - Absolute
8F - Future Expansion
9Ø - BCC
91 - STA - (Indirect),Y
92 - Future Expansion
93 - Future Expansion
94 - STY - Zero Page,X
95 - STA - Zero Page,X
96 - STX - Zero Page,Y
97 - Future Expansion
98 - TYA
99 - STA - Absolute,Y
9A - TXS
9B - Future Expansion
9C - Future Expansion
9D - STA - Absolute,X
9E - Future Expansion
9F - Future Expansion

AØ - LDY - Immediate
A1 - LDA - (Indirect,X)
A2 - LDX - Immediate
A3 - Future Expansion
A4 - LDY - Zero Page
A5 - LDA - Zero Page
A6 - LDX - Zero Page
A7 - Future Expansion
A8 - TAY
A9 - LDA - Immediate
AA - TAX
AB - Future Expansion
AC - LDY - Absolute
AD - LDA - Absolute
AE - LDX - Absolute
AF - Future Expansion
BØ - BCS
B1 - LDA - (Indirect),Y
B2 - Future Expansion
B3 - Future Expansion
B4 - LDY - Zero Page,X
B5 - LDA - Zero Page,X
B6 - LDX - Zero Page,Y
B7 - Future Expansion
B8 - CLV
B9 - LDA - Absolute,Y
BA - TSX
BB - Future Expansion
BC - LDY - Absolute,X
BD - LDA - Absolute,X
BE - LDX - Absolute,Y
BF - Future Expansion

CØ - CPY - Immediate
C1 - CMP - (Indirect,X)
C2 - Future Expansion
C3 - Future Expansion
C4 - CPY - Zero Page
C5 - CMP - Zero Page
C6 - DEC - Zero Page
C7 - Future Expansion
C8 - INY
C9 - CMP - Immediate
CA - DEX
CB - Future Expansion
CC - CPY - Absolute
CD - CMP - Absolute
CE - DEC - Absolute
CF - Future Expansion
DØ - BNE
D1 - CMP - (Indirect),Y
D2 - Future Expansion
D3 - Future Expansion
D4 - Future Expansion
D5 - CMP - Zero Page,X
D6 - DEC - Zero Page,X
D7 - Future Expansion
D8 - CLD
D9 - CMP - Absolute,Y
DA - Future Expansion
DB - Future Expansion
DC - Future Expansion
DD - CMP - Absolute,X
DE - DEC - Absolute,X
DF - Future Expansion

EØ - CPX - Immediate
E1 - SBC - (Indirect,X)
E2 - Future Expansion
E3 - Future Expansion
E4 - CPX - Zero Page
E5 - SBC - Zero Page
E6 - INC - Zero Page
E7 - Future Expansion
E8 - INX
E9 - SBC - Immediate
EA - NOP
EB - Future Expansion
EC - CPX - Absolute
ED - SBC - Absolute
EE - INC - Absolute
EF - Future Expansion
FØ - BEQ
F1 - SBC - (Indirect),Y
F2 - Future Expansion
F3 - Future Expansion
F4 - Future Expansion
F5 - SBC - Zero Page,X
F6 - INC - Zero Page,X
F7 - Future Expansion
F8 - SED
F9 - SBC - Absolute,Y
FA - Future Expansion
FB - Future Expansion
FC - Future Expansion
FD - SBC - Absolute,X
FE - INC - Absolute,X
FF - Future Expansion

MEMORY MANAGEMENT ON THE COMMODORE 64

The Commodore 64 has 64K bytes of RAM. It also has 20K bytes of ROM, containing BASIC, the operating system, and the standard character set. It also accesses input/output devices as a 4K chunk of memory. How is this all possible on a computer with a 16-bit address bus, that is normally only capable of addressing 64K?

The secret is in the 6510 processor chip itself. On the chip is an input/output port. This port is used to control whether RAM or ROM or I/O will appear in certain portions of the system's memory. The port is also used to control the Datassette™, so it is important to affect only the proper bits.

The 6510 input/output port appears at location 1. The data direction register for this port appears at location 0. The port is controlled like any of the other input/output ports in the system . . . the data direction controls whether a given bit will be an input or an output, and the actual data transfer occurs through the port itself.

The lines in the 6510 control port are defined as follows:

NAME	BIT	DIRECTION	DESCRIPTION
LORAM	0	OUTPUT	Control for RAM/ROM at $A000–$BFFF (BASIC)
HIRAM	1	OUTPUT	Control for RAM/ROM at $E000–$FFFF (KERNAL)
CHAREN	2	OUTPUT	Control for I/O/ROM at $D000–$DFFF
	3	OUTPUT	Cassette write line
	4	INPUT	Cassette switch sense
	5	OUTPUT	Cassette motor control

The proper value for the data direction register is as follows:

BITS	5	4	3	2	1	0
	1	0	1	1	1	1

(where 1 is an output, and 0 is an input).

This gives a value of 47 decimal. The Commodore 64 automatically sets the data direction register to this value.

The control lines, in general, perform the function given in their descriptions. However, a combination of control lines are occasionally used to get a particular memory configuration.

LORAM (bit 0) can generally be thought of as a control line which banks the 8K byte BASIC ROM in and out of the microprocessor address space. Normally, this line is HIGH for BASIC operation. If this line is programmed LOW, the BASIC ROM will disappear from the memory map and be replaced by 8K bytes of RAM from $A000–$BFFF.

HIRAM (bit 1) can generally be thought of as a control line which banks the 8K byte KERNAL ROM in and out of the microprocessor address space. Normally, this line is HIGH for BASIC operation. If this line is programmed LOW, the KERNAL ROM will disappear from the memory map and be replaced by 8K bytes of RAM from $E000–$FFFF.

CHAREN (bit 2) is used only to bank the 4K byte character generator ROM in or out of the microprocessor address space. From the processor point of view, the character ROM occupies the same address space as the I/O devices ($D000–$DFFF). When the CHAREN line is set to 1 (as is normal), the I/O devices appear in the microprocessor address space, and the character ROM is not accessable. When the CHAREN bit is cleared to 0, the character ROM appears in the processor address space, and the I/O devices are not accessable. (The microprocessor only needs to access the character ROM when downloading the character set from ROM to RAM. Special care is needed for this . . . see the section on PROGRAMMABLE CHARACTERS in the GRAPHICS chapter). CHAREN can be overridden by other control lines in certain memory configurations. CHAREN will have no effect on any memory configuration without I/O devices. RAM will appear from $D000–$DFFF instead.

NOTE: In any memory map containing ROM, a WRITE (a POKE) to a ROM location will store data in the RAM "under" the ROM. Writing to a ROM location stores data in the "hidden" RAM. For example, this allows a hi-resolution screen to be kept underneath a ROM, and be changed without having to bank the screen back into the processor address space. Of course a READ of a ROM location will return the contents of the ROM, not the "hidden" RAM.

COMMODORE 64 FUNDAMENTAL MEMORY MAP

E000-FFFF	8K KERNAL ROM OR RAM
D000-DFFF	4K I/O OR RAM OR CHARACTER ROM
C000-CFFF	4K RAM
A000-BFFF	8K BASIC ROM OR RAM OR ROM PLUG-IN
8000-9FFF	8K RAM OR ROM PLUG-IN
4000-7FFF	16K RAM
0000-3FFF	16K RAM

I/O BREAKDOWN

D000-D3FF	VIC (Video Controller)	1K Bytes
D400-D7FF	SID (Sound Synthesizer)	1K Bytes
D800-DBFF	Color RAM	1K Nybbles
DC00-DCFF	CIA1 (Keyboard)	256 Bytes
DD00-DDFF	CIA2 (Serial Bus, User Port/RS-232)	256 Bytes
DE00-DEFF	Open I/O slot #1 (CP/M Enable)	256 Bytes
DF00-DFFF	Open I/O slot #2 (Disk)	256 Bytes

The two open I/O slots are for general purpose user I/O, special purpose I/O cartridges (such as IEEE), and have been tentatively designated for enabling the Z-80 cartridge (CP/M option) and for interfacing to a low-cost high-speed disk system.

The system provides for "auto-start" of the program in a Commodore 64 Expansion Cartridge. The cartridge program is started if the first nine bytes of the cartridge ROM starting at location 32768 ($8000) contain specific data. The first two bytes must hold the Cold Start vector to be used by the cartridge program. The next two bytes at 32770 ($8002) must be the Warm Start vector used by the cartridge program. The next three bytes must be the letters, CBM, with bit 7 set in each letter. The last two bytes must be the digits "80" in PET ASCII.

COMMODORE 64 MEMORY MAPS

The following tables list the various memory configurations available on the COMMODORE 64, the states of the control lines which select each memory map, and the intended use of each map.

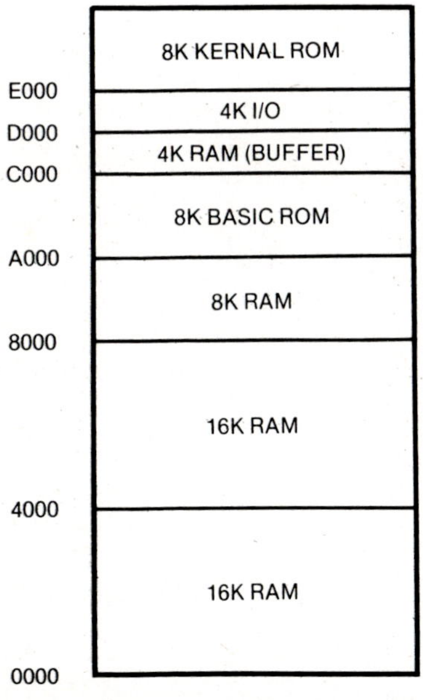

X = DON'T CARE
0 = LOW
1 = HIGH

LORAM = 1
HIRAM = 1
GAME = 1
EXROM = 1

This is the default BASIC memory map which provides BASIC 2.0 and 38K contiguous bytes of user RAM.

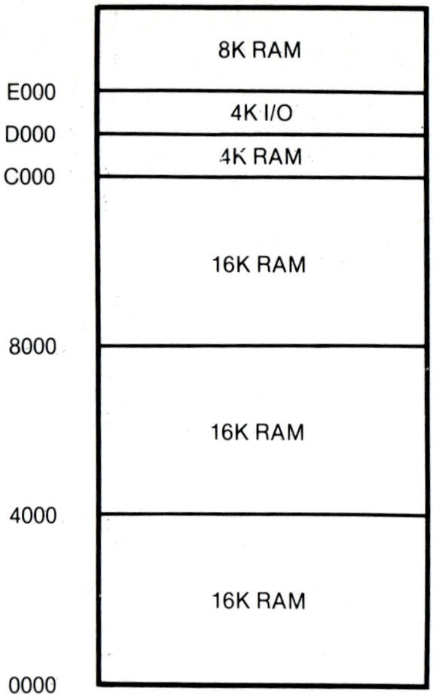

X = DON'T CARE
0 = LOW
1 = HIGH

LORAM = 1
HIRAM = 0
GAME = 1
EXROM = X
OR
LORAM = 1
HIRAM = 0
GAME = 0
(THE CHARACTER ROM IS NOT ACCESSIBLE BY THE CPU IN THIS MAP)
EXROM = 0

This map provides 60K bytes of RAM and I/O devices. The user must write his own I/O driver routines.

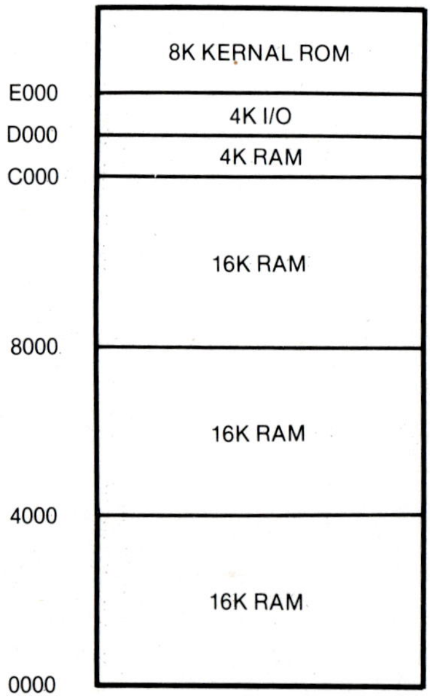

X = DON'T CARE
0 = LOW
1 = HIGH

LORAM = 0
HIRAM = 1
GAME = 1
EXROM = X

This map is intended for use with softload languages (including CP/M), providing 52K contiguous bytes of user RAM, I/O devices, and I/O driver routines.

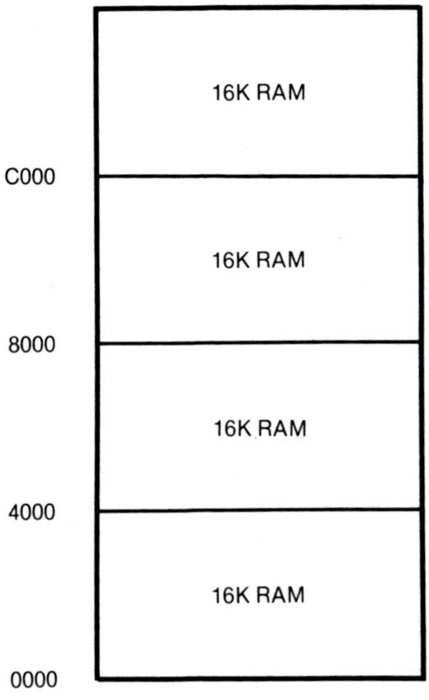

X = DON'T CARE
0 = LOW
1 = HIGH

LORAM = 0
HIRAM = 0
GAME = 1
EXROM = X
OR
LORAM = 0
HIRAM = 0
GAME = X
EXROM = 0

This map gives access to all 64K bytes of RAM. The I/O devices must be banked back into the processor's address space for any I/O operation.

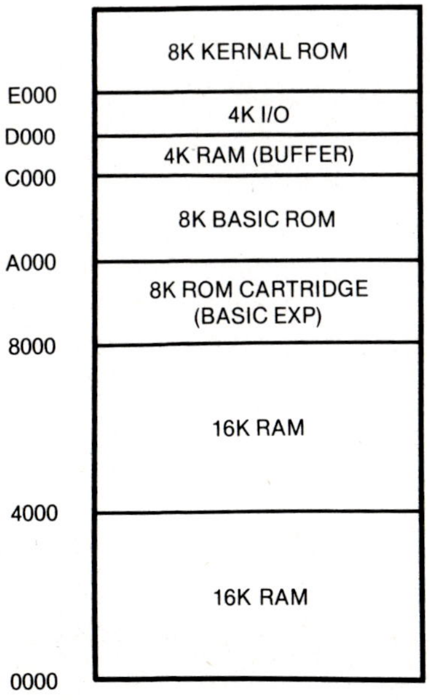

X = DON'T CARE
0 = LOW
1 = HIGH

LORAM = 1
HIRAM = 1
GAME = 1
EXROM = 0

This is the standard configuration for a BASIC system with a BASIC expansion ROM. This map provides 32K contiguous bytes of user RAM and up to 8K bytes of BASIC "enhancement."

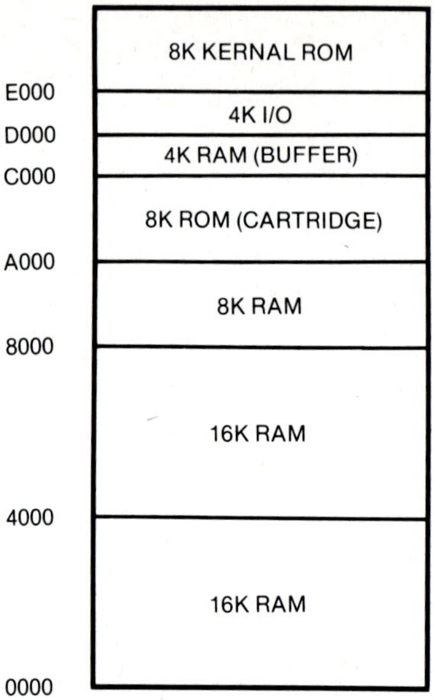

X = DON'T CARE
0 = LOW
1 = HIGH

LORAM = 0
HIRAM = 1
GAME = 0
EXROM = 0

This map provides 40K contiguous bytes of user RAM and up to 8K bytes of plug-in ROM for special ROM-based applications which don't require BASIC.

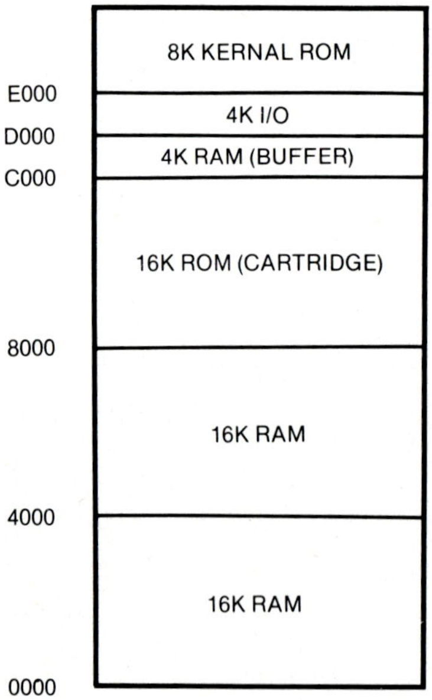

X = DON'T CARE
0 = LOW
1 = HIGH

LORAM = 1
HIRAM = 1
GAME = 0
EXROM = 0

This map provides 32K contiguous bytes of user RAM and up to 16K bytes of plug-in ROM for special ROM-based applications which don't require BASIC (word processors, other languages, etc.).

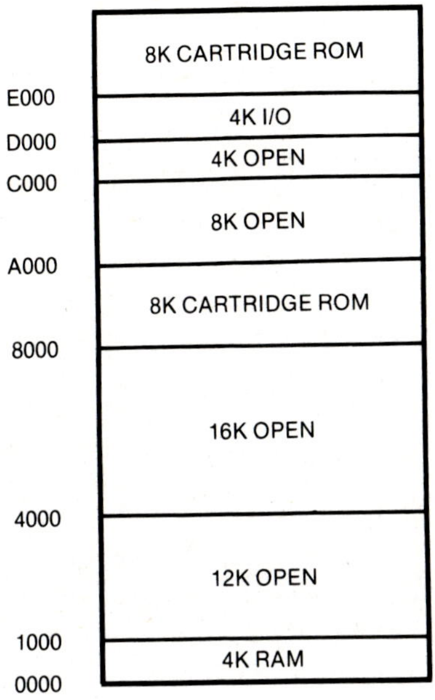

X = DON'T CARE
0 = LOW
1 = HIGH

LORAM = X
HIRAM = X
GAME = 0
EXROM = 1

This is the ULTIMAX video game memory map. Note that the 2K byte "expansion RAM" for the ULTIMAX, if required, is accessed out of the COMMODORE 64 and any RAM in the cartridge is ignored.

THE KERNAL

One of the problems facing programmers in the microcomputer field is the question of what to do when changes are made to the operating system of the computer by the company. Machine language programs which took much time to develop might no longer work, forcing major revisions in the program. To alleviate this problem, Commodore has developed a method of protecting software writers called the **KERNAL**.

Essentially, the KERNAL is a standardized **JUMP TABLE** to the input, output, and memory management routines in the operating system. The locations of each routine in ROM may change as the system is upgraded. But the KERNAL jump table will always be changed to match. If your machine language routines only use the system ROM routines through the KERNAL, it will take much less work to modify them, should that need ever arise.

The KERNAL is the operating system of the Commodore 64 computer. All input, output, and memory management is controlled by the KERNAL.

To simplify the machine language programs you write, and to make sure that future versions of the Commodore 64 operating system don't make your machine language programs obsolete, the KERNAL contains a jump table for you to use. By taking advantage of the 39 input/output routines and other utilities available to you from the table, not only do you save time, you also make it easier to translate your programs from one Commodore computer to another.

The jump table is located on the last page of memory, in read-only memory (ROM).

To use the KERNAL jump table, first you set up the parameters that the KERNAL routine needs to work. Then **JSR** (Jump to SubRoutine) to the proper place in the KERNAL jump table. After performing its function, the KERNAL transfers control back to your machine language program. Depending on which KERNAL routine you are using, certain registers may pass parameters back to your program. The particular registers for each KERNAL routine may be found in the individual descriptions of the KERNAL subroutines.

A good question at this point is why use the jump table at all? Why not just JSR directly to the KERNAL subroutine involved? The jump table is used so that if the KERNAL or BASIC is changed, your machine language programs will still work. In future operating systems the routines may have their memory locations moved around to a different position in the memory map . . . but the jump table will still work correctly!

KERNAL POWER-UP ACTIVITIES

1) On power-up, the KERNAL first resets the stack pointer, and clears decimal mode.
2) The KERNAL then checks for the presence of an autostart ROM cartridge at location $8000 HEX (32768 decimal). If this is present, normal initialization is suspended, and control is transferred to the cartridge code. If an autostart ROM is not present, normal system initialization continues.
3) Next, the KERNAL initializes all INPUT/OUTPUT devices. The serial bus is initialized. Both 6526 CIA chips are set to the proper values for keyboard scanning, and the 60-Hz timer is activated. The SID chip is cleared. The BASIC memory map is selected and the cassette motor is switched off.
4) Next, the KERNAL performs a RAM test, setting the top and bottom of memory pointers. Also, page zero is initialized, and the tape buffer is set up.

   The RAM TEST routine is a nondestructive test starting at location $0300 and working upward. Once the test has found the first non-RAM location, the top of RAM has its pointer set. The bottom of memory is always set to $0800, and the screen setup is always set at $0400.
5) Finally, the KERNAL performs these other activities. I/O vectors are set to default values. The indirect jump table in low memory is established. The screen is then cleared, and all screen editor variables reset. Then the indirect at $A000 is used to start BASIC.

HOW TO USE THE KERNAL

When writing machine language programs it is often convenient to use the routines which are already part of the operating system for input/output, access to the system clock, memory management, and other similar operations. It is an unnecessary duplication of effort to write these routines over and over again, so easy access to the operating system helps speed machine language programming.

As mentioned before, the KERNAL is a jump table. This is just a collection of JMP instructions to many operating system routines.

To use a KERNAL routine you must first make all of the preparations that the routine demands. If one routine says that you must call another KERNAL routine first, then that routine must be called. If the routine expects you to put a number in the accumulator, then that number must be there. Otherwise your routines have little chance of working the way you expect them to work.

After all preparations are made, you must call the routine by means of the JSR instruction. All KERNAL routines you can access are structured as SUBROUTINES, and must end with an RTS instruction. When the KERNAL routine has finished its task, control is returned to your program at the instruction after the JSR.

Many of the KERNAL routines return error codes in the status word or the accumulator if you have problems in the routine. Good programming practice and the success of your machine language programs demand that you handle this properly. If you ignore an error return, the rest of your program might "bomb."

That's all there is to do when you're using the KERNAL. Just these three simple steps:

1) Set up
2) Call the routine
3) Error handling

The following conventions are used in describing the KERNAL routines:

—**FUNCTION NAME:** Name of the KERNAL routine.

—**CALL ADDRESS:** This is the call address of the KERNAL routine, given in hexadecimal.

—**COMMUNICATION REGISTERS:** Registers listed under this heading are used to pass parameters to and from the KERNAL routines.

—**PREPARATORY ROUTINES:** Certain KERNAL routines require that data be set up before they can operate. The routines needed are listed here.

—**ERROR RETURNS:** A return from a KERNAL routine with the CARRY set indicates that an error was encountered in processing. The accumulator will contain the number of the error.

—**STACK REQUIREMENTS:** This is the actual number of stack bytes used by the KERNAL routine.

—**REGISTERS AFFECTED:** All registers used by the KERNAL routine are listed here.

—**DESCRIPTION:** A short tutorial on the function of the KERNAL routine is given here.

The list of the KERNAL routines follows.

USER CALLABLE KERNAL ROUTINES

NAME	ADDRESS		FUNCTION
	HEX	DECIMAL	
ACPTR	$FFA5	65445	Input byte from serial port.
CHKIN	$FFC6	65478	Open channel for input
CHKOUT	$FFC9	65481	Open channel for output
CHRIN	$FFCF	65487	Input character from channel
CHROUT	$FFD2	65490	Output character to channel
CIOUT	$FFA8	65448	Output byte to serial port
CINT	$FF81	65409	Initialize screen editor
CLALL	$FFE7	65511	Close all channels and files
CLOSE	$FFC3	65475	Close a specified logical file
CLRCHN	$FFCC	65484	Close input and output channels
GETIN	$FFE4	65508	Get character from keyboard queue (keyboard buffer)
IOBASE	$FFF3	65523	Returns base address of I/O devices
IOINIT	$FF84	65412	Initialize input/output
LISTEN	$FFB1	65457	Command devices on the serial bus to LISTEN
LOAD	$FFD5	65493	Load RAM from a device
MEMBOT	$FF9C	65436	Read/set the bottom of memory
MEMTOP	$FF99	65433	Read/set the top of memory
OPEN	$FFC0	65472	Open a logical file

NAME	ADDRESS		FUNCTION
	HEX	DECIMAL	
PLOT	$FFF0	65520	Read/set X,Y cursor position
RAMTAS	$FF87	65415	Initialize RAM, allocate tape buffer, set screen $0400
RDTIM	$FFDE	65502	Read real time clock
READST	$FFB7	65463	Read I/O status word
RESTOR	$FF8A	65418	Restore default I/O vectors
SAVE	$FFD8	65496	Save RAM to device
SCNKEY	$FF9F	65439	Scan keyboard
SCREEN	$FFED	65517	Return X,Y organization of screen
SECOND	$FF93	65427	Send secondary address after LISTEN
SETLFS	$FFBA	65466	Set logical, first, and second addresses
SETMSG	$FF90	65424	Control KERNAL messages
SETNAM	$FFBD	65469	Set file name
SETTIM	$FFDB	65499	Set real time clock
SETTMO	$FFA2	65442	Set timeout on serial bus
STOP	$FFE1	65505	Scan stop key
TALK	$FFB4	65460	Command serial bus device to TALK
TKSA	$FF96	65430	Send secondary address after TALK
UDTIM	$FFEA	65514	Increment real time clock
UNLSN	$FFAE	65454	Command serial bus to UNLISTEN
UNTLK	$FFAB	65451	Command serial bus to UNTALK
VECTOR	$FF8D	65421	Read/set vectored I/O

B-1. Function Name: ACPTR

Purpose: Get data from the serial bus
Call address: $FFA5 (hex) 65445 (decimal)
Communication registers: .A
Preparatory routines: TALK, TKSA
Error returns: See READST
Stack requirements: 13
Registers affected: .A, .X

Description: This is the routine to use when you want to get information from a device on the serial bus, like a disk. This routine gets a byte of data off the serial bus using full handshaking. The data is returned in the accumulator. To prepare for this routine the TALK routine must be called first to command the device on the serial bus to send data through the bus. If the input device needs a secondary command, it must be sent by using the TKSA KERNAL routine before calling this routine. Errors are returned in the status word. The READST routine is used to read the status word.

How to Use:

0) Command a device on the serial bus to prepare to send data to the Commodore 64. (Use the TALK and TKSA KERNAL routines.)
1) Call this routine (using JSR).
2) Store or otherwise use the data.

EXAMPLE:

```
;GET A BYTE FROM THE BUS
JSR ACPTR
STA DATA
```

B-2. Function Name: CHKIN

Purpose: Open a channel for input
Call address: $FFC6 (hex) 65478 (decimal)
Communication registers: .X
Preparatory routines: (OPEN)
Error returns:
Stack requirements: None
Registers affected: .A, .X

Description: Any logical file that has already been opened by the KERNAL OPEN routine can be defined as an input channel by this routine. Naturally, the device on the channel must be an input device. Otherwise an error will occur, and the routine will abort.

If you are getting data from anywhere other than the keyboard, this routine must be called before using either the CHRIN or the GETIN KERNAL routines for data input. If you want to use the input from the keyboard, and no other input channels are opened, then the calls to this routine, and to the OPEN routine are not needed.

When this routine is used with a device on the serial bus, it automatically sends the talk address (and the secondary address if one was specified by the OPEN routine) over the bus.

How to Use:

0) OPEN the logical file (if necessary; see description above).
1) Load the .X register with number of the logical file to be used.
2) Call this routine (using a JSR command).

Possible errors are:

#3: File not open
#5: Device not present
#6: File not an input file

EXAMPLE:

```
; PREPARE FOR INPUT FROM LOGICAL FILE 2
LDX #2
JSR CHKIN
```

B-3. Function Name: CHKOUT

Purpose: Open a channel for output
Call address: $FFC9 (hex) 65481 (decimal)
Communication registers: .X
Preparatory routines: (OPEN)
Error returns: 0,3,5,7 (See READST)
Stack requirements: 4+
Registers affected: .A, .X

Description: Any logical file number that has been created by the KERNAL routine OPEN can be defined as an output channel. Of course, the device you intend opening a channel to must be an output device. Otherwise an error will occur, and the routine will be aborted.

This routine must be called before any data is sent to any output device unless you want to use the Commodore 64 screen as your output device. If screen output is desired, and there are no other output channels already defined, then calls to this routine, and to the OPEN routine are not needed.

When used to open a channel to a device on the serial bus, this routine will automatically send the LISTEN address specified by the OPEN routine (and a secondary address if there was one).

How to Use:

REMEMBER: this routine is NOT NEEDED to send data to the screen.

0) Use the KERNAL OPEN routine to specify a logical file number, a LISTEN address, and a secondary address (if needed).
1) Load the .X register with the logical file number used in the open statement.
2) Call this routine (by using the JSR instruction).

EXAMPLE:

```
LDX #3          ;DEFINE LOGICAL FILE 3 AS AN OUTPUT CHANNEL
JSR CHKOUT
```

Possible errors are:

#3: FIle not open
#5: Device not present
#7: Not an output file

B-4. Function Name: CHRIN

Purpose: Get a character from the input channel
Call address: $FFCF (hex) 65487 (decimal)
Communication registers: .A
Preparatory routines: (OPEN, CHKIN)
Error returns: 0 (See READST)
Stack requirements: 7+
Registers affected: .A, .X

Description: This routine gets a byte of data from a channel already set up as the input channel by the KERNAL routine CHKIN. If the CHKIN has NOT been used to define another input channel, then all your data is expected from the keyboard. The data byte is returned in the accumulator. The channel remains open after the call.

Input from the keyboard is handled in a special way. First, the cursor is turned on, and blinks until a carriage return is typed on the keyboard. All characters on the line (up to 88 characters) are stored in the BASIC input buffer. These characters can be retrieved one at a time by calling this routine once for each character. When the carriage return is retrieved, the entire line has been processed. The next time this routine is called, the whole process begins again, i.e., by flashing the cursor.

How to Use:

FROM THE KEYBOARD

1) Retrieve a byte of data by calling this routine.
2) Store the data byte.
3) Check if it is the last data byte (is it a CR ?).
4) If not, go to step 1.

EXAMPLE:

```
     LDY $#00      ;PREPARE THE .Y REGISTER TO STORE THE DATA
RD   JSR CHRIN
     STA DATA,Y    ;STORE THE YTH DATA BYTE IN THE YTH
                   ;LOCATION IN THE DATA AREA.
     INY
     CMP #CR       ;IS IT A CARRIAGE RETURN?
     BNE RD        ;NO, GET ANOTHER DATA BYTE
```

EXAMPLE:

```
JSR CHRIN
STA DATA
```

FROM OTHER DEVICES

0) Use the KERNAL OPEN and CHKIN routines.
1) Call this routine (using a JSR instruction).
2) Store the data.

EXAMPLE:

```
JSR CHRIN
STA DATA
```

B-5. Function Name: CHROUT

Purpose: Output a character
Call address: $FFD2 (hex) 65490 (decimal)
Communication registers: .A
Preparatory routines: (CHKOUT,OPEN)
Error returns: 0 (See READST)
Stack requirements: 8+
Registers affected: .A

Description: This routine outputs a character to an already opened channel. Use the KERNAL OPEN and CHKOUT routines to set up the output channel before calling this routine. If this call is omitted, data is sent to the default output device (number 3, the screen). The data byte to be output is loaded into the accumulator, and this routine is called. The data is then sent to the specified output device. The channel is left open after the call.

NOTE: Care must be taken when using this routine to send data to a specific serial device since data will be sent to all open output channels on the bus. Unless this is desired, all open output channels on the serial bus other than the intended destination channel must be closed by a call to the KERNAL CLRCHN routine.

How to Use:

0) Use the CHKOUT KERNAL routine if needed (see description above).
1) Load the data to be output into the accumulator.
2) Call this routine.

EXAMPLE:

```
;DUPLICATE THE BASIC INSTRUCTION CMD 4,"A";
LDX #4                 ;LOGICAL FILE #4
JSR CHKOUT             ;OPEN CHANNEL OUT
LDA #'A
JSR CHROUT             ;SEND CHARACTER
```

B-6. Function Name: CIOUT

Purpose: Transmit a byte over the serial bus
Call address: $FFA8 (hex) 65448 (decimal)
Communication registers: .A
Preparatory routines: LISTEN, [SECOND]
Error returns: See READST
Stack requirements: 5
Registers affected: None

Description: This routine is used to send information to devices on the serial bus. A call to this routine will put a data byte onto the serial bus using full serial handshaking. Before this routine is called, the LISTEN KERNAL routine must be used to command a device on the serial bus to get ready to receive data. (If a device needs a secondary address, it must also be sent by using the SECOND KERNAL routine.) The accumulator is loaded with a byte to handshake as data on the serial bus. A device must be listening or the status word will return a timeout. This routine always buffers one character. (The routine holds the previous character to be sent back.) So when a call to the KERNAL UNLSN routine is made to end the data transmission, the buffered character is sent with an End Or Identify (EOI) set. Then the UNLSN command is sent to the device.

How to Use:

0) Use the LISTEN KERNAL routine (and the SECOND routine if needed).
1) Load the accumulator with a byte of data.
2) Call this routine to send the data byte.

EXAMPLE:

```
LDA #'X                    ;SEND AN X TO THE SERIAL BUS
JSR CIOUT
```

B-7. Function Name: CINT

Purpose: Initialize screen editor & 6567 video chip
Call address: $FF81 (hex) 65409 (decimal)
Communication registers: None
Preparatory routines: None
Error returns: None
Stack requirements: 4
Registers affected: .A, .X, .Y

Description: This routine sets up the 6567 video controller chip in the Commodore 64 for normal operation. The KERNAL screen editor is also initialized. This routine should be called by a Commodore 64 program cartridge.

How to Use:

1) Call this routine.

EXAMPLE:

```
JSR CINT
JMP RUN                    ;BEGIN EXECUTION
```

B-8. Function Name: CLALL

Purpose: Close all files
Call address: $FFE7 (hex) 65511 (decimal)
Communication registers: None
Preparatory routines: None
Error returns: None
Stack requirements: 11
Registers affected: .A, .X

Description: This routine closes all open files. When this routine is called, the pointers into the open file table are reset, closing all files. Also, the CLRCHN routine is automatically called to reset the I/O channels.

How to Use:

1) Call this routine.

EXAMPLE:

```
JSR CLALL ;CLOSE ALL FILES AND SELECT DEFAULT I/O CHANNELS
JMP RUN   ;BEGIN EXECUTION
```

B-9. Function Name: CLOSE

Purpose: Close a logical file
Call address: $FFC3 (hex) 65475 (decimal)
Communication registers: .A
Preparatory routines: None
Error returns: 0,240 (See READST)
Stack requirements: 2+
Registers affected: .A, .X, .Y

Description: This routine is used to close a logical file after all I/O operations have been completed on that file. This routine is called after the accumulator is loaded with the logical file number to be closed (the same number used when the file was opened using the OPEN routine).

How to Use:

1) Load the accumulator with the number of the logical file to be closed.
2) Call this routine.

EXAMPLE:

```
;CLOSE 15
LDA #15
JSR CLOSE
```

B-10. Function Name: CLRCHN

Purpose: Clear I/O channels
Call address: $FFCC (hex) 65484 (decimal)
Communication registers: None
Preparatory routines: None
Error returns:
Stack requirements: 9
Registers affected: .A, .X

Description: This routine is called to clear all open channels and restore the I/O channels to their original default values. It is usually called after opening other I/O channels (like a tape or disk drive) and using them for input/output operations. The default input device is 0 (keyboard). The default output device is 3 (the Commodore 64 screen).

If one of the channels to be closed is to the serial port, an UNTALK signal is sent first to clear the input channel or an UNLISTEN is sent to clear the output channel. By not calling this routine (and leaving listener(s) active on the serial bus) several devices can receive the same data from the Commodore 64 at the same time. One way to take advantage of this would be to command the printer to TALK and the disk to LISTEN. This would allow direct printing of a disk file.

This routine is automatically called when the KERNAL CLALL routine is executed.

How to Use:

1) Call this routine using the JSR instruction.

EXAMPLE:

```
JSR CLRCHN
```

B-11. Function Name: GETIN

Purpose: Get a character
Call address: $FFE4 (hex) 65508 (decimal)
Communication registers: .A
Preparatory routines: CHKIN, OPEN
Error returns: See READST
Stack requirements: 7+
Registers affected: .A (.X, .Y)

Description: If the channel is the keyboard, this subroutine removes one character from the keyboard queue and returns it as an ASCII value in the accumulator. If the queue is empty, the value returned in the accumulator will be zero. Characters are put into the queue automatically by an interrupt driven keyboard scan routine which calls the SCNKEY routine. The keyboard buffer can hold up to ten characters. After the buffer is filled, additional characters are ignored until at least one character has been removed from the queue. If the channel is RS-232, then only the .A register is used and a single character is returned. See READST to check validity. If the channel is serial, cassette, or screen, call BASIN routine.

How to Use:

1) Call this routine using a JSR instruction.
2) Check for a zero in the accumulator (empty buffer).
3) Process the data.

EXAMPLE:

```
;WAIT FOR A CHARACTER
WAIT JSR GETIN
CMP #0
BEQ WAIT
```

B-12. Function Name: IOBASE

Purpose: Define I/O memory page
Call address: $FFF3 (hex) 65523 (decimal)
Communication registers: .X, .Y
Preparatory routines: None
Error returns:
Stack requirements: 2
Registers affected: .X, .Y

Description: This routine sets the X and Y registers to the address of the memory section where the memory mapped I/O devices are located. This address can then be used with an offset to access the memory mapped I/O devices in the Commodore 64. The offset is the number of locations from the beginning of the page on which the I/O register you want is located. The .X register contains the low order address byte, while the .Y register contains the high order address byte.

This routine exists to provide compatibility between the Commodore 64, VIC-20, and future models of the Commodore 64. If the I/O locations for a machine language program are set by a call to this routine, they should still remain compatible with future versions of the Commodore 64, the KERNAL and BASIC.

How to Use:

1) Call this routine by using the JSR instruction.
2) Store the .X and the .Y registers in consecutive locations.
3) Load the .Y register with the offset.
4) Access that I/O location.

EXAMPLE:

```
; SET THE DATA DIRECTION REGISTER OF THE USER PORT TO 0 (INPUT)
JSR IOBASE
STX POINT      ;SET BASE REGISTERS
STY POINT+1
LDY #2
LDA #0         ;OFFSET FOR DDR OF THE USER PORT
STA (POINT), Y ;SET DDR TO 0
```

B-13. Function Name: IOINIT

Purpose: Initialize I/O devices
Call Address: $FF84 (hex) 65412 (decimal)
Communication registers: None
Preparatory routines: None
Error returns:
Stack requirements: None
Registers affected: .A, .X, .Y

Description: This routine initializes all input/output devices and routines. It is normally called as part of the initialization procedure of a Commodore 64 program cartridge.

EXAMPLE:

```
JSR IOINIT
```

B-14. Function Name: LISTEN

Purpose: Command a device on the serial bus to listen
Call Address: $FFB1 (hex) 65457 (decimai)
Communication registers: .A
Preparatory routines: None
Error returns: See READST
Stack requirements: None
Registers affected: .A

Description: This routine will command a device on the serial bus to receive data. The accumulator must be loaded with a device number between 0 and 31 before calling the routine. LISTEN will OR the number bit by bit to convert to a listen address, then transmits this data as a command on the serial bus. The specified device will then go into listen mode, and be ready to accept information.

How to Use:

1) Load the accumulator with the number of the device to command to LISTEN.
2) Call this routine using the JSR instruction.

EXAMPLE:

```
;COMMAND DEVICE #8 TO LISTEN
LDA #8
JSR LISTEN
```

B-15. Function Name: LOAD

Purpose: Load RAM from device
Call address: $FFD5 (hex) 65493 (decimal)
Communication registers: .A,.X,.Y
Preparatory routines: SETLFS, SETNAM
Error returns: 0,4,5,8,9, READST
Stack requirements: None
Registers affected: .A, .X, .Y

Description: This routine LOADs data bytes from any input device directly into the memory of the Commodore 64. It can also be used for a verify operation, comparing data from a device with the data already in memory, while leaving the data stored in RAM unchanged.

The accumulator (.A) must be set to 0 for a LOAD operation, or 1 for a verify. If the input device is OPENed with a secondary address (SA) of 0 the header information from the device is ignored. In this case, the .X and .Y registers must contain the starting address for the load. If the device is addressed with a secondary address of 1, then the data is loaded into memory starting at the location specified by the header. This routine returns the address of the highest RAM location loaded.

Before this routine can be called, the KERNAL SETLFS, and SETNAM routines must be called.

> **NOTE:** You can NOT LOAD from the keyboard (0), RS-232 (2), or the screen (3).

How to Use:

0) Call the SETLFS, and SETNAM routines. If a relocated load is desired, use the SETLFS routine to send a secondary address of 0.
1) Set the .A register to 0 for load, 1 for verify.
2) If a relocated load is desired, the .X and .Y registers must be set to the start address for the load.
3) Call the routine using the JSR instruction.

EXAMPLE:

```
            ;LOAD A FILE FROM TAPE
            LDA   #DEVICE1        ;SET DEVICE NUMBER
            LDX   #FILENO         ;SET LOGICAL FILE NUMBER
            LDY   CMD1            ;SET SECONDARY ADDRESS
            JSR   SETLFS
            LDA   #NAME1-NAME     ;LOAD .A WITH NUMBER OF
                                  ;CHARACTERS IN FILE NAME
            LDX   #<NAME          ;LOAD .X AND .Y WITH
                                  ;ADDRESS OF
            LDY   #>NAME          ;FILE NAME
            JSR   SETNAM
            LDA   #0              ;SET FLAG FOR A LOAD
            LDX   #$FF            ;ALTERNATE START
            LDY   #$FF
            JSR   LOAD
            STX   VARTAB          ;END OF LOAD
            STY   VARTAB+1
            JMP   START
NAME        .BYT  'FILE NAME'
NAME 1      ;
```

B-16. Function Name: MEMBOT

Purpose: Set bottom of memory
Call address: $FF9C (hex) 65436 (decimal)
Communication registers: .X,.Y
Preparatory routines: None
Error returns: None
Stack requirements: None
Registers affected: .X, .Y

Description: This routine is used to set the bottom of the memory. If the accumulator carry bit is set when this routine is called, a pointer to the lowest byte of RAM is returned in the .X and .Y registers. On the unexpanded Commodore 64 the initial value of this pointer is $0800 (2048 in decimal). If the accumulator carry bit is clear (=0) when this routine is called, the values of the .X and .Y registers are transferred to the low and high bytes, respectively, of the pointer to the beginning of RAM.

How to Use:

TO READ THE BOTTOM OF RAM

1) Set the carry.
2) Call this routine.

TO SET THE BOTTOM OF MEMORY

1) Clear the carry.
2) Call this routine.

EXAMPLE:

```
; MOVE BOTTOM OF MEMORY UP 1 PAGE
SEC            ;READ MEMORY BOTTOM
JSR MEMBOT
INY
CLC            ;SET MEMORY BOTTOM TO NEW VALUE
JSR MEMBOT
```

B-17. Function Name: MEMTOP

Purpose: Set the top of RAM
Call address: $FF99 (hex) 65433 (decimal)
Communication registers: .X, .Y
Preparatory routines: None
Error returns: None
Stack requirements: 2
Registers affected: .X, .Y

Description: This routine is used to set the top of RAM. When this routine is called with the carry bit of the accumulator set, the pointer to the top of RAM will be loaded into the .X and .Y registers. When this routine is called with the accumulator carry bit clear, the contents of the .X and .Y registers are loaded in the top of memory pointer, changing the top of memory.

EXAMPLE:

```
;DEALLOCATE THE RS-232 BUFFER
SEC
JSR MEMTOP  ;READ TOP OF MEMORY
DEX
CLC
JSR MEMTOP  ;SET NEW TOP OF MEMORY
```

B-18. Function Name: OPEN

Purpose: Open a logical file
Call address: $FFC0 (hex) 65472 (decimal)
Communication registers: None
Preparatory routines: SETLFS, SETNAM
Error returns: 1,2,4,5,6,240, READST
Stack requirements: None
Registers affected: .A, .X, .Y

Description: This routine is used to OPEN a logical file. Once the logical file is set up, it can be used for input/output operations. Most of the I/O KERNAL routines call on this routine to create the logical files to operate on. No arguments need to be set up to use this routine, but both the SETLFS and SETNAM KERNAL routines must be called before using this routine.

How to Use:

0) Use the SETLFS routine.
1) Use the SETNAM routine.
2) Call this routine.

EXAMPLE:

This is an implementation of the BASIC statement: OPEN 15,8,15,"I/ O"

```
        LDA #NAME2-NAME   ;LENGTH OF FILE NAME FOR SETLFS
        LDY #>NAME        ;ADDRESS OF FILE NAME
        LDX #<NAME
        JSR SETNAM
        LDA #15
        LDX #8
        LDY #15
        JSR SETLFS
        JSR OPEN
NAME    .BYT 'I/O'
NAME2
```

B-19. Function Name: PLOT

Purpose: Set cursor location
Call address: $FFF0 (hex) 65520 (decimal)
Communication registers: .A, .X, .Y
Preparatory routines: None
Error returns: None
Stack requirements: 2
Registers affected: .A, .X, .Y

Description: A call to this routine with the accumulator carry flag set loads the current position of the cursor on the screen (in X,Y coordinates) into the .Y and .X registers. Y is the column number of the cursor location (6–39), and X is the row number of the location of the cursor (0–24). A call with the carry bit clear moves the cursor to X,Y as determined by the .Y and .X registers.

How to Use:

READING CURSOR LOCATION

1) Set the carry flag.
2) Call this routine.
3) Get the X and Y position from the .Y and .X registers, respectively.

SETTING CURSOR LOCATION

1) Clear carry flag.
2) Set the .Y and .X registers to the desired cursor location.
3) Call this routine.

EXAMPLE:

```
; MOVE THE CURSOR TO ROW 10, COLUMN 5 (5,10)
LDX #10
LDY #5
CLC
JSR PLOT
```

B-20. Function Name: RAMTAS

Purpose: Perform RAM test
Call address: $FF87 (hex) 65415 (decimal)
Communication registers: .A, .X, .Y
Preparatory routines: None
Error returns: None
Stack requirements: 2
Registers affected: .A, .X, .Y

Description: This routine is used to test RAM and set the top and bottom of memory pointers accordingly. It also clears locations $0000 to $0101 and $0200 to $03FF. It also allocates the cassette buffer, and sets the screen base to $0400. Normally, this routine is called as part of the initialization process of a Commodore 64 program cartridge.

EXAMPLE:

```
JSR RAMTAS
```

B-21. Function Name: RDTIM

Purpose: Read system clock
Call address: $FFDE (hex) 65502 (decimal)
Communication registers: .A, .X, .Y
Preparatory routines: None
Error returns: None
Stack requirements: 2
Registers affected: .A, .X, .Y

Description: This routine is used to read the system clock. The clock's resolution is a 60th of a second. Three bytes are returned by the routine. The accumulator contains the most significant byte, the X index register contains the next most significant byte, and the Y index register contains the least significant byte.

EXAMPLE:

```
JSR RDTIM
STY TIME
STX TIME+1
STA TIME+2
. . .
TIME *=*+3
```

B-22. Function Name: READST

Purpose: Read status word
Call address: $FFB7 (hex) 65463 (decimal)
Communication registers: .A
Preparatory routines: None
Error returns: None
Stack requirements: 2
Registers affected: .A

Description: This routine returns the current status of the I/O devices in the accumulator. The routine is usually called after new communication to an I/O device. The routine gives you information about device status, or errors that have occurred during the I/O operation.

The bits returned in the accumulator contain the following information: (see table below)

ST BIT POSITION	ST NUMERIC VALUE	CASSETTE READ	SERIAL/RW	TAPE VERIFY + LOAD
0	1		Time out write	
1	2		Time out read	
2	4	Short block		Short block
3	8	Long block		Long block
4	16	Unrecoverable read error		Any mismatch
5	32	Checksum error		Checksum error
6	64	End of file	EOI line	
7	−128	End of tape	Device not present	End of tape

How to Use:

1) Call this routine.
2) Decode the information in the .A register as it refers to your program.

EXAMPLE:

```
;CHECK FOR END OF FILE DURING READ
JSR READST
AND #64                    ;CHECK EOF BIT (EOF=END OF FILE)
BNE EOF                    ;BRANCH ON EOF
```

B-23. Function Name: RESTOR

Purpose: Restore default system and interrupt vectors
Call address: $FF8A (hex) 65418 (decimal)
Preparatory routines: None
Error returns: None
Stack requirements: 2
Registers affected: .A, .X, .Y

Description: This routine restores the default values of all system vectors used in KERNAL and BASIC routines and interrupts. (See the Memory Map for the default vector contents). The KERNAL VECTOR routine is used to read and alter individual system vectors.

How to Use:

1) Call this routine.

EXAMPLE:

```
JSR RESTOR
```

B-24. Function Name: SAVE

Purpose: Save memory to a device
Call address: $FFD8 (hex) 65496 (decimal)
Communication registers: .A,.X,.Y
Preparatory routines: SETLFS, SETNAM
Error returns: 5,8,9, READST
Stack requirements: None
Registers affected: .A, .X, .Y

Description: This routine saves a section of memory. Memory is saved from an indirect address on page 0 specified by the accumulator to the address stored in the .X and .Y registers. It is then sent to a logical file on an input/output device. The SETLFS and SETNAM routines must be used before calling this routine. However, a file name is not required to SAVE to device 1 (the Datassette™ recorder). Any attempt to save to other devices without using a file name results in an error.

> **NOTE:** Device 0 (the keyboard), device 2 (RS-232), and device 3 (the screen) cannot be SAVEd to. If the attempt is made, an error occurs, and the SAVE is stopped.

How to Use:

0) Use the SETLFS routine and the SETNAM routine (unless a SAVE with no file name is desired on "a save to the tape recorder").
1) Load two consecutive locations on page 0 with a pointer to the start of your save (in standard 6502 low byte first, high byte next format).
2) Load the accumulator with the single byte page zero offset to the pointer.
3) Load the .X and .Y registers with the low byte and high byte respectively of the location of the end of the save.
4) Call this routine.

EXAMPLE:

```
LDA #1            ;DEVICE=1:CASSETTE
JSR SETLFS
LDA #0            ;NO FILE NAME
JSR SETNAM
LDA PROG          ;LOAD START ADDRESS OF SAVE
STA TXTTAB        ; (LOW BYTE)
LDA PROG+1
STA TXTTAB+1      ; (HIGH BYTE)
LDX VARTAB        ;LOAD .X WITH LOW BYTE OF END OF SAVE
LDY VARTAB+1      ;LOAD .Y WITH HIGH BYTE
LDA #<TXTTAB      ;LOAD ACCUMULATOR WITH PAGE 0 OFFSET
JSR SAVE
```

B-25. Function Name: SCNKEY

Purpose: Scan the keyboard
Call address: $FF9F (hex) 65439 (decimal)
Communication registers: None
Preparatory routines: IOINIT
Error returns: None
Stack requirements: 5
Registers affected: .A, .X, .Y

Description: This routine scans the Commodore 64 keyboard and checks for pressed keys. It is the same routine called by the interrupt handler. If a key is down, its ASCII value is placed in the keyboard queue. This routine is called only if the normal IRQ interrupt is bypassed.

How to Use:

1) Call this routine.

EXAMPLE:

```
GET  JSR SCNKEY    ;SCAN KEYBOARD
     JSR GETIN     ;GET CHARACTER
     CMP #0        ;IS IT NULL?
     BEQ GET       ;YES . . . SCAN AGAIN
     JSR CHROUT    ;PRINT IT
```

B-26. Function Name: SCREEN

Purpose: Return screen format
Call address: $FFED (hex) 65517 (decimal)
Communication registers: .X,.Y
Preparatory routines: None
Stack requirements: 2
Registers affected: .X, .Y

Description: This routine returns the format of the screen, e.g., 40 columns in .X and 25 lines in .Y. The routine can be used to determine what machine a program is running on. This function has been implemented on the Commodore 64 to help upward compatibility of your programs.

How to Use:

1) Call this routine.

EXAMPLE:

```
JSR SCREEN
STX MAXCOL
STY MAXROW
```

B-27. Function Name: SECOND

Purpose: Send secondary address for LISTEN
Call address: $FF93 (hex) 65427 (decimal)
Communication registers: .A
Preparatory routines: LISTEN
Error returns: See READST
Stack requirements: 8
Registers affected: .A

Description: This routine is used to send a secondary address to an I/O device after a call to the LISTEN routine is made, and the device is commanded to LISTEN. The routine canNOT be used to send a secondary address after a call to the TALK routine.

A secondary address is usually used to give setup information to a device before I/O operations begin.

When a secondary address is to be sent to a device on the serial bus, the address must first be ORed with $60.

How to Use:

1) Load the accumulator with the secondary address to be sent.
2) Call this routine.

EXAMPLE:

```
;ADDRESS DEVICE #8 WITH COMMAND (SECONDARY ADDRESS) #15
LDA #8
JSR LISTEN
LDA #15
JSR SECOND
```

B-28. Function Name: SETLFS

Purpose: Set up a logical file
Call address: $FFBA (hex) 65466 (decimal)
Communication registers: .A, .X, .Y
Preparatory routines: None
Error returns: None
Stack requirements: 2
Registers affected: None

Description: This routine sets the logical file number, device address, and secondary address (command number) for other KERNAL routines.

The logical file number is used by the system as a key to the file table created by the OPEN file routine. Device addresses can range from 0 to 31. The following codes are used by the Commodore 64 to stand for the CBM devices listed below:

ADDRESS	DEVICE
0	Keyboard
1	Datassette™ #1
2	RS-232C device
3	CRT display
4	Serial bus printer
8	CBM serial bus disk drive

Device numbers 4 or greater automatically refer to devices on the serial bus.

A command to the device is sent as a secondary address on the serial bus after the device number is sent during the serial attention handshaking sequence. If no secondary address is to be sent, the .Y index register should be set to 255.

How to Use:

1) Load the accumulator with the logical file number.
2) Load the .X index register with the device number.
3) Load the .Y index register with the command.

EXAMPLE:

```
FOR LOGICAL FILE 32, DEVICE #4, AND NO COMMAND:
LDA #32
LDX #4
LDY #255
JSR SETLFS
```

B-29. Function Name: SETMSG

Purpose: Control system message output
Call address: $FF90 (hex) 65424 (decimal)
Communication registers: .A
Preparatory routines: None
Error returns: None
Stack requirements: 2
Registers affected: .A

Description: This routine controls the printing of error and control messages by the KERNAL. Either print error messages or print control messages can be selected by setting the accumulator when the routine is called. FILE NOT FOUND is an example of an error message. PRESS PLAY ON CASSETTE is an example of a control message.

Bits 6 and 7 of this value determine where the message will come from. If bit 7 is 1, one of the error messages from the KERNAL is printed. If bit 6 is set, control messages are printed.

How to Use:

1) Set accumulator to desired value.
2) Call this routine.

EXAMPLE:

```
LDA #$40
JSR SETMSG                    ;TURN ON CONTROL MESSAGES
LDA #$80
JSR SETMSG                    ;TURN ON ERROR MESSAGES
LDA #0
JSR SETMSG                    ;TURN OFF ALL KERNAL MESSAGES
```

B-30. Function Name: SETNAM

Purpose: Set up file name
Call address: $FFBD (hex) 65469 (decimal)
Communication registers: .A, .X, .Y
Preparatory routines: None
Stack requirements: None
Registers affected: None

Description: This routine is used to set up the file name for the OPEN, SAVE, or LOAD routines. The accumulator must be loaded with the length of the file name. The .X and .Y registers must be loaded with the address of the file name, in standard 6502 low-byte/high-byte format. The address can be any valid memory address in the system where a string of characters for the file name is stored. If no file name is desired, the accumulator must be set to 0, representing a zero file length. The .X and .Y registers can be set to any memory address in that case.

How to Use:

1) Load the accumulator with the length of the file name.
2) Load the .X index register with the low order address of the file name.
3) Load the .Y index register with the high order address.
4) Call this routine.

EXAMPLE:

```
LDA #NAME2-NAME      ;LOAD LENGTH OF FILE NAME
LDX #<NAME           ;LOAD ADDRESS OF FILE NAME
LDY #>NAME
JSR SETNAM
```

B-31. Function Name: SETTIM

Purpose: Set the system clock
Call address: $FFDB (hex) 65499 (decimal)
Communication registers: .A, .X, .Y
Preparatory routines: None
Error returns: None
Stack requirements: 2
Registers affected: None

Description: A system clock is maintained by an interrupt routine that updates the clock every 1/60th of a second (one "jiffy"). The clock is three bytes long, which gives it the capability to count up to 5,184,000 jiffies (24 hours). At that point the clock resets to zero. Before calling this routine to set the clock, the accumulator must contain the most significant byte, the .X index register the next most significant byte, and the .Y index register the least significant byte of the initial time setting (in jiffies).

How to Use:

1) Load the accumulator with the MSB of the 3-byte number to set the clock.
2) Load the .X register with the next byte.
3) Load the .Y register with the LSB.
4) Call this routine.

EXAMPLE:

```
;SET THE CLOCK TO 10 MINUTES = 3600 JIFFIES
LDA #0                 ; MOST SIGNIFICANT
LDX #>3600
LDY #<3600             ; LEAST SIGNIFICANT
JSR SETTIM
```

B-32. Function Name: SETTMO

Purpose: Set IEEE bus card timeout flag
Call address: $FFA2 (hex) 65442 (decimal)
Communication registers: .A
Preparatory routines: None
Error returns: None
Stack requirements: 2
Registers affected: None

NOTE: This routine is used ONLY with an IEEE add-on card!

Description: This routine sets the timeout flag for the IEEE bus. When the timeout flag is set, the Commodore 64 will wait for a device on the IEEE port for 64 milliseconds. If the device does not respond to the Commodore 64's Data Address Valid (DAV) signal within that time the Commodore 64 will recognize an error condition and leave the handshake sequence. When this routine is called when the accumulator contains a 0 in bit 7, timeouts are enabled. A 1 in bit 7 will disable the timeouts.

> **NOTE:** The Commodore 64 uses the timeout feature to communicate that a disk file is not found on an attempt to OPEN a file only with an IEEE card.

How to Use:

TO SET THE TIMEOUT FLAG

1) Set bit 7 of the accumulator to 0.
2) Call this routine.

TO RESET THE TIMEOUT FLAG

1) Set bit 7 of the accumulator to 1.
2) Call this routine.

EXAMPLE:

```
;DISABLE TIMEOUT
LDA #0
JSR SETTMO
```

B-33. Function Name: STOP

Purpose: Check if STOP key is pressed
Call address: $FFE1 (hex) 65505 (decimal)
Communication registers: .A
Preparatory routines: None
Error returns: None
Stack requirements: None
Registers affected: .A, .X

Description: If the STOP key on the keyboard was pressed during a UDTIM call, this call returns the Z flag set. In addition, the channels will be reset to default values. All other flags remain unchanged. If the STOP key is not pressed then the accumulator will contain a byte representing the last row of the keyboard scan. The user can also check for certain other keys this way.

How to Use:

0) UDTIM should be called before this routine.
1) Call this routine.
2) Test for the zero flag.

EXAMPLE:

```
JSR UDTIM ;SCAN FOR STOP
JSR STOP
BNE *+5   ;KEY NOT DOWN
JMP READY ;= . . . STOP
```

B-34. Function Name: TALK

Purpose: Command a device on the serial bus to TALK
Call address: $FFB4 (hex) 65460 (decimal)
Communication registers: .A
Preparatory routines: None
Error returns: See READST
Stack requirements: 8
Registers affected: .A

Description: To use this routine the accumulator must first be loaded with a device number between 0 and 31. When called, this routine then ORs bit by bit to convert this device number to a talk address. Then this data is transmitted as a command on the serial bus.

How to Use:

1) Load the accumulator with the device number.
2) Call this routine.

EXAMPLE:

```
;COMMAND DEVICE #4 TO TALK
LDA #4
JSR TALK
```

B-35. Function Name: TKSA

Purpose: Send a secondary address to a device commanded to TALK
Call address: $FF96 (hex) 65430 (decimal)
Communication registers: .A
Preparatory routines: TALK
Error returns: See READST
Stack requirements: 8
Registers affected: .A

Description: This routine transmits a secondary address on the serial bus for a TALK device. This routine must be called with a number between 0 and 31 in the accumulator. The routine sends this number as a secondary address command over the serial bus. This routine can only be called after a call to the TALK routine. It will not work after a LISTEN.

How to Use:

0) Use the TALK routine.
1) Load the accumulator with the secondary address.
2) Call this routine.

EXAMPLE:

```
;TELL DEVICE #4 TO TALK WITH COMMAND #7
LDA #4
JSR TALK
LDA #7
JSR TALKSA
```

B-36. Function Name: UDTIM

Purpose: Update the system clock
Call address: $FFEA (hex) 65514 (decimal)
Communication registers: None
Preparatory routines: None
Error returns: None
Stack requirements: 2
Registers affected: .A, .X

Description: This routine updates the system clock. Normally this routine is called by the normal KERNAL interrupt routine every 1/60th of a second. If the user program processes its own interrupts this routine must be called to update the time. In addition, the STOP key routine must be called, if the STOP key is to remain functional.

How to Use:

1) Call this routine.

EXAMPLE:

```
JSR UDTIM
```

B-37. Function Name: UNLSN

Purpose: Send an UNLISTEN command
Call address: $FFAE (hex) 65454 (decimal)
Communication registers: None
Preparatory routines: None
Error returns: See READST
Stack requirements: 8
Registers affected: .A

Description: This routine commands all devices on the serial bus to stop receiving data from the Commodore 64 (i.e., UNLISTEN). Calling this routine results in an UNLISTEN command being transmitted on the serial bus. Only devices previously commanded to listen are affected. This routine is normally used after the Commodore 64 is finished sending data to external devices. Sending the UNLISTEN commands the listening devices to get off the serial bus so it can be used for other purposes.

How to Use:

1) Call this routine.

EXAMPLE:

```
JSR UNLSN
```

B-38. Function Name: UNTLK

Purpose: Send an UNTALK command
Call address: $FFAB (hex) 65451 (decimal)
Communication registers: None
Preparatory routines: None
Error returns: See READST
Stack requirements: 8
Registers affected: .A

Description: This routine transmits an UNTALK command on the serial bus. All devices previously set to TALK will stop sending data when this command is received.

How to Use:

1) Call this routine.

EXAMPLE:

```
JSR UNTALK
```

B-39. Function Name: VECTOR

Purpose: Manage RAM vectors
Call address: $FF8D (hex) 65421 (decimal)
Communication registers: .X,.Y
Preparatory routines: None
Error returns: None
Stack requirements: 2
Registers affected: .A, .X, .Y

Description: This routine manages all system vector jump addresses stored in RAM. Calling this routine with the the accumulator carry bit set stores the current contents of the RAM vectors in a list pointed to by the .X and .Y registers. When this routine is called with the carry clar, the user list pointed to by the .X and .Y registers is transferred to the system RAM vectors. The RAM vectors are listed in the memory map.

> **NOTE:** This routine requires caution in its use. The best way to use it is to first read the entire vector contents into the user area, alter the desired vectors, and then copy the contents back to the system vectors.

How to Use:

READ THE SYSTEM RAM VECTORS

1) Set the carry.
2) Set the .X and .y registers to the address to put the vectors.
3) Call this routine.

LOAD THE SYSTEM RAM VECTORS

1) Clear the carry bit.
2) Set the .X and .Y registers to the address of the vector list in RAM that must be loaded.
3) Call this routine.

EXAMPLE:

```
;CHANGE THE INPUT ROUTINES TO NEW SYSTEM
LDX #<USER
LDY #>USER
SEC
JSR VECTOR        ;READ OLD VECTORS
LDA #<MYINP       ;CHANGE INPUT
STA USER+10
LDA #>MYINP
STA USER+11
LDX #<USER
LDY #>USER
CLC
JSR VECTOR        ;ALTER SYSTEM
. . .
USER *=*+26
```

ERROR CODES

The following is a list of error messages which can occur when using the KERNAL routines. If an error occurs during a KERNAL routine, the carry bit of the accumulator is set, and the number of the error message is returned in the accumulator.

> **NOTE:** Some KERNAL I/O routines do not use these codes for error messages. Instead, errors are identified using the KERNAL READST routine.

NUMBER	MEANING
0	Routine terminated by the STOP key
1	Too many open files
2	File already open
3	File not open
4	File not found
5	Device not present
6	File is not an input file
7	File is not an output file
8	File name is missing
9	Illegal device number
240	Top-of-memory change RS-232 buffer allocation/deallocation

USING MACHINE LANGUAGE FROM BASIC

There are several methods of using BASIC and machine language on the Commodore 64, including special statements as part of CBM BASIC as well as key locations in the machine. There are five main ways to use machine language routines from BASIC on the Commodore 64. They are:

1) The BASIC SYS statement
2) The BASIC USR function
3) Changing one of the RAM I/O vectors
4) Changing one of the RAM interrupt vectors
5) Changing the CHRGET routine

1) The BASIC statement **SYS X** causes a **JUMP** to a machine language subroutine located at address X. The routine must end with an **RTS** (ReTurn from Subroutine) instruction. This will transfer control back to BASIC.

   Parameters are generally passed between the machine language routine and the BASIC program using the BASIC PEEK and POKE statements, and their machine language equivalents.

   The **SYS** command is the most useful method of combining BASIC with machine language. PEEKs and POKEs make multiple parameter passing easy. There can be many SYS statements in a program, each to a different (or even the same) machine language routine.

2) The BASIC function **USR(X)** transfers control to the machine language subroutine located at the address stored in locations 785 and 786. (The address is stored in standard low-byte/high-byte format.) The value X is evaluated and passed to the machine language subroutine through floating point accumulator #1, located beginning at address $61 (see memory map for more details). A value may be returned back to the BASIC program by placing it in the floating point accumulator. The machine language routine must end with an RTS instruction to return to BASIC.

   This statement is different from the **SYS,** because you have to set up an indirect vector. Also different is the format through which the variable is passed (floating point format). The indirect vector must be changed if more than one machine language routine is used.

3) Any of the input/output or BASIC internal routines accessed through the vector table located on page 3 (see **ADDRESSING MODES, ZERO PAGE**) can be replaced, or amended by user code. Each 2-byte vector consists of a low byte and a high byte address which is used by the operating system.

The **KERNAL VECTOR** routine is the most reliable way to change any of the vectors, but a single vector can be changed by POKEs. A new vector will point to a user prepared routine which is meant to replace or augment the standard system routine. When the appropriate BASIC command is executed, the user routine will be executed. If after executing the user routine, it is necessary to execute the normal system routine, the user program must **JMP** (JuMP) to the address formerly contained in the vector. If not, the routine must end with a RTS to transfer control back to BASIC.

4) The **HARDWARE INTERRUPT (IRQ) VECTOR** can be changed. Every 1/60th of a second, the operating system transfers control to the routine specified by this vector. The KERNAL normally uses this for timing, keyboard scanning, etc. If this technique is used, you should always transfer control to the normal **IRQ** handling routine, unless the replacement routine is prepared to handle the CIA chip. (REMEMBER to end the routine with an **RTI** (ReTurn from Interrupt) if the CIA is handled by the routine).

This method is useful for tasks which must happen concurrently with a BASIC program, but has the drawback of being more difficult.

NOTE: ALWAYS DISABLE INTERRUPTS BEFORE CHANGING THIS VECTOR!

5) The **CHRGET** routine is used by BASIC to get each character/token. This makes it simple to add new BASIC commands. Naturally, each new command must be executed by a user written machine language subroutine. A common way to use this method is to specify a character (@ for example) which will occur before any of the new commands. The new CHRGET routine will search for the special character. If none is present, control is passed to the normal BASIC CHRGET routine. If the special character is present, the new command is interpreted and executed by your machine language program. This minimizes the extra execution time added by the need to search for additional commands. This technique is often called a *wedge*.

WHERE TO PUT MACHINE LANGUAGE ROUTINES

The best place for machine language routines on the Commodore 64 is from $C000–$CFFF, assuming the routines are smaller than 4K bytes long. This section of memory is not disturbed by BASIC.

If for some reason it's not possible or desirable to put the machine language routine at $C000, for instance if the routine is larger than 4K bytes, it then becomes necessary to reserve an area at the top of memory from BASIC for the routine. The top of memory is normally $9FFF. The top of memory can be changed through the KERNAL routine **MEMTOP,** or by the following BASIC statements:

```
10 POKE51,L:POKE52,H:POKE55,L:POKE56,H:CLR
```

Where H and L are the high and low portions, respectively, of the new top of memory. For example, to reserve the area from $9000 to $9FFF for machine language, use the following:

```
10 POKE51,0:POKE52,144:POKE55,0:POKE56,144:CLR
```

HOW TO ENTER MACHINE LANGUAGE

There are 3 common methods to add the machine language programs to a BASIC program. They are:

1) DATA STATEMENTS:

By READing DATA statements, and POKEing the values into memory at the start of the program, machine language routines can be added. This is the easiest method. No special methods are needed to save the two parts of the program, and it is fairly easy to debug. The drawbacks include taking up more memory space, and the wait while the program is POKEd in. Therefore, this method is better for smaller routines.

EXAMPLE:

```
10 RESTORE:FORX=1TO9:READA:POKE12*4096+X,A:NEXT
.
.
.
BASIC PROGRAM
.
.
.
1000 DATA 161,1,204,204,204,204,204,204,96
```

2) MACHINE LANGUAGE MONITOR (64MON):

This program allows you to enter a program in either HEX or SYMBOLIC codes, and save the portion of memory the program is in. Advantages of this method include easier entry of the machine language routines, debugging aids, and a much faster means of saving and loading. The drawback to this method is that it generally requires the BASIC program to load the machine language routine from tape or disk when it is started. (For more details on 64MON see the machine language section.)

EXAMPLE:

The following is an example of a BASIC program using a machine language routine prepared by 64MON. The routine is stored on tape:

```
10 IF FLAG=1 THEN 20
15 FLAG=1:LOAD "MACHINE LANGUAGE ROUTINE NAME",1,1
20
.
.
.
REST OF BASIC PROGRAM
```

3) EDITOR/ASSEMBLER PACKAGE:

Advantages are similar to using a machine language monitor, but programs are even easier to enter. Disadvantages are also similar to the use of a machine language monitor.

COMMODORE 64 MEMORY MAP

LABEL	HEX ADDRESS	DECIMAL LOCATION	DESCRIPTION
D6510	0000	0	6510 On-Chip Data-Direction Register
R6510	0001	1	6510 On-Chip 8-Bit Input/Output Register
	0002	2	Unused
ADRAY1	0003–0004	3–4	Jump Vector: Convert Floating—Integer

LABEL	HEX ADDRESS	DECIMAL LOCATION	DESCRIPTION
ADRAY2	0005–0006	5–6	Jump Vector: Convert Integer—Floating
CHARAC	0007	7	Search Character
ENDCHR	0008	8	Flag: Scan for Quote at End of String
TRMPOS	0009	9	Screen Column From Last TAB
VERCK	000A	10	Flag: 0 = Load, 1 = Verify
COUNT	000B	11	Input Buffer Pointer / No. of Subscripts
DIMFLG	000C	12	Flag: Default Array DI-Mension
VALTYP	000D	13	Data Type: $FF = String, $00 = Numeric
INTFLG	000E	14	Data Type: $80 = Integer, $00 = Floating
GARBFL	000F	15	Flag: DATA scan/LIST quote/Garbage Coll
SUBFLG	0010	16	Flag: Subscript Ref / User Function Call
INPFLG	0011	17	Flag: $00 = INPUT, $40 = GET, $98 = READ
TANSGN	0012	18	Flag: TAN sign / Comparison Result
	0013	19	Flag: INPUT Prompt
LINNUM	0014–0015	20–21	Temp: Integer Value
TEMPPT	0016	22	Pointer: Temporary String Stack
LASTPT	0017–0018	23–24	Last Temp String Address
TEMPST	0019–0021	25–33	Stack for Temporary Strings
INDEX	0022–0025	34–37	Utility Pointer Area
RESHO	0026–002A	38–42	Floating-Point Product of Multiply
TXTTAB	002B–002C	43–44	Pointer: Start of BASIC Text

LABEL	HEX ADDRESS	DECIMAL LOCATION	DESCRIPTION
VARTAB	002D–002E	45–46	Pointer: Start of BASIC Variables
ARYTAB	002F–0030	47–48	Pointer: Start of BASIC Arrays
STREND	0031–0032	49–50	Pointer: End of BASIC Arrays (+1)
FRETOP	0033–0034	51–52	Pointer: Bottom of String Storage
FRESPC	0035–0036	53–54	Utility String Pointer
MEMSIZ	0037–0038	55–56	Pointer: Highest Address Used by BASIC
CURLIN	0039–003A	57–58	Current BASIC Line Number
OLDLIN	003B–003C	59–60	Previous BASIC Line Number
OLDTXT	003D–003E	61–62	Pointer: BASIC Statement for CONT
DATLIN	003F–0040	63–64	Current DATA Line Number
DATPTR	0041–0042	65–66	Pointer: Current DATA Item Address
INPPTR	0043–0044	67–68	Vector: INPUT Routine
VARNAM	0045–0046	69–70	Current BASIC Variable Name
VARPNT	0047–0048	71–72	Pointer: Current BASIC Variable Data
FORPNT	0049–004A	73–74	Pointer: Index Variable for FOR/NEXT
	004B–0060	75–96	Temp Pointer / Data Area
FACEXP	0061	97	Floating-Point Accumulator #1: Exponent
FACHO	0062–0065	98–101	Floating Accum. #1: Mantissa
FACSGN	0066	102	Floating Accum. #1: Sign
SGNFLG	0067	103	Pointer: Series Evaluation Constant

LABEL	HEX ADDRESS	DECIMAL LOCATION	DESCRIPTION
BITS	0068	104	Floating Accum. #1: Overflow Digit
ARGEXP	0069	105	Floating-Point Accumulator #2: Exponent
ARGHO	006A–006D	106–109	Floating Accum. #2: Mantissa
ARGSGN	006E	110	Floating Accum. #2: Sign
ARISGN	006F	111	Sign Comparison Result: Accum. #1 vs #2
FACOV	0070	112	Floating Accum. #1. Low-Order (Rounding)
FBUFPT	0071–0072	113–114	Pointer: Cassette Buffer
CHRGET	0073–008A	115–138	Subroutine: Get Next Byte of BASIC Text
CHRGOT	0079	121	Entry to Get Same Byte of Text Again
TXTPTR	007A–007B	122–123	Pointer: Current Byte of BASIC Text
RNDX	008B–008F	139–143	Floating RND Function Seed Value
STATUS	0090	144	Kernal I/O Status Word: ST
STKEY	0091	145	Flag: STOP key / RVS key
SVXT	0092	146	Timing Constant for Tape
VERCK	0093	147	Flag: 0 = Load, 1 = Verify
C3PO	0094	148	Flag: Serial Bus—Output Char. Buffered
BSOUR	0095	149	Buffered Character for Serial Bus
SYNO	0096	150	Cassette Sync No.
	0097	151	Temp Data Area
LDTND	0098	152	No. of Open Files / Index to File Table
DFLTN	0099	153	Default Input Device (0)
DFLTO	009A	154	Default Output (CMD) Device (3)

LABEL	HEX ADDRESS	DECIMAL LOCATION	DESCRIPTION
PRTY	009B	155	Tape Character Parity
DPSW	009C	156	Flag: Tape Byte-Received
MSGFLG	009D	157	Flag: $80 = Direct Mode, $00 = Program
PTR1	009E	158	Tape Pass 1 Error Log
PTR2	009F	159	Tape Pass 2 Error Log
TIME	00A0–00A2	160–162	Real-Time Jiffy Clock (approx) 1/60 Sec
	00A3–00A4	163–164	Temp Data Area
CNTDN	00A5	165	Cassette Sync Countdown
BUFPNT	00A6	166	Pointer: Tape I/O Buffer
INBIT	00A7	167	RS-232 Input Bits / Cassette Temp
BITCI	00A8	168	RS-232 Input Bit Count / Cassette Temp
RINONE	00A9	169	RS-232 Flag: Check for Start Bit
RIDATA	00AA	170	RS-232 Input Byte Buffer/Cassette Temp
RIPRTY	00AB	171	RS-232 Input Parity / Cassette Short Cnt
SAL	00AC–00AD	172–173	Pointer: Tape Buffer/ Screen Scrolling
EAL	00AE–00AF	174–175	Tape End Addresses/End of Program
CMP0	00B0–00B1	176–177	Tape Timing Constants
TAPE1	00B2–00B3	178–179	Pointer: Start of Tape Buffer
BITTS	00B4	180	RS-232 Out Bit Count / Cassette Temp
NXTBIT	00B5	181	RS-232 Next Bit to Send/ Tape EOT Flag
RODATA	00B6	182	RS-232 Out Byte Buffer
FNLEN	00B7	183	Length of Current File Name
LA	00B8	184	Current Logical File Number

LABEL	HEX ADDRESS	DECIMAL LOCATION	DESCRIPTION
SA	00B9	185	Current Secondary Address
FA	00BA	186	Current Device Number
FNADR	00BB–00BC	187–188	Pointer: Current File Name
ROPRTY	00BD	189	RS-232 Out Parity / Cassette Temp
FSBLK	00BE	190	Cassette Read/Write Block Count
MYCH	00BF	191	Serial Word Buffer
CAS1	00C0	192	Tape Motor Interlock
STAL	00C1–00C2	193–194	I/O Start Address
MEMUSS	00C3–00C4	195–196	Tape Load Temps
LSTX	00C5	197	Current Key Pressed: CHR$(n) 0 = No Key
NDX	00C6	198	No. of Chars. in Keyboard Buffer (Queue)
RVS	00C7	199	Flag: Print Reverse Chars.—1=Yes, 0=No Used
INDX	00C8	200	Pointer: End of Logical Line for INPUT
LXSP	00C9–00CA	201–202	Cursor X-Y Pos. at Start of INPUT
SFDX	00CB	203	Flag: Print Shifted Chars.
BLNSW	00CC	204	Cursor Blink enable: 0 = Flash Cursor
BLNCT	00CD	205	Timer: Countdown to Toggle Cursor
GDBLN	00CE	206	Character Under Cursor
BLNON	00CF	207	Flag: Last Cursor Blink On/Off
CRSW	00D0	208	Flag: INPUT or GET from Keyboard
PNT	00D1–00D2	209–210	Pointer: Current Screen Line Address

LABEL	HEX ADDRESS	DECIMAL LOCATION	DESCRIPTION
PNTR	00D3	211	Cursor Column on Current Line
QTSW	00D4	212	Flag: Editor in Quote Mode, $00 = NO
LNMX	00D5	213	Physical Screen Line Length
TBLX	00D6	214	Current Cursor Physical Line Number
	00D7	215	Temp Data Area
INSRT	00D8	216	Flag: Insert Mode, >0 = # INSTs
LDTB1	00D9–00F2	217–242	Screen Line Link Table / Editor Temps
USER	00F3–00F4	243–244	Pointer: Current Screen Color RAM loc.
KEYTAB	00F5–00F6	245–246	Vector: Keyboard Decode Table
RIBUF	00F7–00F8	247–248	RS-232 Input Buffer Pointer
ROBUF	00F9–00FA	249–250	RS-232 Output Buffer Pointer
FREKZP	00FB–00FE	251–254	Free 0-Page Space for User Programs
BASZPT	00FF	255	BASIC Temp Data Area
	0100–01FF	256–511	Micro-Processor System Stack Area
	0100–010A	256–266	Floating to String Work Area
BAD	0100–013E	256–318	Tape Input Error Log
BUF	0200–0258	512–600	System INPUT Buffer
LAT	0259–0262	601–610	KERNAL Table: Active Logical File No's.
FAT	0263–026C	611–620	KERNAL Table: Device No. for Each File
SAT	026D–0276	621–630	KERNAL Table: Second Address Each File
KEYD	0277–0280	631–640	Keyboard Buffer Queue (FIFO)

LABEL	HEX ADDRESS	DECIMAL LOCATION	DESCRIPTION
MEMSTR	0281–0282	641–642	Pointer: Bottom of Memory for O.S.
MEMSIZ	0283–0284	643–644	Pointer: Top of Memory for O.S.
TIMOUT	0285	645	Flag: Kernal Variable for IEEE Timeout
COLOR	0286	646	Current Character Color Code
GDCOL	0287	647	Background Color Under Cursor
HIBASE	0288	648	Top of Screen Memory (Page)
XMAX	0289	649	Size of Keyboard Buffer
RPTFLG	028A	650	Flag: REPEAT Key Used, $80 = Repeat
KOUNT	028B	651	Repeat Speed Counter
DELAY	028C	652	Repeat Delay Counter
SHFLAG	028D	653	Flag: Keyb'rd SHIFT Key/ CTRL Key/C= Key
LSTSHF	028E	654	Last Keyboard Shift Pattern
KEYLOG	028F–0290	655–656	Vector: Keyboard Table Setup
MODE	0291	657	Flag: $00=Disable SHIFT Keys, $80 = Enable SHIFT Keys
AUTODN	0292	658	Flag: Auto Scroll Down, 0 = ON
M51CTR	0293	659	RS-232: 6551 Control Register Image
M51CDR	0294	660	RS-232: 6551 Command Register Image
M51AJB	0295–0296	661–662	RS-232 Non-Standard BPS (Time/2-100) USA
RSSTAT	0297	663	RS-232: 6551 Status Register Image
BITNUM	0298	664	RS-232 Number of Bits Left to Send

LABEL	HEX ADDRESS	DECIMAL LOCATION	DESCRIPTION
BAUDOF	0299–029A	665–666	RS-232 Baud Rate: Full Bit Time (μs)
RIDBE	029B	667	RS-232 Index to End of Input Buffer
RIDBS	029C	668	RS-232 Start of Input Buffer (Page)
RODBS	029D	669	RS-232 Start of Output Buffer (Page)
RODBE	029E	670	RS-232 Index to End of Output Buffer
IRQTMP	029F–02A0	671–672	Holds IRQ Vector During Tape I/O
ENABL	02A1	673	RS-232 Enables
	02A2	674	TOD Sense During Cassette I/O
	02A3	675	Temp Storage For Cassette Read
	02A4	676	Temp D1IRQ Indicator For Cassette Read
	02A5	677	Temp For Line Index
	02A6	678	PAL/NTSC Flag, 0= NTSC, 1= PAL
	02A7–02FF	679–767	Unused
IERROR	0300–0301	768–769	Vector: Print BASIC Error Message
IMAIN	0302–0303	770–771	Vector: BASIC Warm Start
ICRNCH	0304–0305	772–773	Vector: Tokenize BASIC Text
IQPLOP	0306–0307	774–775	Vector: BASIC Text LIST
IGONE	0308–0309	776–777	Vector: BASIC Char. Dispatch
IEVAL	030A–030B	778–779	Vector: BASIC Token Evaluation
SAREG	030C	780	Storage for 6502 .A Register
SXREG	030D	781	Storage for 6502 .X Register

LABEL	HEX ADDRESS	DECIMAL LOCATION	DESCRIPTION
SYREG	030E	782	Storage for 6502 .Y Register
SPREG	030F	783	Storage for 6502 .SP Register
USRPOK	0310	784	USR Function Jump Instr (4C)
USRADD	0311–0312	785–786	USR Address Low Byte/ High Byte
	0313	787	Unused
CINV	0314–0315	788–789	Vector: Hardware IRQ Interrupt
CBINV	0316–0317	790–791	Vector: BRK Instr. Interrupt
NMINV	0318–0319	792–793	Vector: Non-Maskable Interrupt
IOPEN	031A–031B	794–795	KERNAL OPEN Routine Vector
ICLOSE	031C–031D	796–797	KERNAL CLOSE Routine Vector
ICHKIN	031E–031F	798–799	KERNAL CHKIN Routine Vector
ICKOUT	0320–0321	800–801	KERNAL CHKOUT Routine Vector
ICLRCH	0322–0323	802–803	KERNAL CLRCHN Routine Vector
IBASIN	0324–0325	804–805	KERNAL CHRIN Routine Vector
IBSOUT	0326–0327	806–807	KERNAL CHROUT Routine Vector
ISTOP	0328–0329	808–809	KERNAL STOP Routine Vector
IGETIN	032A–032B	810–811	KERNAL GETIN Routine Vector
ICLALL	032C–032D	812–813	KERNAL CLALL Routine Vector
USRCMD	032E–032F	814–815	User-Defined Vector
ILOAD	0330–0331	816–817	KERNAL LOAD Routine Vector

LABEL	HEX ADDRESS	DECIMAL LOCATION	DESCRIPTION
ISAVE	0332–0333	818–819	KERNAL SAVE Routine Vector
	0334–033B	820–827	Unused
TBUFFR	033C–03FB	828–1019	Tape I/O Buffer
	03FC–03FF	1020–1023	Unused
VICSCN	0400–07FF	1024–2047	1024 Byte Screen Memory Area
	0400–07E7	1024–2023	Video Matrix: 25 Lines × 40 Columns
	07F8–07FF	2040–2047	Sprite Data Pointers
	0800–9FFF	2048–40959	Normal BASIC Program Space
	8000–9FFF	32768–40959	VSP Cartridge ROM—8192 Bytes
	A000–BFFF	40960–49151	BASIC ROM—8192 Bytes (or 8K RAM)
	C000–CFFF	49152–53247	RAM—4096 Bytes
	D000–DFFF	53248–57343	Input/Output Devices and Color RAM or Character Generator ROM or RAM—4096 Bytes
	E000–FFFF	57344–65535	KERNAL ROM—8192 Bytes (or 8K RAM)

COMMODORE 64 INPUT/OUTPUT ASSIGNMENTS

HEX	DECIMAL	BITS	DESCRIPTION
0000	0	7–0	MOS 6510 Data Direction Register (xx101111) Bit=1: Output, Bit=0: Input, x=Don't Care
0001	1		MOS 6510 Micro-Processor On-Chip I/O Port
		0	/LORAM Signal (0=Switch BASIC ROM Out)

HEX	DECIMAL	BITS	DESCRIPTION
		1	/HIRAM Signal (0=Switch Kernal ROM Out)
		2	/CHAREN Signal (0=Switch Char. ROM In)
		3	Cassette Data Output Line
		4	Cassette Switch Sense 1 = Switch Closed
		5	Cassette Motor Control 0 = ON, 1 = OFF
		6–7	Undefined
D000–D02E	53248–54271		MOS 6566 VIDEO INTERFACE CONTROLLER (VIC)
D000	53248		Sprite 0 X Pos
D001	53249		Sprite 0 Y Pos
D002	53250		Sprite 1 X Pos
D003	53251		Sprite 1 Y Pos
D004	53252		Sprite 2 X Pos
D005	53253		Sprite 2 Y Pos
D006	53254		Sprite 3 X Pos
D007	53255		Sprite 3 Y Pos
D008	53256		Sprite 4 X Pos
D009	53257		Sprite 4 Y Pos
D00A	53258		Sprite 5 X Pos
D00B	53259		Sprite 5 Y Pos
D00C	53260		Sprite 6 X Pos
D00D	53261		Sprite 6 Y Pos
D00E	53262		Sprite 7 X Pos
D00F	53263		Sprite 7 Y Pos
D010	53264		Sprites 0–7 X Pos (msb of X coord.)
D011	53265		VIC Control Register
		7	Raster Compare: (Bit 8) See 53266
		6	Extended Color Text Mode: 1 = Enable

HEX	DECIMAL	BITS	DESCRIPTION
		5	Bit-Map Mode: 1 = Enable
		4	Blank Screen to Border Color: 0 = Blank
		3	Select 24/25 Row Text Display: 1 = 25 Rows
		2–0	Smooth Scroll to Y Dot-Position (0-7)
D012	53266		Read Raster / Write Raster Value for Compare IRQ
D013	53267		Light-Pen Latch X Pos
D014	53268		Light-Pen Latch Y Pos
D015	53269		Sprite Display Enable: 1 = Enable
D016	53270		VIC Control Register
		7–6	Unused
		5	ALWAYS SET THIS BIT TO 0!
		4	Multi-Color Mode: 1 = Enable (Text or Bit-Map)
		3	Select 38/40 Column Text Display: 1 = 40 Cols
		2–0	Smooth Scroll to X Pos
D017	53271		Sprites 0–7 Expand 2× Vertical (Y)
D018	53272		VIC Memory Control Register
		7–4	Video Matrix Base Address (inside VIC)
		3–1	Character Dot-Data Base Address (inside VIC)
D019	53273		VIC Interrupt Flag Register (Bit = 1: IRQ Occurred)
		7	Set on Any Enabled VIC IRQ Condition
		3	Light-Pen Triggered IRQ Flag

HEX	DECIMAL	BITS	DESCRIPTION
		2	Sprite to Sprite Collision IRQ Flag
		1	Sprite to Background Collision IRQ Flag
		0	Raster Compare IRQ Flag
D01A	53274		IRQ Mask Register: 1 = Interrupt Enabled
D01B	53275		Sprite to Background Display Priority: 1 = Sprite
D01C	53276		Sprites 0–7 Multi-Color Mode Select: 1 = M.C.M.
D01D	53277		Sprites 0–7 Expand 2× Horizontal (X)
D01E	53278		Sprite to Sprite Collision Detect
D01F	53279		Sprite to Background Collision Detect
D020	53280		Border Color
D021	53281		Background Color 0
D022	53282		Background Color 1
D023	53283		Background Color 2
D024	53284		Background Color 3
D025	53285		Sprite Multi-Color Register 0
D026	53286		Sprite Multi-Color Register 1
D027	53287		Sprite 0 Color
D028	53288		Sprite 1 Color
D029	53289		Sprite 2 Color
D02A	53290		Sprite 3 Color
D02B	53291		Sprite 4 Color
D02C	53292		Sprite 5 Color
D02D	53293		Sprite 6 Color
D02E	53294		Sprite 7 Color
D400–D7FF	54272–55295		MOS 6581 SOUND INTERFACE DEVICE (SID)

HEX	DECIMAL	BITS	DESCRIPTION
D400	54272		Voice 1: Frequency Control—Low-Byte
D401	54273		Voice 1: Frequency Control—High-Byte
D402	54274		Voice 1: Pulse Waveform Width—Low-Byte
D403	54275	7–4	Unused
		3–0	Voice 1: Pulse Waveform Width—High-Nybble
D404	54276		Voice 1: Control Register
		7	Select Random Noise Waveform, 1 = On
		6	Select Pulse Waveform, 1 = On
		5	Select Sawtooth Waveform, 1 = On
		4	Select Triangle Waveform, 1 = On
		3	Test Bit: 1 = Disable Oscillator 1
		2	Ring Modulate Osc. 1 with Osc. 3 Output, 1 = On
		1	Synchronize Osc. 1 with Osc. 3 Frequency, 1 = On
		0	Gate Bit: 1 = Start Att/Dec/Sus, 0 = Start Release
D405	54277		Envelope Generator 1: Attack / Decay Cycle Control
		7–4	Select Attack Cycle Duration: 0–15
		3–0	Select Decay Cycle Duration: 0–15
D406	54278		Envelope Generator 1: Sustain / Release Cycle Control

HEX	DECIMAL	BITS	DESCRIPTION
		7–4	Select Sustain Cycle Duration: 0–15
		3–0	Select Release Cycle Duration: 0–15
D407	54279		Voice 2: Frequency Control—Low-Byte
D408	54280		Voice 2: Frequency Control—High-Byte
D409	54281		Voice 2: Pulse Waveform Width—Low-Byte
D40A	54282	7–4	Unused
		3–0	Voice 2: Pulse Waveform Width—High-Nybble
D40B	54283		Voice 2: Control Register
		7	Select Random Noise Waveform, 1 = On
		6	Select Pulse Waveform, 1 = On
		5	Select Sawtooth Waveform, 1 = On
		4	Select Triangle Waveform, 1 = On
		3	Test Bit: 1 = Disable Oscillator 2
		2	Ring Modulate Osc. 2 with Osc. 1 Output, 1 = On
		1	Synchronize Osc. 2 with Osc. 1 Frequency, 1 = On
		0	Gate Bit: 1 = Start Att/Dec/Sus, 0 = Start Release
D40C	54284		Envelope Generator 2: Attack / Decay Cycle Control
		7–4	Select Attack Cycle Duration: 0–15

HEX	DECIMAL	BITS	DESCRIPTION
		3–0	Select Decay Cycle Duration: 0–15
D40D	54285		Envelope Generator 2: Sustain / Release Cycle Control
		7–4	Select Sustain Cycle Duration: 0–15
		3–0	Select Release Cycle Duration: 0–15
D40E	54286		Voice 3: Frequency Control—Low-Byte
D40F	54287		Voice 3: Frequency Control—High-Byte
D410	54288		Voice 3: Pulse Waveform Width—Low-Byte
D411	54289	7–4	Unused
		3–0	Voice 3: Pulse Waveform Width—High-Nybble
D412	54290		Voice 3: Control Register
		7	Select Random Noise Waveform, 1 = On
		6	Select Pulse Waveform, 1 = On
		5	Select Sawtooth Waveform, 1 = On
		4	Select Triangle Waveform, 1 = On
		3	Test Bit: 1 = Disable Oscillator 3
		2	Ring Modulate Osc. 3 with Osc. 2 Output, 1 = On
		1	Synchronize Osc. 3 with Osc. 2 Frequency, 1 = On
		0	Gate Bit: 1 = Start Att/Dec/Sus, 0 = Start Release

HEX	DECIMAL	BITS	DESCRIPTION
D413	54291		Envelope Generator 3: Attack / Decay Cycle Control
		7–4	Select Attack Cycle Duration: 0–15
		3–0	Select Decay Cycle Duration: 0–15
D414	54292		Envelope Generator 3: Sustain / Release Cycle Control
		7–4	Select Sustain Cycle Duration: 0–15
		3–0	Select Release Cycle Duration: 0–15
D415	54293		Filter Cutoff Frequency: Low-Nybble (Bits 2–0)
D416	54294		Filter Cutoff Frequency: High-Byte
D417	54295		Filter Resonance Control / Voice Input Control
		7–4	Select Filter Resonance: 0–15
		3	Filter External Input: 1 = Yes, 0 = No
		2	Filter Voice 3 Output: 1 = Yes, 0 = No
		1	Filter Voice 2 Output: 1 = Yes, 0 = No
		0	Filter Voice 1 Output: 1 = Yes, 0 = No
D418	54296		Select Filter Mode and Volume
		7	Cut-Off Voice 3 Output: 1 = Off, 0 = On
		6	Select Filter High-Pass Mode: 1 = On
		5	Select Filter Band-Pass Mode: 1 = On

HEX	DECIMAL	BITS	DESCRIPTION
		4	Select Filter Low-Pass Mode: 1 = On
		3–0	Select Output Volume: 0–15
D419	54297		Analog/Digital Converter: Game Paddle 1 (0–255)
D41A	54298		Analog/Digital Converter: Game Paddle 2 (0–255)
D41B	54299		Oscillator 3 Random Number Generator
D41C	54230		Envelope Generator 3 Output
D500–D7FF	54528–55295		SID IMAGES
D800–DBFF	55296–56319		Color RAM (Nybbles)
DC00–DCFF	56320–56575		MOS 6526 Complex Interface Adapter (CIA) #1
DC00	56320		Data Port A (Keyboard, Joystick, Paddles, Light-Pen)
		7–0	Write Keyboard Column Values for Keyboard Scan
		7–6	Read Paddles on Port A / B (01 = Port A, 10 = Port B)
		4	Joystick A Fire Button: 1 = Fire
		3–2	Paddle Fire Buttons
		3–0	Joystick A Direction (0–15)
DC01	56321		Data Port B (Keyboard, Joystick, Paddles): Game Port 1

HEX	DECIMAL	BITS	DESCRIPTION
		7–0	Read Keyboard Row Values for Keyboard Scan
		7	Timer B: Toggle/Pulse Output
		6	Timer A: Toggle/Pulse Output
		4	Joystick 1 Fire Button: 1 = Fire
		3–2	Paddle Fire Buttons
		3–0	Joystick 1 Direction
DC02	56322		Data Direction Register—Port A (56320)
DC03	56323		Data Direction Register—Port B (56321)
DC04	56324		Timer A: Low-Byte
DC05	56325		Timer A: High-Byte
DC06	56326		Timer B: Low-Byte
DC07	56327		Timer B: High-Byte
DC08	56328		Time-of-Day Clock: 1/10 Seconds
DC09	56329		Time-of-Day Clock: Seconds
DC0A	56330		Time-of-Day Clock: Minutes
DC0B	56331		Time-of-Day Clock: Hours + AM/PM Flag (Bit 7)
DC0C	56332		Synchronous Serial I/O Data Buffer
DC0D	56333		CIA Interrupt Control Register (Read IRQs/ Write Mask)
		7	IRQ Flag (1 = IRQ Occurred) / Set-Clear Flag
		4	FLAG1 IRQ (Cassette Read / Serial Bus SRQ Input)

HEX	DECIMAL	BITS	DESCRIPTION
		3	Serial Port Interrupt
		2	Time-of-Day Clock Alarm Interrupt
		1	Timer B Interrupt
		0	Timer A Interrupt
DC0E	56334		CIA Control Register A
		7	Time-of-Day Clock Frequency: 1 = 50 Hz, 0 = 60 Hz
		6	Serial Port I/O Mode: 1 = Output, 0 = Input
		5	Timer A Counts: 1 = CNT Signals, 0 = System 02 Clock
		4	Force Load Timer A: 1 = Yes
		3	Timer A Run Mode: 1 = One-Shot, 0 = Continuous
		2	Timer A Output Mode to PB6: 1 = Toggle, 0 = Pulse
		1	Timer A Output on PB6: 1 = Yes, 0 = No
		0	Start/Stop Timer A: 1 = Start, 0 = Stop
DC0F	56335		CIA Control Register B
		7	Set Alarm/TOD-Clock: 1 = Alarm, 0 = Clock

HEX	DECIMAL	BITS	DESCRIPTION
		6–5	Timer B Mode Select: 00 = Count System 02 Clock Pulses 01 = Count Positive CNT Transitions 10 = Count Timer A Underflow Pulses 11 = Count Timer A Underflows While CNT Positive
		4–0	Same as CIA Control Reg. A–for Timer B
DD00–DDFF	56576–56831		MOS 6526 Complex Interface Adapter (CIA) #2
DD00	56576		Data Port A (Serial Bus, RS-232, VIC Memory Control)
		7	Serial Bus Data Input
		6	Serial Bus Clock Pulse Input
		5	Serial Bus Data Output
		4	Serial Bus Clock Pulse Output
		3	Serial Bus ATN Signal Output
		2	RS-232 Data Output (User Port)
		1–0	VIC Chip System Memory Bank Select (Default = 11)
DD01	56577		Data Port B (User Port, RS-232)
		7	User / RS-232 Data Set Ready

HEX	DECIMAL	BITS	DESCRIPTION
		6	User / RS-232 Clear to Send
		5	User
		4	User / RS-232 Carrier Detect
		3	User / RS-232 Ring Indicator
		2	User / RS-232 Data Terminal Ready
		1	User / RS-232 Request to Send
		0	User / RS-232 Received Data
DD02	56578		Data Direction Register—Port A
DD03	56579		Data Direction Register—Port B
DD04	56580		Timer A: Low-Byte
DD05	56581		Timer A: High-Byte
DD06	56582		Timer B: Low-Byte
DD07	56583		Timer B: High-Byte
DD08	56584		Time-of-Day Clock: 1/10 Seconds
DD09	56585		Time-of-Day Clock: Seconds
DD0A	56586		Time-of-Day Clock: Minutes
DD0B	56587		Time-of-Day Clock: Hours + AM/PM Flag (Bit 7)
DD0C	56588		Synchronous Serial I/O Data Buffer
DD0D	56589		CIA Interrupt Control Register (Read NMIs/ Write Mask)

HEX	DECIMAL	BITS	DESCRIPTION
		7	NMI Flag (1 = NMI Occurred) / Set-Clear Flag
		4	FLAG1 NMI (User/RS-232 Received Data Input)
		3	Serial Port Interrupt
		1	Timer B Interrupt
		0	Timer A Interrupt
DD0E	56590		CIA Control Register A
		7	Time-of-Day Clock Frequency: 1 = 50 Hz, 0 = 60 Hz
		6	Serial Port I/O Mode: 1 = Output, 0 = Input
		5	Timer A Counts: 1 = CNT Signals, 0 = System 02 Clock
		4	Force Load Timer A: 1 = Yes
		3	Timer A Run Mode: 1 = One-Shot, 0 = Continuous
		2	Timer A Output Mode to PB6: 1 = Toggle, 0 = Pulse
		1	Timer A Output on PB6: 1 = Yes, 0 = No
		0	Start/Stop Timer A: 1 = Start, 0 = Stop
DD0F	56591		CIA Control Register B
		7	Set Alarm/TOD-Clock: 1 = Alarm, 0 = Clock

HEX	DECIMAL	BITS	DESCRIPTION
		6–5	Timer B Mode Select: 00 = Count System 02 Clock Pulses 01 = Count Positive CNT Transitions 10 = Count Timer A Underflow Pulses 11 = Count Timer A Underflows While CNT Positive
		4–0	Same as CIA Control Reg. A–for Timer B
DE00–DEFF	56832–57087		Reserved for Future I/O Expansion
DF00–DFFF	57088–57343		Reserved for Future I/O Expansion

CHAPTER 6

INPUT/OUTPUT GUIDE

- Introduction
- Output to the TV
- Output to Other Devices
- The Game Ports
- RS-232 Interface Description
- The User Port
- The Serial Bus
- The Expansion Port
- Z-80 Microprocessor Cartridge

INTRODUCTION

Computers have three basic abilities: they can calculate, make decisions, and communicate. Calculation is probably the easiest to program. Most of the rules of mathematics are familiar to us. Decision making is not too difficult, since the rules of logic are relatively few, even if you don't know them too well yet.

Communication is the most complex, because it involves the least exacting set of rules. This is not an oversight in the design of computers. The rules allow enough flexibility to communicate virtually anything, and in many possible ways. The only real rule is this: whatever sends information must present the information so that it can be understood by the receiver.

OUTPUT TO THE TV

The simplest form of output in BASIC is the PRINT statement. PRINT uses the TV screen as the output device, and your eyes are the input device because they use the information on the screen.

When PRINTing on the screen, your main objective is to format the information on the screen so it's easy to read. You should try to think like a graphic artist, using colors, placement of letters, capital and lower case letters, as well as graphics to best communicate the information. Remember, no matter how smart your program, you want to be able to understand what the results mean to you.

The PRINT statement uses certain character codes as "commands" to the cursor. The **CRSR** key doesn't actually display anything, it just makes the cursor change position. Other commands change colors, clear the screen, and insert or delete spaces. The **RETURN** key has a character code number (CHR$) of 13. A complete table of these codes is contained in Appendix C.

There are two functions in the BASIC language that work with the PRINT statement. TAB positions the cursor on the given position from the left edge of the screen, SPC moves the cursor right a given number of spaces from the current position.

Punctuation marks in the PRINT statement serve to separate and format information. The semicolon (;) separates 2 items without any spaces in between. If it is the last thing on a line, the cursor remains after the last thing PRINTed instead of going down to the next line. It suppresses (replaces) the RETURN character that is normally PRINTed at the end of the line.

The comma (,) separates items into columns. The Commodore 64 has 4 columns of 10 characters each on the screen. When the computer PRINTs a comma, it moves the cursor right to the start of the next column. If it is past the last column of the line, it moves the cursor down to the next line. Like the semicolon, if it is the last item on a line the RETURN is suppressed.

The quote marks (" ") separate literal text from variables. The first quote mark on the line starts the literal area, and the next quote mark ends it. By the way, you don't have to have a final quote mark at the end of the line.

The RETURN code (CHR$ code of 13) makes the cursor go to the next *logical* line on the screen. This is not always the very next line. When you type past the end of a line, that line is linked to the next line. The computer knows that both lines are really one long line. The links are held in the *line link table* (see the memory map for how this is set up).

A logical line can be 1 or 2 screen lines long, depending on what was typed or PRINTed. The logical line the cursor is on determines where the RETURN key sends it. The logical line at the top of the screen determines if the screen scrolls 1 or 2 lines at a time.

There are other ways to use the TV as an output device. The chapter on graphics describes the commands to create objects that move across the screen. The VIC chip section tells how the screen and border colors and sizes are changed. And the sound chapter tells how the TV speaker creates music and special effects.

OUTPUT TO OTHER DEVICES

It is often necessary to send output to devices other than the screen, like a cassette deck, printer, disk drive, or modem. The OPEN statement in BASIC creates a "channel" to talk to one of these devices. Once the channel is OPEN, the PRINT# statement will send characters to that device.

EXAMPLE of OPEN and PRINT# Statements:

```
100 OPEN 4, 4: PRINT# 4, "WRITING ON PRINTER"
110 OPEN 3, 8, 3, "0:DISK-FILE,S,W": PRINT# 3, "SEND TO DISK"
120 OPEN 1, 1, 1, "TAPE-FILE": PRINT# 1, "WRITE ON TAPE"
130 OPEN 2, 2, 0, CHR$(10): PRINT# 2, "SEND TO MODEM"
```

The OPEN statement is somewhat different for each device. The parameters in the OPEN statement are shown in the table below for each device.

TABLE of OPEN Statement Parameters:

FORMAT: OPEN file#, device#, number, string

DEVICE	DEVICE#	NUMBER	STRING
CASSETTE	1	0 = Input 1 = Output 2 = Output with EOT	File Name
MODEM	2	0	Control Registers
SCREEN	3	0,1	
PRINTER	4 or 5	0 = Upper/Graphics 7 = Upper/Lower Case	Text Is PRINTed
DISK	8 to 11	2–14 = Data Channel 15 = Command Channel	Drive #, File Name, File Type, Read/Write Command

OUTPUT TO PRINTER

The printer is an output device similar to the screen. Your main concern when sending output to the printer is to create a format that is easy on the eyes. Your tools here include reversed, double-width, capital and lower case letters, as well as dot-programmable graphics.

The SPC function works for the printer in the same way it works for the screen. However, the TAB function does not work correctly on the printer, because it calculates the current position on the line based on the cursor's position on the screen, not on the paper.

The OPEN statement for the printer creates the channel for communication. It also specifies which character set will be used, either upper case with graphics or upper and lower case.

EXAMPLES of OPEN Statement for Printer:

```
OPEN 1, 4: REM UPPER CASE/GRAPHICS
OPEN 1, 4, 7: REM UPPER AND LOWER CASE
```

When working with one character set, individual lines can be PRINTed in the opposite character set. When in upper case with graphics, the cursor down character (CHR$(17)) switches the characters to the upper and lower case set. When in upper and lower case, the cursor up character (CHR$(145)) allows upper case and graphics characters to be PRINTed.

Other special functions in the printer are controlled through character codes. All these codes are simply PRINTed just like any other character.

TABLE of Printer Control Character Codes:

CHR$ CODE	PURPOSE
10	Line feed
13	RETURN (automatic line feed on CBM printers)
14	Begin double-width character mode
15	End double-width character mode
18	Begin reverse character mode
146	End reverse character mode
17	Switch to upper/lower case character set
145	Switch to upper case/graphics character set
16	Tab to position in next 2 characters
27	Move to specified dot position
8	Begin dot-programmable graphic mode
26	Repeat graphics data

See your Commodore printer's manual for details on using the command codes.

OUTPUT TO MODEM

The modem is a simple device that can translate character codes into audio pulses and vice-versa, so that computers can communicate over telephone lines. The OPEN statement for the modem sets up the parameters to match the speed and format of the other computer you are communicating with. Two characters can be sent in the string at the end of the OPEN statement.

The bit positions of the first character code determine the baud rate, number of data bits, and number of stop bits. The second code is optional, and its bits specify the parity and duplex of the transmission. See the RS-232 section or your **VICMODEM** manual for specific details on this device.

EXAMPLE of OPEN Statement for Modem:

```
OPEN 1, 2, 0, CHR$(6): REM 300 BAUD
100 OPEN 2, 2, 0, CHR$(163) CHR$(112): REM 110 BAUD, ETC.
```

Most computers use the American Standard Code for Information Interchange, known as ASCII (pronounced ASK-KEY). This standard set of character codes is somewhat different from the codes used in the Commodore 64. When communicating with other computers, the Commodore character codes must be translated into their ASCII counterparts. A table of standard ASCII codes is included in this book in Appendix C.

Output to the modem is a fairly uncomplicated task, aside from the need for character translation. However, you must know the receiving device fairly well, especially when writing programs where your computer "talks" to another computer without human intervention. An example of this would be a terminal program that automatically types in your account number and secret password. To do this successfully, you must carefully count the number of characters and RETURN characters. Otherwise, the computer receiving the characters won't know what to do with them.

WORKING WITH CASSETTE TAPE

Cassette tapes have an almost unlimited capacity for data. The longer the tape, the more information it can store. However, tapes are limited in time. The more data on the tape, the longer the time it takes to find the information.

The programmer must try to minimize the time factor when working with tape storage. One common practice is to read the entire cassette data file into RAM, then process it, and then re-write all the data on the tape. This allows you to sort, edit, and examine your data. However, this limits the size of your files to the amount of available RAM.

If your data file is larger than the available RAM, it is probably time to switch to using the floppy disk. The disk can read data at any position on the disk, without needing to read through all the other data. You can write data over old data without disturbing the rest of the file. That's why the disk is used for all business applications like ledgers and mailing lists.

The PRINT# statement formats data just like the PRINT statement does. All punctuation works the same. But remember, you're not working with the screen now. The formatting must be done with the INPUT# statement constantly in mind.

Consider the statement PRINT# 1, A$, B$, C$. When used with the screen, the commas between the variables provide enough blank space between items to format them into columns ten characters wide. On cassette, anywhere from 1 to 10 spaces will be added, depending on the length of the strings. This wastes space on your tape.

Even worse is what happens when the INPUT# statement tries to read these strings. The statement INPUT# 1, A$, B$, C$ will discover no data for B$ and C$. A$ will contain all three variables, plus the spaces between them. What happens? Here's a look at the tape file:

```
A$="DOG" B$="CAT" C$="TREE"
PRINT# 1, A$, B$, C$
```

1	2	3	4	5	6	7	8	9	10	11	12	13	14	15	16	17	18	19	20	21	22	23	24	25
D	O	G								C	A	T								T	R	E	E	RETURN

The INPUT# statement works like the regular INPUT statement. When typing data into the INPUT statement, the data items are separated, either by hitting the RETURN key or using commas to separate them. The PRINT# statement puts a RETURN at the end of a line just like the PRINT statement. A$ fills up with all three values because there's no separator on the tape between them, only after all three.

A proper separator would be a comma (,) or a RETURN on the tape. The RETURN code is automatically put at the end of a PRINT or PRINT # statement. One way to put the RETURN code between each item is to use only one item per PRINT# statement. A better way is to set a variable to the RETURN CHR$ code, which is CHR$(13), or use a comma. The statement for this is R$= "," : PRINT# 1, A$ R$ B$ R$ C$. Don't use commas or any other punctuation between the variable names, since the Commodore 64 can tell them apart and they'll only use up space in your program.

A proper tape file looks like this:

1	2	3	4	5	6	7	8	9	10	11	12	13
D	O	G	,	C	A	T	,	T	R	E	E	RETURN

The GET# statement will pick data from the tape one character at a time. It will receive each character, including the RETURN code and other punctuation. The CHR$(0) code is received as an empty string, not as a one character string with a code of 0. If you try to use the ASC function on an empty string, you get the error message **ILLEGAL QUANTITY ERROR**.

The line GET# 1, A$: A= ASC(A$) is commonly used in programs to examine tape data. To avoid error messages, the line should be modified to GET#1, A$: A= ASC(A$+ CHR$(0)). The CHR$(0) at the end acts as insurance against empty strings, but doesn't affect the ASC function when there are other characters in A$.

DATA STORAGE ON FLOPPY DISKETTES

Diskettes allow 3 different forms of data storage. Sequential files are similar to those on tape, but several can can be used at the same time. Relative files let you organize the data into records, and then read and replace individual records within the file. Random files let you work with data anywhere on the disk. They are organized into 256 byte sections called blocks.

The PRINT# statement's limitations are discussed in the section on cassette tape. The same limitations to format apply on the disk. RETURNs or commas are needed to separate your data. The CHR$(0) is still read by the GET# statement as an empty string.

Relative and random files both make use of separate data and command "channels." Data written to the disk goes through the data channel, where it is stored in a temporary buffer in the disk's RAM. When the record or block is complete, a command is sent through the command channel that tells the drive where to put the data, and the entire buffer is written.

Applications that require large amounts of data to be processed are best stored in relative disk files. These will use the least amount of time and provide the best flexibility for the programmer. Your disk drive manual gives a complete programming guide to use of disk files.

THE GAME PORTS

The Commodore 64 has two 9-pin Game Ports which allow the use of joysticks, paddles, or a light pen. Each port will accept either one joystick or one paddle pair. A light pen can be plugged into Port A (only) for special graphic control, etc. This section gives you examples of how to use the joysticks and paddles from both BASIC and machine language.

The digital joystick is connected to CIA #1 (MOS 6526 Complex Interface Adapter). This input/output device also handles the paddle fire buttons and keyboard scanning. The 6526 CIA chip has 16 registers which are in memory locations 56320 through 56335 inclusive ($DC00 to $DC0F). Port A data appears at location 56320 (DC00) and Port B data is found at location 56321 ($DC01).

A digital joystick has five distinct switches, four of the switches are used for direction and one of the switches is used for the fire button. The joystick switches are arranged as shown:

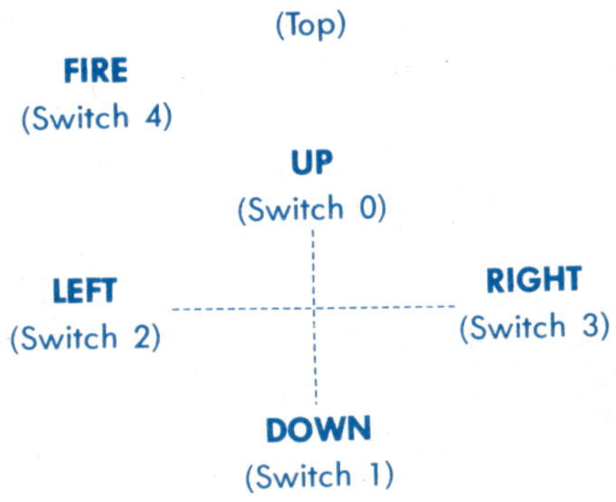

These switches correspond to the lower 5 bits of the data in location 56320 or 56321. Normally the bit is set to a one if a direction is NOT chosen or the fire button is NOT pressed. When the fire button is pressed, the bit (bit 4 in this case) changes to a 0. To read the joystick from BASIC, the following subroutine should be used:

```
10 FORK=0TO10:REM SET UP DIRECTION STRING
20 READDR$(K):NEXT
30 DATA"","N","S","","W","NW"
40 DATA"SW","","E","NE","SE"
50 PRINT"GOING...";
60 GOSUB100:REM READ THE JOYSTICK
65 IFDR$(JV)=""THEN80:REM CHECK IF A DIRECTION WAS
CHOSEN
70 PRINTDR$(JV);" ";:REM OUTPUT WHICH DIRECTION
80 IFFR=16THEN60:REM CHECK IF FIRE BUTTON WAS
PUSHED
90 PRINT"------F------I------R------E------!!!":GOTO60
100 JV=PEEK(56320):REM GET JOYSTICK VALUE
110 FR=JVAND16:REM FORM FIRE BUTTON STATUS
120 JV=15-(JVAND15):REM FORM DIRECTION VALUE
130 RETURN
```

NOTE: For the second joystick, set JV = PEEK (56321).

The values for JV correspond to these directions:

JV EQUAL TO	DIRECTION
0	NONE
1	UP
2	DOWN
3	—
4	LEFT
5	UP & LEFT
6	DOWN & LEFT
7	—
8	RIGHT
9	UP & RIGHT
10	DOWN & RIGHT

A small machine code routine which accomplishes the same task is as follows:

```
1000 .PAGE (JOYSTICK.8/5)  JOYSTICK - BUTTON READ ROUTINE
1010 ;
1020 ;AUTHOR - BILL HINDORFF
1030 ;
1040 DX=$C110
1050 DY=$C111
1060 *=$C200
1070 DJRR   LDA $DC00     ;    (GET INPUT FROM PORT A ONLY)
1080 DJRRB  LDY #0        ;THIS ROUTINE READS AND DECODES THE
1090        LDX #0        ;JOYSTICK/FIREBUTTON INPUT DATA IN
1100        LSR A         ;THE ACCUMULATOR. THIS LEAST SIGNIFICANT
1110        BCS DJR0      ;5 BITS CONTAIN THE SWITCH CLOSURE
1120        DEY           ;INFORMATION. IF A SWITCH IS CLOSED THEN IT
1130 DJR0   LSR A         ;PRODUCES A ZERO BIT. IF A SWITCH IS OPEN THEN
1140        BCS DJR1      ;IT PRODUCES A ONE BIT. THE JOYSTICK DIR-
1150        INY           ;ECTIONS ARE RIGHT, LEFT, FORWARD, BACKWARD
1160 DJR1   LSR A         ;BIT3=RIGHT, BIT2=LEFT, BIT1=BACKWARD,
1170        BCS DJR2      ;BIT0=FORWARD AND BIT4=FIRE BUTTON.
1180        DEX           ;AT RTS TIME DX AND DY CONTAIN 2'S COMPLIMENT
1190 DJR2   LSR A         ;DIRECTION NUMBERS I.E. $FF=-1, $00=0, $01=1.
1200        BCS DJR3      ;DX=1 (MOVE RIGHT), DX=-1 (MOVE LEFT),
1210        INX           ;DX=0 (NO X CHANGE). DY=-1 (MOVE UP SCREEN),
1220 DJR3   LSR A         ;DY=1 (MOVE DOWN SCREEN), DY=0 (NO Y CHANGE).
1230        STX DX        ;THE FORWARD JOYSTICK POSITION CORRESPONDS
1240        STY DY        ;TO MOVE UP THE SCREEN AND THE BACKWARD
1250        RTS           ;POSITION TO MOVE DOWN SCREEN.
1260 ;
1270 ;AT RTS TIME THE CARRY FLAG CONTAINS THE FIRE BUTTON STATE.
1280 ;IF C=1 THEN BUTTON NOT PRESSED. IF C=0 THEN PRESSED.
1290 ;
1300 .END
```

PADDLES

A paddle is connected to both CIA #1 and the SID chip (MOS 6581 Sound Interface Device) through a game port. The paddle value is read via the SID registers 54297 ($D419) and 54298 ($D41A). PADDLES ARE NOT RELIABLE WHEN READ FROM BASIC ALONE!!!! The best way to use paddles, from BASIC or machine code, is to use the following machine language routine. . . . (SYS to it from BASIC then PEEK the memory locations used by the subroutine).

```
1000
;*****************************************************
1010 ;* FOUR PADDLE READ ROUTINE (CAN ALSO BE USED
FOR TWO)
1020
;*****************************************************
1030 ;AUTHOR - BILL HINDORFF
1040 PORTA=$DC00
1050 CIDDRA=$DC02
1060 SID=$D400
1070 *=$C100
1080 BUFFER *=*+1
1090 PDLX *=*+2
1100 PDLY *=*+2
1110 BTNA *=*+1
1120 BTNB *=*+1
1130 *=$C000
1140 PDLRD
1150      LDX #1                        ;FOR FOUR PADDLES
OR TWO ANALOG JOYSTICKS
1160 PDLRD0                             ;ENTRY POINT FOR
ONE PAIR (CONDITION X 1ST)
1170      SEI
1180      LDA CIDDRA                    ;GET CURRENT VALUE
OF DDR
1190      STA BUFFER                    ;SAVE IT AWAY
1200      LDA #$C0
1210      STA CIDDRA                    ;SET PORT A FOR
INPUT
1220      LDA #$80
1230 PDLRD1
1240      STA PORTA                     ;ADDRESS A PAIR OF
PADDLES
1250      LDY #$80                      ;WAIT A WHILE
1260 PDLRD2
1270      NOP
1280      DEY
1290      BPL PDLRD2
1300      LDA SID+25                    ;GET X VALUE
1310      STA PDLX,X
1320      LDA SID+26                    ;GET Y VALUE
1330      STA PDLY,X
```

```
1340      LDA PORTA                  ;TIME TO READ
PADDLE FIRE BUTTONS
1350      ORA #$80                   ;MAKE IT THE SAME
AS OTHER PAIR
1360      STA BTNA                   ;BIT 2 IS PDL X,
BIT 3 IS PDL Y
1370      LDA #$40
1380      DEX                        ;ALL PAIRS DONE?
1390      BPL PDLRD1                 ;NO
1400      LDA BUFFER
1410      STA CIDDRA                 ;RESTORE PREVIOUS
VALUE OF DDR
1420      LDA PORTA+1                ;FOR 2ND PAIR -
1430      STA BTNB                   ;BIT 2 IS PDL X,
BIT 3 IS PDL Y
1440      CLI
1450      RTS
1460 .END
```

The paddles can be read by using the following BASIC program:

```
10 C=12*4096:REM SET PADDLE ROUTINE START
11 REM POKE IN THE PADDLE READING ROUTINE
15 FORI=0TO63:READA:POKEC+I,A:NEXT
20 SYSC:REM CALL THE PADDLE ROUTINE
30 P1=PEEK(C+257):REM SET PADDLE ONE VALUE
40 P2=PEEK(C+258):REM  "     "    TWO   "
50 P3=PEEK(C+259):REM  "     "   THREE  "
60 P4=PEEK(C+260):REM  "     "    FOUR  "
61 REM READ FIRE BUTTON STATUS
62 S1=PEEK(C+261):S2=PEEK(C+262)
70 PRINTP1,P2,P3,P4:REM PRINT PADDLE VALUES
72 REM PRINT FIRE BUTTON STATUS
75 PRINT:PRINT"FIRE A ";S1,"FIRE B ";S2
80 FORW=1TO50:NEXT:REM WAIT A WHILE

          SHIFT CLR/HOME
90 PRINT"♥":PRINT:GOTO 20:REM CLEAR SCREEN AND DO
AGAIN
95 REM DATA FOR MACHINE CODE ROUTINE
100 DATA162,1,120,173,2,220,141,0,193,169,192,141,
2,220,169
110 DATA128,141,0,220,160,128,234,136,16,252,173,
25,212,157
120 DATA1,193,173,26,212,157,3,193,173,0,220,9,128,
141,5,193
130 DATA169,64,202,16,222,173,0,193,141,2,220,173,
1,220,141
140 DATA6,193,88,96
```

LIGHT PEN

The light pen input latches the current screen position into a pair of registers (LPX, LPY) on a low-going edge. The X position register 19 ($13) will contain the 8 MSB of the X position at the time of transition. Since the X position is defined by a 512-state counter (9 bits), resolution to 2 horizontal dots is provided. Similarly, the Y position is latched in its register 20 ($14), but here 8 bits provide single raster resolution within the visible display. The light pen latch may be triggered only once per frame, and subsequent triggers within the same frame will have no effect. Therefore, you must take several samples before turning the pen to the screen (3 or more samples average), depending upon the characteristics of your light pen.

RS-232 INTERFACE DESCRIPTION

GENERAL OUTLINE

The Commodore 64 has a built-in RS-232 interface for connection to any RS-232 modem, printer, or other device. To connect a device to the Commodore 64, all you need is a cable and a little bit of programming.

RS-232 on the Commodore 64 is set-up in the standard RS-232 format, but the voltages are TTL levels (0 to 5V) rather than the normal RS-232 −12 to 12 volt range. The cable between the Commodore 64 and the RS-232 device should take care of the necessary voltage conversions. The Commodore RS-232 interface cartridge handles this properly.

The RS-232 interface software can be accessed from BASIC or from the KERNAL for machine language programming.

RS-232 on the BASIC level uses the normal BASIC commands: OPEN, CLOSE, CMD, INPUT#, GET#, PRINT#, and the reserved variable ST. INPUT# and GET# fetch data from the receiving buffer, while PRINT# and CMD place data into the transmitting buffer. The use of these commands (and examples) will be described in more detail later in this chapter.

The RS-232 KERNAL byte and bit level handlers run under the control of the 6526 CIA #2 device timers and interrupts. The 6526 chip generates NMI (Non-Maskable Interrupt) requests for RS-232 processing. This allows background RS-232 processing to take place during BASIC and machine language programs. There are built-in hold-offs in the KERNAL, cassette, and serial bus routines to prevent the disruption of data storage or transmission by the NMIs that are generated by the RS-232 routines. During cassette or serial bus activities, data can NOT be received from RS-232 devices. But because these hold-offs are only local (assuming you're careful about your programming) no interference should result.

There are two buffers in the Commodore 64 RS-232 interface to help prevent the loss of data when transmitting or receiving RS-232 information.

The Commodore 64 RS-232 KERNAL buffers consist of two first-in/first-out (FIFO) buffers, each 256 bytes long, at the top of memory. The OPENing of an RS-232 channel automatically allocates 512 bytes of memory for these buffers. If there is not enough free space beyond the end of your BASIC program no error message will be printed, and the end of your program will be destroyed. **SO BE CAREFUL!**

These buffers are automatically removed by using the CLOSE command.

OPENING AN RS-232 CHANNEL

Only one RS-232 channel should be open at any time; a second OPEN statement will cause the buffer pointers to be reset. Any characters in either the transmit buffer or the receive buffer will be lost.

Up to 4 characters can be sent in the filename field. The first two are the control and command register characters; the other two are reserved for future system options. Baud rate, parity, and other options can be selected through this feature.

No error-checking is done on the control word to detect a non-implemented baud rate. Any illegal control word will cause the system output to operate at a very slow rate (below 50 baud).

BASIC SYNTAX:

OPEN lfn,2,0,"<control register><command register><opt baud low><opt baud high>"

lfn—The logical file number (lfn) then can be any number from 1 through 255. But be aware of the fact that if you choose a logical file number that is greater than 127, then a line feed will follow all carriage returns.

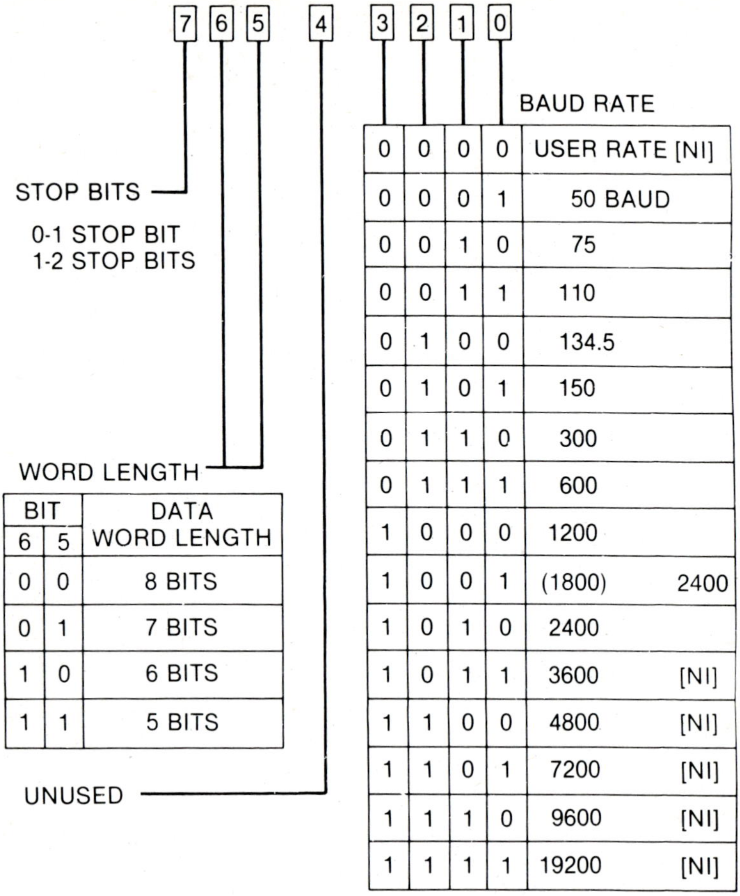

Figure 6-1. Control Register Map.

<control register>—Is a single byte character (see Figure 6-1, Control Register Map) required to specify the baud rates. If the lower 4 bits of the baud rate is equal to zero (0), the <opt baud low><opt baud high> characters give you a rate based on the following:

<opt baud low>=<system frequency/rate/2−100−<opt baud high>*256

<opt baud high>=INT((system frequency/rate/2−100)/256

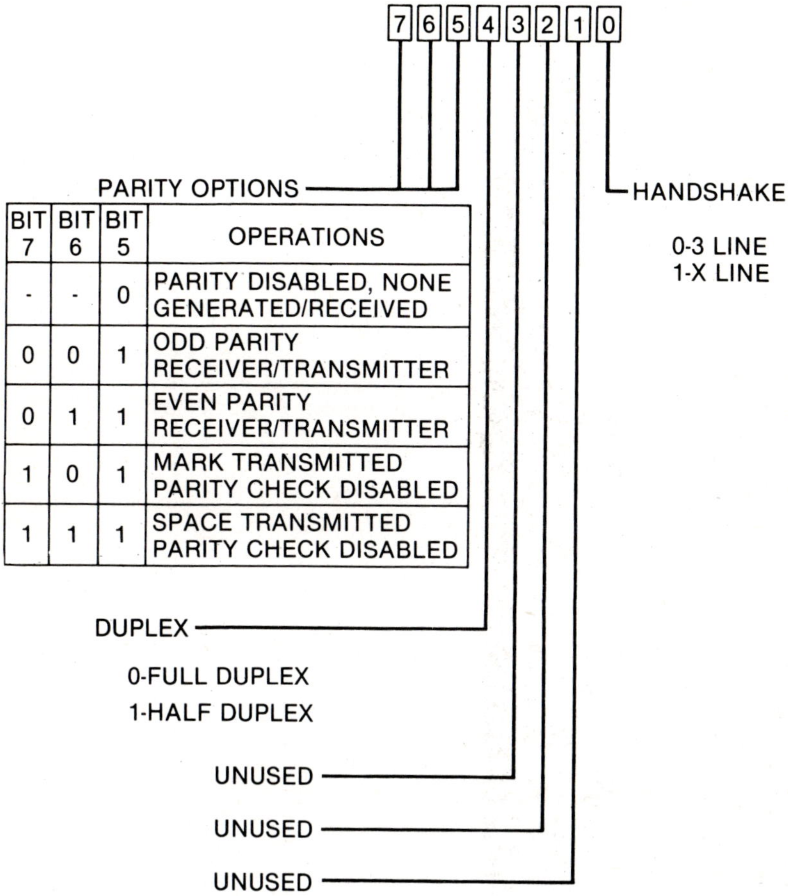

BIT 7	BIT 6	BIT 5	OPERATIONS
-	-	0	PARITY DISABLED, NONE GENERATED/RECEIVED
0	0	1	ODD PARITY RECEIVER/TRANSMITTER
0	1	1	EVEN PARITY RECEIVER/TRANSMITTER
1	0	1	MARK TRANSMITTED PARITY CHECK DISABLED
1	1	1	SPACE TRANSMITTED PARITY CHECK DISABLED

Figure 6-2. Command Register Map.

The formulas above are based on the fact that:

system frequency = 1.02273E6 NTSC (North American TV standard)
= 0.98525E6 PAL (U.K. and most European TV standard)

<command register>—Is a single byte character (see Figure 6-2, Command Register Map) that defines other terminal parameters. This character is NOT required.

KERNAL ENTRY:

OPEN ($FFC0) (See KERNAL specifications for more information on entry conditions and instructions.)

> **IMPORTANT NOTE:** In a BASIC program, the RS-232 OPEN command should be performed before creating any variables or arrays because an automatic CLR is performed when an RS-232 channel is OPENed (This is due to the allocation of 512 bytes at the top of memory.) Also remember that your program will be destroyed if 512 bytes of space are not available at the time of the OPEN statement.

GETTING DATA FROM AN RS-232 CHANNEL

When getting data from an RS-232 channel, the Commodore 64 receiver buffer will hold up to 255 characters before the buffer overflows. This is indicated in the RS-232 status word (ST in BASIC, or RSSTAT in machine language). If an overflow occurs, then all characters received during a full buffer condition, from that point on, are lost. Obviously, it pays to keep the buffer as clear as possible.

If you wish to receive RS-232 data at high speeds (BASIC can only go so fast, especially considering garbage collects. This can cause the receiver buffer to overflow), you will have to use machine language routines to handle this type of data burst.

BASIC SYNTAX:

Recommended: GET#lfn, <string variable>
NOT Recommended: INPUT#lfn ,<variable list>

KERNAL ENTRIES:

CHKIN ($FFC6)—See Memory Map for more information on entry and exit conditions.

GETIN ($FFE4)—See Memory Map for more information on entry and exit conditions.

CHRIN ($FFCF)—See Memory Map for more information on entry and exit conditions.

NOTES:

If the word length is less than 8 bits, all unused bit(s) will be assigned a value of zero.

If a GET# does not find any data in the buffer, the character "" (a null) is returned.

If INPUT# is used, then the system will hang in a waiting condition until a non-null character and a following carriage return is received. Therefore, if the Clear To Send (CTS) or DataSsette Ready (DSR) line(s) disappear during character INPUT#, the system will hang in a RESTORE-only state. This is why the INPUT# and CHRIN routines are NOT recommended.

The routine CHKIN handles the x-line handshake which follows the EIA standard (August 1979) for RS-232-C interfaces. (The Request To Send (RTS), CTS, and Received line signal (DCD) lines are implemented with the Commodore 64 computer defined as the Data Terminal device.)

SENDING DATA TO AN RS-232 CHANNEL

When sending data, the output buffer can hold 255 characters before a full buffer hold-off occurs. The system will wait in the CHROUT routine until transmission is allowed or the RUN/STOP and RESTORE keys are used to recover the system through a WARM START.

BASIC SYNTAX:

CMD lfn—acts same as in the BASIC specifications.
PRINT#lfn,<variable list>

KERNAL ENTRIES:

CHKOUT ($FFC9)—See Memory Map for more information on entry and exit conditions.

CHROUT ($FFD2)—See Memory Map for more information on entry conditions.

IMPORTANT NOTES: There is no carriage-return delay built into the output channel. This means that a normal RS-232 printer cannot correctly print, unless some form of hold-off (asking the Commodore 64 to wait) or internal buffering is implemented by the printer. The hold-off can easily be implemented in your program. If a CTS (x-line) handshake is implemented, the Commodore 64 buffer will fill, and then hold-off more output until transmission is allowed by the RS-232 device. X-line handshaking is a handshake routine that uses multi-lines for receiving and transmitting data.

The routine CHKOUT handles the x-line handshake, which follows the EIA standard (August 1979) for RS-232-C interfaces. The RTS, CTS, and DCD lines are implemented with the Commodore 64 defined as the Data Terminal Device.

CLOSING AN RS-232 DATA CHANNEL

Closing an RS-232 file discards all data in the buffers at the time of execution (whether or not it had been transmitted or printed out), stops all RS-232 transmitting and receiving, sets the RTS and transmitted data (S_{out}) lines high, and removes both RS-232 buffers.

BASIC SYNTAX:

CLOSE lfn

KERNAL ENTRY:

CLOSE ($FFC3)—See Memory Map for more information on entry and exit conditions.

NOTE: Care should be taken to ensure all data is transmitted before closing the channel. A way to check this from BASIC is:

```
100 SS=ST: IF(SS=0 OR SS=8) THEN 100
110 CLOSE lfn
```

Table 6-1. User-Port Lines

(6526 DEVICE #2 Loc. $DD00–$DD0F)						
PIN ID	**6526 ID**	**DESCRIPTION**	**EIA**	**ABV**	**IN/ OUT**	**MODES**
C	PB0	RECEIVED DATA	(BB)	S_{in}	IN	1 2
D	PB1	REQUEST TO SEND	(CA)	RTS	OUT	1*2
E	PB2	DATA TERMINAL READY	(CD)	DTR	OUT	1*2
F	PB3	RING INDICATOR	(CE)	RI	IN	3
H	PB4	RECEIVED LINE SIGNAL	(CF)	DCD	IN	2
J	PB5	UNASSIGNED	( )	XXX	IN	3
K	PB6	CLEAR TO SEND	(CB)	CTS	IN	2
L	PB7	DATA SET READY	(CC)	DSR	IN	2
B	FLAG2	RECEIVED DATA	(BB)	S_{in}	IN	1 2
M	PA2	TRANSMITTED DATA	(BA)	S_{out}	OUT	1 2
A	GND	PROTECTIVE GROUND	(AA)	GND		1 2
N	GND	SIGNAL GROUND	(AB)	GND		1 2 3

MODES:

1) 3-LINE INTERFACE (S_{in},S_{out},GND)
2) X-LINE INTERFACE
3) USER AVAILABLE ONLY (Unused/unimplemented in code.)

* These lines are held high during 3-LINE mode.

```
[7] [6] [5] [4] [3] [2] [1] [0] (Machine Lang.—RSSTAT
 :   :   :   :   :   :   :   :_PARITY ERROR BIT
 :   :   :   :   :   :   :_____FRAMING ERROR BIT
 :   :   :   :   :   :_________RECEIVER BUFFER OVERRUN BIT
 :   :   :   :   :_____________RECEIVER BUFFER—EMPTY
                               (USE TO TEST AFTER A GET#)
 :   :   :   :_________________CTS SIGNAL MISSING BIT
 :   :   :_____________________UNUSED BIT
 :   :_________________________DSR SIGNAL MISSING BIT
 :_____________________________BREAK DETECTED BIT
```

Figure 6-3. RS-232 Status Register.

NOTES:

If the BIT=0, then no error has been detected.

The RS-232 status register can be read from BASIC using the variable ST.

If ST is read by BASIC or by using the KERNAL READST routine the RS-232 status word is cleared when you exit. If multiple uses of the STATUS word are necessary the ST should be assigned to another variable. For example:

SR=ST: REM ASSIGNS ST TO SR

The RS-232 status is read (and cleared) only when the RS-232 channel was the last external I/O used.

SAMPLE BASIC PROGRAMS

```
10 REM THIS PROGRAM SENDS AND RECEIVES DATA
TO/FROM A SILENT 700
11 REM TERMINAL MODIFIED FOR PET ASCII
20 REM TI SILENT 700 SET-UP: 300 BAUD, 7-BIT ASCII,
 MARK PARITY,
21 REM FULL DUPLEX
30 REM SAME SET-UP AT COMPUTER USING 3-LINE
INTERFACE
100 OPEN 2,2,3,CHR$(6+32)+CHR$(32+128):REM OPEN
THE CHANNEL
110 GET#2,A$:REM TURN ON THE RECEIVER CHANNEL
(TOSS A NULL)
200 REM MAIN LOOP
210 GET B$:REM GET FROM COMPUTER KEYBOARD
220 IF B$<>"" THEN PRINT#2,B$;:REM IF A KEY
PRESSED, SEND TO TERMINAL
230 GET#2,C$:REM GET A KEY FROM THE TERMINAL
240 PRINT B$;C$;:REM PRINT ALL INPUTS TO COMPUTER
SCREEN
250 SR=ST: IF SR=0 OR SR=8 THEN 200:REM CHECK
STATUS, IF GOOD THEN CONTINUE
300 REM ERROR REPORTING
310 PRINT "ERROR: ";
320 IF SR AND 1 THEN PRINT "PARITY"
330 IF SR AND 2 THEN PRINT "FRAME"
340 IF SR AND 4 THEN PRINT "RECEIVER BUFFER FULL"
350 IF SR AND 128 THEN PRINT "BREAK"
360 IF (PEEK(673) AND 1) THEN 360:REM WAIT UNTIL
ALL CHARS TRANSMITTED
370 CLOSE 2: END
```

```
10 REM THIS PROGRAM SENDS AND RECEIVES TRUE ASCII
DATA
100 OPEN 5,2,3,CHR$(6)
110 DIM F%(255),T%(255)
200 FOR J=32 TO 64:T%(J)=J:NE
210 T%(13)=13:T%(20)=8:RV=18:CT=0
220 FOR J=65 TO 90:K=J+32:T%(J)=K:NEXT
230 FOR J=91 TO 95:T%(J)=J:NEXT
240 FOR J=193 TO 218:K=J-128:T%(J)=K:NEXT
250 T%(146)=16:T%(133)=16
260 FOR J=0 TO 255
270 K=T%(J)
280 IF K<>0THEN F%(K)=J:F%(K+128)=J
290 NEXT
300 PRINT " "CHR$(147)
310 GET#5,A$
320 IF A$=""OR ST<>0 THEN 360
330 PRINT " "CHR$(157);CHR$(F%(ASC(A$)));
340 IF F%(ASC(A$))=34 THEN POKE212,0
350 GOTO 310
360 PRINTCHR$(RV)" "CHR$(157);CHR$(146);:GET A$
370 IF A$<>""THENPRINT#5,CHR$(T%(ASC(A$)));
380 CT=CT+1
390 IF CT=8 THENCT=0:RV=164-RV
410 GOTO310
```

RECEIVER/TRANSMITTER BUFFER BASE LOCATION POINTERS

$00F7–RIBUF—A two-byte pointer to the Receiver Buffer base location.

$00F9–ROBUF—A two-byte pointer to the Transmitter Buffer base location.

The two locations above are set up by the OPEN KERNAL routine, each pointing to a different 256-byte buffer. They are de-allocated by writing a zero into the high order bytes ($00F8 and $00FA), which is done by the CLOSE KERNAL entry. They may also be allocated/de-allocated by the machine language programmer for his/her own purposes, removing/creating only the buffer(s) required. When using a machine language program that allocates these buffers, care must be taken to make sure that the top of memory pointers stay correct, especially if BASIC programs are expected to run at the same time.

ZERO-PAGE MEMORY LOCATIONS AND USAGE FOR RS-232 SYSTEM INTERFACE

$00A7–INBIT—Receiver input bit temp storage.
$00A8–BITCI—Receiver bit count in.
$00A9–RINONE—Receiver flag Start bit check.
$00AA–RIDATA—Receiver byte buffer/assembly location.
$00AB–RIPRTY—Receiver parity bit storage.
$00B4–BITTS—Transmitter bit count out.
$00B5–NXTBIT—Transmitter next bit to be sent.
$00B6–RODATA—Transmitter byte buffer/disassembly location.

All the above zero-page locations are used locally and are only given as a guide to understand the associated routines. These cannot be used directly by the BASIC or KERNAL level programmer to do RS-232 type things. The system RS-232 routines must be used.

NONZERO-PAGE MEMORY LOCATIONS AND USAGE FOR RS-232 SYSTEM INTERFACE

General RS-232 storage:

$0293–M51CTR—Pseudo 6551 control register (see Figure 6-1).
$0294–M51COR—Pseudo 6551 command register (see Figure 6-2).
$0295–M51AJB—Two bytes following the control and command registers in the file name field. These locations contain the baud rate for the start of the bit test during the interface activity, which, in turn, is used to calculate baud rate.
$0297–RSSTAT—The RS-232 status register (see Figure 6-3).
$0298–BITNUM—The number of bits to be sent/received.
$0299–BAUDOF—Two bytes that are equal to the time of one bit cell. (Based on system clock/baud rate.)

$029B–RIDBE—The byte index to the end of the receiver FIFO buffer.

$029C–RIDBS—The byte index to the start of the receiver FIFO buffer.

$029D–RODBS—The byte index to the start of the transmitter FIFO buffer.

$029E–RODBE—The byte index to the end of the transmitter FIFO buffer.

$02A1–ENABL—Holds current active interrupts in the CIA #2 ICR. When bit 4 is turned on means that the system is waiting for the Receiver Edge. When bit 1 is turned on then the system is receiving data. When bit 0 is turned on then the system is transmitting data.

THE USER PORT

The user port is meant to connect the Commodore 64 to the outside world. By using the lines available at this port, you can connect the Commodore 64 to a printer, a Votrax Type and Talk, a MODEM, even another computer.

The port on the Commodore 64 is directly connected to one of the 6526 CIA chips. By programming, the CIA will connect to many other devices.

PORT PIN DESCRIPTION

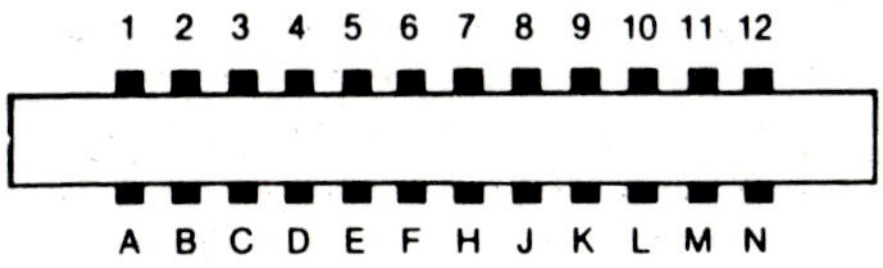

PORT PIN DESCRIPTION

PIN TOP SIDE	DESCRIPTION	NOTES
1	GROUND	
2	+5V	(100 mA MAX.)
3	RESET	By grounding this pin, the Commodore 64 will do a COLD START, resetting completely. The pointers to a BASIC program will be reset, but memory will not be cleared. This is also a RESET output for the external devices.
4	CNT1	Serial port counter from CIA #1 (SEE CIA SPECS).
5	SP1	Serial port from CIA #1 (SEE 6526 CIA SPECS).
6	CNT2	Serial port counter from CIA #2 (SEE CIA SPECS).
7	SP2	Serial port from CIA #1 (SEE 6526 CIA SPECS).
8	PC2	Handshaking line from CIA #2 (SEE CIA SPECS).
9	SERIAL ATN	This pin is connected to the ATN line of the serial bus.
10	9 VAC+phase	Connected directly to the Commodore
11	9 VAC−phase	64 transformer (50 mA MAX.).
12	GND	
BOTTOM SIDE		
A	GND	The Commodore 64 gives you control over PORT B on CIA chip #1. Eight lines for input or output are available, as well as 2 lines for handshaking with an outside device. The I/O lines for PORT B are controlled by two locations. One is the PORT itself, and is located at 56577 ($DD01 HEX). Naturally you PEEK it to read an INPUT, or POKE it to set an OUTPUT. Each of the eight I/O lines can be set up as either an INPUT or an OUTPUT by setting the DATA DIRECTION REGISTER properly.
B	FLAG2	
C	PB0	
D	PB1	
E	PB2	
F	PB3	
H	PB4	
J	PB5	
K	PB6	
L	PB7	
M	PA2	
N	GND	

The **DATA DIRECTION REGISTER** has its location at 56579 ($DD03 hex). Each of the eight lines in the PORT has a BIT in the eight-bit DATA DIRECTION REGISTER (DDR) which controls whether that line will be an input or an output. If a bit in the DDR is a ONE, the corresponding line of the PORT will be an OUTPUT. If a bit in the DDR is a ZERO, the corresponding line of the PORT will be an INPUT. For example, if bit 3 of the DDR is set to 1, then line 3 of the PORT will be an output. A further example:

If the DDR is set like this:

BIT #: 7 6 5 4 3 2 1 0
VALUE: 0 0 1 1 1 0 0 0

You can see that lines 5,4, and 3 will be outputs since those bits are ones. The rest of the lines will be inputs, since those lines are zeros.

To PEEK or POKE tne USER port, it is necessary to use both the DDR and the PORT itself.

Remember that the PEEK and POKE statements want a number from 0–255. The numbers given in the example must be translated into decimal before they can be used. The value would be:

$$2^5 + 2^4 + 2^3 = 32 + 16 + 8 = 56$$

Notice that the bit # for the DDR is the same number that = 2 raised to a power to turn the bit value on.

(16 = 2↑4=2×2×2×2, 8 = 2↑3=2×2×2)

The two other lines, FLAG1 and PA2 are different from the rest of the USER PORT. These two lines are mainly for HANDSHAKING, and are programmed differently from port B.

Handshaking is needed when two devices communicate. Since one device may run at a different speed than another device it is necessary to give the devices some way of knowing what the other device is doing. Even when the devices are operating at the same speed, handshaking is necessary to let the other know when data is to be sent, and if it has been received. The **FLAG1** line has special characteristics which make it well suited for handshaking.

FLAG1 is a negative edge sensitive input which can be used as a general purpose interrupt input. Any negative transition on the FLAG line will set the FLAG interrupt bit. If the FLAG interrupt is enabled, this will cause an INTERRUPT REQUEST. If the FLAG bit is not enabled, it can be polled from the interrupt register under program control.

PA2 is bit 2 of PORT A of the CIA. It is controlled like any other bit in the port. The port is located at 56576 ($DD00). The data direction register is located at 56578 ($DD02.)

FOR MORE INFORMATION ON THE 6526 SEE THE CHIP SPECIFICATIONS IN APPENDIX M.

THE SERIAL BUS

The serial bus is a daisy chain arrangement designed to let the Commodore 64 communicate with devices such as the VIC-1541 DISK DRIVE and the VIC-1525 GRAPHICS PRINTER. The advantage of the serial bus is that more than one device can be connected to the port. Up to 5 devices can be connected to the serial bus at one time.

There are three types of operation over a serial bus—CONTROL, TALK, and LISTEN. A CONTROLLER device is one which controls operation of the serial bus. A TALKER transmits data onto the bus. A LISTENER receives data from the bus.

The Commodore 64 is the controller of the bus. It also acts as a TALKER (when sending data to the printer, for example) and as a LISTENER (when loading a program from the disk drive, for example). Other devices may be either LISTENERS (the printer), TALKERS, or both (the disk drive). Only the Commodore 64 can act as the controller.

All devices connected on the serial bus will receive all the data transmitted over the bus. To allow the Commodore 64 to route data to its intended destination, each device has a bus ADDRESS. By using this device address, the Commodore 64 can control access to the bus. Addresses on the serial bus range from 4 to 31.

The Commodore 64 can COMMAND a particular device to TALK or LISTEN. When the Commodore 64 commands a device to TALK, the device will begin putting data onto the serial bus. When the Commodore 64 commands a device to LISTEN, the device addressed will get ready to receive data (from the Commodore 64 or from another device on the bus). Only one device can TALK on the bus at a time; otherwise, the data will collide and the system will crash in confusion. However, any number of devices can LISTEN at the same time to one TALKER.

COMMON SERIAL BUS ADDRESSES

NUMBER	DEVICE
4 or 5	VIC-1525 GRAPHIC PRINTER
8	VIC-1541 DISK DRIVE

Other device addresses are possible. Each device has its own address. Certain devices (like the Commodore 64 printer) provide a choice between two addresses for the convenience of the user.

The SECONDARY ADDRESS is to let the Commodore 64 transmit setup information to a device. For example, to OPEN a connection on the bus to the printer, and have it print in UPPER/LOWER case, use the following:

```
OPEN 1,4,7
```

where,

1 is the logical file number (the number you PRINT# to),
4 is the ADDRESS of the printer, and
7 is the SECONDARY ADDRESS that tells the printer to go into UPPER/LOWER case mode.

There are 6 lines used in serial bus operation—3 input and 3 output. The 3 input lines bring data, control, and timing signals into the Commodore 64. The 3 output lines send data, control, and timing signals from the Commodore 64 to external devices on the serial bus.

SERIAL BUS PINOUTS

PIN	DESCRIPTION
1	SERIAL SRQ IN
2	GND
3	SERIAL ATN IN/OUT
4	SERIAL CLK IN/OUT
5	SERIAL DATA IN/OUT
6	NO CONNECTION

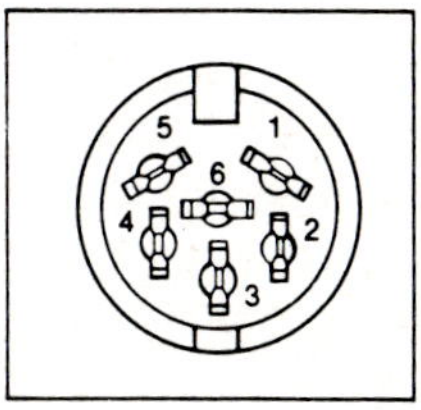

SERIAL SRQ IN: (SERIAL SERVICE REQUEST IN)

Any device on the serial bus can bring this signal LOW when it requires attention from the Commodore 64. The Commodore 64 will then take care of the device. (See Figure 6-4).

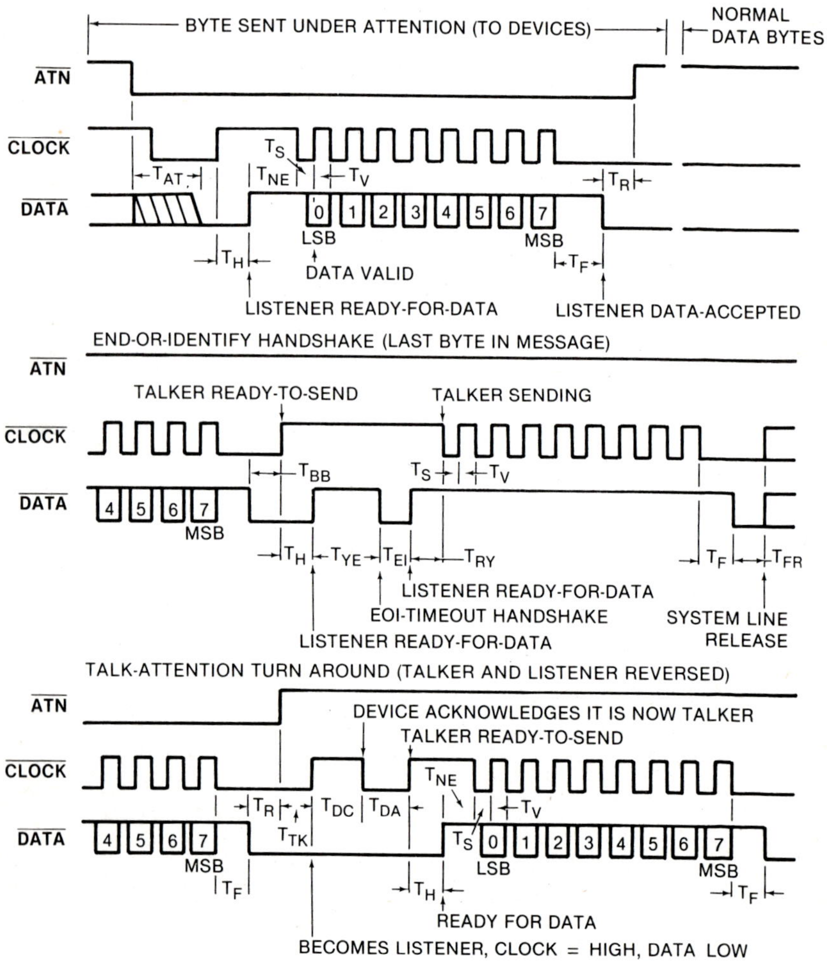

Figure 6-4. Serial

SERIAL ATN IN/OUT: (SERIAL ATTENTION IN/OUT)

The Commodore 64 uses this signal to start a command sequence for a device on the serial bus. When the Commodore 64 brings this signal LOW, all other devices on the bus start listening for the Commodore 64 to transmit an address. The device addressed must respond in a preset period of time; otherwise, the Commodore 64 will assume that the device addressed is not on the bus, and will return an error in the STATUS WORD. (See Figure 6-4).

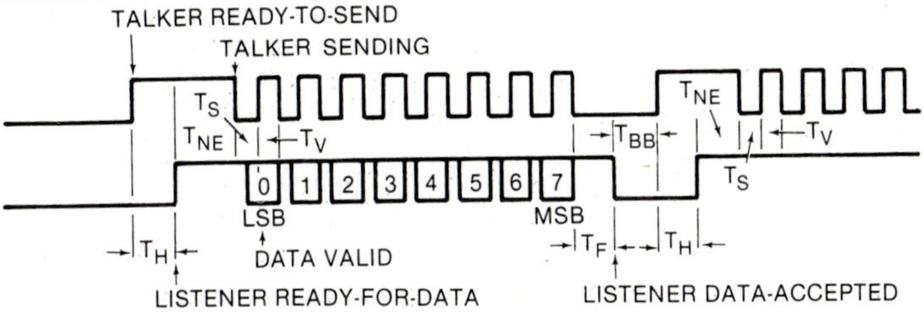

SERIAL BUS TIMING

Description	Symbol	Min.	Typ.	Max.
ATN RESPONSE (REQUIRED)[1]	T_{AT}	—	—	1000μ
LISTENER HOLD-OFF	T_H	0	—	∞
NON-EOI RESPONSE TO RFD[2]	T_{NE}	—	40μs	200μs
BIT SET-UP TALKER[4]	T_S	20μs	70μs	—
DATA VALID	T_V	20μs	20μs	—
FRAME HANDSHAKE[3]	T_F	0	20	1000μs
FRAME TO RELEASE OF ATN	T_R	20μs	—	—
BETWEEN BYTES TIME	T_{BB}	100μs	—	—
EOI RESPONSE TIME	T_{YE}	200μs	250μs	—
EOI RESPONSE HOLD TIME[5]	T_{EI}	60μs	—	—
TALKER RESPONSE LIMIT	T_{RY}	0	30μs	60μs
BYTE-ACKNOWLEDGE[4]	T_{PR}	20μs	30μs	—
TALK-ATTENTION RELEASE	T_{TK}	20μs	30μs	100μs
TALK-ATTENTION ACKNOWLEDGE	T_{DC}	0	—	—
TALK-ATTENTION ACK. HOLD	T_{DA}	80μs	—	—
EOI ACKNOWLEDGE	T_{FR}	60μs	—	—

Notes:
1. If maximum time exceeded, device not present error.
2. If maximum time exceeded, EOI response required.
3. If maximum time exceeded, frame error.
4. T_V and T_{PR} minimum must be 60μs for external device to be a talker.
5. T_{EI} minimum must be 80μs for external device to be a listener.

Bus Timing.

SERIAL CLK IN/OUT: (SERIAL CLOCK IN/OUT)

This signal is used for timing the data sent on the serial bus. (See Figure 6-4).

SERIAL DATA IN/OUT:

Data on the serial bus is transmitted one bit at a time on this line. (See Figure 6-4.)

THE EXPANSION PORT

The expansion connector is a 44-pin (22/22) female edge connector on the back of the Commodore 64. With the Commodore 64 facing you, the expansion connector is on the far right of the back of the computer. To use the connector, a 44-pin (22/22) male edge connector is required.

This port is used for expansions of the Commodore 64 system which require access to the address bus or the data bus of the computer. Caution is necessary when using the expansion bus, because it's possible to damage the Commodore 64 by a malfunction of your equipment.

The expansion bus is arranged as follows:

The signals available on the connector are as follows:

NAME	PIN	DESCRIPTION
GND	1	System ground
+5 VDC	2	(Total USER PORT and CARTRIDGE devices can
+5 VDC	3	draw no more than 450 mA.)
$\overline{\text{IRQ}}$	4	Interrupt Request line to 6502 (active low)
R/$\overline{\text{W}}$	5	Read/Write
DOT CLOCK	6	8.18 MHz video dot clock
$\overline{\text{I/O1}}$	7	I/O block 1 @ \$DE00–\$DEFF (active low) unbuffered I/O
$\overline{\text{GAME}}$	8	active low ls ttl input
$\overline{\text{EXROM}}$	9	active low ls ttl input
$\overline{\text{I/O2}}$	10	I/O block 2 @ \$DF00–\$DFFF (active low) buff'ed ls ttl output

NAME	PIN	DESCRIPTION
$\overline{\text{ROML}}$	11	8K decoded RAM/ROM block @ $8000 (active low) buffered ls ttl output
BA	12	Bus available signal from the VIC-II chip unbuffered 1 ls load max.
$\overline{\text{DMA}}$	13	Direct memory access request line (active low input) ls ttl input
D7	14	Data bus bit 7
D6	15	Data bus bit 6
D5	16	Data bus bit 5
D4	17	Data bus bit 4 — unbuffered, 1 ls ttl load max (D7–D0)
D3	18	Data bus bit 3
D2	19	Data bus bit 2
D1	20	Data bus bit 1
D0	21	Data bus bit 0
GND	22	System ground
GND	A	
$\overline{\text{ROMH}}$	B	8K decoded RAM/ROM block @ $E000 buffered
$\overline{\text{RESET}}$	C	6502 RESET pin (active low) buff'ed ttl out/unbuff'ed in
$\overline{\text{NMI}}$	D	6502 Non Maskable Interrupt (active low) buff'ed ttl out, unbuff'ed in
$\phi 2$	E	Phase 2 system clock
A15	F	Address bus bit 15
A14	H	Address bus bit 14
A13	J	Address bus bit 13
A12	K	Address bus bit 12
A11	L	Address bus bit 11
A10	M	Address bus bit 10
A9	N	Address bus bit 9
A8	P	Address bus bit 8 — unbuffered, 1 ls ttl load max (A15–A0)
A7	R	Address bus bit 7
A6	S	Address bus bit 6
A5	T	Address bus bit 5
A4	U	Address bus bit 4
A3	V	Address bus bit 3
A2	W	Address bus bit 2
A1	X	Address bus bit 1
A0	Y	Address bus bit 0
GND	Z	System ground

Overbar means active low

Following is a description of some important lines on the expansion port:

Pins 1,22,A,Z are connected to the system ground.

Pin 6 is the DOT CLOCK. This is the 8.18-MHz video dot clock. All system timing is derived from this clock.

Pin 12 is the BA (BUS AVAILABLE) signal from the VIC-II chip. This line will go low 3 cycles before the VIC-II takes over the system busses, and remains low until the VIC-II is finished fetching display information.

Pin 13 is the DMA (DIRECT MEMORY ACCESS) line. When this line is pulled low, the address bus, the data bus, and the Read/Write line of the 6510 processor chip enter high-impedance state mode. This allows an external processor to take control of the system busses. This line should only be pulled low when the $\phi 2$ clock is low. Also, since the VIC-II chip will continue to perform display DMA, the external device must conform to the VIC-II timing. (See VIC-II timing diagram.) This line is pulled up on the Commodore 64.

Z-80 MICROPROCESSOR CARTRIDGE

Reading this book and using your computer has shown you just how versatile your Commodore 64 really is. But what makes this machine even more capable of meeting your needs is the addition of peripheral equipment. Peripherals are things like Datassette™ recorders, disk drives, printers, and modems. All these items can be added to your Commodore 64 through the various ports and sockets on the back of your machine. The thing that makes Commodore peripherals so good is the fact that our peripherals are "intelligent." That means that they don't take up valuable Random Access Memory space when they're in use. You're free to use all 64K of memory in your Commodore 64.

Another advantage of your Commodore 64 is the fact most programs you write on your Commodore 64 today will be upwardly compatible with any new Commodore computer you buy in the future. This is partially because of the qualities of the computer's Operating System (OS).

However, there is one thing that the Commodore OS can't do: make your programs compatible with a computer made by another company.

Most of the time you won't even have to think about using another company's computer, because your Commodore 64 is so easy to use. But for the occasional user who wants to take advantage of software that may not be available in Commodore 64 format we have created a Commodore CP/M® cartridge.

CP/M® is not a "computer dependent" operating system. Instead it uses some of the memory space normally available for programming to run its own operating system. There are advantages and disadvantages to this. The disadvantages are that the programs you write will have to be shorter than the programs you can write using the Commodore 64's built-in operating system. In addition, you can NOT use the Commodore 64's powerful screen editing capabilities. The advantages are that you can now use a large amount of software that has been specifically designed for CP/M® and the Z-80 microprocessor, and the programs that you write using the CP/M® operating system can be transported and run on any other computer that has CP/M® and a Z-80 card.

By the way, most computers that have a Z-80 microprocessor require that you go inside the computer to actually install a Z-80 card. With this method you have to be very careful not to disturb the delicate circuitry that runs the rest of the computer. The Commodore CP/M® cartridge eliminates this hassle because our Z-80 cartridge plugs into the back of your Commodore 64 quickly and easily, without any messy wires that can cause problems later.

USING COMMODORE CP/M®

The Commodore Z-80 cartridge let's you run programs designed for a Z-80 microprocessor on your Commodore 64. The cartridge is provided with a diskette containing the Commodore CP/M® operating system.

RUNNING COMMODORE CP/M®

To run CP/M®:

1) LOAD the CP/M® program from your disk drive.
2) Type RUN.
3) Hit the RETURN key.

At this point the 64K bytes of RAM in the Commodore 64 are accessible by the built-in 6510 central processor, OR 48K bytes of RAM are available for the Z-80 central processor. You can shift back and forth between these two processors, but you can NOT use them at the same time in a single program. This is possible because of your Commodore 64's sophisticated timing mechanism.

Below is the memory address translation that is performed on the Z-80 cartridge. You should notice that by adding 4096 bytes to the memory locations used in CP/M® $1000 (hex) you equal the memory addresses of the normal Commodore 64 operating system. The correspondence between Z-80 and 6510 memory addresses is as follows:

Z-80 ADDRESSES		6510 ADDRESSES	
DECIMAL	HEX	DECIMAL	HEX
0000–4095	0000–0FFF	4096–8191	1000–1FFF
4096–8191	1000–1FFF	8192–12287	2000–2FFF
8192–12287	2000–2FFF	12288–16383	3000–3FFF
12288–16383	3000–3FFF	16384–20479	4000–4FFF
16384–20479	4000–4FFF	20480–24575	5000–5FFF
20480–24575	5000–5FFF	24576–28671	6000–6FFF
24576–28671	6000–6FFF	28672–32767	7000–7FFF
28672–32767	7000–7FFF	32768–36863	8000–8FFF
32768–36863	8000–8FFF	36864–40959	9000–9FFF
36864–40959	9000–9FFF	40960–45055	A000–AFFF
40960–45055	A000–AFFF	45056–49151	B000–BFFF
45056–49151	B000–BFFF	49152–53247	C000–CFFF
49152–53247	C000–CFFF	53248–57343	D000–DFFF
53248–57343	D000–DFFF	57344–61439	E000–EFFF
57344–61439	E000–EFFF	61440–65535	F000–FFFF
61440–65535	F000–FFFF	0000–4095	0000–0FFF

To TURN ON the Z-80 and TURN OFF the 6510 chip, type in the following program:

```
10 REM THIS PROGRAM IS TO BE USED WITH THE Z80 CARD
20 REM IT FIRST STORES Z80 DATA AT $1000
(Z80=$0000)
30 REM THEN IT TURNS OFF THE 6510 IRQ'S AND ENABLES
40 REM THE Z80 CARD.  THE Z80 CARD MUST BE TURNED
OFF
50 REM TO REENABLE THE 6510 SYSTEM.
100 REM STORE Z80 DATA
110 READ B: REM GET SIZE OF Z80 CODE TO BE MOVED
120 FOR I=4096 TO 4096+B-1:REM MOVE CODE
130 READ A:POKE I,A
140 NEXT I
200 REM RUN Z80 CODE
210 POKE 56333,127 : REM TURN OF 6510 IRQ'S
220 POKE 56832,00  : REM TURN ON Z80 CARD
230 POKE 56333,129 : REM TURN ON 6510 IRQ'S WHEN
Z80 DONE
240 END
1000 REM Z80 MACHINE LANGUAGE CODE DATA SECTION
1010 DATA 18 : REM SIZE OF DATA TO BE PASSED
1100 REM Z80 TURN ON CODE
1110 DATA 00,00,00 : REM OUR Z80 CARD REQUIRES
TURN ON TIME AT $0000
1200 REM Z80 TASK DATA HERE
1210 DATA 33,02,245 : REM LD HL,NN (LOCATION ON
SCREEN)
1220 DATA 52 : REM INC HL (INCREMENT THAT LOCATION)
1300 REM Z80 SELF-TURN OFF DATA HERE
1310 DATA 62,01 : REM LD A,N
1320 DATA 50,00,206 : REM LD (NN),A :I/O LOCATION
1330 DATA 00,00,00 : REM NOP: NOP: NOP
1340 DATA 195,00,00 : REM JMP $0000
```

For more details about Commodore CP/M® and the Z-80 microprocessor look for the cartridge and the Z-80 Reference Guide at your local Commodore computer dealer.

APPENDICES

ABBREVIATIONS FOR BASIC KEYWORDS

As a time-saver when typing in programs and commands, Commodore 64 BASIC allows the user to abbreviate most keywords. The abbreviation for PRINT is a question mark. The abbreviations for other words are made by typing the first one or two letters of the word, followed by the SHIFTed next letter of the word. If the abbreviations are used in a program line, the keyword will LIST in the full form.

Command	Abbreviation	Looks like this on screen
ABS	A SHIFT B	A ▎
AND	A SHIFT N	A ╱
ASC	A SHIFT S	A ♥
ATN	A SHIFT T	A ▏
CHR$	C SHIFT H	C ▕
CLOSE	CL SHIFT O	CL ▏
CLR	C SHIFT L	C ▁
CMD	C SHIFT M	C ╲
CONT	C SHIFT O	C ▏
COS	NONE	COS
DATA	D SHIFT A	D ♠
DEF	D SHIFT E	D ▔
DIM	D SHIFT I	D ╮
END	E SHIFT N	E ╱
EXP	E SHIFT X	E ♣
FN	NONE	FN
FOR	F SHIFT O	F ▏
FRE	F SHIFT R	F ▁
GET	G SHIFT E	G ▔
GET#	NONE	GET#
GOSUB	GO SHIFT S	GO ♥
GOTO	G SHIFT O	G ▏
IF	NONE	IF
INPUT	NONE	INPUT
INPUT#	I SHIFT N	I ╱
INT	NONE	INT

Command	Abbreviation	Looks like this on screen	Command	Abbreviation	Looks like this on screen
LEFT$	LE SHIFT F	LE	RIGHT$	R SHIFT I	R
LEN	NONE	LEN	RND	R SHIFT N	R
LET	L SHIFT E	L	RUN	R SHIFT U	R
LIST	L SHIFT I	L	SAVE	S SHIFT A	S ♠
LOAD	L SHIFT O	L	SGN	S SHIFT G	S
LOG	NONE	LOG	SIN	S SHIFT I	S
MID$	M SHIFT I	M	SPC(	S SHIFT P	S
NEW	NONE	NEW	SQR	S SHIFT Q	S ●
NEXT	N SHIFT E	N	STATUS	ST	ST
NOT	N SHIFT O	N	STEP	ST SHIFT E	ST
ON	NONE	ON	STOP	S SHIFT T	S
OPEN	O SHIFT P	O	STR$	ST SHIFT R	ST
OR	NONE	OR	SYS	S SHIFT Y	S
PEEK	P SHIFT E	P	TAB(	T SHIFT A	T ♠
POKE	P SHIFT O	P	TAN	NONE	TAN
POS	NONE	POS	THEN	T SHIFT H	T
PRINT	?	?	TIME	TI	TI
PRINT#	P SHIFT R	P	TIME$	TI$	TI$
READ	R SHIFT E	R	USR	U SHIFT S	U ♥
REM	NONE	REM	VAL	V SHIFT A	V ♠
RESTORE	RE SHIFT S	RE ♥	VERIFY	V SHIFT E	V
RETURN	RE SHIFT T	RE	WAIT	W SHIFT A	W ♠

SCREEN DISPLAY CODES

The following chart lists all of the characters built into the Commodore 64 character sets. It shows which numbers should be POKEd into screen memory (locations 1024-2023) to get a desired character. Also shown is which character corresponds to a number PEEKed from the screen.

Two character sets are available, but only one set at a time. This means that you cannot have characters from one set on the screen at the same time you have characters from the other set displayed. The sets are switched by holding down the SHIFT and C= keys simultaneously.

From BASIC, POKE 53272,21 will switch to upper case mode and POKE 53272,23 switches to lower case.

Any number on the chart may also be displayed in REVERSE. The reverse character code may be obtained by adding 128 to the values shown.

If you want to display a solid circle at location 1504, POKE the code for the circle (81) into location 1504: POKE 1504,81.

There is a corresponding memory location to control the color of each character displayed on the screen (locations 55296-56295). To change the color of the circle to yellow (color code 7) you would POKE the corresponding memory location (55776) with the character color: POKE 55776,7.

Refer to Appendix D for the complete screen and color memory maps, along with color codes.

NOTE: The following POKEs display the same symbol in set 1 and 2: 1, 27–64, 91–93, 96–104, 106–121, 123–127.

SCREEN CODES

SET 1	SET 2	POKE	SET 1	SET 2	POKE	SET 1	SET 2	POKE
@		0	C	c	3	F	f	6
A	a	1	D	d	4	G	g	7
B	b	2	E	e	5	H	h	8

SET 1	SET 2	POKE	SET 1	SET 2	POKE	SET 1	SET 2	POKE
I	i	9	%		37	♠	A	65
J	j	10	&		38	│	B	66
K	k	11	'		39	─	C	67
L	l	12	(		40	─	D	68
M	m	13	)		41	▔	E	69
N	n	14	*		42	▁	F	70
O	o	15	+		43	▏	G	71
P	p	16	,		44	▕	H	72
Q	q	17	–		45	╮	I	73
R	r	18	.		46	╰	J	74
S	s	19	/		47	╯	K	75
T	t	20	0		48	└	L	76
U	u	21	1		49	╲	M	77
V	v	22	2		50	╱	N	78
W	w	23	3		51	┌	O	79
X	x	24	4		52	┐	P	80
Y	y	25	5		53	●	Q	81
Z	z	26	6		54	▁	R	82
[		27	7		55	♥	S	83
£		28	8		56	▏	T	84
]		29	9		57	╭	U	85
↑		30	:		58	╳	V	86
←		31	;		59	○	W	87
SPACE		32	<		60	♣	X	88
!		33	=		61	▕	Y	89
"		34	>		62	♦	Z	90
#		35	?		63	┼		91
$		36	─		64	▒		92

SET 1	SET 2	POKE	SET 1	SET 2	POKE	SET 1	SET 2	POKE
		93			105			117
		94			106			118
		95			107			119
SPACE		96			108			120
		97			109			121
		98			110			122
		99			111			123
		100			112			124
		101			113			125
		102			114			126
		103			115			127
		104			116			

Codes from 128-255 are reversed images of codes 0-127.

APPENDIX C

ASCII AND CHR$ CODES

This appendix shows you what characters will appear if you PRINT CHR$(X), for all possible values of X. It will also show the values obtained by typing PRINT ASC("x"), where x is any character you can type. This is useful in evaluating the character received in a GET statement, converting upper/lower case, and printing character based commands (like switch to upper/lower case) that could not be enclosed in quotes.

PRINTS	CHR$	PRINTS	CHR$	PRINTS	CHR$	PRINTS	CHR$
	0	CRSR ↓	17	"	34	3	51
	1	RVS ON	18	#	35	4	52
	2	CLR HOME	19	$	36	5	53
	3	INST DEL	20	%	37	6	54
	4		21	&	38	7	55
WHT	5		22	'	39	8	56
	6		23	(	40	9	57
	7		24	)	41	:	58
DISABLES SHIFT C=	8		25	*	42	;	59
ENABLES SHIFT C=	9		26	+	43	<	60
	10		27	,	44	=	61
	11	RED	28	–	45	>	62
	12	CRSR →	29	.	46	?	63
RETURN	13	GRN	30	/	47	@	64
SWITCH TO LOWER CASE	14	BLU	31	0	48	A	65
	15	SPACE	32	1	49	B	66
	16	!	33	2	50	C	67

PRINTS	CHR$	PRINTS	CHR$	PRINTS	CHR$	PRINTS	CHR$
D	68	♠	97		126	Grey 3	155
E	69		98		127	PUR	156
F	70		99		128	CRSR	157
G	71		100	Orange	129	YEL	158
H	72		101		130	CYN	159
I	73		102		131	SPACE	160
J	74		103		132		161
K	75		104	f1	133		162
L	76		105	f3	134		163
M	77		106	f5	135		164
N	78		107	f7	136		165
O	79		108	f2	137		166
P	80		109	f4	138		167
Q	81		110	f6	139		168
R	82		111	f8	140		169
S	83		112	SHIFT RETURN	141		170
T	84	●	113	SWITCH TO UPPER CASE	142		171
U	85		114		143		172
V	86	♥	115	BLK	144		173
W	87		116	CRSR	145		174
X	88		117	RVS OFF	146		175
Y	89		118	CLR HOME	147		176
Z	90	○	119	INST DEL	148		177
[	91	♣	120	Brown	149		178
£	92		121	Lt. Red	150		179
]	93	♦	122	Grey 1	151		180
↑	94		123	Grey 2	152		181
←	95		124	Lt. Green	153		182
	96		125	Lt. Blue	154		183

PRINTS	CHR$	PRINTS	CHR$	PRINTS	CHR$	PRINTS	CHR$
	184		186		188		190
	185		187		189		191

CODES	**192-223**	**SAME AS**	**96-127**
CODES	**224-254**	**SAME AS**	**160-190**
CODE	**255**	**SAME AS**	**126**

APPENDIX D

SCREEN AND COLOR MEMORY MAPS

The following charts list which memory locations control placing characters on the screen, and the locations used to change individual character colors, as well as showing character color codes.

SCREEN MEMORY MAP

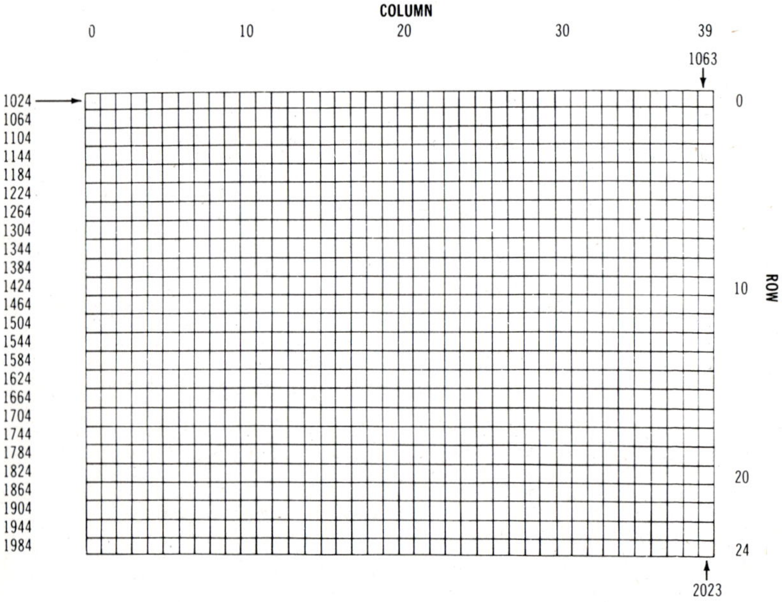

The actual values to POKE into a color memory location to change a character's color are:

Ø	BLACK	8	ORANGE
1	WHITE	9	BROWN
2	RED	1Ø	Light RED
3	CYAN	11	GRAY 1
4	PURPLE	12	GRAY 2
5	GREEN	13	Light GREEN
6	BLUE	14	Light BLUE
7	YELLOW	15	GRAY 3

For example, to change the color of a character located at the upper left-hand corner of the screen to red, type: POKE 55296,2.

COLOR MEMORY MAP

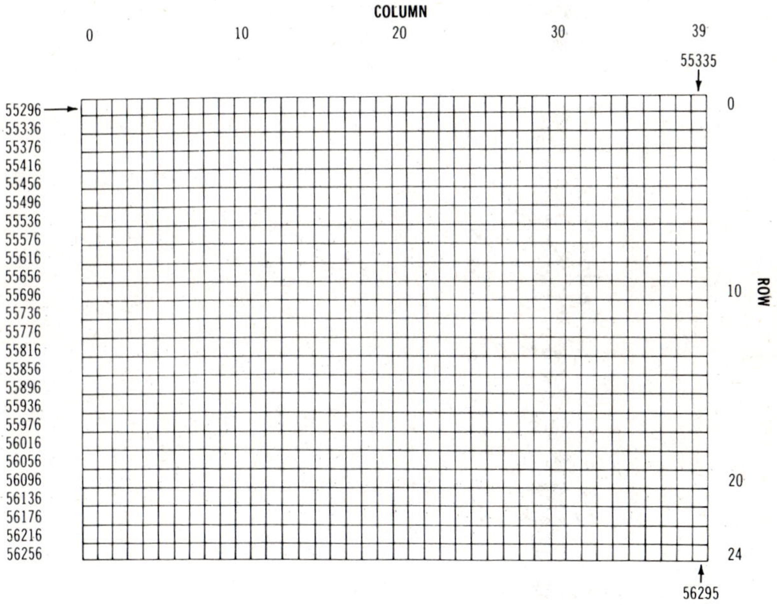

MUSIC NOTE VALUES

This appendix contains a complete list of Note#, actual note, and the values to be POKEd into the HI FREQ and LOW FREQ registers of the sound chip to produce the indicated note.

MUSICAL NOTE		OSCILLATOR FREQ		
NOTE	OCTAVE	DECIMAL	HI	LOW
0	C–0	268	1	12
1	C#–0	284	1	28
2	D–0	301	1	45
3	D#–0	318	1	62
4	E–0	337	1	81
5	F–0	358	1	102
6	F#–0	379	1	123
7	G–0	401	1	145
8	G#–0	425	1	169
9	A–0	451	1	195
10	A#–0	477	1	221
11	B–0	506	1	250
16	C–1	536	2	24
17	C#–1	568	2	56
18	D–1	602	2	90
19	D#–1	637	2	125
20	E–1	675	2	163
21	F–1	716	2	204
22	F#–1	758	2	246
23	G–1	803	3	35
24	G#–1	851	3	83
25	A–1	902	3	134
26	A#–1	955	3	187
27	B–1	1012	3	244
32	C–2	1072	4	48

MUSICAL NOTE		OSCILLATOR FREQ		
NOTE	OCTAVE	DECIMAL	HI	LOW
33	C#–2	1136	4	112
34	D–2	1204	4	180
35	D#–2	1275	4	251
36	E–2	1351	5	71
37	F–2	1432	5	152
38	F#–2	1517	5	237
39	G–2	1607	6	71
40	G#–2	1703	6	167
41	A–2	1804	7	12
42	A#–2	1911	7	119
43	B–2	2025	7	233
48	C–3	2145	8	97
49	C#–3	2273	8	225
50	D–3	2408	9	104
51	D#–3	2551	9	247
52	E–3	2703	10	143
53	F–3	2864	11	48
54	F#–3	3034	11	218
55	G–3	3215	12	143
56	G#–3	3406	13	78
57	A–3	3608	14	24
58	A#–3	3823	14	239
59	B–3	4050	15	210
64	C–4	4291	16	195
65	C#–4	4547	17	195
66	D–4	4817	18	209
67	D#–4	5103	19	239
68	E–4	5407	21	31
69	F–4	5728	22	96
70	F#–4	6069	23	181
71	G–4	6430	25	30
72	G#–4	6812	26	156
73	A–4	7217	28	49
74	A#–4	7647	29	223
75	B–4	8101	31	165
80	C–5	8583	33	135
81	C#–5	9094	35	134

MUSICAL NOTE		OSCILLATOR FREQ		
NOTE	OCTAVE	DECIMAL	HI	LOW
82	D–5	9634	37	162
83	D#–5	10207	39	223
84	E–5	10814	42	62
85	F–5	11457	44	193
86	F#–5	12139	47	107
87	G–5	12860	50	60
88	G#–5	13625	53	57
89	A–5	14435	56	99
90	A#–5	15294	59	190
91	B–5	16203	63	75
96	C–6	17167	67	15
97	C#–6	18188	71	12
98	D–6	19269	75	69
99	D#–6	20415	79	191
100	E–6	21629	84	125
101	F–6	22915	89	131
102	F#–6	24278	94	214
103	G–6	25721	100	121
104	G#–6	27251	106	115
105	A–6	28871	112	199
106	A#–6	30588	119	124
107	B–6	32407	126	151
112	C–7	34334	134	30
113	C#–7	36376	142	24
114	D–7	38539	150	139
115	D#–7	40830	159	126
116	E–7	43258	168	250
117	F–7	45830	179	6
118	F#–7	48556	189	172
119	G–7	51443	200	243
120	G#–7	54502	212	230
121	A–7	57743	225	143
122	A#–7	61176	238	248
123	B–7	64814	253	46

FILTER SETTINGS

Location	Contents
54293	Low cutoff frequency (0–7)
54294	High cutoff frequency (0–255)
54295	Resonance (bits 4–7) Filter voice 3 (bit 2) Filter voice 2 (bit 1) Filter voice 1 (bit 0)
54296	High pass (bit 6) Bandpass (bit 5) Low pass (bit 4) Volume (bits 0–3)

APPENDIX F

BIBLIOGRAPHY

Addison-Wesley	"BASIC and the Personal Computer", Dwyer and Critchfield
Compute	"Compute's First Book of PET/CBM"
Cowbay Computing	"Feed Me, I'm Your PET Computer", Carol Alexander
	"Looking Good with Your PET", Carol Alexander
	"Teacher's PET—Plans, Quizzes, and Answers"
Creative Computing	"Getting Acquainted With Your VIC 20", T. Hartnell
Dilithium Press	"BASIC Basic-English Dictionary for the PET", Larry Noonan
	"PET BASIC", Tom Rugg and Phil Feldman
Faulk Baker Associates	"MOS Programming Manual", MOS Technology
Hayden Book Co.	"BASIC From the Ground Up", David E. Simon
	"I Speak BASIC to My PET", Aubrey Jones, Jr.
	"Library of PET Subroutines", Nick Hampshire
	"PET Graphics", Nick Hampshire
	"BASIC Conversions Handbook, Apple, TRS-80, and PET", David A. Brain, Phillip R. Oviatt, Paul J. Paquin, and Chandler P. Stone

Howard W. Sams	"The Howard W. Sams Crash Course in Microcomputers", Louis E. Frenzel, Jr.
	"Mostly BASIC: Applications for Your PET", Howard Berenbon
	"PET Interfacing", James M. Downey and Steven M. Rogers
	"VIC 20 Programmer's Reference Guide", A. Finkel, P. Higginbottom, N. Harris, and M. Tomczyk
Little, Brown & Co.	"Computer Games for Businesses, Schools, and Homes", J. Victor Nagigian, and William S. Hodges
	"The Computer Tutor: Learning Activities for Homes and Schools", Gary W. Orwig, University of Central Florida, and William S. Hodges
McGraw-Hill	"Hands-On BASIC With a PET", Herbert D. Peckman
	"Home and Office Use of VisiCalc", D. Castlewitz, and L. Chisauki
Osborne/McGraw-Hill	"PET/CBM Personal Computer Guide", Carroll S. Donahue
	"PET Fun and Games", R. Jeffries and G. Fisher
	"PET and the IEEE", A. Osborne and C. Donahue
	"Some Common BASIC Programs for the PET", L. Poole, M. Borchers, and C. Donahue
	"Osborne CP/M User Guide", Thom Hogan
	"CBM Professional Computer Guide"
	"The PET Personal Guide"
	"The 8086 Book", Russell Rector and George Alexy
P. C. Publications	"Beginning Self-Teaching Computer Lessons"

Prentice-Hall	"The PET Personal Computer for Beginners", S. Dunn and V. Morgan
Reston Publishing Co.	"PET and the IEEE 488 Bus (GPIB)", Eugene Fisher and C. W. Jensen
	"PET BASIC—Training Your PET Computer", Ramon Zamora, Wm. F. Carrie, and B. Allbrecht
	"PET Games and Recreation", M. Ogelsby, L. Lindsey, and D. Kunkin
	"PET BASIC", Richard Huskell
	"VIC Games and Recreation"
Telmas Courseware Ratings	"BASIC and the Personal Computer", T. A. Dwyer, and M. Critchfield
Total Information Services	"Understanding Your PET/CBM, Vol. 1, BASIC Programming"
	"Understanding Your VIC", David Schultz

Commodore Magazines provide you with the most up-to-date information for your Commodore 64. Two of the most popular publications that you should seriously consider subscribing to are:

COMMODORE—*The Microcomputer Magazine* is published bi-monthly and is available by subscription ($15.00 per year, U.S., and $25.00 per year, worldwide).

POWER/PLAY—*The Home Computer Magazine* is published quarterly and is available by subscription ($10.00 per year, U.S., and $15.00 per year worldwide).

VIC CHIP REGISTER MAP

53248 ($D000) Starting (Base) Address

Register # Dec	Hex	DB7	DB6	DB5	DB4	DB3	DB2	DB1	DB0	
0	0	S0X7							S0X0	SPRITE 0 X Component
1	1	S0Y7							S0Y0	SPRITE 0 Y Component
2	2	S1X7							S1X0	SPRITE 1 X
3	3	S1Y7							S1Y0	SPRITE 1 Y
4	4	S2X7							S2X0	SPRITE 2 X
5	5	S2Y7							S2Y0	SPRITE 2 Y
6	6	S3X7							S3X0	SPRITE 3 X
7	7	S3Y7							S3Y0	SPRITE 3 Y
8	8	S4X7							S4X0	SPRITE 4 X
9	9	S4Y7							S4Y0	SPRITE 4 Y
10	A	S5X7							S5X0	SPRITE 5 X
11	B	S5Y7							S5Y0	SPRITE 5 Y
12	C	S6X7							S6X0	SPRITE 6 X
13	D	S6Y7							S6Y0	SPRITE 6 Y
14	E	S7X7							S7X0	SPRITE 7 X Component
15	F	S7Y7							S7Y0	SPRITE 7 Y Component
16	10	S7X8	S6X8	S5X8	S4X8	S3X8	S2X8	S1X8	S0X8	MSB of X COORD.
17	11	RC8	ECM	BMM	BLNK	RSEL	YSCL2	YSCL1	YSCL0	Y SCROLL MODE
18	12	RC7	RC6	RC5	RC4	RC3	RC2	RC1	RC0	RASTER
19	13	LPX7							LPX0	LIGHT PEN X
20	14	LPY7							LPY0	LIGHT PEN Y

Register # Dec	Hex	DB7	DB6	DB5	DB4	DB3	DB2	DB1	DB0	
21	15	SE7							SE0	SPRITE ENABLE (ON/OFF)
22	16	N.C.	N.C.	RST	MCM	CSEL	XSCL2	XSCL1	XSCL0	X SCROLL MODE
23	17	SEXY7							SEXY0	SPRITE EXPAND Y
24	18	VS13	VS12	VS11	VS10	CB13	CB12	CB11	N.C.	SCREEN and Character Memory Base Address
25	19	IRQ	N.C.	N.C.	N.C.	LPIRQ	ISSC	ISBC	RIRQ	Interrupt Request's
26	1A	N.C.	N.C.	N.C.	N.C.	MLPI	MISSC	MISBC	MRIRQ	Interrupt Request MASKS
27	1B	BSP7							BSP0	Background-Sprite PRIORITY
28	1C	SCM7							SCM0	MULTICOLOR SPRITE SELECT
29	1D	SEXX7							SEXX0	SPRITE EXPAND X
30	1E	SSC7							SSC0	Sprite-Sprite COLLISION
31	1F	SBC7							SBC0	Sprite-Background COLLISION

Register # Dec	Hex	Color
32	20	BORDER COLOR
33	21	BACKGROUND COLOR 0
34	22	BACKGROUND COLOR 1
35	23	BACKGROUND COLOR 2
36	24	BACKGROUND COLOR 3
37	25	SPRITE MULTICOLOR 0
38	26	SPRITE MULTICOLOR 1

Register # Dec	Hex	Color
39	27	SPRITE 0 COLOR
40	28	SPRITE 1 COLOR
41	29	SPRITE 2 COLOR
42	2A	SPRITE 3 COLOR
43	2B	SPRITE 4 COLOR
44	2C	SPRITE 5 COLOR
45	2D	SPRITE 6 COLOR
46	2E	SPRITE 7 COLOR

COLOR CODES

Dec	Hex	Color
0	0	BLACK
1	1	WHITE
2	2	RED
3	3	CYAN
4	4	PURPLE
5	5	GREEN
6	6	BLUE
7	7	YELLOW

Dec	Hex	Color
8	8	ORANGE
9	9	BROWN
10	A	LT RED
11	B	GRAY 1
12	C	GRAY 2
13	D	LT GREEN
14	E	LT BLUE
15	F	GRAY 3

LEGEND:
ONLY COLORS 0-7 MAY BE USED IN MULTICOLOR CHARACTER MODE

APPENDIX H

DERIVING MATHEMATICAL FUNCTIONS

Functions that are not intrinsic to Commodore 64 BASIC may be calculated as follows:

FUNCTION	BASIC EQUIVALENT
SECANT	SEC(X)=1/COS(X)
COSECANT	CSC(X)=1/SIN(X)
COTANGENT	COT(X)=1/TAN(X)
INVERSE SINE	ARCSIN(X)=ATN(X/SQR(−X*X+1))
INVERSE COSINE	ARCCOS(X)=−ATN(X/SQR (−X*X +1)) +π/2
INVERSE SECANT	ARCSEC(X)=ATN(X/SQR(X*X−1))
INVERSE COSECANT	ARCCSC(X)=ATN(X/SQR(X*X−1)) +(SGN(X)−1*π/2
INVERSE COTANGENT	ARCOT(X)=ATN(X)+π/2
HYPERBOLIC SINE	SINH(X)=(EXP(X)−EXP(−X))/2
HYPERBOLIC COSINE	COSH(X)=(EXP(X)+EXP(−X))/2
HYPERBOLIC TANGENT	TANH(X)=EXP(−X)/(EXP(x)+EXP (−X))*2+1
HYPERBOLIC SECANT	SECH(X)=2/(EXP(X)+EXP(−X))
HYPERBOLIC COSECANT	CSCH(X)=2/(EXP(X)−EXP(−X))
HYPERBOLIC COTANGENT	COTH(X)=EXP(−X)/(EXP(X) −EXP(−X))*2+1
INVERSE HYPERBOLIC SINE	ARCSINH(X)=LOG(X+SQR(X*X+1))
INVERSE HYPERBOLIC COSINE	ARCCOSH(X)=LOG(X+SQR(X*X−1))
INVERSE HYPERBOLIC TANGENT	ARCTANH(X)=LOG((1+X)/(1−X))/2
INVERSE HYPERBOLIC SECANT	ARCSECH(X)=LOG((SQR (−X*X+1)+1/X)
INVERSE HYPERBOLIC COSECANT	ARCCSCH(X)=LOG((SGN(X)*SQR (X*X+1/x)
INVERSE HYPERBOLIC COTANGENT	ARCCOTH(X)=LOG((X+1)/(X−1))/2

APPENDIX I

PINOUTS FOR INPUT/OUTPUT DEVICES

This appendix is designed to show you what connections may be made to the Commodore 64.

1) Game I/O
2) Cartridge Slot
3) Audio/Video
4) Serial I/O (Disk/Printer)
5) Modulator Output
6) Cassette
7) User Port

Control Port 1

Pin	Type	Note
1	JOYA0	
2	JOYA1	
3	JOYA2	
4	JOYA3	
5	POT AY	
6	BUTTON A/LP	
7	+5V	MAX. 50mA
8	GND	
9	POT AX	

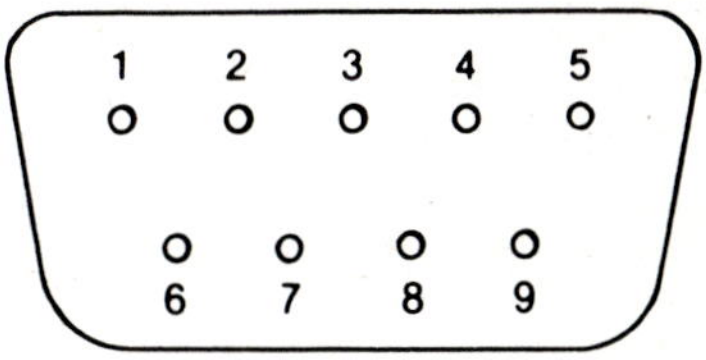

Control Port 2

Pin	Type	Note
1	JOYB0	
2	JOYB1	
3	JOYB2	
4	JOYB3	
5	POT BY	
6	BUTTON B	
7	+5V	MAX. 50mA
8	GND	
9	POT BX	

Cartridge Expansion Slot

Pin	Type
1	GND
2	+5V
3	+5V
4	$\overline{IRQ}$
5	R/$\overline{W}$
6	Dot Clock
7	I/O 1
8	$\overline{GAME}$
9	$\overline{EXROM}$
10	I/O 2
11	$\overline{ROML}$

Pin	Type
12	BA
13	$\overline{DMA}$
14	D7
15	D6
16	D5
17	D4
18	D3
19	D2
20	D1
21	D0
22	GND

Pin	Type
A	GND
B	$\overline{ROMH}$
C	$\overline{RESET}$
D	$\overline{NMI}$
E	S 02
F	A15
H	A14
J	A13
K	A12
L	A11
M	A10

Pin	Type
N	A9
P	A8
R	A7
S	A6
T	A5
U	A4
V	A3
W	A2
X	A1
Y	A0
Z	GND

Audio/Video

Pin	Type	Note
1	LUMINANCE	
2	GND	
3	AUDIO OUT	
4	VIDEO OUT	
5	AUDIO IN	

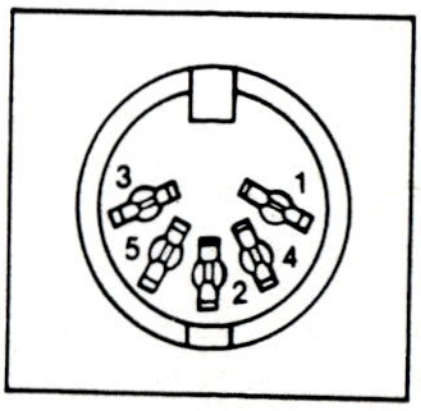

Serial I/O

Pin	Type
1	SERIAL $\overline{SRQIN}$
2	GND
3	SERIAL ATN IN/OUT
4	SERIAL CLK IN/OUT
5	SERIAL DATA IN/OUT
6	$\overline{RESET}$

Cassette

Pin	Type
A-1	GND
B-2	+5V
C-3	CASSETTE MOTOR
D-4	CASSETTE READ
E-5	CASSETTE WRITE
F-6	CASSETTE SENSE

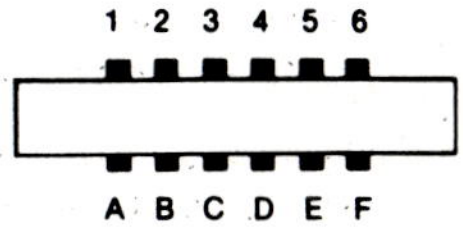

User I/O

Pin	Type	Note
1	GND	
2	+5V	MAX. 100 mA
3	$\overline{\text{RESET}}$	
4	CNT1	
5	SP1	
6	CNT2	
7	SP2	
8	$\overline{\text{PC2}}$	
9	SER. ATN IN	
10	9 VAC	MAX. 100 mA
11	9 VAC	MAX. 100 mA
12	GND	

Pin	Type	Note
A	GND	
B	$\overline{\text{FLAG2}}$	
C	PB0	
D	PB1	
E	PB2	
F	PB3	
H	PB4	
J	PB5	
K	PB6	
L	PB7	
M	PA2	
N	GND	

APPENDIX J

CONVERTING STANDARD BASIC PROGRAMS TO COMMODORE 64 BASIC

If you have programs written in a BASIC other than Commodore BASIC, some minor adjustments may be necessary before running them on the Commodore-64. We've included some hints to make the conversion easier.

String Dimensions

Delete all statements that are used to declare the length of strings. A statement such as DIM A$(I,J), which dimensions a string array for J elements of length I, should be converted to the Commodore BASIC statement DIM A$(J).

Some BASICs use a comma or an ampersand for string concatenation. Each of these must be changed to a plus sign, which is the Commodore BASIC operator for string concatenation.

In Commodore-64 BASIC, the MID$, RIGHT$, and LEFT$ functions are used to take substrings of strings. Forms such as A$(I) to access the Ith character in A$, or A$(I,J) to take a substring of A$ from position I to J, must be changed as follows:

Other BASIC	Commodore 64 BASIC
A$(I) = X$	A$ = LEFT$(A$,I−1)+X$+MID$(A$,I+1)
A$(I,J) = X$	A$ = LEFT$(A$,I−1)+X$+MID$(A$,J+1)

Multiple Assignments

To set B and C equal to zero, some BASICs allow statements of the form:

```
1Ø LET B=C=Ø
```

Commodore 64 BASIC would interpret the second equal sign as a logical operator and set B = −1 if C = 0. Instead, convert this statement to:

```
1Ø C=Ø : B=Ø
```

Multiple Statements

Some BASICs use a backslash (\ ) to separate multiple statements on a line. With Commodore 64 BASIC, separate all statements by a colon (:).

MAT Functions

Programs using the MAT functions available on some BASICs must be rewritten using FOR. . .NEXT loops to execute properly.

APPENDIX K

ERROR MESSAGES

This appendix contains a complete list of the error messages generated by the Commodore-64, with a description of causes.

BAD DATA String data was received from an open file, but the program was expecting numeric data.

BAD SUBSCRIPT The program was trying to reference an element of an array whose number is outside of the range specified in the DIM statement.

BREAK Program execution was stopped because you hit the STOP key.

CAN'T CONTINUE The CONT command will not work, either because the program was never RUN, there has been an error, or a line has been edited.

DEVICE NOT PRESENT The required I/O device was not available for an OPEN, CLOSE, CMD, PRINT#, INPUT#, or GET#.

DIVISION BY ZERO Division by zero is a mathematical oddity and not allowed.

EXTRA IGNORED Too many items of data were typed in response to an INPUT statement. Only the first few items were accepted.

FILE NOT FOUND If you were looking for a file on tape, and END-OF-TAPE marker was found. If you were looking on disk, no file with that name exists.

FILE NOT OPEN The file specified in a CLOSE, CMD, PRINT#, INPUT#, or GET#, must first be OPENed.

FILE OPEN An attempt was made to open a file using the number of an already open file.

FORMULA TOO COMPLEX The string expression being evaluated should be split into at least two parts for the system to work with, or a formula has too many parentheses.

ILLEGAL DIRECT The INPUT statement can only be used within a program, and not in direct mode.

ILLEGAL QUANTITY A number used as the argument of a function or statement is out of the allowable range.

LOAD There is a problem with the program on tape.

NEXT WITHOUT FOR This is caused by either incorrectly nesting loops or having a variable name in a NEXT statement that doesn't correspond with one in a FOR statement.

NOT INPUT FILE An attempt was made to INPUT or GET data from a file which was specified to be for output only.

NOT OUTPUT FILE An attempt was made to PRINT data to a file which was specified as input only.

OUT OF DATA A READ statement was executed but there is no data left unREAD in a DATA statement.

OUT OF MEMORY There is no more RAM available for program or variables. This may also occur when too many FOR loops have been nested, or when there are too many GOSUBs in effect.

OVERFLOW The result of a computation is larger than the largest number allowed, which is 1.70141884E+38.

REDIM'D ARRAY An array may only be DIMensioned once. If an array variable is used before that array is DIM'd, an automatic DIM operation is performed on that array setting the number of elements to ten, and any subsequent DIMs will cause this error.

REDO FROM START Character data was typed in during an INPUT statement when numeric data was expected. Just re-type the entry so that it is correct, and the program will continue by itself.

RETURN WITHOUT GOSUB A RETURN statement was encountered, and no GOSUB command has been issued.

STRING TOO LONG A string can contain up to 255 characters.

?SYNTAX ERROR A statement is unrecognizable by the Commodore 64. A missing or extra parenthesis, misspelled keywords, etc.

TYPE MISMATCH This error occurs when a number is used in place of a string, or vice-versa.

UNDEF'D FUNCTION A user defined function was referenced, but it has never been defined using the DEF FN statement.

UNDEF'D STATEMENT An attempt was made to GOTO or GOSUB or RUN a line number that doesn't exist.

VERIFY The program on tape or disk does not match the program currently in memory.

APPENDIX L

6510 MICROPROCESSOR CHIP SPECIFICATIONS

DESCRIPTION

The 6510 is a low-cost microcomputer system capable of solving a broad range of small-systems and peripheral-control problems at minimum cost to the user.

An 8-bit Bi-Directional I/O Port is located on-chip with the Output Register at Address 0000 and the Data-Direction Register at Address 0001. The I/O Port is bit-by-bit programmable.

The Three-State sixteen-bit Address Bus allows Direct Memory Accessing (DMA) and multiprocessor systems sharing a common memory.

The internal processor architecture is identical to the MOS Technology 6502 to provide software compatibility.

FEATURES OF THE 6510 . . .

- Eight-Bit Bi-Directional I/O Port
- Single +5-volt supply
- N-channel, silicon gate, depletion load technology
- Eight-bit parallel processing
- 56 Instructions
- Decimal and binary arithmetic
- Thirteen addressing modes
- True indexing capability
- Programmable stack pointer
- Variable length stack
- Interrupt capability
- Eight-Bit Bi-Directional Data Bus
- Addressable memory range of up to 65K bytes
- Direct memory access capability
- Bus compatible with M6800
- Pipeline architecture
- 1-MHz and 2-MHz operation
- Use with any type or speed memory

PIN CONFIGURATION

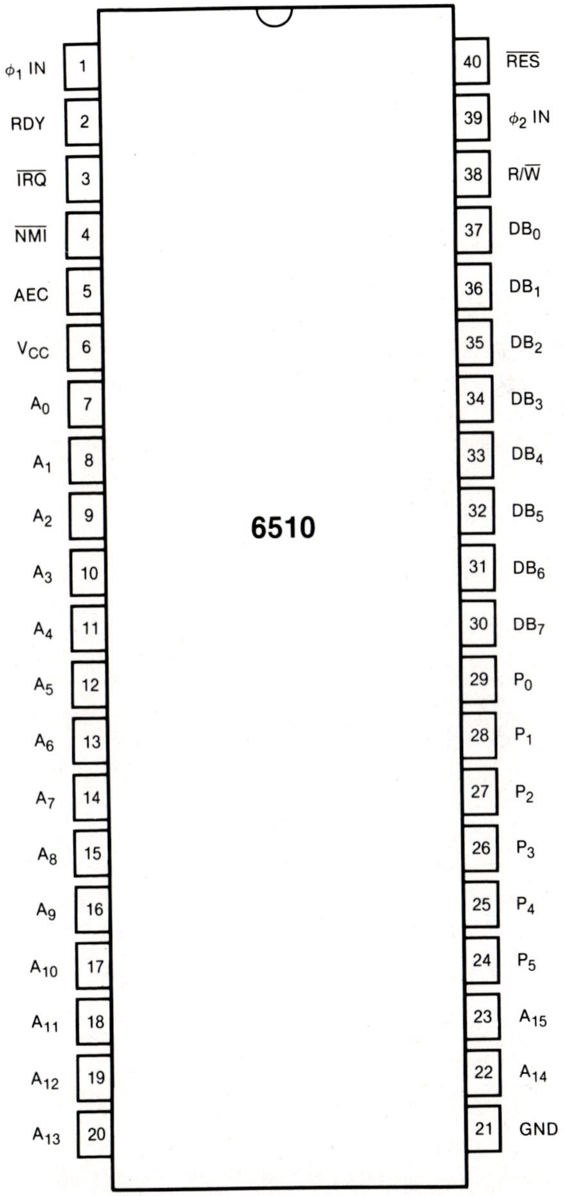

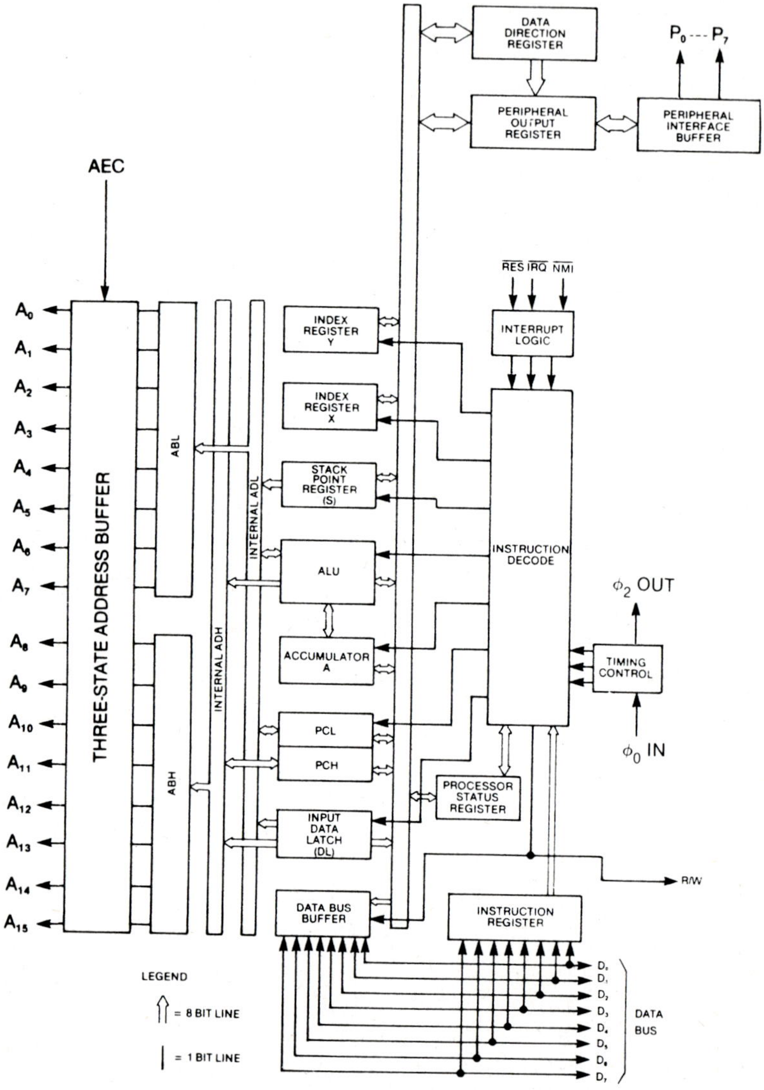

6510 BLOCK DIAGRAM

6510 CHARACTERISTICS

MAXIMUM RATINGS

RATING	SYMBOL	VALUE	UNIT
SUPPLY VOLTAGE	V_{CC}	−0.3 to +7.0	V_{DC}
INPUT VOLTAGE	V_{in}	−0.3 to +7.0	V_{DC}
OPERATING TEMPERATURE	T_A	0 to +70	°C
STORAGE TEMPERATURE	T_{STG}	−55 to +150	°C

NOTE: This device contains input protection against damage due to high static voltages or electric fields; however, precautions should be taken to avoid application of voltages higher than the maximum rating.

ELECTRICAL CHARACTERISTICS (VCC = 5.0 V ±5%, VSS = 0, T_A = 0° to +70°C)

CHARACTERISTIC	SYMBOL	MIN.	TYP.	MAX.	UNIT
Input High Voltage ϕ_1, $\phi_{2(in)}$	V_{IH}	V_{CC} − 0.2	—	V_{CC} + 1.0V	V_{DC}
Input High Voltage $\overline{RES}$, P_0-P_7 $\overline{IRQ}$, Data		V_{SS} + 2.0	—	—	V_{DC}
Input Low Voltage ϕ_1, $\phi_{2(in)}$	V_{IL}	V_{SS} − 0.3	—	V_{SS} + 0.2	V_{DC}
$\overline{RES}$, P_0-P_7 $\overline{IRQ}$, Data		—	—	V_{SS} + 0.8	V_{DC}
Input Leakage Current (V_{in} = 0 to 5.25V, V_{CC} = 5.25V) Logic	I_{in}	—	—	2.5	μA
ϕ_1, $\phi_{2(in)}$		—	—	100	μA
Three State (Off State) Input Current (V_{in} = 0.4 to 2.4V, V_{CC} = 5.25V) Data Lines	I_{TSI}	—	—	10	μA
Output High Voltage (I_{OH} = −100μA_{DC}, V_{CC} = 4.75V) Data, A0-A15, R/W, P_0-P_7	V_{OH}	V_{SS} + 2.4	—	—	V_{DC}

CHARACTERISTIC	SYMBOL	MIN.	TYP.	MAX.	UNIT
Out Low Voltage (I_{OL} = 1.6mA_{DC}, V_{CC} = 4.75V) Data, A0-A15, R/W, P_0-P_7	V_{OL}	—	—	V_{SS} + 0.4	V_{DC}
Power Supply Current	I_{CC}	—	125		mA
Capacitance V_{in} = 0, T_A = 25°C, f = 1MHz)	C				pF
Logic, P_0-P_7	C_{in}	—	—	10	
Data		—	—	15	
A0-A15, R/W	C_{out}	—	—	12	
ϕ_1	$C\phi_1$	—	30	50	
ϕ_2	$C\phi_2$	—	50	80	

CLOCK TIMING

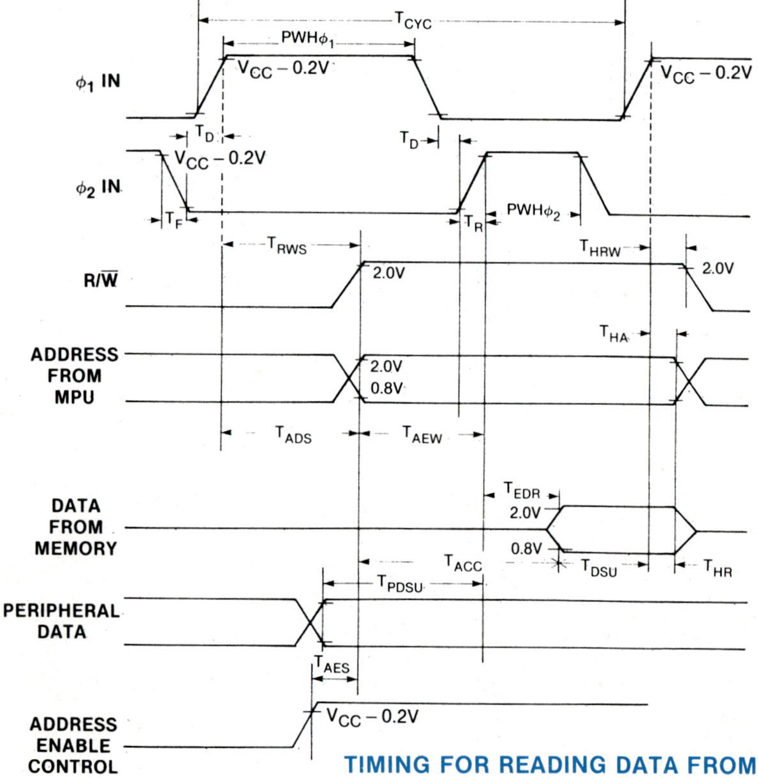

TIMING FOR READING DATA FROM MEMORY OR PERIPHERALS

CLOCK TIMING

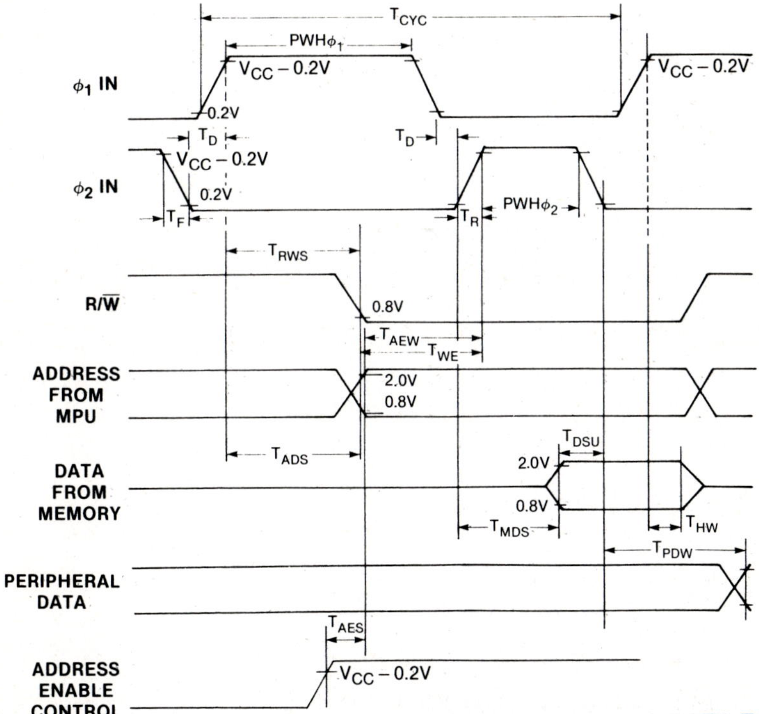

TIMING FOR WRITING DATA TO MEMORY OR PERIPHERALS

AC CHARACTERISTICS

ELECTRICAL CHARACTERISTICS (V_{CC} = 5 V ±5%, V_{SS} = 0 V, T_A = 0°–70°C)

CLOCK TIMING		1MHz TIMING			2 MHz TIMING			
CHARACTERISTIC	SYMBOL	MIN.	TYP.	MAX.	MIN.	TYP.	MAX.	UNITS
Cycle Time	T_{CYC}	1000	—	—	500	—	—	ns
Clock Pulse Width φ1	PWHφ1	430	—	—	215	—	—	ns
(Measured at V_{CC} − 0.2V) φ2	PWHφ2	470	—	—	235	—	—	ns
Fall Time, Rise Time (Measured from 0.2V to V_{CC} − 0.2V)	T_F, T_R	—	—	25	—	—	15	ns
Delay Time between Clocks (Measured at 0.2V)	T_D	0	—	—	0	—	—	ns

READ/WRITE TIMING (LOAD = 1TTL)		1 MHz TIMING			2 MHz TIMING			
CHARACTERISTIC	SYMBOL	MIN.	TYP.	MAX.	MIN.	TYP.	MAX.	UNITS
Read/Write Setup Time from 6508	T_{RWS}	—	100	300	—	100	150	ns
Address Setup Time from 6508	T_{ADS}	—	100	300	—	100	150	ns
Memory Read Access Time	T_{ACC}	—	—	575	—	—	300	ns

Data Stability Time Period	T_{DSU}	100	—	—	50			ns
Data Hold Time-Read	T_{HR}		—	—				ns
Data Hold Time-Write	T_{HW}	10	30	—	10	30		ns
Data Setup Time from 6510	T_{MDS}	—	150	200	—	75	100	ns
Address Hold Time	T_{HA}	10	30	—	10	30		ns
R/W Hold Time	T_{HRW}	10	30	—	10	30		ns
Delay Time, Address valid to $\phi 2$ positive transition	T_{AEW}	180	—	—				ns
Delay Time, $\phi 2$ positive transition to Data valid on bus	T_{EDR}	—	—	395				ns
Delay Time, Data valid to $\phi 2$ negative transition	T_{DSU}	300	—	—				ns
Delay Time, R/W negative transition to $\phi 2$ positive transition	T_{WE}	130	—	—				ns
Delay Time, $\phi 2$ negative transition to Peripheral Data valid	T_{PDW}	—	—	1				μs
Peripheral Data Setup Time	T_{PDSU}	300	—	—				ns
Address Enable Setup Time	T_{AES}			60			60	ns

SIGNAL DESCRIPTION

Clocks (ϕ_1, ϕ_2)

The 6510 requires a two-phase non-overlapping clock that runs at the V_{CC} voltage level.

Address Bus (A_0-A_{15})

These outputs are TTL compatible, capable of driving one standard TTL load and 130 pf.

Data Bus (D_0-D_7)

Eight pins are used for the data bus. This is a Bi-Directional bus, transferring data to and from the device and peripherals. The outputs are tri-state buffers capable of driving one standard TTL load and 130 pf.

Reset

This input is used to reset or start the microprocessor from a power down condition. During the time that this line is held low, writing to or from the microprocessor is inhibited. When a positive edge is detected on the input, the microprocessor will immediately begin the reset sequence.

After a system initialization time of six clock cycles, the mask interrupt flag will be set and the microprocessor will load the program counter from the memory vector locations FFFC and FFFD. This is the start location for program control.

After V_{CC} reaches 4.75 volts in a power-up routine, reset must be held low for at least two clock cycles. At this time the R/W signal will become valid.

When the reset signal goes high following these two clock cycles, the microprocessor will proceed with the normal reset procedure detailed above.

Interrupt Request ($\overline{IRQ}$)

This TTL level input requests that an interrupt sequence begin within the microprocessor. The microprocessor will complete the current instruction being executed before recognizing the request. At that time, the interrupt mask bit in the Status Code Register will be examined. If the interrupt mask flag is not set, the microprocessor will begin an interrupt sequence. The Program Counter and Processor Status Register are stored in the stack. The microprocessor will then set the interrupt mask flag high so that no further interrupts may occur. At the end of this cycle, the program counter low will be loaded from address FFFE, and program counter high from location FFFF, therefore transferring program control to the memory vector located at these addresses.

Address Enable Control (AEC)

The Address Bus is valid only when the Address Enable Control line is high. When low, the Address Bus is in a high-impedance state. This feature allows easy DMA and multiprocessor systems.

I/O Port (P_0-P_5)

Six pins are used for the peripheral port, which can transfer data to or from peripheral devices. The Output Register is located in RAM at Address 0001, and the Data Direction Register is at Address 0000. The outputs are capable at driving one standard TTL load and 130 pf.

Read/Write (R/W)

This signal is generated by the microprocessor to control the direction of data transfers on the Data Bus. This line is high except when the microprocessor is writing to memory or a peripheral device.

ADDRESSING MODES

ACCUMULATOR ADDRESSING—This form of addressing is represented with a one byte instruction, implying an operation on the accumulator.

IMMEDIATE ADDRESSING—In immediate addressing, the operand is contained in the second byte of the instruction, with no further memory addressing required.

ABSOLUTE ADDRESSING—In absolute addressing, the second byte of the instruction specifies the eight low order bits of the effective address while the third byte specifies the eight high order bits. Thus, the absolute addressing mode allows access to the entire 65K bytes of addressable memory.

ZERO PAGE ADDRESSING—The zero page instructions allow for shorter code and execution times by only fetching the second byte of the instruction and assuming a zero high address byte. Careful use of the zero page can result in significant increase in code efficiency.

INDEXED ZERO PAGE ADDRESSING—(X, Y indexing)—This form of addressing is used in conjunction with the index register and is referred to as "Zero Page, X" or "Zero Page, Y." The effective address is calculated by adding the second byte to the contents of the index register. Since this is a form of "Zero Page" addressing, the content of the second byte references a location in page zero. Additonally, due to the "Zero Page" addressing nature of this mode, no carry is added to the high order 8 bits of memory and crossing of page boundaries does not occur.

INDEXED ABSOLUTE ADDRESSING—(X, Y indexing)—This form of addressing is used in conjunction with X and Y index register and is referred to as "Absolute, X," and "Absolute, Y." The effective address is formed by adding the contents of X and Y to the address contained in the second and third bytes of the instruction. This mode allows the index register to contain the index or count value and the instruction to contain the base address. This type of indexing allows any location referencing and the index to modify multiple fields resulting in reduced coding and execution time.

IMPLIED ADDRESSING—In the implied addressing mode, the address containing the operand is implicitly stated in the operation code of the instruction.

RELATIVE ADDRESSING—Relative addressing is used only with branch instructions and establishes a destination for the conditional branch.

The second byte of the instruction becomes the operand which is an "Offset" added to the contents of the lower eight bits of the program counter when the counter is set at the next instruction. The range of the offset is −128 to +127 bytes from the next instruction.

INDEXED INDIRECT ADDRESSING—In indexed indirect addressing (referred to as [Indirect, X]), the second byte of the instruction is added to the contents of the X index register, discarding the carry. The result of this addition points to a memory location on page zero whose contents is the low order eight bits of the effective address. The next memory location in page zero contains the high order eight bits of the effective address. Both memory locations specifying the high and low order bytes of the effective address must be in page zero.

INDIRECT INDEXED ADDRESSING—In indirect indexed addressing (referred to as [Indirect], Y), the second byte of the instruction points to a memory location in page zero. The contents of this memory location is added to the contents of the Y index register, the result being the low order eight bits of the effective address. The carry from this addition is added to the contents of the next page zero memory location, the result being the high order eight bits of the effective address.

ABSOLUTE INDIRECT—The second byte of the instruction contains the low order eight bits of a memory location. The high order eight bits of that memory location is contained in the third byte of the instruction. The contents of the fully specified memory location is the low order byte of the effective address. The next memory location contains the high order byte of the effective address which is loaded into the sixteen bits of the program counter.

INSTRUCTION SET—ALPHABETIC SEQUENCE

ADC Add Memory to Accumulator with Carry
AND "AND" Memory with Accumulator
ASL Shift Left One Bit (Memory or Accumulator)

BCC Branch on Carry Clear
BCS Branch on Carry Set
BEQ Branch on Result Zero
BIT Test Bits in Memory with Accumulator
BMI Branch on Result Minus
BNE Branch on Result not Zero
BPL Branch on Result Plus
BRK Force Break
BVC Branch on Overflow Clear
BVS Branch on Overflow Set

CLC Clear Carry Flag
CLD Clear Decimal Mode
CLI Clear Interrupt Disable Bit
CLV Clear Overflow Flag
CMP Compare Memory and Accumulator
CPX Compare Memory and Index X
CPY Compare Memory and Index Y

DEC	Decrement Memory by One
DEX	Decrement Index X by One
DEY	Decrement Index Y by One
EOR	"Exclusive-OR" Memory with Accumulator
INC	Increment Memory by One
INX	Increment Index X by One
INY	Increment Index Y by One
JMP	Jump to New Location
JSR	Jump to New Location Saving Return Address
LDA	Load Accumulator with Memory
LDX	Load Index X with Memory
LDY	Load Index Y with Memory
LSR	Shift One Bit Right (Memory or Accumulator)
NOP	No Operation
ORA	"OR" Memory with Accumulator
PHA	Push Accumulator on Stack
PHP	Push Processor Status on Stack
PLA	Pull Accumulator from Stack
PLP	Pull Processor Status from Stack
ROL	Rotate One Bit Left (Memory or Accumulator)
ROR	Rotate One Bit Right (Memory or Accumulator)
RTI	Return from Interrupt
RTS	Return from Subroutine
SBC	Subtract Memory from Accumulator with Borrow
SEC	Set Carry Flag
SED	Set Decimal Mode
SEI	Set Interrupt Disable Status
STA	Store Accumulator in Memory
STX	Store Index X in Memory
STY	Store Index Y in Memory

TAX	Transfer Accumulator to Index X
TAY	Transfer Accumulator to Index Y
TSX	Transfer Stack Pointer to Index X
TXA	Transfer Index X to Accumulator
TXS	Transfer Index X to Stack Register
TYA	Transfer Index Y to Accumulator

PROGRAMMING MODEL

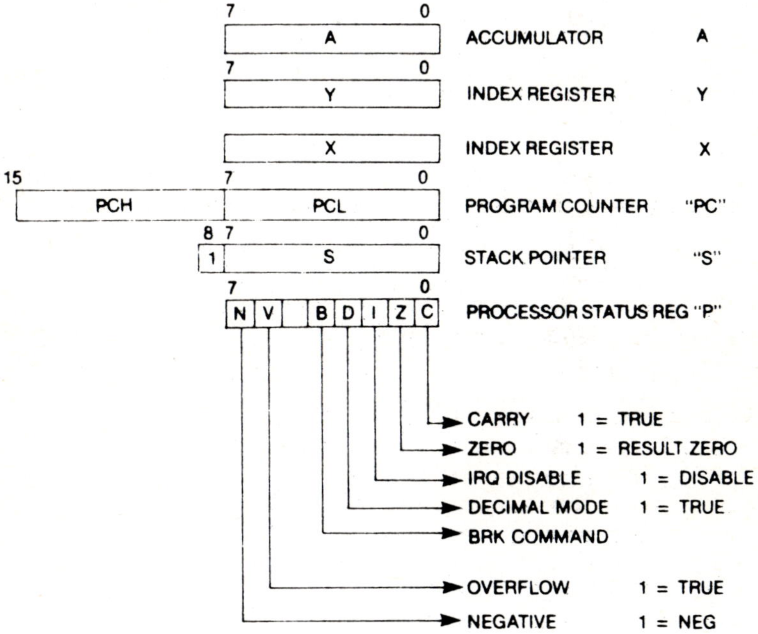

INSTRUCTION SET—OP CODES, EXECUTION

INSTRUCTIONS		Immediate			Absolute			Zero Page			Accum.			Implied			(Ind.) X			(Ind.) Y			Z, Page, X			Abs. X			Abs. Y			Relative			Indirect			Z, Page, Y			CONDITION CODES					
Mnemonic	Operation	OP	N	#	OP	N	#	OP	N	#	OP	N	#	OP	N	#	OP	N	#	OP	N	#	OP	N	#	OP	N	#	OP	N	#	OP	N	#	OP	N	#	OP	N	#	N	Z	C	I	D	V
ADC	A + M + C→A (4) (1)	69	2	2	6D	4	3	65	3	2							61	6	2	71	5	2	75	4	2	7D	4	3	79	4	3										✓	✓	✓	—	—	✓
AND	A∧M→A (1)	29	2	2	2D	4	3	25	3	2							21	6	2	31	5	2	35	4	2	3D	4	3	39	4	3										✓	✓	—	—	—	—
ASL	C←[7 0]←0				0E	6	3	06	5	2	0A	2	1										16	6	2	1E	7	3													✓	✓	✓	—	—	—
BCC	BRANCH ON C = 0 (2)																															90	2	2							—	—	—	—	—	—
BCS	BRANCH ON C = 1 (2)																															B0	2	2							—	—	—	—	—	—
BEO	BRANCH ON Z = 1 (2)																															F0	2	2							—	—	—	—	—	—
BIT	A∧M				2C	4	3	24	3	2																															M_7	✓	—	—	—	M_6
BMI	BRANCH ON N = 1 (2)																															30	2	2							—	—	—	—	—	—
BNE	BRANCH ON Z = 0 (2)																															D0	2	2							—	—	—	—	—	—
BPL	BRANCH ON N = 0 (2)																															10	2	2							—	—	—	—	—	—
BRK	(See Fig. 1)													00	7	1																									—	—	—	1	—	—
BVC	BRANCH ON V = 0 (2)																															50	2	2							—	—	—	—	—	—
BVS	BRANCH ON V = 1 (2)																															70	2	2							—	—	—	—	—	—
CLC	0→C													18	2	1																									—	—	0	—	—	—
CLD	0→D													D8	2	1																									—	—	—	—	0	—
CLI	0→I													58	2	1																									—	—	—	0	—	—
CLV	0→V													B8	2	1																									—	—	—	—	—	0
CMP	A − M (1)	C9	2	2	CD	4	3	C5	3	2							C1	6	2	D1	5	2	D5	4	2	DD	4	3	D9	4	3										✓	✓	✓	—	—	—
CPX	X − M	E0	2	2	EC	4	3	E4	3	2																															✓	✓	✓	—	—	—
CPY	Y − M	C0	2	2	CC	4	3	C4	3	2																															✓	✓	✓	—	—	—
DEC	M − 1→M				CE	6	3	C6	5	2													D6	6	2	DE	7	3													✓	✓	—	—	—	—
DEX	X − 1→X													CA	2	1																									✓	✓	—	—	—	—
DEY	Y − 1→Y													B8	2	1																									✓	✓	—	—	—	—
EOR	A∀M→A (1)	49	2	2	4D	4	3	45	3	2							41	6	2	51	5	2	55	4	2	5D	4	3	59	4	3										✓	✓	—	—	—	—
INC	M + 1→M				EE	6	3	E6	5	2													F6	6	2	FE	7	3													✓	✓	—	—	—	—
INX	X + 1→X													E8	2	1																									✓	✓	—	—	—	—
INY	Y + 1→Y													C8	2	1																									✓	✓	—	—	—	—
JMP	JUMP TO NEW LOC.				4C	3	3																												6C	5	3				—	—	—	—	—	—
JSR	(See Fig. 2) JUMP SUB				20	6	3																																		—	—	—	—	—	—
LDA	M→A (1)	A9	2	2	AD	4	3	A5	3	2							A1	6	2	B1	5	2	B5	4	2	BD	4	3	B9	4	3										✓	✓	—	—	—	—

TIME, MEMORY REQUIREMENTS

INSTRUCTIONS		Immediate			Absolute			Zero Page			Accum.			Implied			(Ind.) X			(Ind.) Y			Z, Page, X			Abs. X			Abs. Y			Relative			Indirect			Z, Page, Y			CONDITION CODES					
Mnemonic	Operation	OP	N	#	OP	N	#	OP	N	#	OP	N	#	OP	N	#	OP	N	#	OP	N	#	OP	N	#	OP	N	#	OP	N	#	OP	N	#	OP	N	#	OP	N	#	N	Z	C	I	D	V
LDX	M→X (1)	A2	2	2	AE	4	3	A6	3	2																			BE	4	3							B6	4	2	✓	✓	—	—	—	—
LDY	M→Y (1)	A0	2	2	AC	4	3	A4	3	2													B4	4	2	BC	4	3													✓	✓	—	—	—	—
LSR	0→[7 0]→C				4E	6	3	46	5	2	4A	2	1										56	6	2	5E	7	3													0	✓	✓	—	—	—
NOP	NO OPERATION													EA	2	1																									—	—	—	—	—	—
ORA	AVM→A	09	2	2	0D	4	3	05	3	2							01	6	2	11	5	2	15	4	2	1D	4	3	19	4	3										✓	✓	—	—	—	—
PHA	$A \to M_S$ $S-1 \to S$													48	3	1																									—	—	—	—	—	—
PHP	$P \to M_S$ $S-1 \to S$													08	3	1																									—	—	—	—	—	—
PLA	$S+1 \to S$ $M_S \to A$													68	4	1																									✓	✓	—	—	—	—
PLP	$S+1 \to S$ $M_S \to P$													28	4	1																									(RESTORED)					
ROL	←[7 0]←[C]←				2E	6	3	26	5	2	2A	2	1										36	6	2	3E	7	3													✓	✓	✓	—	—	—
ROR	→[C]→[7 0]→				6E	6	3	66	5	2	6A	2	1										76	6	2	7E	7	3													✓	✓	✓	—	—	—
RTI	(See Fig. 1) RTRN INT													40	6	1																									(RESTORED)					
RTS	(See Fig. 2) RTRN SUB													60	6	1																									—	—	—	—	—	—
SBC	$A-M-\overline{C} \to A$ (1)	E9	2	2	ED	4	3	E5	3	2							E1	6	2	F1	5	2	F5	4	2	FD	4	3	F9	4	3										✓	✓	(3)	—	—	✓
SEC	1→C													38	2	1																									—	—	1	—	—	—
SED	1→D													F8	2	1																									—	—	—	—	1	—
SEI	1→I													78	2	1																									—	—	—	1	—	—
STA	A→M				8D	4	3	85	3	2							81	6	2	91	6	2	95	4	2	9D	5	3	99	5	3										—	—	—	—	—	—
STX	X→M				8E	4	3	86	3	2																												96	4	2	—	—	—	—	—	—
STY	Y→M				8C	4	3	84	3	2													94	4	2																—	—	—	—	—	—
TAX	A→X													AA	2	1																									✓	✓	—	—	—	—
TAY	A→Y													A8	2	1																									✓	✓	—	—	—	—
TSX	S→X													BA	2	1																									✓	✓	—	—	—	—
TXA	X→A													8A	2	1																									✓	✓	—	—	—	—
TXS	X→S													9A	2	1																									—	—	—	—	—	—
TYA	Y→A													98	2	1																									✓	✓	—	—	—	—

(1) ADD 1 TO "N" IF PAGE BOUNDARY IS CROSSED.
(2) ADD 1 TO "N" IF BRANCH OCCURS TO SAME PAGE.
ADD 2 TO "N" IF BRANCH OCCURS TO DIFFERENT PAGE.
(3) CARRY NOT = BORROW.
(4) IF IN DECIMAL MODE Z FLAG IS INVALID
ACCUMULATOR MUST BE CHECKED FOR ZERO RESULT.

X INDEX X
Y INDEX Y
A ACCUMULATOR
M MEMORY PER EFFECTIVE ADDRESS
M_S MEMORY PER STACK POINTER

+ ADD
− SUBTRACT
∧ AND
∨ OR
∀ EXCLUSIVE OR

✓ MODIFIED
— NOT MODIFIED
M_7 MEMORY BIT 7
M_6 MEMORY BIT 6
N NO. CYCLES
NO. BYTES

NOTE: COMMODORE SEMICONDUCTOR GROUP cannot assume liability for the use of undefined OP CODES.

6510 MEMORY MAP

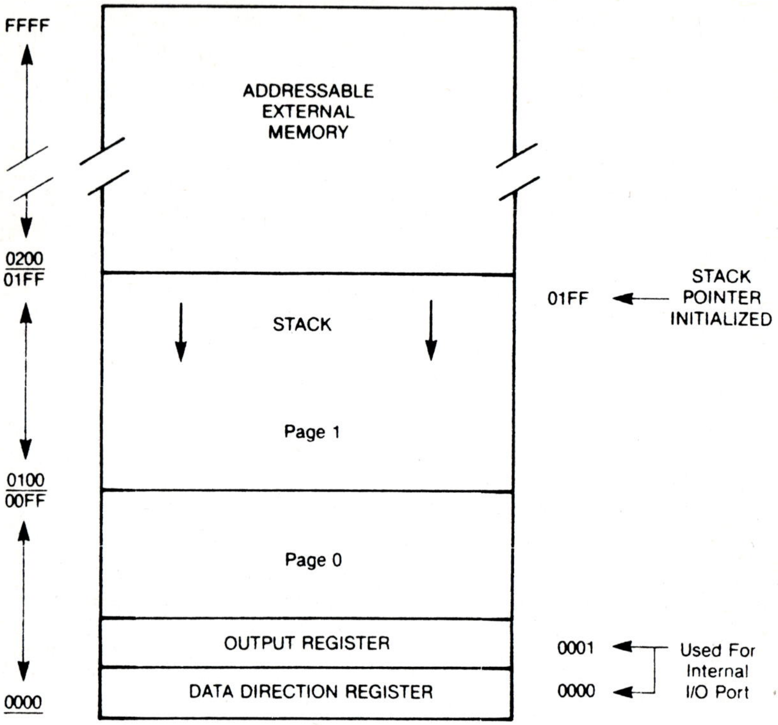

APPLICATIONS NOTES

Locating the Output Register at the internal I/O Port in Page Zero enhances the powerful Zero Page Addressing instructions of the 6510.

By assigning the I/O Pins as inputs (using the Data Direction Register) the user has the ability to change the contents of address 0001 (the Output Register) using peripheral devices. The ability to change these contents using peripheral inputs, together with Zero Page Indirect Addressing instructions, allows novel and versatile programming techniques not possible earlier.

COMMODORE SEMICONDUCTOR GROUP reserves the right to make changes to any products herein to improve reliability, function or design. **COMMODORE SEMICONDUCTOR GROUP** does not assume any liability arising out of the application or use of any product or circuit described herein; neither does it convey any license under its patent rights nor the rights of others.

6526 COMPLEX INTERFACE ADAPTER (CIA) CHIP SPECIFICATIONS

DESCRIPTION

The 6526 Complex Interface Adapter (CIA) is a 65XX bus compatible peripheral interface device with extremely flexible timing and I/O capabilities.

FEATURES

- 16 Individually programmable I/O lines
- 8 or 16-Bit handshaking on read or write
- 2 independent, linkable 16-Bit interval timers
- 24-hour (AM/PM) time of day clock with programmable alarm
- 8-Bit shift register for serial I/O
- 2TTL Load capability
- CMOS compatible I/O lines
- 1 or 2 MHz operation available

PIN CONFIGURATION

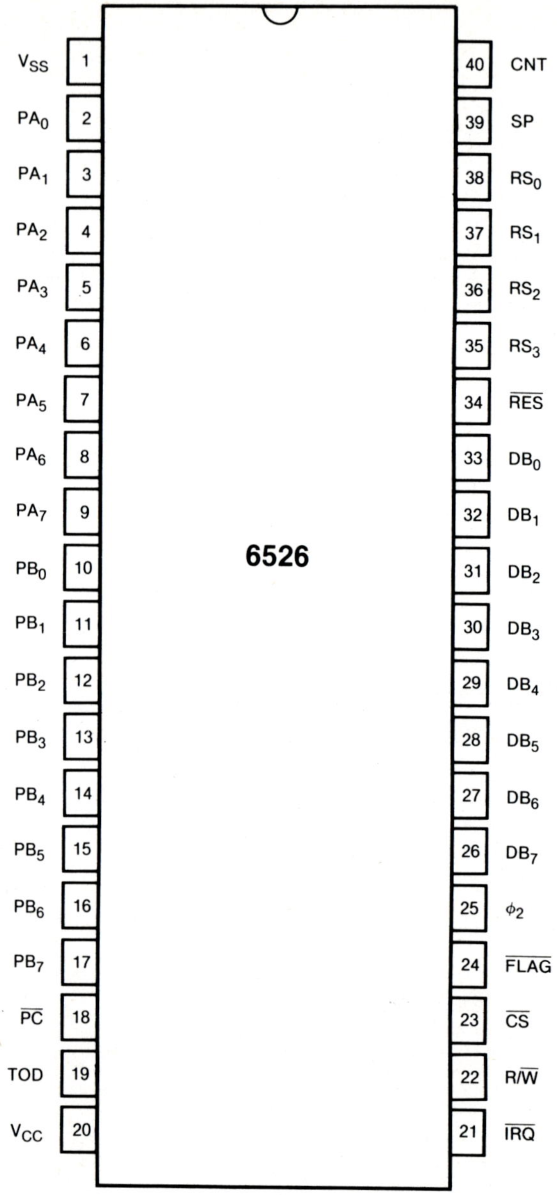

6526
BLOCK DIAGRAM

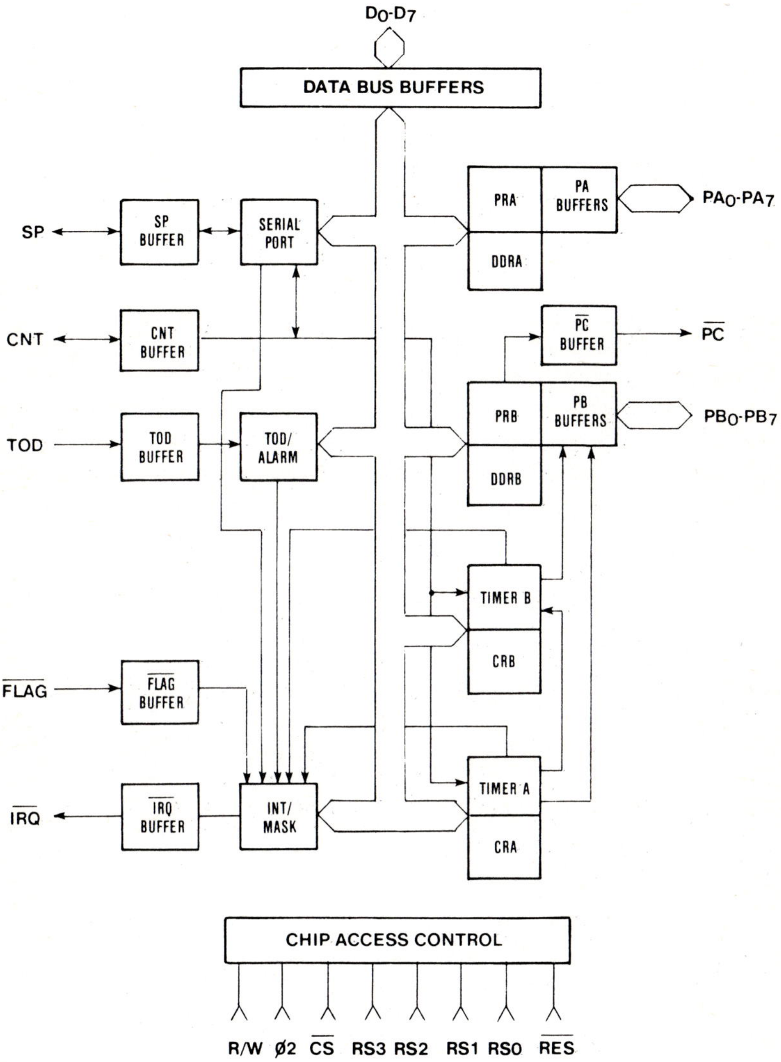

MAXIMUM RATINGS

Supply Voltage, V_{CC}	−0.3V to +7.0V
Input/Output Voltage, V_{IN}	−0.3V to +7.0V
Operating Temperature, T_{OP}	0° C to 70° C
Storage Temperature, T_{STG}	−55° C to 150° C

All inputs contain protection circuitry to prevent damage due to high static discharges. Care should be exercised to prevent unnecessary application of voltages in excess of the allowable limits.

COMMENT

Stresses above those listed under "Absolute Maximum Ratings" may cause permanent damage to the device. These are stress ratings only. Functional operation of this device at these or any other conditions above those indicated in the operational sections of this specification is not implied and exposure to absolute maximum rating conditions for extended periods may affect device reliability.

ELECTRICAL CHARACTERISTICS (V_{CC} ± 5%, V_{SS} = 0 V, T_A = 0–70°C)

CHARACTERISTIC	SYMBOL	MIN.	TYP.	MAX.	UNIT
Input High Voltage	V_{IH}	+2.4	—	V_{CC}	V
Input Low Voltage	V_{IL}	−0.3	—	—	V
Input Leakage Current; $V_{IN}=V_{SS}$ +5V (TOD, R/W, $\overline{FLAG}$, ϕ2, $\overline{RES}$, RS0-RS3, $\overline{CS}$)	I_{IN}	—	1.0	2.5	μA

CHARACTERISTIC	SYMBOL	MIN.	TYP.	MAX.	UNIT
Port Input Pull-up Resistance	R_{PI}	3.1	5.0	—	KΩ
Output Leakage Current for High Impedance State (Three State); V_{IN} = 4V to 2.4V; (DB0–DB7, SP, CNT, $\overline{IRQ}$)	I_{TSI}	—	±1.0	±10.0	μA
Output High Voltage V_{CC}=MIN, I_{LOAD} < −200μA (PA0–PA7, $\overline{PC}$ PB0–PB7, DB0–DB7)	V_{OH}	+2.4	—	V_{CC}	V
Output Low Voltage V_{CC}= MIN, I_{LOAD} < 3.2 mA	V_{OL}	—	—	+0.40	V
Output High Current (Sourcing); V_{OH} > 2.4V (PA0–PA7, PB0–PB7, PC, DB0–DB7	I_{OH}	−200	−1000	—	μA
Output Low Current (Sinking); V_{OL} < .4V (PA0–PA7, $\overline{PC}$, PB0–PB7, DB0–DB7)	I_{OL}	3.2	—	—	mA
Input Capacitance	C_{IN}	—	7	10	pf
Output Capacitance	C_{OUT}	—	7	10	pf
Power Supply Current	I_{CC}	—	70	100	mA

6526 WRITE TIMING DIAGRAM

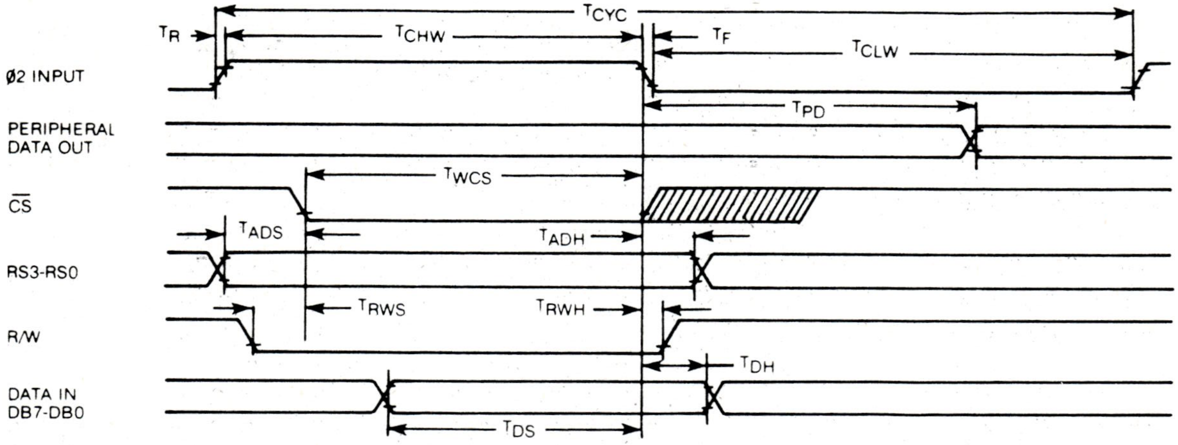

6526 READ TIMING DIAGRAM

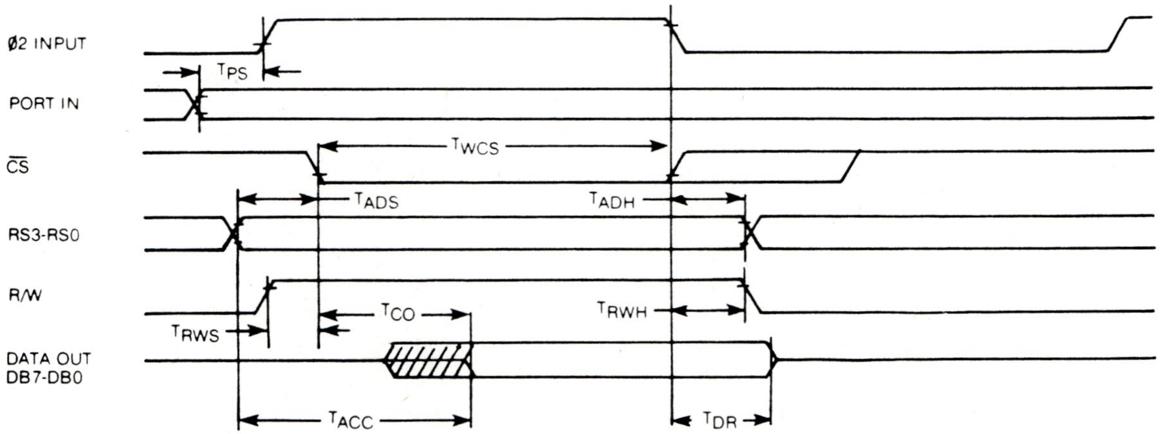

6526 INTERFACE SIGNALS

ϕ2—Clock Input

The ϕ2 clock is a TTL compatible input used for internal device operation and as a timing reference for communicating with the system data bus.

$\overline{\text{CS}}$—Chip Select Input

The $\overline{\text{CS}}$ input controls the activity of the 6526. A low level on $\overline{\text{CS}}$ while ϕ2 is high causes the device to respond to signals on the R/W and address (RS) lines. A high on $\overline{\text{CS}}$ prevents these lines from controlling the 6526. The $\overline{\text{CS}}$ line is normally activated (low) at ϕ2 by the appropriate address combination.

R/W—Read/Write Input

The R/W signal is normally supplied by the microprocessor and controls the direction of data transfers of the 6526. A high on R/W indicates a read (data transfer out of the 6526), while a low indicates a write (data transfer into the 6526).

RS3–RS0—Address Inputs

The address inputs select the internal registers as described by the Register Map.

DB7–BD0—Data Bus Inputs/Outputs

The eight data bus pins transfer information between the 6526 and the system data bus. These pins are high impedance inputs unless $\overline{\text{CS}}$ is low and R/W and ϕ2 are high to read the device. During this read, the data bus output buffers are enabled, driving the data from the selected register onto the system data bus.

$\overline{\text{IRQ}}$—Interrupt Request Output

$\overline{\text{IRQ}}$ is an open drain output normally connected to the processor interrupt input. An external pullup resistor holds the signal high, allowing multiple $\overline{\text{IRQ}}$ outputs to be connected together. The $\overline{\text{IRQ}}$ output is normally off (high impedance) and is activated low as indicated in the functional description.

$\overline{RES}$—Reset Input

A low on the $\overline{RES}$ pin resets all internal registers. The port pins are set as inputs and port registers to zero (although a read of the ports will return all highs because of passive pullups). The timer control registers are set to zero and the timer latches to all ones. All other registers are reset to zero.

6526 TIMING CHARACTERISTICS

Symbol	Characteristic	1MHz MIN	1MHz MAX	2MHz MIN	2MHz MAX	Unit
	$\phi 2$ Clock					
T_{CYC}	Cycle Time	1000	20,000	500	20,000	ns
T_R, T_F	Rise and Fall Time	—	25	—	25	ns
T_{CHW}	Clock Pulse Width (High)	420	10,000	200	10,000	ns
T_{CLW}	Clock Pulse Width (Low)	420	10,000	200	10,000	ns
	Write Cycle					
T_{PD}	Output Delay From $\phi 2$	—	1000	—	500	ns
T_{WCS}	$\overline{CS}$ low while $\phi 2$ high	420	—	200	—	ns
T_{ADS}	Address Setup Time	0	—	0	—	ns
T_{ADH}	Address Hold Time	10	—	5	—	ns
T_{RWS}	R/W Setup Time	0	—	0	—	ns
T_{RWH}	R/W Hold Time	0	—	0	—	ns
T_{DS}	Data Bus Setup Time	150	—	75	—	ns
T_{DH}	Data Bus Hold Time	0	—	0	—	ns
	Read Cycle					
T_{PS}	Port Setup Time	300	—	150	—	ns
$T_{WCS}(2)$	$\overline{CS}$ low while $\phi 2$ high	420	—	20	—	ns
T_{ADS}	Address Setup Time	0	—	0	—	ns
T_{ADH}	Address Hold Time	10	—	5	—	ns
T_{RWS}	R/W Setup Time	0	—	0	—	ns
T_{RWH}	R/W Hold Time	0	—	0	—	ns

Symbol	Characteristic	1MHz		2MHz		Unit
		MIN	MAX	MIN	MAX	
T_{ACC}	Data Access from RS3-RS0	—	550	—	275	ns
$T_{CO}(3)$	Data Access from $\overline{CS}$	—	320	—	150	ns
T_{DR}	Data Release Time	50	—	25	—	ns

NOTES: 1—All timings are referenced from V_{IL} max and V_{IH} min on inputs and V_{OL} max and V_{OH} min on outputs.

2—T_{WCS} is measured from the later of $\phi 2$ high or $\overline{CS}$ low. $\overline{CS}$ must be low at least until the end of $\phi 2$ high.

3—T_{CO} is measured from the later of $\phi 2$ high or $\overline{CS}$ low. Valid data is available only after the later of T_{ACC} or T_{CO}.

REGISTER MAP

RS3	RS2	RS1	RS0	REG	NAME	
0	0	0	0	0	PRA	PERIPHERAL DATA REG A
0	0	0	1	1	PRB	PERIPHERAL DATA REG B
0	0	1	0	2	DDRA	DATA DIRECTION REG A
0	0	1	1	3	DDRB	DATA DIRECTION REG B
0	1	0	0	4	TA LO	TIMER A LOW REGISTER
0	1	0	1	5	TA HI	TIMER A HIGH REGISTER
0	1	1	0	6	TB LO	TIMER B LOW REGISTER
0	1	1	1	7	TB HI	TIMER B HIGH REGISTER
1	0	0	0	8	TOD 10THS	10THS OF SECONDS REGISTER
1	0	0	1	9	TOD SEC	SECONDS REGISTER
1	0	1	0	A	TOD MIN	MINUTES REGISTER
1	0	1	1	B	TOD HR	HOURS—AM/PM REGISTER
1	1	0	0	C	SDR	SERIAL DATA REGISTER
1	1	0	1	D	ICR	INTERRUPT CONTROL REGISTER
1	1	1	0	E	CRA	CONTROL REG A
1	1	1	1	F	CRB	CONTROL REG B

6526 FUNCTIONAL DESCRIPTION

I/O Ports (PRA, PRB, DDRA, DDRB).

Ports A and B each consist of an 8-bit Peripheral Data Register (PR) and an 8-bit Data Direction Register (DDR). If a bit in the DDR is set to a one, the corresponding bit in the PR is an output; if a DDR bit is set to a zero, the corresponding PR bit is defined as an input. On a READ, the PR reflects the information present on the actual port pins (PA0–PA7, PB0–PB7) for both input and output bits. Port A and Port B have passive pull-up devices as well as active pull-ups, providing both CMOS and TTL compatibility. Both ports have two TTL load drive capability. In addition to normal I/O operation, PB6 and PB7 also provide timer output functions.

Handshaking

Handshaking on data transfers can be accomplished using the $\overline{PC}$ output pin and the $\overline{FLAG}$ input pin. $\overline{PC}$ will go low for one cycle following a read or write of PORT B. This signal can be used to indicate "data ready" at PORT B or "data accepted" from PORT B. Handshaking on 16-bit data transfers (using both PORT A and PORT B) is possible by always reading or writing PORT A first. $\overline{FLAG}$ is a negative edge sensitive input which can be used for receiving the $\overline{PC}$ output from another 6526, or as a general purpose interrupt input. Any negative transition of $\overline{FLAG}$ will set the FLAG interrupt bit.

REG	NAME	D_7	D_6	D_5	D_4	D_3	D_2	D_1	D_0
0	PRA	PA_7	PA_6	PA_5	PA_4	PA_3	PA_2	PA_1	PA_0
1	PRB	PB_7	PB_6	PB_5	PB_4	PB_3	PB_2	PB_1	PB_0
2	DDRA	DPA_7	DPA_6	DPA_5	DPA_4	DPA_3	DPA_2	DPA_1	DPA_0
3	DDRB	DPB_7	DPB_6	DPB_5	DPB_4	DPB_3	DPB_2	DPB_1	DPB_0

Interval Timers (Timer A, Timer B)

Each interval timer consists of a 16-bit read-only Timer Counter and a 16-bit write-only Timer Latch. Data written to the timer are latched in the Timer Latch, while data read from the timer are the present contents of the Time Counter. The timers can be used independently or linked for extended operations. The various timer modes allow generation of long time delays, variable width pulses, pulse trains and variable frequency waveforms. Utilizing the CNT input, the timers can count external pulses or measure frequency, pulse width and delay times of external signals. Each timer has an associated control register, providing independent control of the following functions:

Start/Stop

A control bit allows the timer to be started or stopped by the microprocessor at any time.

PB On/Off:

A control bit allows the timer output to appear on a PORT B output line (PB6 for TIMER A and PB7 for TIMER B). This function overrides the DDRB control bit and forces the appropriate PB line to an output.

Toggle/Pulse

A control bit selects the output applied to PORT B. On every timer underflow the output can either toggle or generate a single positive pulse of one cycle duration. The Toggle output is set high whenever the timer is started and is set low by $\overline{\text{RES}}$.

One-Shot/Continuous

A control bit selects either timer mode. In one-shot mode, the timer will count down from the latched value to zero, generate an interrupt, reload the latched value, then stop. In continuous mode, the timer will count from the latched value to zero, generate an interrupt, reload the latched value and repeat the procedure continuously.

Force Load

A strobe bit allows the timer latch to be loaded into the timer counter at any time, whether the timer is running or not.

Input Mode:

Control bits allow selection of the clock used to decrement the timer. TIMER A can count $\phi 2$ clock pulses or external pulses applied to the CNT pin. TIMER B can count $\phi 2$ pulses, external CNT pulses, TIMER A underflow pulses or TIMER A underflow pulses while the CNT pin is held high.

The timer latch is loaded into the timer on any timer underflow, on a force load or following a write to the high byte of the prescaler while the timer is stopped. If the timer is running, a write to the high byte will load the timer latch, but not reload the counter.

READ (TIMER)

REG	NAME								
4	TA LO	TAL_7	TAL_6	TAL_5	TAL_4	TAL_3	TAL_2	TAL_1	TAL_0
5	TA HI	TAH_7	TAH_6	TAH_5	TAH_4	TAH_3	TAH_2	TAH_1	TAH_0
6	TB LO	TBL_7	TBL_6	TBL_5	TBL_4	TBL_3	TBL_2	TBL_1	TBL_0
7	TB HI	TBH_7	TBH_6	TBH_5	TBH_4	TBH_3	TBH_2	TBH_1	TBH_0

WRITE (PRESCALER)

REG	NAME								
4	TA LO	PAL_7	PAL_6	PAL_5	PAL_4	PAL_3	PAL_2	PAL_1	PAL_0
5	TA HI	PAH_7	PAH_6	PAH_5	PAH_4	PAH_3	PAH_2	PAH_1	PAH_0
6	TB LO	PBL_7	PBL_6	PBL_5	PBL_4	PBL_3	PBL_2	PBL_1	PBL_0
7	TB HI	PBH_7	PBH_6	PBH_5	PBH_4	PBH_3	PBH_2	PBH_1	PBH_0

Time of Day Clock (TOD)

The TOD clock is a special purpose timer for real-time applications. TOD consists of a 24-hour (AM/PM) clock with 1/10th second resolution. It is organized into 4 registers: 10ths of seconds, Seconds, Minutes and Hours. The AM/PM flag is in the MSB of the Hours register for easy bit testing. Each register reads out in BCD format to simplify conversion for driving displays, etc. The clock requires an external 60 Hz or 50 Hz (programmable) TTL level input on the TOD pin for accurate time-keeping. In addition to time-keeping, a programmable ALARM is provided for generating an interrupt at a desired time. The ALARM registers are located at the same addresses as the corresponding TOD registers. Access to the ALARM is governed by a Control Register bit. The ALARM is write-only; any read of a TOD address will read time regardless of the state of the ALARM access bit.

A specific sequence of events must be followed for proper setting and reading of TOD. TOD is automatically stopped whenever a write to the Hours register occurs. The clock will not start again until after a write to the 10ths of seconds register. This assures TOD will always start at the desired time. Since a carry from one stage to the next can occur at any time with respect to a read operation, a latching function is included to keep all Time Of Day information constant during a read sequence. All four TOD registers latch on a read of Hours and remain latched until after a read of 10ths of seconds. The TOD clock continues to count when the output registers are latched. If only one register is to be read, there is no carry problem and the register can be read "on the fly," provided that any read of Hours is followed by a read of 10ths of seconds to disable the latching.

READ

REG	NAME								
8	TOD 10THS	0	0	0	0	T_8	T_4	T_2	T_1
9	TOD SEC	0	SH_4	SH_2	SH_1	SL_8	SL_4	SL_2	SL_1
A	TOD MIN	0	MH_4	MH_2	MH_1	ML_8	ML_4	ML_2	ML_1
B	TOD HR	PM	0	0	HH	HL_8	HL_4	HL_2	HL_1

WRITE

$CRB_7=0$ TOD
$CRB_7=1$ ALARM
(SAME FORMAT AS READ)

Serial Port (SDR)

The serial port is a buffered, 8-bit synchronous shift register system. A control bit selects input or output mode. In input mode, data on the SP pin is shifted into the shift register on the rising edge of the signal applied to the CNT pin. After 8 CNT pulses, the data in the shift register is dumped into the Serial Data Register and an interrupt is generated. In the output mode, TIMER A is used for the baud rate generator. Data is shifted out on the SP pin at ½ the underflow rate of TIMER A. The maximum baud rate possible is $\phi 2$ divided by 4, but the maximum useable baud rate will be determined b:, line loading and the speed at which the receiver responds to input data. Transmission will start following a write to the Serial Data Register (provided TIMER A is running and in continuous mode). The clock signal derived from TIMER A appears as an output on the CNT pin. The data in the Serial Data Register will be loaded into the shift register then shift out to the SP pin when a CNT pulse occurs. Data shifted out becomes valid on the falling edge of CNT and remains valid until the next falling edge. After 8 CNT pulses, an interrupt is generated to indicate more data can be sent. If the Serial Data Register was loaded with new information prior to this interrupt, the new data will automatically be loaded into the shift register and transmission will continue. If the microprocessor stays one byte ahead of the shift register, transmission will be continuous. If no further data is to be transmitted, after the 8th CNT pulse, CNT will return high and SP will remain at the level of the last data bit transmitted. SDR data is shifted out MSB first and serial input data should also appear in this format.

The bidirectional capability of the Serial Port and CNT clock allows many 6526 devices to be connected to a common serial communication bus on which one 6526 acts as a master, sourcing data and shift clock, while all other 6526 chips act as slaves. Both CNT and SP outputs are open drain to allow such a common bus. Protocol for master/slave selection can be transmitted over the serial bus, or via dedicated handshaking lines.

REG	NAME								
C	SDR	S_7	S_6	S_5	S_4	S_3	S_2	S_1	S_0

Interrupt Control (ICR)

There are five sources of interrupts on the 6526: underflow from TIMER A, underflow from TIMER B, TOD ALARM, Serial Port full/empty and $\overline{\text{FLAG}}$. A single register provides masking and interrupt information. The interrupt Control Register consists of a write-only MASK register and a read-only DATA register. Any interrupt will set the corresponding bit in the DATA register. Any interrupt which is enabled by the MASK register will set the IR bit (MSB) of the DATA register and bring the $\overline{\text{IRQ}}$ pin low. In a multi-chip system, the IR bit can be polled to detect which chip has generated an interrupt request. The interrupt DATA register is cleared and the $\overline{\text{IRQ}}$ line returns high following a read of the DATA register. Since each interrupt sets an interrupt bit regardless of the MASK, and each interrupt bit can be selectively masked to prevent the generation of a processor interrupt, it is possible to intermix polled interrupts with true interrupts. However, polling the IR bit will cause the DATA register to clear, therefore, it is up to the user to preserve the information contained in the DATA register if any polled interrupts were present.

The MASK register provides convenient control of individual mask bits. When writing to the MASK register, if bit 7 (SET/$\overline{\text{CLEAR}}$) of the data written is a ZERO, any mask bit written with a one will be cleared, while those mask bits written with a zero will be unaffected. If bit 7 of the data written is a ONE, any mask bit written with a one will be set, while those mask bits written with a zero will be unaffected. In order for an interrupt flag to set IR and generate an Interrupt Request, the corresponding MASK bit must be set.

READ (INT DATA)

REG	NAME								
D	ICR	IR	0	0	FLG	SP	ALRM	TB	TA

WRITE (INT MASK)

REG	NAME								
D	ICR	S/$\overline{C}$	X	X	FLG	SP	ALRM	TB	TA

CONTROL REGISTERS

There are two control registers in the 6526, CRA and CRB. CRA is associated with TIMER A and CRB is associated with TIMER B. The register format is as follows:

CRA:

Bit	Name	Function
0	START	1=START TIMER A, 0=STOP TIMER A. This bit is automatically reset when underflow occurs during one-shot mode.
1	PBON	1=TIMER A output appears on PB6, 0=PB6 normal operation.
2	OUTMODE	1=TOGGLE, 0=PULSE
3	RUNMODE	1=ONE-SHOT, 0=CONTINUOUS
4	LOAD	1=FORCE LOAD (this is a STROBE input, there is no data storage, bit 4 will always read back a zero and writing a zero has no effect).
5	INMODE	1=TIMER A counts positive CNT transitions, 0=TIMER A counts $\phi 2$ pulses.
6	SPMODE	1=SERIAL PORT output (CNT sources shift clock), 0=SERIAL PORT input (external shift clock required).
7	TODIN	1=50 Hz clock required on TOD pin for accurate time, 0=60 Hz clock required on TOD pin for accurate time.

CRB:

Bit	Name	Function
		(Bits CRB0-CRB4 are identical to CRA0-CRA4 for TIMER B with the exception that bit 1 controls the output of TIMER B on PB7).
5,6	INMODE	Bits CRB5 and CRB6 select one of four input modes for TIMER B as:

CRB6	CRB5	
0	0	TIMER B counts $\phi 2$ pulses.
0	1	TIMER B counts positive CNT transistions.
1	0	TIMER B counts TIMER A underflow pulses.
1	1	TIMER B counts TIMER A underflow pulses while CNT is high.

Bit	Name	Function
7	ALARM	1=writing to TOD registers sets ALARM, 0=writing to TOD registers sets TOD clock.

REG	NAME	TOD IN	SP MODE	IN MODE	LOAD	RUN MODE	OUT MODE	PB ON	START
E	CRA	0=60Hz 1=50Hz	0=INPUT 1=OUTPUT	0=$\phi 2$ 1=CNT	1=FORCE LOAD (STROBE)	0=CONT. 1=O.S.	0=PULSE 1=TOGGLE	0=PB_6OFF 1=PB_6 ON	0=STOP 1=START

TA (IN MODE through START)

REG	NAME	ALARM	IN	MODE	LOAD	RUN MODE	OUT MODE	PB ON	START
F	CRB	0=TOD 1= ALARM	0 1 1 1	0=$\phi 2$ 1=CNT 0=TA 1=CNT·TA	1=FORCE LOAD (STROBE)	0=CONT. 1=O.S.	0=PULSE 1=TOGGLE	0=PB_7 OFF 1=PB_7 ON	0=STOP 1=START

TB (IN through START)

All unused register bits are unaffected by a write and are forced to zero on a read.

COMMODORE SEMICONDUCTOR GROUP reserves the right to make changes to any products herein to improve reliability, function or design. **COMMODORE SEMICONDUCTOR GROUP** does not assume any liability arising out of the application or use of any product or circuit described herein; neither does it convey any license under its patent rights nor the rights of others.

APPENDIX N

6566/6567 (VIC-II) CHIP SPECIFICATIONS

The 6566/6567 are multi-purpose color video controller devices for use in both computer video terminals and video game applications. Both devices contain 47 control registers which are accessed via a standard 8-bit microprocessor bus (65XX) and will access up to 16K of memory for display information. The various operating modes and options within each mode are described.

CHARACTER DISPLAY MODE

In the character display mode, the 6566/6567 fetches CHARACTER POINTERs from the VIDEO MATRIX area of memory and translates the pointers to character dot location addresses in the 2048 byte CHARACTER BASE area of memory. The video matrix is comprised of 1000 consecutive locations in memory which each contain an eight-bit character pointer. The location of the video matrix within memory is defined by VM13–VM10 in register 24 ($18) which are used as the 4 MSB of the video matrix address. The lower order 10 bits are provided by an internal counter (VC3–VC0) which steps through the 1000 character locations. Note that the 6566/6567 provides 14 address outputs; therefore, additional system hardware may be required for complete system memory decodes.

CHARACTER POINTER ADDRESS

A13	A12	A11	A10	A09	A08	A07	A06	A05	A04	A03	A02	A01	A00
VM13	VM12	VM11	VM10	VC9	VC8	VC7	VC6	VC5	VC4	VC3	VC2	VC1	VC0

The eight-bit character pointer permits up to 256 different character definitions to be available simultaneously. Each character is an 8×8 dot matrix stored in the character base as eight consecutive bytes. The location of the character base is defined by CB13–CB11 also in register 24 ($18) which are used for the 3 most significant bits (MSB) of the character base address. The 11 lower order addresses are formed by the 8-bit character pointer from the video matrix (D7–D0) which selects a particular character, and a 3-bit raster counter (RC2–RC0) which selects one of the eight character bytes. The resulting characters are formatted as 25 rows of 40 characters each. In addition to the 8-bit character pointer, a 4-bit COLOR NYBBLE is associated with each video matrix location (the video matrix memory must be 12 bits wide) which defines one of sixteen colors for each character.

CHARACTER DATA ADDRESS

A13	A12	A11	A10	A09	A08	A07	A06	A05	A04	A03	A02	A01	A00
CB13	CB12	CB11	D7	D6	D5	D4	D3	D2	D1	D0	RC2	RC1	RC0

STANDARD CHARACTER MODE (MCM = BMM = ECM = 0)

In the standard character mode, the 8 sequential bytes from the character base are displayed directly on the 8 lines in each character region. A "0" bit causes the background #0 color (from register 33 ($21)) to be displayed while the color selected by the color nybble (foreground) is displayed for a "1" bit (see Color Code Table).

FUNCTION	CHARACTER BIT	COLOR DISPLAYED
Background	0	Background #0 color (register 33 ($21))
Foreground	1	Color selected by 4-bit color nybble

Therefore, each character has a unique color determined by the 4-bit color nybble (1 of 16) and all characters share the common background color.

MULTI-COLOR CHARACTER MODE (MCM = 1, BMM = ECM = 0

Multi-color mode provides additional color flexibility allowing up to four colors within each character but with reduced resolution. The multi-color mode is selected by setting the MCM bit in register 22 ($16) to "1," which causes the dot data stored in the character base to be interpreted in a different manner. If the MSB of the color nybble is a "0," the character will be displayed as described in standard character mode, allowing the two modes to be inter-mixed (however, only the lower order 8 colors are available). When the MSB of the color nybble is a "1" (if MCM:MSB(CM) = 1) the character bits are interpreted in the multi-color mode:

FUNCTION	CHARACTER BIT PAIR	COLOR DISPLAYED
Background	00	Background #0 Color (register 33 ($21))
Background	01	Background #1 Color (register 34 ($22))
Foreground	10	Background #2 Color (register 35 ($23))
Foreground	11	Color specified by 3 LSB of color nybble

Since two bits are required to specify one dot color, the character is now displayed as a 4 × 8 matrix with each dot twice the horizontal size as in standard mode. Note, however, that each character region can now contain 4 different colors, two as foreground and two as background (see MOB priority).

EXTENDED COLOR MODE (ECM = 1, BMM = MCM = 0)

The extended color mode allows the selection of individual background colors for each character region with the normal 8 × 8 character resolution. This mode is selected by setting the ECM bit of register 17 ($11) to "1." The character dot data is displayed as in the standard mode (foreground color determined by the color nybble is displayed for a "1" data bit), but the 2 MSB of the character pointer are used to select the background color for each character region as follows:

CHAR. POINTER MS BIT PAIR	BACKGROUND COLOR DISPLAYED FOR 0 BIT
00	Background #0 color (register 33 ($21))
01	Background #1 color (register 34 ($22))
10	Background #2 color (register 35 ($23))
11	Background #3 color (register 36 ($24))

Since the two MSB of the character pointers are used for color information, only 64 different character definitions are available. The 6566/6567 will force CB10 and CB9 to "0" regardless of the original pointer values, so that only the first 64 character definitions will be accessed. With extended color mode each character has one of sixteen individually defined foreground colors and one of the four available background colors.

NOTE: Extended color mode and multi-color mode should not be enabled simultaneously.

BIT MAP MODE

In bit map mode, the 6566/6567 fetches data from memory in a different fashion, so that a one-to-one correspondence exists between each displayed dot and a memory bit. The bit map mode provides a screen resolution of 320H × 200V individually controlled display dots. Bit map mode is selected by setting the BMM bit in register 17 ($11) to a "1." The VIDEO MATRIX is still accessed as in character mode, but the video matrix data is no longer interpreted as character pointers, but rather as color data. The VIDEO MATRIX COUNTER is then also used as an address to fetch the dot data for display from the 8000-byte DISPLAY BASE. The display base address is formed as follows:

A13	A12	A11	A10	A09	A08	A07	A06	A05	A04	A03	A02	A01	A00
CB13	VC9	VC8	VC7	VC6	VC5	VC4	VC3	VC2	VC1	VC0	RC2	RC1	RC0

VCx denotes the video matrix counter outputs, RCx denotes the 3-bit raster line counter and CB13 is from register 24 ($18). The video matrix counter steps through the same 40 locations for eight raster lines, continuing to the next 40 locations every eighth line, while the raster counter increments once for each horizontal video line (raster line). This addressing results in each eight sequential memory locations being formatted as an 8 × 8 dot block on the video display.

STANDARD BIT MAP MODE (BMM =1, MCM = 0)

When standard bit map mode is in use, the color information is derived only from the data stored in the video matrix (the color nybble is disregarded). The 8 bits are divided into two 4-bit nybbles which allow two colors to be independently selected in each 8 × 8 dot block. When a bit in the display memory is a "0" the color of the output dot is set by the least significant (lower) nybble (LSN). Similarly, a display memory bit of "1" selects the output color determined by the MSN (upper nybble).

BIT	DISPLAY COLOR
0	Lower nybble of video matrix pointer
1	Upper nybble of video matrix pointer

MULTI-COLOR BIT MAP MODE (BMM = MCM = 1)

Multi-colored bit map mode is selected by setting the MCM bit in register 22 ($16) to a "1" in conjunction with the BMM bit. Multi-color mode uses the same memory access sequences as standard bit map mode, but interprets the dot data as follows:

BIT PAIR	DISPLAY COLOR
00	Background #0 color (register 33 ($21))
01	Upper nybble of video matrix pointer
10	Lower nybble of video matrix pointer
11	Video matrix color nybble

Note that the color nybble (DB11–DB8) IS used for the multi-color bit map mode. Again, as two bits are used to select one dot color, the horizontal dot size is doubled, resulting in a screen resolution of 160H × 200V. Utilizing multi-color bit map mode, three independently selected colors can be displayed in each 8 × 8 block in addition to the background color.

MOVABLE OBJECT BLOCKS

The movable object block (MOB) is a special type of character which can be displayed at any one position on the screen without the block constraints inherent in character and bit map mode. Up to 8 unique MOBs can be displayed simultaneously, each defined by 63 bytes in memory which are displayed as a 24×21 dot array (shown below). A number of special features make MOBs especially suited for video graphics and game applications.

MOB DISPLAY BLOCK

BYTE	BYTE	BYTE
00	01	02
03	04	05
.	.	.
.	.	.
.	.	.
57	58	59
60	61	62

ENABLE

Each MOB can be selectively enabled for display by setting its corresponding enable bit (MnE) to "1" in register 21 ($15). If the MnE bit is "0," no MOB operations will occur involving the disabled MOB.

POSITION

Each MOB is positioned via its X and Y position register (see register map) with a resolution of 512 horizontal and 256 vertical positions. The position of a MOB is determined by the upper-left corner of the array. X locations 23 to 347 ($17–$157) and Y locations 50 to 249 ($32–$F9) are visible. Since not all available MOB positions are entirely visible on the screen, MOBs may be moved smoothly on and off the display screen.

COLOR

Each MOB has a separate 4-bit register to determine the MOB color. The two MOB color modes are:

STANDARD MOB (MnMC = 0)

In the standard mode, a "0" bit of MOB data allows any background data to show through (transparent) and a "1" bit is displayed as the MOB color determined by the corresponding MOB Color register.

MULTI-COLOR MOB (MnMC = 1)

Each MOB can be individually selected as a multi-color MOB via MnMC bits in the MOB Multi-color register 28 ($1C). When the MnMC bit is "1," the corresponding MOB is displayed in the multi-color mode. In the multi-color mode, the MOB data is interpreted in pairs (similar to the other multi-color modes) as follows:

BIT PAIR	COLOR DISPLAYED
00	Transparent
01	MOB Multi-color #0 (register 37 ($25))
10	MOB Color (registers 39-46 ($27-$2E))
11	MOB Multi-color #1 (register 38 ($26))

Since two bits of data are required for each color, the resolution of the MOB is reduced to 12×21, with each horizontal dot expanded to twice standard size so that the overall MOB size does not change. Note that up to 3 colors can be displayed in each MOB (in addition to transparent) but that two of the colors are shared among all the MOBs in the multi-color mode.

MAGNIFICATION

Each MOB can be selectively expanded (2×) in both the horizontal and vertical directions. Two registers contain the control bits (MnXE,MnYE) for the magnification control:

REGISTER	FUNCTION
23 ($17)	Horizontal expand MnXE—"1"=expand; "0"=normal
29 ($1D)	Vertical expand MnYE—"1"=expand; "0"=normal

When MOBs are expanded, no increase in resolution is realized. The same 24×21 array (12×21 if multi-colored) is displayed, but the overall MOB dimension is doubled in the desired direction (the smallest MOB dot may be up to 4× standard dot dimension if a MOB is both multi-colored and expanded).

PRIORITY

The priority of each MOB may be individually controlled with respect to the other displayed information from character or bit map modes. The priority of each MOB is set by the corresponding bit (MnDP) of register 27 ($1B) as follows:

REG BIT	PRIORITY TO CHARACTER OR BIT MAP DATA
0	Non-transparent MOB data will be displayed (MOB in front)
1	Non-transparent MOB data will be displayed only instead of Bkgd #0 or multi-color bit pair 01 (MOB behind)

MOB—DISPLAY DATA PRIORITY

MnDP = 1	MnDP = 0
MOBn Foreground Background	Foreground MOBn Background

MOB data bits of "0" ("00" in multi-color mode) are transparent, always permitting any other information to be displayed.

The MOBs have a fixed priority with respect to each other, with MOB 0 having the highest priority and MOB 7 the lowest. When MOB data (except transparent data) of two MOBs are coincident, the data from the lower number MOB will be displayed. MOB vs. MOB data is prioritized before priority resolution with character or bit map data.

COLLISION DETECTION

Two types of MOB collision (coincidence) are detected, MOB to MOB collision and MOB to display data collision:

1) A collision between two MOBs occurs when non-transparent output data of two MOBs are coincident. Coincidence of MOB transparent areas will not generate a collision. When a collision occurs, the MOB bits (MnM) in the MOB–MOB COLLISION register 30 ($1E) will be set to "1" for both colliding MOBs. As a collision between two (or more) MOBs occurs, the MOB–MOB collision bit for each collided MOB will be set. The collision bits remain set until a read of the collision register, when all bits are automatically cleared. MOBs collisions are detected even if positioned off-screen.
2) The second type of collision is a MOB–DATA collision between a MOB and foreground display data from the character or bit map modes. The MOB-DATA COLLISION register 31 ($1F) has a bit (MnD) for each MOB which is set to "1" when both the MOB and non-background display data are coincident. Again, the coincidence of only transparent data does not generate a collision. For special applications, the display data from the 0–1 multicolor bit pair also does not cause a collision. This feature permits their use as background display data without interfering with true MOB collisions. A MOB–DATA collision can occur off-screen in the horizontal direction if actual display data has been scrolled to an off-screen position (see scrolling). The MOB–DATA COLLISION register also automatically clears when read.

The collision interrupt latches are set whenever the first bit of either register is set to "1." Once any collision bit within a register is set high, subsequent collisions will not set the interrupt latch until that collision register has been cleared to all "0s" by a read.

MOB MEMORY ACCESS

The data for each MOB is stored in 63 consecutive bytes of memory. Each block of MOB data is defined by a MOB pointer, located at the end of the VIDEO MATRIX. Only 1000 bytes of the video matrix are used in the normal display modes, allowing the video matrix locations 1016–1023 (VM base+$3F8 to VM base+$3FF) to be used for MOB pointers 0–7, respectively. The eight-bit MOB pointer from the video matrix together with the six bits from the MOB byte counter (to address 63 bytes) define the entire 14–bit address field:

A13	A12	A11	A10	A09	A08	A07	A06	A05	A04	A03	A02	A01	A00
MP7	MP6	MP5	MP4	MP3	MP2	MP1	MP0	MC5	MC4	MC3	MC2	MC1	MC0

Where MPx are the MOB pointer bits from the video matrix and MCx are the internally generated MOB counter bits. The MOB pointers are read from the video matrix at the end of every raster line. When the Y position register of a MOB matches the current raster line count, the actual fetches of MOB data begin. Internal counters automatically step through the 63 bytes of MOB data, displaying three bytes on each raster line.

OTHER FEATURES

SCREEN BLANKING

The display screen may be blanked by setting the DEN bit in register 17 ($11) to a "0." When the screen is blanked, the entire screen will be filled with the exterior color as set in register 32 ($20). When blanking is active, only transparent (Phase 1) memory accesses are required, permitting full processor utilization of the system bus. MOB data, however, will be accessed if the MOBs are not also disabled. The DEN bit must be set to "1" for normal video display.

ROW/COLUMN SELECT

The normal display consists of 25 rows of 40 characters (or character regions) per row. For special display purposes, the display window may be reduced to 24 rows and 38 characters. There is no change in the format of the displayed information, except that characters (bits) adjacent to the exterior border area will now be covered by the border. The select bits operate as follows:

RSEL	NUMBER OF ROWS	CSEL	NUMBER OF COLUMNS
0	24 rows	0	38 columns
1	25 rows	1	40 columns

The RSEL bit is in register 17 ($11) and the CSEL bit is in register 22 ($16). For standard display the larger display window is normally used, while the smaller display window is normally used in conjunction with scrolling.

SCROLLING

The display data may be scrolled up to one entire character space in both the horizontal and vertical direction. When used in conjunction with the smaller display window (above), scrolling can be used to create a smooth panning motion of display data while updating the system memory only when a new character row (or column) is required. Scrolling is also used to center a fixed display within the display window.

BITS	REGISTER	FUNCTION
X2,X1,X0	22 ($16)	Horizontal Position
Y2,Y1,Y0	17 ($11)	Vertical Position

LIGHT PEN

The light pen input latches the current screen position into a pair of registers (LPX,LPY) on a low-going edge. The X position register 19 ($13) will contain the 8 MSB of the X position at the time of transition. Since the X position is defined by a 512-state counter (9 bits) resolution to 2 horizontal dots is provided. Similarly, the Y position is latched to its register 20 ($14) but here 8 bits provide single raster resolution within the visible display. The light pen latch may be triggered only once per frame, and subsequent triggers within the same frame will have no effect. Therefore, you must take several samples before turning the light pen to the screen (3 or more samples, average), depending upon the characteristics of your light pen.

RASTER REGISTER

The raster register is a dual-function register. A read of the raster register 18 ($12) returns the lower 8 bits of the current raster position (the MSB–RC8 is located in register 17 ($11)). The raster register can be interrogated to implement display changes outside the visible area to prevent display flicker. The visible display window is from raster 51 through raster 251 ($033–$0FB). A write to the raster bits (including RC8) is latched for use in an internal raster compare. When the current raster matches the written value, the raster interrupt latch is set.

INTERRUPT REGISTER

The interrupt register shows the status of the four sources of interrupt. An interrupt latch in register 25 ($19) is set to "1" when an interrupt source has generated an interrupt request. The four sources of interrupt are:

LATCH BIT	ENABLE BIT	WHEN SET
IRST	ERST	Set when (raster count) = (stored raster count)
IMDC	EMDC	Set by MOB–DATA collision register (first collision only)
IMMC	EMMC	Set by MOB–MOB collision register (first collision only)
ILP	ELP	Set by negative transition of LP input (once per frame)
IRQ		Set high by latch set and enabled (invert of IRQ/ output)

To enable an interrupt request to set the IRQ/ output to "0," the corresponding interrupt enable bit in register 26 ($1A) must be set to "1." Once an interrupt latch has been set, the latch may be cleared only by writing a "1" to the desired latch in the interrupt register. This feature allows selective handling of video interrupts without software required to "remember" active interrupts.

DYNAMIC RAM REFRESH

A dynamic ram refresh controller is built in to the 6566/6567 devices. Five 8-bit row addresses are refreshed every raster line. This rate guarantees a maximum delay of 2.02 ms between the refresh of any single row address in a 128 refresh scheme. (The maximum delay is 3.66 ms in a 256 address refresh scheme.) This refresh is totally transparent to the system, since the refresh occurs during Phase 1 of the system clock. The 6567 generates both RAS/ and CAS/ which are normally connected directly to the dynamic rams. RAS/ and CAS/ are generated for every Phase 2 and every video data access (including refresh) so that external clock generation is not required.

THEORY OF OPERATION

SYSTEM INTERFACE

The 6566/6567 video controller devices interact with the system data bus in a special way. A 65XX system requires the system buses only during the Phase 2 (clock high) portion of the cycle. The 6566/6567 devices take advantage of this feature by normally accessing system memory during the Phase 1 (clock low) portion of the clock cycle. Therefore, operations such as character data fetches and memory refresh are totally transparent to the processor and do not reduce the processor throughput. The video chips provide the interface control signals required to maintain this bus sharing.

The video devices provide the signal AEC (address enable control) which is used to disable the processor address bus drivers allowing the video device to access the address bus. AEC is active low which permits direct connection to the AEC input of the 65XX family. The AEC signal is normally activated during Phase 1 so that processor operation is not affected. Because of this bus "sharing," all memory accesses must be completed in 1/2 cycle. Since the video chips provide a 1-MHz clock (which must be used as system Phase 2), a memory cycle is 500 ns including address setup, data access and, data setup to the reading device.

Certain operations of the 6566/6567 require data at a faster rate than available by reading only during the Phase 1 time; specifically, the access of character pointers from the video matrix and the fetch of MOB data. Therefore, the processor must be disabled and the data accessed during the Phase 2 clock. This is accomplished via the BA (bus available) signal. The BA line is normally high but is brought low during Phase 1 to indicate that the video chip will require a Phase 2 data access. Three Phase-2 times are allowed after BA low for the processor to complete any current memory accesses. On the fourth Phase 2 after BA low, the AEC signal will remain low during Phase 2 as the video chip fetches data. The BA line is normally connected to the RDY input of a 65XX processor. The character pointer fetches occur every eighth raster line during the display window and require 40 consecutive Phase 2 accesses to fetch the video matrix pointers. The MOB data fetches require 4 memory accesses as follows:

PHASE	DATA	CONDITION
1	MOB Pointer	Every raster
2	MOB Byte 1	Each raster while MOB is displayed
1	MOB Byte 2	Each raster while MOB is displayed
2	MOB Byte 3	Each raster while MOB is displayed

The MOB pointers are fetched every other Phase 1 at the end of each raster line. As required, the additional cycles are used for MOB data fetches. Again, all necessary bus control is provided by the 6566/6567 devices.

MEMORY INTERFACE

The two versions of the video interface chip, 6566 and 6567, differ in address output configurations. The 6566 has thirteen fully decoded addresses for direct connection to the system address bus. The 6567 has multiplexed addresses for direct connection to 64K dynamic RAMs. The least significant address bits, A06–A00, are present on A06–A00 while RAS/ is brought low, while the most significant bits, A13–A08, are present on A05–A00 while CAS/ is brought low. The pins A11–A07 on the 6567 are static address outputs to allow direct connection of these bits to a conventional 16K (2K×8) ROM. (The lower order addresses require external latching.)

PROCESSOR INTERFACE

Aside from the special memory accesses described above, the 6566/6567 registers can be accessed similar to any other peripheral device. The following processor interface signals are provided:

DATA BUS (DB7–DB0)

The eight data bus pins are the bi-directional data port, controlled by CS/, RW, and Phase 0. The data bus can only be accessed while AEC and Phase 0 are high and CS/ is low.

CHIP SELECT (CS/)

The chip select pin, CS/, is brought low to enable access to the device registers in conjunction with the address and RW pins. CS/ low is recognized only while AEC and Phase 0 are high.

READ/WRITE (R/W)

The read/write input, R/W, is used to determine the direction of data transfer on the data bus, in conjunction with CS/. When R/W is high ("1") data is transferred from the selected register to the data bus output. When R/W is low ("0") data presented on the data bus pins is loaded into the selected register.

ADDRESS BUS (A05–A00)

The lower six address pins, A5–A0, are bi-directional. During a processor read or write of the video device, these address pins are inputs. The data on the address inputs selects the register for read or write as defined in the register map.

CLOCK OUT (PHO)

The clock output, Phase 0, is the 1-MHz clock used as the 65XX processor Phase 0 in. All system bus activity is referenced to this clock. The clock frequency is generated by dividing the 8-MHz video input clock by eight.

INTERRUPTS (IRQ/)

The interrupt output, IRQ/, is brought low when an enabled source of interrupt occurs within the device. The IRQ/ output is open drain, requiring an external pull-up resistor.

VIDEO INTERFACE

The video output signal from the 6566/6567 consists of two signals which must be externally mixed together. SYNC/LUM output contains all the video data, including horizontal and vertical syncs, as well as the luminance information of the video display. SYNC/LUM is open drain, requiring an external pull-up of 500 ohms. The COLOR output contains all the chrominance information, including the color reference burst and the color of all display data. The COLOR output is open source and should be terminated with 1000 ohms to ground. After appropriate mixing of these two signals, the resulting signal can directly drive a video monitor or be fed to a modulator for use with a standard television.

SUMMARY OF 6566/6567 BUS ACTIVITY

AEC	PHO	CS/	R/W	ACTION
0	0	X	X	PHASE 1 FETCH, REFRESH
0	1	X	X	PHASE 2 FETCH (PROCESSOR OFF)
1	0	X	X	NO ACTION
1	1	0	0	WRITE TO SELECTED REGISTER
1	1	0	1	READ FROM SELECTED REGISTER
1	1	1	X	NO ACTION

PIN CONFIGURATION

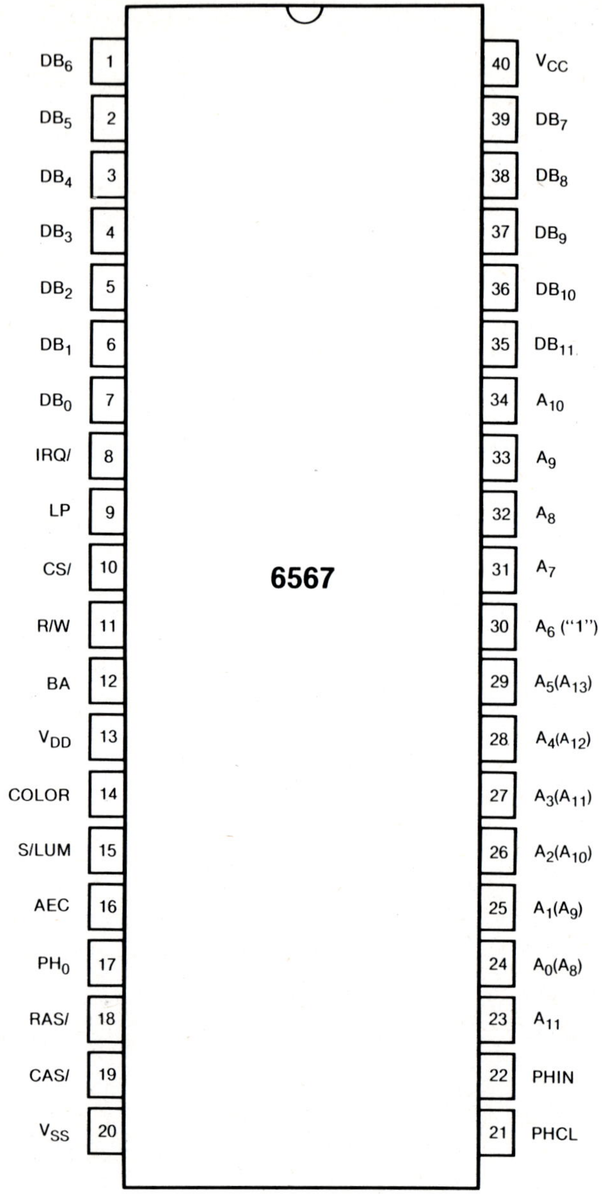

(Multiplexed addresses in parentheses)

PIN CONFIGURATION

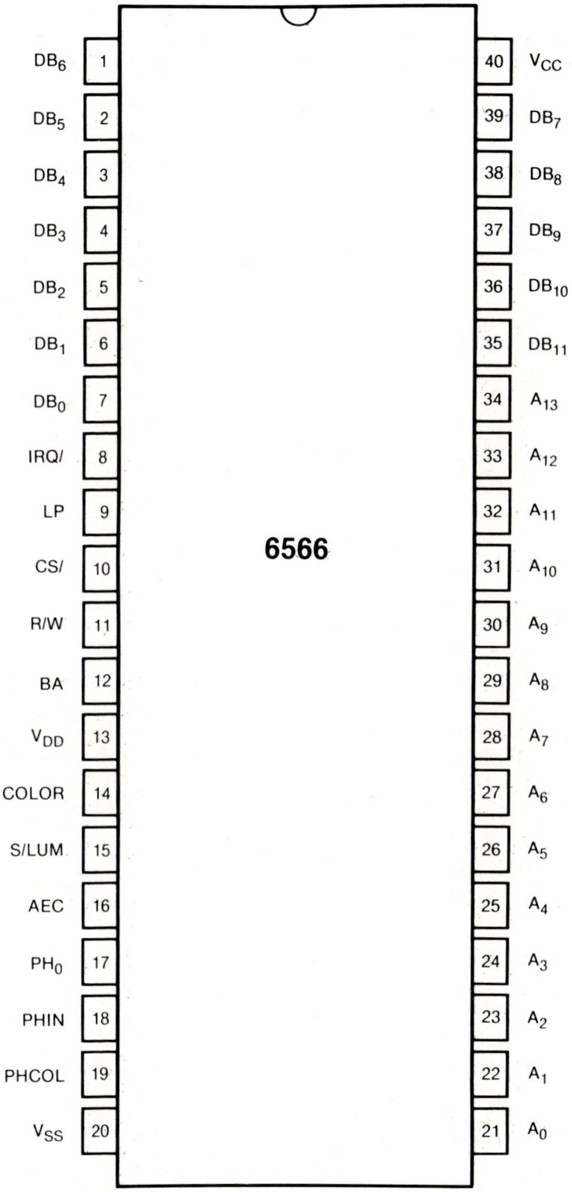

REGISTER MAP

ADDRESS		DB7	DB6	DB5	DB4	DB3	DB2	DB1	DB0	DESCRIPTION
00	($00)	M0X7	M0X6	M0X5	M0X4	M0X3	M0X2	M0X1	M0X0	MOB 0 X-position
01	($01)	M0Y7	M0Y6	M0Y5	M0Y4	M0Y3	M0Y2	M0Y1	M0Y0	MOB 0 Y-position
02	($02)	M1X7	M1X6	M1X5	M1X4	M1X3	M1X2	M1X1	M1X0	MOB 1 X-position
03	($03)	M1Y7	M1Y6	M1Y5	M1Y4	M1Y3	M1Y2	M1Y1	M1Y0	MOB 1 Y-position
04	($04)	M2X7	M2X6	M2X5	M2X4	M2X3	M2X2	M2X1	M2X0	MOB 2 X-position
05	($05)	M2Y7	M2Y6	M2Y5	M2Y4	M2Y3	M2Y2	M2Y1	M2Y0	MOB 2 Y-position
06	($06)	M3X7	M3X6	M3X5	M3X4	M3X3	M3X2	M3X1	M3X0	MOB 3 X-position
07	($07)	M3Y7	M3Y6	M3Y5	M3Y4	M3Y3	M3Y2	M3Y1	M3Y0	MOB 3 Y-position
08	($08)	M4X7	M4X6	M4X5	M4X4	M4X3	M4X2	M4X1	M4X0	MOB 4 X-position
09	($09)	M4Y7	M4Y6	M4Y5	M4Y4	M4Y3	M4Y2	M4Y1	M4Y0	MOB 4 Y-position
10	($0A)	M5X7	M5X6	M5X5	M5X4	M5X3	M5X2	M5X1	M5X0	MOB 5 X-position
11	($0B)	M5Y7	M5Y6	M5Y5	M5Y4	M5Y3	M5Y2	M5Y1	M5Y0	MOB 5 Y-position
12	($0C)	M6X7	M6X6	M6X5	M6X4	M6X3	M6X2	M6X1	M6X0	MOB 6 X-position
13	($0D)	M6Y7	M6Y6	M6Y5	M6Y4	M6Y3	M6Y2	M6Y1	M6Y0	MOB 6 Y-position
14	($0E)	M7X7	M7X6	M7X5	M7X4	M7X3	M7X2	M7X1	M7X0	MOB 7 X-position
15	($0F)	M7Y7	M7Y6	M7Y5	M7Y4	M7Y3	M7Y2	M7Y1	M6Y0	MOB 7 Y-position
16	($10)	M7X8	M6X8	M5X8	M4X8	M3X8	M2X8	M1X8	M0X8	MSB of X-position
17	($11)	RC8	ECM	BMM	DEN	RSEL	Y2	Y1	Y0	See text
18	($12)	RC7	RC6	RC5	RC4	RC3	RC2	RC1	RC0	Raster register
19	($13)	LPX8	LPX7	LPX6	LPX5	LPX4	LPX3	LPX2	LPX1	Light Pen X
20	($14)	LPY7	LPY6	LPY5	LPY4	LPY3	LPY2	LPY1	LPY0	Light Pen Y
21	($15)	M7E	M6E	M5E	M4E	M3E	M2E	M1E	M0E	MOB Enable
22	($16)	—	—	RES	MCM	CSEL	X2	X1	X0	See text
23	($17)	M7YE	M6YE	M5YE	M4YE	M3YE	M2YE	M1YE	M0YE	MOB Y-expand

24	($18)	VM13	VM12	VM11	VM10	CB13	CB12	CB11	—	Memory Pointers
25	($19)	IRQ	—	—	—	ILP	IMMC	IMBC	IRST	Interrupt Register
26	($1A)	—	—	—	—	ELP	EMMC	EMBC	ERST	Enable Interrupt
27	($1B)	M7DP	M6DP	M5DP	M4DP	M3DP	M2DP	M1DP	M0DP	MOB-DATA Priority
28	($1C)	M7MC	M6MC	M5MC	M4MC	M3MC	M2MC	M1MC	M0MC	MOB Multicolor Sel
29	($1D)	M7XE	M6XE	M5XE	M4XE	M3XE	M2XE	M1XE	M0XE	MOB X-expand
30	($1E)	M7M	M6M	M5M	M4M	M3M	M2M	M1M	M0M	MOB-MOB Collision
31	($1F)	M7D	M6D	M5D	M4D	M3D	M2D	M1D	M0D	MOB-DATA Collision
32	($20)	—	—	—	—	EC3	EC2	EC1	EC0	Exterior Color
33	($21)	—	—	—	—	B0C3	B0C2	B0C1	B0C0	Bkgd #0 Color
34	($22)	—	—	—	—	B1C3	B1C2	B1C1	B1C0	Bkgd #1 Color
35	($23)	—	—	—	—	B2C3	B2C2	B2C1	B2C0	Bkgd #2 Color
36	($24)	—	—	—	—	B3C3	B3C2	B3C1	B3C0	Bkgd #3 Color
37	($25)	—	—	—	—	MM03	MM02	MM01	MM00	MOB Multicolor #0
38	($26)	—	—	—	—	MM13	MM12	MM11	MM10	MOB Multicolor #1
39	($27)	—	—	—	—	M0C3	M0C2	M0C1	M0C0	MOB 0 Color
40	($28)	—	—	—	—	M1C3	M1C2	M1C1	M1C0	MOB 1 Color
41	($29)	—	—	—	—	M2C3	M2C2	M2C1	M2C0	MOB 2 Color
42	($2A)	—	—	—	—	M3C3	M3C2	M3C1	M3C0	MOB 3 Color
43	($2B)	—	—	—	—	M4C3	M4C2	M4C1	M4C0	MOB 4 Color
44	($2C)	—	—	—	—	M5C3	M5C2	M5C1	M5C0	MOB 5 Color
45	($2D)	—	—	—	—	M6C3	M6C2	M6C1	M6C0	MOB 6 Color
46	($2E)	—	—	—	—	M7C3	M7C2	M7C1	M7C0	MOB 7 Color

NOTE: A dash indicates a no connect. All no connects are read as a "1."

COLOR CODES

D4	D3	D1	D0	HEX	DEC	COLOR
0	0	0	0	0	0	BLACK
0	0	0	1	1	1	WHITE
0	0	1	0	2	2	RED
0	0	1	1	3	3	CYAN
0	1	0	0	4	4	PURPLE
0	1	0	1	5	5	GREEN
0	1	1	0	6	6	BLUE
0	1	1	1	7	7	YELLOW
1	0	0	0	8	8	ORANGE
1	0	0	1	9	9	BROWN
1	0	1	0	A	10	LT RED
1	0	1	1	B	11	DARK GREY
1	1	0	0	C	12	MED GREY
1	1	0	1	D	13	LT GREEN
1	1	1	0	E	14	LT BLUE
1	1	1	1	F	15	LT GREY

6581 SOUND INTERFACE DEVICE (SID) CHIP SPECIFICATIONS

CONCEPT

The 6581 Sound Interface Device (SID) is a single-chip, 3-voice electronic music synthesizer/sound effects generator compatible with the 65XX and similar microprocessor families. SID provides wide-range, high-resolution control of pitch (frequency), tone color (harmonic content), and dynamics (volume). Specialized control circuitry minimizes software overhead, facilitating use in arcade/home video games and low-cost musical instruments.

FEATURES

- 3 TONE OSCILLATORS
  Range: 0–4 kHz
- 4 WAVEFORMS PER OSCILLATOR
  Triangle, Sawtooth,
  Variable Pulse, Noise
- 3 AMPLITUDE MODULATORS
  Range: 48 dB
- 3 ENVELOPE GENERATORS
  Exponential response
  Attack Rate: 2 ms–8 s
  Decay Rate: 6 ms–24 s
  Sustain Level: 0–peak volume
  Release Rate: 6 ms–24 s
- OSCILLATOR SYNCHRONIZATION
- RING MODULATION

- PROGRAMMABLE FILTER
  - Cutoff range: 30 Hz–12 kHz
  - 12 dB/octave Rolloff
  - Low pass, Bandpass,
  - High pass, Notch outputs
  - Variable Resonance
- MASTER VOLUME CONTROL
- 2 A/D POT INTERFACES
- RANDOM NUMBER/MODULATION GENERATOR
- EXTERNAL AUDIO INPUT

PIN CONFIGURATION

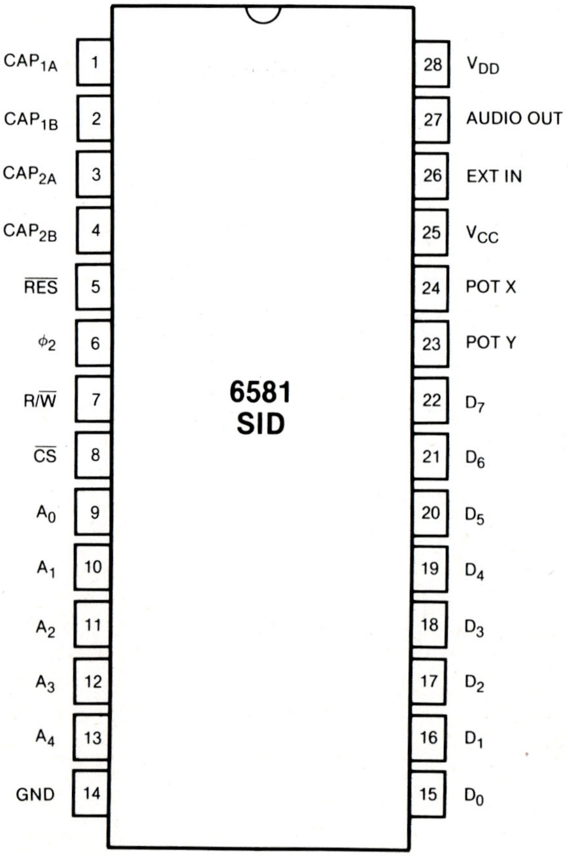

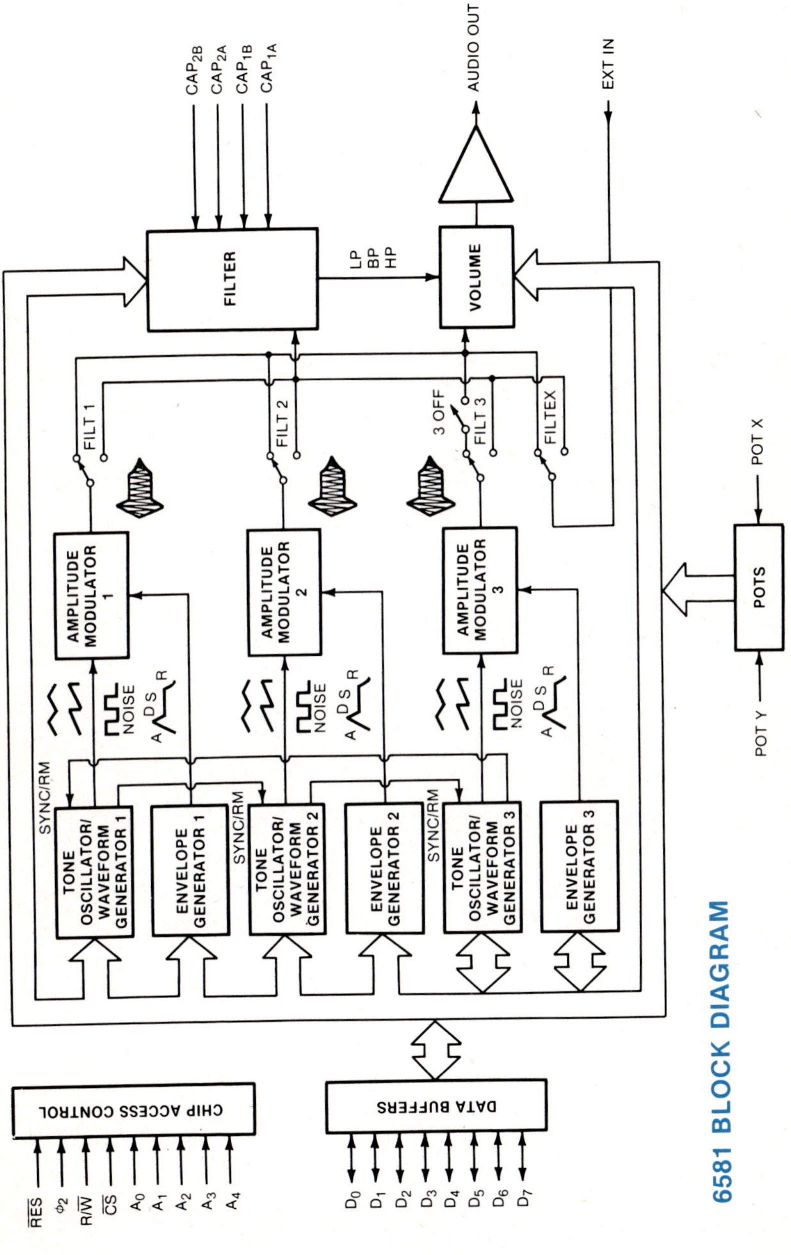

6581 BLOCK DIAGRAM

DESCRIPTION

The 6581 consists of three synthesizer "voices" which can be used independently or in conjunction with each other (or external audio sources) to create complex sounds. Each voice consists of a Tone Oscillator/Waveform Generator, an Envelope Generator and an Amplitude Modulator. The Tone Oscillator controls the pitch of the voice over a wide range. The Oscillator produces four waveforms at the selected frequency, with the unique harmonic content of each waveform providing simple control of tone color. The volume dynamics of the oscillator are controlled by the Amplitude Modulator under the direction of the Envelope Generator. When triggered, the Envelope Generator creates an amplitude envelope with programmable rates of increasing and decreasing volume. In addition to the three voices, a programmable Filter is provided for generating complex, dynamic tone colors via subtractive synthesis.

SID allows the microprocessor to read the changing output of the third Oscillator and third Envelope Generator. These outputs can be used as a source of modulation information for creating vibrato, frequency/filter sweeps and similar effects. The third oscillator can also act as a random number generator for games. Two A/D converters are provided for interfacing SID with potentiometers. These can be used for "paddles" in a game environment or as front panel controls in a music synthesizer. SID can process external audio signals, allowing multiple SID chips to be daisy-chained or mixed in complex polyphonic systems.

SID CONTROL REGISTERS

There are 29 eight-bit registers in SID which control the generation of sound. These registers are either WRITE-only or READ-only and are listed below in Table 1.

Table 1. SID Register Map

	ADDRESS A4	A3	A2	A1	A0	REG # (HEX)	DATA D7	D6	D5	D4	D3	D2	D1	D0	REG NAME	REG TYPE
															Voice 1	
0	0	0	0	0	0	00	F_7	F_6	F_5	F_4	F_3	F_2	F_1	F_0	FREQ LO	WRITE-ONLY
1	0	0	0	0	1	01	F_{15}	F_{14}	F_{13}	F_{12}	F_{11}	F_{10}	F_9	F_8	FREQ HI	WRITE-ONLY
2	0	0	0	1	0	02	PW_7	PW_6	PW_5	PW_4	PW_3	PW_2	PW_1	PW_0	PW LO	WRITE-ONLY
3	0	0	0	1	1	03	—	—	—	—	PW_{11}	PW_{10}	PW_9	PW_8	PW HI	WRITE-ONLY
4	0	0	1	0	0	04	NOISE	⊓⊔⊓	/|/|	/\/\	TEST	RING MOD	SYNC	GATE	CONTROL REG	WRITE-ONLY
5	0	0	1	0	1	05	ATK_3	ATK_2	ATK_1	ATK_0	DCY_3	DCY_2	DCY_1	DCY_0	ATTACK/DECAY	WRITE-ONLY
6	0	0	1	1	0	06	STN_3	STN_2	STN_1	STN_0	RLS_3	RLS_2	RLS_1	RLS_0	SUSTAIN/RELEASE	WRITE-ONLY
															Voice 2	
7	0	0	1	1	1	07	F_7	F_6	F_5	F_4	F_3	F_2	F_1	F_0	FREQ LO	WRITE-ONLY
8	0	1	0	0	0	08	F_{15}	F_{14}	F_{13}	F_{12}	F_{11}	F_{10}	F_9	F_8	FREQ HI	WRITE-ONLY
9	0	1	0	0	1	09	PW_7	PW_6	PW_5	PW_4	PW_3	PW_2	PW_1	PW_0	PW LO	WRITE-ONLY
10	0	1	0	1	0	0A	—	—	—	—	PW_{11}	PW_{10}	PW_9	PW_8	PW HI	WRITE-ONLY
11	0	1	0	1	1	0B	NOISE	⊓⊔⊓	/|/|	/\/\	TEST	RING MOD	SYNC	GATE	CONTROL REG	WRITE-ONLY
12	0	1	1	0	0	0C	ATK_3	ATK_2	ATK_1	ATK_0	DCY_3	DCY_2	DCY_1	DCY_0	ATTACK/DECAY	WRITE-ONLY
13	0	1	1	0	1	0D	STN_3	STN_2	STN_1	STN_0	RLS_3	RLS_2	RLS_1	RLS_0	SUSTAIN/RELEASE	WRITE-ONLY
															Voice 3	
14	0	1	1	1	0	0E	F_7	F_6	F_5	F_4	F_3	F_2	F_1	F_0	FREQ LO	WRITE-ONLY
15	0	1	1	1	1	0F	F_{15}	F_{14}	F_{13}	F_{12}	F_{11}	F_{10}	F_9	F_8	FREQ HI	WRITE-ONLY
16	1	0	0	0	0	10	PW_7	PW_6	PW_5	PW_4	PW_3	PW_2	PW_1	PW_0	PW LO	WRITE-ONLY
17	1	0	0	0	1	11	—	—	—	—	PW_{11}	PW_{10}	PW_9	PW_8	PW HI	WRITE-ONLY
18	1	0	0	1	0	12	NOISE	⊓⊔⊓	/|/|	/\/\	TEST	RING MOD	SYNC	GATE	CONTROL REG	WRITE-ONLY
19	1	0	0	1	1	13	ATK_3	ATK_2	ATK_1	ATK_0	DCY_3	DCY_2	DCY_1	DCY_0	ATTACK/DECAY	WRITE-ONLY
20	1	0	1	0	0	14	STN_3	STN_2	STN_1	STN_0	RLS_3	RLS_2	RLS_1	RLS_0	SUSTAIN/RELEASE	WRITE-ONLY
															Filter	
21	1	0	1	0	1	15	—	—	—	—	—	FC_2	FC_1	FC_0	FC LO	WRITE-ONLY
22	1	0	1	1	0	16	FC_{10}	FC_9	FC_8	FC_7	FC_6	FC_5	FC_4	FC_3	FC HI	WRITE-ONLY
23	1	0	1	1	1	17	RES_3	RES_2	RES_1	RES_0	FILTEX	FILT 3	FILT 2	FILT 1	RES/FILT	WRITE-ONLY
24	1	1	0	0	0	18	3 OFF	HP	BP	LP	VOL_3	VOL_2	VOL_1	VOL_0	MODE/VOL	WRITE-ONLY
															Misc.	
25	1	1	0	0	1	19	PX_7	PX_6	PX_5	PX_4	PX_3	PX_2	PX_1	PX_0	POT X	READ-ONLY
26	1	1	0	1	0	1A	PY_7	PY_6	PY_5	PY_4	PY_3	PY_2	PY_1	PY_0	POT Y	READ-ONLY
27	1	1	0	1	1	1B	O_7	O_6	O_5	O_4	O_3	O_2	O_1	O_0	OSC_3/RANDOM	READ-ONLY
28	1	1	1	0	0	1C	E_7	E_6	E_5	E_4	E_3	E_2	E_1	E_0	ENV_3	READ-ONLY

SID REGISTER DESCRIPTION

VOICE 1

FREQ LO/FREQ HI (Registers 00,01)

Together these registers form a 16-bit number which linearly controls the frequency of Oscillator 1. The frequency is determined by the following equation:

$$F_{out} = (F_n \times F_{clk}/16777216)\ \text{Hz}$$

Where F_n is the 16-bit number in the Frequency registers and F_{clk} is the system clock applied to the $\phi 2$ input (pin 6). For a standard 1.0-MHz clock, the frequency is given by:

$$F_{out} = (F_n \times 0.059604645)\ \text{Hz}$$

A complete table of values for generating 8 octaves of the equally tempered musical scale with concert A (440 Hz) tuning is provided in Appendix E. It should be noted that the frequency resolution of SID is sufficient for any tuning scale and allows sweeping from note to note (portamento) with no discernable frequency steps.

PW LO/PW HI (Registers 02,03)

Together these registers form a 12-bit number (bits 4–7 of PW HI are not used) which linearly controls the Pulse Width (duty cycle) of the Pulse waveform on Oscillator 1. The pulse width is determined by the following equation:

$$PW_{out} = (PW_n/40.95)\ \%$$

Where PWn is the 12-bit number in the Pulse Width registers.

The pulse width resolution allows the width to be smoothly swept with no discernable stepping. Note that the Pulse waveform on Oscillator 1 must be selected in order for the Pulse Width registers to have any audible effect. A value of 0 or 4095 ($FF) in the Pulse Width registers will produce a constant DC output, while a value of 2048 ($800) will produce a square wave.

CONTROL REGISTER (Register 04)

This register contains eight control bits which select various options on Oscillator 1.

GATE (Bit 0): The GATE bit controls the Envelope Generator for Voice 1. When this bit is set to a one, the Envelope Generator is Gated (triggered) and the ATTACK/DECAY/SUSTAIN cycle is initiated. When the bit is reset to a zero, the RELEASE cycle begins. The Envelope Generator controls the amplitude of Oscillator 1 appearing at the audio output, therefore, the GATE bit must be set (along with suitable envelope parameters) for the selected output of Oscillator 1 to be audible. A detailed discussion of the Envelope Generator can be found at the end of this Appendix.

SYNC (Bit 1): The SYNC bit, when set to a one, synchronizes the fundamental frequency of Oscillator 1 with the fundamental frequency of Oscillator 3, producing "Hard Sync" effects.

Varying the frequency of Oscillator 1 with respect to Oscillator 3 produces a wide range of complex harmonic structures from Voice 1 at the frequency of Oscillator 3. In order for sync to occur, Oscillator 3 must be set to some frequency other than zero but preferably lower than the frequency of Oscillator 1. No other parameters of Voice 3 have any effect on sync.

RING MOD (Bit 2): The RING MOD bit, when set to a one, replaces the Triangle waveform output of Oscillator 1 with a "Ring Modulated" combination of Oscillators 1 and 3. Varying the frequency of Oscillator 1 with respect to Oscillator 3 produces a wide range of non-harmonic overtone structures for creating bell or gong sounds and for special effects. In order for ring modulation to be audible, the Triangle waveform of Oscillator 1 must be selected and Oscillator 3 must be set to some frequency other than zero. No other parameters of Voice 3 have any effect on ring modulation.

TEST (Bit 3): The TEST bit, when set to a one, resets and locks Oscillator 1 at zero until the TEST bit is cleared. The Noise waveform output of Oscillator 1 is also reset and the Pulse waveform output is held at a DC level. Normally this bit is used for testing purposes, however, it can be used to synchronize Oscillator 1 to external events, allowing the generation of highly complex waveforms under real-time software control.

(Bit 4): When set to a one, the Triangle waveform output of Oscillator 1 is selected. The Triangle waveform is low in harmonics and has a mellow, flute-like quality.

(Bit 5): When set to a one, the Sawtooth waveform output of Oscillator 1 is selected. The Sawtooth waveform is rich in even and odd harmonics and has a bright, brassy quality.

(Bit 6): When set to a one, the Pulse waveform output of Oscillator 1 is selected. The harmonic content of this waveform can be adjusted by the Pulse Width registers, producing tone qualities ranging from a bright, hollow square wave to a nasal, reedy pulse. Sweeping the pulse width in real-time produces a dynamic "phasing" effect which adds a sense of motion to the sound. Rapidly jumping between different pulse widths can produce interesting harmonic sequences.

NOISE (Bit 7): When set to a one, the Noise output waveform of Oscillator 1 is selected. This output is a random signal which changes at the frequency of Oscillator 1. The sound quality can be varied from a low rumbling to hissing white noise via the Oscillator 1 Frequency registers. Noise is useful in creating explosions, gunshots, jet engines, wind, surf and other unpitched sounds, as well as snare drums and cymbals. Sweeping the oscillator frequency with Noise selected produces a dramatic rushing effect.

One of the output waveforms must be selected for Oscillator 1 to be audible, however, it is NOT necessary to de-select waveforms to silence the output of Voice 1. The amplitude of Voice 1 at the final output is a function of the Envelope Generator only.

> **NOTE:** The oscillator output waveforms are NOT additive. If more than one output waveform is selected simultaneously, the result will be a logical ANDing of the waveforms. Although this technique can be used to generate additional waveforms beyond the four listed above, it must be used with care. If any other waveform is selected while Noise is on, the Noise output can "lock up." If this occurs, the Noise output will remain silent until reset by the TEST bit or by bringing RES (pin 5) low.

ATTACK/DECAY (Register 05)

Bits 4–7 of this register (ATK0–ATK3) select 1 of 16 ATTACK rates for the Voice 1 Envelope Generator. The ATTACK rate determines how rapidly the output of Voice 1 rises from zero to peak amplitude when the Envelope Generator is Gated. The 16 ATTACK rates are listed in Table 2.

Bits 0–3 (DCY0–DCY3) select 1 of 16 DECAY rates for the Envelope Generator. The DECAY cycle follows the ATTACK cycle and the DECAY rate determines how rapidly the output falls from the peak amplitude to the selected SUSTAIN level. The 16 DECAY rates are listed in Table 2.

SUSTAIN/RELEASE (Register 06)

Bits 4–7 of this register (STN0–STN3) select 1 of 16 SUSTAIN levels for the Envelope Generator. The SUSTAIN cycle follows the DECAY cycle and the output of Voice 1 will remain at the selected SUSTAIN amplitude as long as the Gate bit remains set. The SUSTAIN levels range from zero to peak amplitude in 16 linear steps, with a SUSTAIN value of 0 selecting zero amplitude and a SUSTAIN value of 15 ($F) selecting the peak amplitude. A SUSTAIN value of 8 would cause Voice 1 to SUSTAIN at an amplitude one-half the peak amplitude reached by the ATTACK cycle.

Bits 0–3 (RLS0–RLS3) select 1 of 16 RELEASE rates for the Envelope Generator. The RELEASE cycle follows the SUSTAIN cycle when the Gate bit is reset to zero. At this time, the output of Voice 1 will fall from the SUSTAIN amplitude to zero amplitude at the selected RELEASE rate. The 16 RELEASE rates are identical to the DECAY rates.

NOTE: The cycling of the Envelope Generator can be altered at any point via the Gate bit. The Envelope Generator can be Gated and Released without restriction. For example, if the Gate bit is reset before the envelope has finished the ATTACK cycle, the RELEASE cycle will immediately begin, starting from whatever amplitude had been reached. If the envelope is then Gated again (before the RELEASE cycle has reached zero amplitude), another ATTACK cycle will begin, starting from whatever amplitude had been reached. This technique can be used to generate complex amplitude envelopes via real-time software control.

Table 2. Envelope Rates

VALUE		ATTACK RATE	DECAY/RELEASE RATE
DEC	(HEX)	(Time/Cycle)	(Time/Cycle)
0	(0)	2 ms	6 ms
1	(1)	8 ms	24 ms
2	(2)	16 ms	48 ms
3	(3)	24 ms	72 ms
4	(4)	38 ms	114 ms
5	(5)	56 ms	168 ms
6	(6)	68 ms	204 ms
7	(7)	80 ms	240 ms
8	(8)	100 ms	300 ms
9	(9)	250 ms	750 ms
10	(A)	500 ms	1.5 s
11	(B)	800 ms	2.4 s
12	(C)	1 s	3 s
13	(D)	3 s	9 s
14	(E)	5 s	15 s
15	(F)	8 s	24 s

NOTE Envelope rates are based on a 1.0-MHz $\phi2$ clock. For other $\phi2$ frequencies, multiply the given rate by 1 MHz/$\phi2$. The rates refer to the amount of time per cycle. For example, given an ATTACK value of 2, the ATTACK cycle would take 16 ms to rise from zero to peak amplitude. The DECAY/RELEASE rates refer to the amount of time these cycles would take to fall from peak amplitude to zero.

VOICE 2

Registers 07–$0D control Voice 2 and are functionally identical to registers 00–06 with these exceptions:

1) When selected, SYNC synchronizes Oscillator 2 with Oscillator 1.
2) When selected, RING MOD replaces the Triangle output of Oscillator 2 with the ring modulated combination of Oscillators 2 and 1.

VOICE 3

Registers $0E–$14 control Voice 3 and are functionally identical to registers 00–06 with these exceptions:

1) When selected, SYNC synchronizes Oscillator 3 with Oscillator 2.
2) When selected, RING MOD replaces the Triangle output of Oscillator 3 with the ring modulated combination of Oscillators 3 and 2.

Typical operation of a voice consists of selecting the desired parameters: frequency, waveform, effects (SYNC, RING MOD) and envelope rates, then gating the voice whenever the sound is desired. The sound can be sustained for any length of time and terminated by clearing the Gate bit. Each voice can be used separately, with independent parameters and gating, or in unison to create a single, powerful voice. When used in unison, a slight detuning of each oscillator or tuning to musical intervals creates a rich, animated sound.

FILTER

FC LO/FC HI (Registers $15,$16)

Together these registers form an 11-bit number (bits 3–7 of FC LO are not used) which linearly controls the Cutoff (or Center) Frequency of the programmable Filter. The approximate Cutoff Frequency ranges from 30 Hz to 12 KHz.

RES/FILT (Register $17)

Bits 4–7 of this register (RES0–RES3) control the resonance of the filter. Resonance is a peaking effect which emphasizes frequency components at the Cutoff Frequency of the Filter, causing a sharper sound. There are 16 resonance settings ranging linearly from no resonance (0) to maximum resonance (15 or $F). Bits 0–3 determine which signals will be routed through the Filter:

FILT 1 (Bit 0): When set to a zero, Voice 1 appears directly at the audio output and the Filter has no effect on it. When set to a one, Voice 1 will be processed through the Filter and the harmonic content of Voice 1 will be altered according to the selected Filter parameters.

FILT 2 (Bit 1): Same as bit 0 for Voice 2.

FILT 3 (Bit 2): Same as bit 0 for Voice 3.

FILTEX (Bit 3): Same as bit 0 for External audio input (pin 26).

MODE/VOL (Register $18)

Bits 4–7 of this register select various Filter mode and output options:

LP (Bit 4): When set to a one, the Low-Pass output of the Filter is selected and sent to the audio output. For a given Filter input signal, all frequency components below the Filter Cutoff Frequency are passed unaltered, while all frequency components above the Cutoff are attenuated at a rate of 12 dB/Octave. The Low-Pass mode produces full-bodied sounds.

BP (Bit 5): Same as bit 4 for the Bandpass output. All frequency components above and below the Cutoff are attenuated at a rate of 6 dB/Octave. The Bandpass mode produces thin, open sounds.

HP (Bit 6): Same as bit 4 for the High-Pass output. All frequency components above the Cutoff are passed unaltered, while all frequency components below the Cutoff are attenuated at a rate of 12 dB/Octave. The High-Pass mode produces tinny, buzzy sounds.

3 OFF (Bit 7): When set to a one, the output of Voice 3 is disconnected from the direct audio path. Setting Voice 3 to bypass the Filter (FILT 3 = 0) and setting 3 OFF to a one prevents Voice 3 from reaching the audio output. This allows Voice 3 to be used for modulation purposes without any undesirable output.

NOTE: The Filter output modes ARE additive and multiple Filter modes may be selected simultaneously. For example, both LP and HP modes can be selected to produce a Notch (or Band Reject) Filter response. In order for the Filter to have any audible effect, at least one Filter output must be selected and at least one Voice must be routed through the Filter. The Filter is, perhaps, the most important element in SID as it allows the generation of complex tone colors via subtractive synthesis (the Filter is used to eliminate specific frequency components from a harmonically rich input signal). The best results are achieved by varying the Cutoff Frequency in real-time.

Bits 0–3 (VOL0–VOL3) select 1 of 16 overall Volume levels for the final composite audio output. The output volume levels range from no output (0) to maximum volume (15 or $F) in 16 linear steps. This control can be used as a static volume control for balancing levels in multi-chip systems or for creating dynamic volume effects, such as Tremolo. Some Volume level other than zero must be selected in order for SID to produce any sound.

MISCELLANEOUS

POTX (Register $19)

This register allows the microprocessor to read the position of the potentiometer tied to POTX (pin 24), with values ranging from 0 at minimum resistance, to 255 ($FF) at maximum resistance. The value is always valid and is updated every 512 $\phi 2$ clock cycles. See the Pin Description section for information on pot and capacitor values.

POTY (Register $1A)

Same as POTX for the pot tied to POTY (pin 23).

OSC 3/RANDOM (Register $1B)

This register allows the microprocessor to read the upper 8 output bits of Oscillator 3. The character of the numbers generated is directly related to the waveform selected. If the Sawtooth waveform of Oscillator 3 is selected, this register will present a series of numbers incrementing from 0 to 255 ($FF) at a rate determined by the frequency of Oscillator 3. If the Triangle waveform is selected, the output will increment from 0 up to 255, then decrement down to 0. If the Pulse waveform is selected, the output will jump between 0 and 255. Selecting the Noise waveform will produce a series of random numbers, therefore, this register can be used as a random number generator for games. There are numerous timing and sequencing applications for the OSC 3 register, however, the chief function is probably that of a modulation generator. The numbers generated by this register can be added, via software, to the Oscillator or Filter Frequency registers or the Pulse Width registers in real-time. Many dynamic effects can be generated in this manner. Siren-like sounds can be created by adding the OSC 3 Sawtooth output to the frequency control of another oscillator. Synthesizer "Sample and Hold" effects can be produced by adding the OSC 3 Noise output to the Filter Frequency control registers. Vibrato can be produced by setting Oscillator 3 to a frequency around 7 Hz and adding the OSC 3 Triangle output (with proper scaling) to the Frequency control of another oscillator. An unlimited range of effects are available by altering the frequency of Oscillator 3 and scaling the OSC 3 output. Normally, when Oscillator 3 is used for modulation, the audio output of Voice 3 should be eliminated (3 OFF = 1).

ENV 3 (Register $1C)

Same as OSC 3, but this register allows the microprocessor to read the output of the Voice 3 Envelope Generator. This output can be added to the Filter Frequency to produce harmonic envelopes, WAH-WAH, and similar effects. "Phaser" sounds can be created by adding this output to the frequency control registers of an oscillator. The Voice 3 Envelope Generator must be Gated in order to produce any output from this register. The OSC 3 register, however, always reflects the changing output of the oscillator and is not affected in any way by the Envelope Generator.

SID PIN DESCRIPTION

CAP1A,CAP1B, (Pins 1,2)/ CAP2A,CAP2B (Pins 3,4)

These pins are used to connect the two integrating capacitors required by the programmable Filter. C1 connects between pins 1 and 2, C2 between pins 3 and 4. Both capacitors should be the same value. Normal operation of the Filter over the audio range (approximately 30 Hz–12 kHz) is accomplished with a value of 2200 pF for C1 and C2. Polystyrene capacitors are preferred and in complex polyphonic systems, where many SID chips must track each other, matched capacitors are recommended.

The frequency range of the Filter can be tailored to specific applications by the choice of capacitor values. For example, a low-cost game may not require full high-frequency response. In this case, larger values for C1 and C2 could be chosen to provide more control over the bass frequencies of the Filter. The maximum Cutoff Frequency of the Filter is given by:

$$FC_{max} = 2.6E-5/C$$

Where C is the capacitor value. The range of the Filter extends 9 octaves below the maximum Cutoff Frequency.

RES (Pin 5)

This TTL-level input is the reset control for SID. When brought low for at least ten $\phi 2$ cycles, all internal registers are reset to zero and the audio output is silenced. This pin is normally connected to the reset line of the microprocessor or a power-on-clear circuit.

$\phi 2$ (Pin 6)

This TTL-level input is the master clock for SID. All oscillator frequencies and envelope rates are referenced to this clock. $\phi 2$ also controls data transfers between SID and the microprocessor. Data can only be transferred when $\phi 2$ is high. Essentially, $\phi 2$ acts as a high-active chip select as far as data transfers are concerned. This pin is normally connected to the system clock, with a nominal operating frequency of 1.0 MHz.

R/W (Pin 7)

This TTL-level input controls the direction of data transfers between SID and the microprocessor. If the chip select conditions have been met, a high on this line allows the microprocessor to Read data from the selected SID register and a low allows the microprocessor to Write data into the selected SID register. This pin is normally connected to the system Read/Write line.

CS (Pin 8)

This TTL-level input is a low active chip select which controls data transfers between SID and the microprocessor. CS must be low for any transfer. A Read from the selected SID register can only occur if CS is low, $\phi 2$ is high and R/W is high. A Write to the selected SID register can only occur if CS is low, $\phi 2$ is high and R/W is low. This pin is normally connected to address decoding circuitry, allowing SID to reside in the memory map of a system.

A0–A4 (Pins 9–13)

These TTL-level inputs are used to select one of the 29 SID registers. Although enough addresses are provided to select 1 of 32 registers, the remaining three register locations are not used. A Write to any of these three locations is ignored and a Read returns invalid data. These pins are normally connected to the corresponding address lines of the microprocessor so that SID may be addressed in the same manner as memory.

GND (Pin 14)

For best results, the ground line between SID and the power supply should be separate from ground lines to other digital circuitry. This will minimize digital noise at the audio output.

D0–D7 (Pins 15–22)

These bidirectional lines are used to transfer data between SID and the microprocessor. They are TTL compatible in the input mode and capable of driving 2 TTL loads in the output mode. The data buffers are usually in the high-impedance off state. During a Write operation, the data buffers remain in the off (input) state and the microprocessor supplies data to SID over these lines. During a Read operation, the data buffers turn on and SID supplies data to the microprocessor over these lines. The pins are normally connected to the corresponding data lines of the microprocessor.

POTX,POTY (Pins 24,23)

These pins are inputs to the A/D converters used to digitize the position of potentiometers. The conversion process is based on the time constant of a capacitor tied from the POT pin to ground, charged by a potentiometer tied from the POT pin to +5 volts. The component values are determined by:

$$RC = 4.7E-4$$

Where R is the maximum resistance of the pot and C is the capacitor.

The larger the capacitor, the smaller the POT value jitter. The recommended values for R and C are 470 kΩ and 1000 pF. Note that a separate pot and cap are required for each POT pin.

V_{CC} (Pin 25)

As with the GND line, a separate +5 VDC line should be run between SID V_{CC} and the power supply in order to minimize noise. A bypass capacitor should be located close to the pin.

EXT IN (Pin 26)

This analog input allows external audio signals to be mixed with the audio output of SID or processed through the Filter. Typical sources include voice, guitar, and organ. The input impedance of this pin is on the order of 100 kΩ. Any signal applied directly to the pin should ride at a DC level of 6 volts and should not exceed 3 volts p–p. In order to prevent any interference caused by DC level differences, external signals should be AC-coupled to EXT IN by an electrolytic capacitor in the 1–10 μF range. As the direct audio path (FILTEX=0) has unity gain, EXT IN can be used to mix outputs of many SID chips by daisy-chaining. The number of chips that can be chained in this manner is determined by the amount of noise and distortion allowable at the final output. Note that the output Volume control will affect not only the three SID voices, but also any external inputs.

AUDIO OUT (Pin 27)

This open-source buffer is the final audio output of SID, comprised of the three SID voices, the Filter and any external input. The output level is set by the output Volume control and reaches a maximum of 2 volts p–p at a DC level of 6 volts. A source resistor from AUDIO OUT to ground is required for proper operation. The recommended resistance is 1 kΩ for a standard output impedance.

As the output of SID rides at a 6-volt DC level, it should be AC-coupled to any audio amplifier with an electrolytic capacitor in the 1–10 μF range.

V_{DD} (Pin 28)

As with V_{CC}, a separate +12 VDC line should be run to SID V_{DD} and a bypass capacitor should be used.

6581 SID CHARACTERISTICS

ABSOLUTE MAXIMUM RATINGS

RATING	SYMBOL	VALUE	UNITS
Supply Voltage	V_{DD}	−0.3 to +17	VDC
Supply Voltage	V_{CC}	−0.3 to +7	VDC
Input Voltage (analog)	V_{ina}	−0.3 to +17	VDC
Input Voltage (digital)	V_{ind}	−0.3 to +7	VDC
Operating Temperature	T_A	0 to +70	°C
Storage Temperature	T_{STG}	−55 to +150	°C

ELECTRICAL CHARACTERISTICS (V_{DD}=12 VDC±5%, V_{CC}=5 VDC±5%, T_A=0 to 70° C)

CHARACTERISTIC		SYMBOL	MIN	TYP	MAX	UNITS
Input High Voltage Input Low Voltage	(RES, ϕ2, R/W, CS, A0–A4, D0–D7)	V_{IH} V_{IL}	2 −0.3	— —	V_{CC} 0.8	VDC VDC
Input Leakage Current	(RES, ϕ2, R/W, CS, A0–A4; V_{in}=0–5 VDC)	I_{in}	—	—	2.5	μA
Three-State (Off)	(D0–D7; V_{CC}=max)	I_{TSI}	—	—	10	μA
Input Leakage Current	V_{in}=0.4–2.4 VDC					
Output High Voltage	(D0–D7; V_{CC}=min, I load=200 μA)	V_{OH}	2.4	—	V_{CC}−0.7	VDC
Output Low Voltage	(D0–D7; V_{CC}=max, I load=3.2 mA)	V_{OL}	GND	—	0.4	VDC
Output High Current	(D0–D7; Sourcing, V_{OH}=2.4 VDC)	I_{OH}	200	—	—	μA

Output Low Current	(D0–D7; Sinking, V_{OL}=0.4 VDC)	I_{OL}	3.2	—	—	mA
Input Capacitance	(RES, ϕ2, R/W, CS, A0–A4, D0–D7)	C_{in}	—	—	10	pF
Pot Trigger Voltage	(POTX, POTY)	V_{pot}	—	$V_{CC}/2$	—	VDC
Pot Sink Current	(POTX, POTY)	I_{pot}	500	—	—	μA
Input Impedance	(EXT IN)	R_{in}	100	150	—	kΩ
Audio Input Voltage	(EXT IN)	V_{in}	5.7 —	6 0.5	6.3 3	VDC VAC
Audio Output Voltage	(AUDIO OUT; 1 kΩ load, volume=max) One Voice on: All Voices on:	V_{out}	5.7 0.4 1.0	6 0.5 1.5	6.3 0.6 2.0	VDC VAC VAC
Power Supply Current	(V_{DD})	I_{DD}	—	20	25	mA
Power Supply Current	(V_{CC})	I_{CC}	—	70	100	mA
Power Dissipation	(Total)	P_D	—	600	1000	mW

6581 SID TIMING

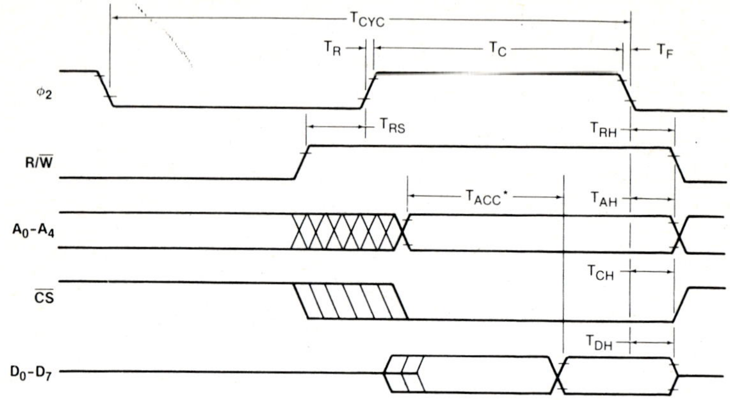

*T_{ACC} is measured from the latest occurring of ϕ_2, $\overline{CS}$, A_0-A_4.

READ CYCLE

SYMBOL	NAME	MIN	TYP	MAX	UNITS
T_{CYC}	Clock Cycle Time	1	—	20	μs
T_C	Clock High Pulse Width	450	500	10,000	ns
T_R, T_F	Clock Rise/Fall Time	—	—	25	ns
T_{RS}	Read Set-Up Time	0	—	—	ns
T_{RH}	Read Hold Time	0	—	—	ns
T_{ACC}	Access Time	—	—	300	ns
T_{AH}	Address Hold Time	10	—	—	ns
T_{CH}	Chip Select Hold Time	0	—	—	ns
T_{DH}	Data Hold Time	20	—	—	ns

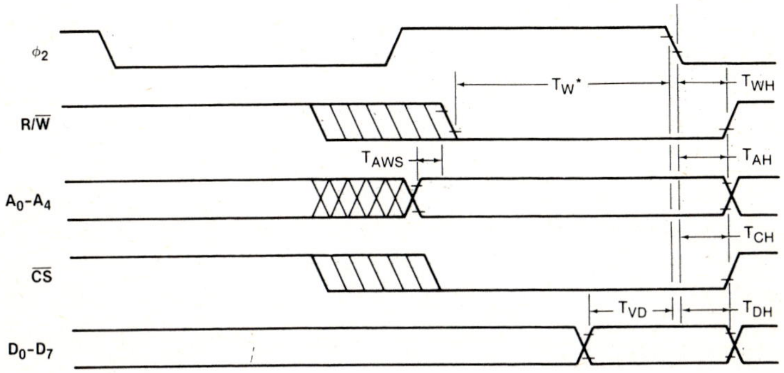

*T_W is measured from the latest occurring of ϕ_2, $\overline{CS}$, R/$\overline{W}$.

WRITE CYCLE

SYMBOL	NAME	MIN	TYP	MAX	UNITS
T_W	Write Pulse Width	300	—	—	ns
T_{WH}	Write Hold Time	0	—	—	ns
T_{AWS}	Address Set-up Time	0	—	—	ns
T_{AH}	Address Hold Time	10	—	—	ns
T_{CH}	Chip Select Hold Time	0	—	—	ns
T_{VD}	Valid Data	80	—	—	ns
T_{DH}	Data Hold Time	10	—	—	ns

EQUAL-TEMPERED MUSICAL SCALE VALUES

The table in Appendix E lists the numerical values which must be stored in the SID Oscillator frequency control registers to produce the notes of the equal-tempered musical scale. The equal-tempered scale consists of an octave containing 12 semitones (notes): C,D,E,F,G,A,B and C#,D#,F#,G#,A#. The frequency of each semitone is exactly the 12th root of 2 ($\sqrt[12]{2}$) times the frequency of the previous semitone. The table is based on a $\phi2$ clock of 1.02 MHz. Refer to the equation given in the Register Description for use of other master clock frequencies. The scale selected is concert pitch, in which A−4 = 440 Hz. Transpositions of this scale and scales other than the equal-tempered scale are also possible.

Although the table in Appendix E provides a simple and quick method for generating the equal-tempered scale, it is very memory inefficient as it requires 192 bytes for the table alone. Memory efficiency can be improved by determining the note value algorithmically. Using the fact that each note in an octave is exactly half the frequency of that note in the next octave, the note look-up table can be reduced from 96 entries to 12 entries, as there are 12 notes per octave. If the 12 entries (24 bytes) consist of the 16-bit values for the eighth octave (C-7 through B-7), then notes in lower octaves can be derived by choosing the appropriate note in the eighth octave and dividing the 16-bit value by two for each octave of difference. As division by two is nothing more than a right-shift of the value, the calculation can easily be accomplished by a simple software routine. Although note B-7 is beyond the range of the oscillators, this value should still be included in the table for calculation purposes (the MSB of B-7 would require a special software case, such as generating this bit in the CARRY before shifting). Each note must be specified in a form which indicates which of the 12 semitones is desired, and which of the eight octaves the semitone is in. Since four bits are necessary to select 1 of 12 semitones and three bits are necessary to select 1 of 8 octaves, the information can fit in one byte, with the lower nybble selecting the semitone (by addressing the look-up table) and the upper nybble being used by the division routine to determine how many times the table value must be right-shifted.

SID ENVELOPE GENERATORS

The four-part ADSR (ATTACK, DECAY, SUSTAIN, RELEASE) envelope generator has been proven in electronic music to provide the optimum trade-off between flexibility and ease of amplitude control. Appropriate selection of envelope parameters allows the simulation of a wide range of percussion and sustained instruments. The violin is a good example of a sustained instrument. The violinist controls the volume by bowing the instrument. Typically, the volume builds slowly, reaches a peak, then drops to an intermediate level. The violinist can maintain this level for as long as desired, then the volume is allowed to slowly die away. A "snapshot" of this envelope is shown below:

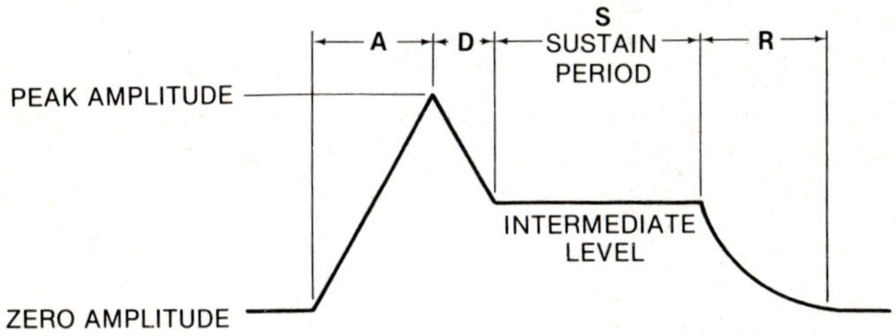

This volume envelope can be easily reproduced by the ADSR as shown below, with typical envelope rates:

ATTACK:	10 ($A)	500 ms
DECAY:	8	300 ms
SUSTAIN:	10 ($A)	
RELEASE:	9	750 ms

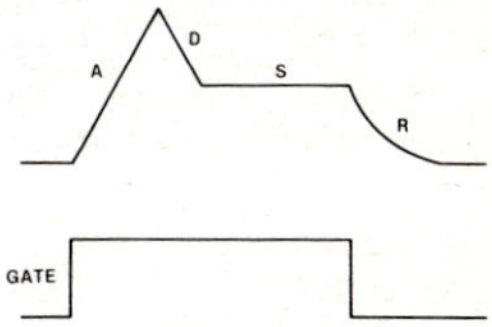

Note that the tone can be held at the intermediate SUSTAIN level for as long as desired. The tone will not begin to die away until GATE is cleared. With minor alterations, this basic envelope can be used for brass and woodwinds as well as strings.

An entirely different form of envelope is produced by percussion instruments such as drums, cymbals and gongs, as well as certain keyboards such as pianos and harpsichords. The percussion envelope is characterized by a nearly instantaneous attack, immediately followed by a decay to zero volume. Percussion instruments cannot be sustained at a constant amplitude. For example, the instant a drum is struck, the sound reaches full volume and decays rapidly regardless of how it was struck. A typical cymbal envelope is shown below:

ATTACK:	0	2ms
DECAY:	9	750ms
SUSTAIN:	0	
RELEASE:	9	750ms

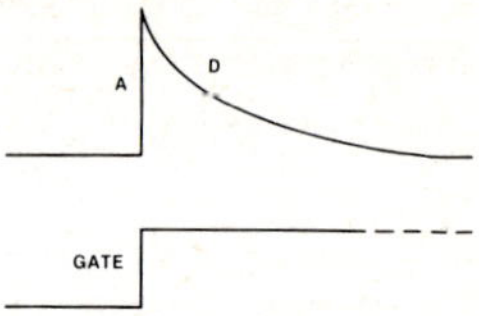

Note that the tone immediately begins to decay to zero amplitude after the peak is reached, regardless of when GATE is cleared. The amplitude envelope of pianos and harpsichords is somewhat more complicated, but can be generated quite easily with the ADSR. These instruments reach full volume when a key is first struck. The amplitude immediately begins to die away slowly as long as the key remains depressed. If the key is released before the sound has fully died away, the amplitude will immediately drop to zero. This envelope is shown below:

ATTACK:	0	2 ms
DECAY:	9	750 ms
SUSTAIN:	0	
RELEASE:	0	6 ms

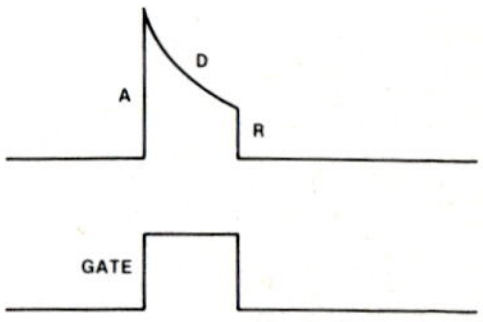

Note that the tone decays slowly until GATE is cleared, at which point the amplitude drops rapidly to zero.

The most simple envelope is that of the organ, When a key is pressed, the tone immediately reaches full volume and remains there. When the key is released, the tone drops immediately to zero volume. This envelope is shown below:

ATTACK:	0	2 ms
DECAY:	0	6 ms
SUSTAIN:	15 ($F)	
RELEASE:	0	6 ms

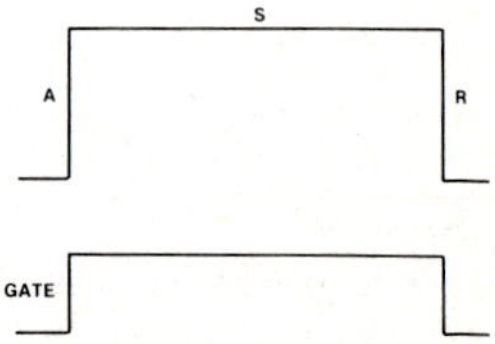

The real power of SID lies in the ability to create original sounds rather than simulations of acoustic instruments. The ADSR is capable of creating envelopes which do not correspond to any "real" instruments. A good example would be the "backwards" envelope. This envelope is characterized by a slow attack and rapid decay which sounds very much like an instrument that has been recorded on tape then played backwards. This envelope is shown below:

ATTACK:	10 ($A)	500 ms
DECAY:	0	6 ms
SUSTAIN:	15 ($F)	
RELEASE:	3	72 ms

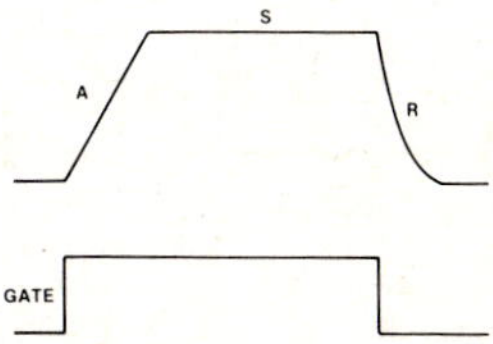

Many unique sounds can be created by applying the amplitude envelope of one instrument to the harmonic structure of another. This produces sounds similar to familiar acoustic instruments, yet notably different. In general, sound is quite subjective and experimentation with various envelope rates and harmonic contents will be necessary in order to achieve the desired sound.

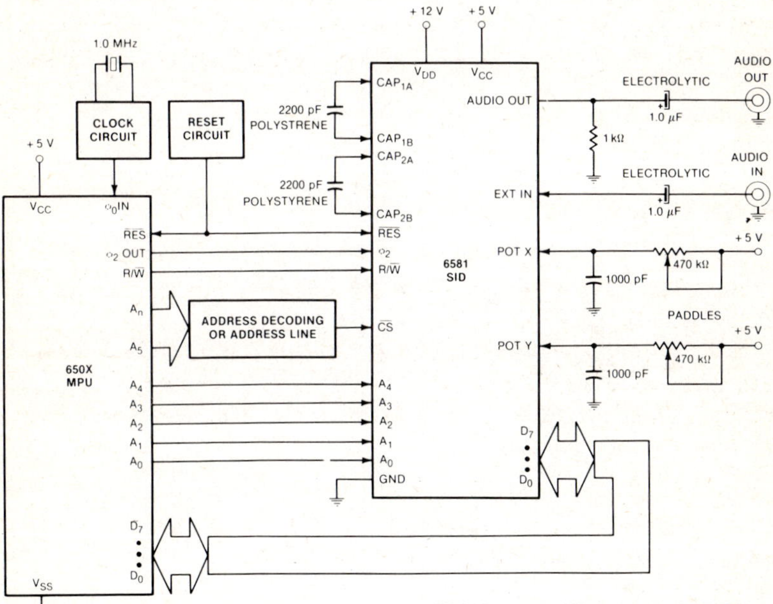

TYPICAL 6581/SID APPLICATION

APPENDIX P

GLOSSARY

ADSR	Attack/Decay/Sustain/Release envelope.
attack	Rate at which musical note reaches peak volume.
binary	Base-2 number system.
Boolean operators	Logical operators.
byte	Memory location.
CHROMA noise	Color distortion.
CIA	Complex Interface Adapter.
DDR	Data Direction Register.
decay	Rate at which musical note falls from peak volume to sustain volume.
decimal	Base-10 number system.
e	Mathematical constant (approx. 2.71828183).
envelope	Shape of the volume of a note over time.
FIFO	First-In/First-Out.
hexadecimal	Base-16 number system.
integer	Whole number (without decimal point).
jiffy clock	Hardware interval timer.
NMI	Non-Maskable Interrupt.
octal	Base-8 number system.
operand	Parameter.
OS	Operating System.
pixel	Dot of resolution on the screen.
queue	Single-file line.
register	Special memory storage location.
release	Rate at which a musical note falls from sustain volume to no volume.
ROM	Read-Only Memory.
SID	Sound Interface Device.
signed numbers	Plus or minus numbers.
subscript	Index variable.
sustain	Volume level for sustain of musical note.
syntax	Programming sentence structure.
truncated	Cut off, eliminated (*not* rounded).
VIC-II	Video Interface Chip.
video screen	Television set.

INDEX

COMMODORE 64 QUICK REFERENCE CARD

SIMPLE VARIABLES

Type	*Name*	*Range*
Real	XY	±1.70141183E+38
		±2.93873588E−39
Integer	XY%	±32767
String	XY$	0 to 255 characters

X is a letter (A-Z), Y is a letter or number (0-9). Variable names can be more than 2 characters, but only the first two are recognized.

ARRAY VARIABLES

Type	*Name*
Single Dimension	XY(5)
Two-Dimension	XY(5,5)
Three-Dimension	XY(5,5,5)

Arrays of up to eleven elements (subscripts 0-10) can be used where needed. Arrays with more than eleven elements need to be DIMensioned.

ALGEBRAIC OPERATORS

- = Assigns value to variable
- − Negation
- ↑ Exponentiation
- * Multiplication
- / Division
- + Addition
- − Subtraction

RELATIONAL AND LOGICAL OPERATORS

=	Equal
<>	Not Equal To
<	Less Than
>	Greater Than
<=	Less Than or Equal To
>=	Greater Than or Equal To
NOT	Logical "Not"
AND	Logical "And"
OR	Logical "Or"

Expression equals 1 if true, 0 if false.

SYSTEM COMMANDS

LOAD "NAME"	Loads a program from tape
SAVE "NAME"	Saves a program on tape
LOAD "NAME",8	Loads a program from disk
SAVE "NAME",8	Saves a program to disk
VERIFY "NAME"	Verifies that program was SAVEd without errors
RUN	Executes a program
RUN xxx	Executes program starting at line xxx
STOP	Halts execution
END	Ends execution
CONT	Continues program execution from line where program was halted
PEEK(X)	Returns contents of memory location X
POKE X,Y	Changes contents of location X to value Y
SYS xxxxx	Jumps to execute a machine language program, starting at xxxxx
WAIT X,Y,Z	Program waits until contents of location X, when EORed with Z and ANDed with Y, is nonzero.
USR(X)	Passes value of X to a machine language subroutine

EDITING AND FORMATTING COMMANDS

LIST	Lists entire program
LIST A-B	Lists from line A to line B
REM Message	Comment message can be listed but is ignored during program execution
TAB(X)	Used in PRINT statements. Spaces X positions on screen
SPC(X)	PRINTs X blanks on line
POS(X)	Returns current cursor position
CLR/HOME	Positions cursor to left corner of screen
SHIFT CLR/HOME	Clears screen and places cursor in "Home" position
SHIFT INST/DEL	Inserts space at current cursor position
INST/DEL	Deletes character at current cursor position
CTRL	When used with numeric color key, selects text color. May be used in PRINT statement.
CRSR Keys	Moves cursor up, down, left, right on screen
Commodore Key	When used with SHIFT selects between upper/lower case and graphic display mode. When used with numeric color key, selects optional text color

ARRAYS AND STRINGS

DIM A(X,Y,Z)	Sets maximum subscripts for A; reserves space for (X+1)*(Y+1)*(Z+1) elements starting at A(0,0,0)
LEN (X$)	Returns number of characters in X$
STR$(X)	Returns numeric value of X, converted to a string
VAL(X$)	Returns numeric value of A$, up to first nonnumeric character
CHR$(X)	Returns ASCII character whose code is X
ASC(X$)	Returns ASCII code for first character of X$
LEFT$(A$,X)	Returns leftmost X characters of A$
RIGHT$(A$,X)	Returns rightmost X characters of A$
MID$(A$,X,Y)	Returns Y characters of A$ starting at character X

INPUT/OUTPUT COMMANDS

INPUT A$ OR A	PRINTs '?' on screen and waits for user to enter a string or value
INPUT "ABC";A	PRINTs message and waits for user to enter value. Can also INPUT A$
GET A$ or A	Waits for user to type one-character value; no RETURN needed
DATA A,"B",C	Initializes a set of values that can be used by READ statement
READ A$ or A	Assigns next DATA value to A$ or A
RESTORE	Resets data pointer to start READing the DATA list again
PRINT "A= ";A	PRINTs string 'A= ' and value of A ';' suppresses spaces - ',' tabs data to next field.

PROGRAM FLOW

GOTO X	Branches to line X
IF A=3 THEN 10	IF assertion is true THEN execute following part of statement. IF false, execute next line number
FOR A=1 TO 10 STEP 2 : NEXT	Executes all statements between FOR and corresponding NEXT, with A going from 1 to 10 by 2. Step size is 1 unless specified
NEXT A	Defines end of loop. A is optional
GOSUB 2000	Branches to subroutine starting at line 2000
RETURN	Marks end of subroutine. Returns to statement following most recent GOSUB
ON X GOTO A,B	Branches to Xth line number on list. If X = 1 branches to A, etc.
ON X GOSUB A,B	Branches to subroutine at Xth line number in list

Get the most out of your Commodore computer with a subscription to Commodore's user magazines

POWER/PLAY

commodore

Fun, Games and Beyond with Commodore Home Computers

Published quarterly in March, June, September and December, POWER/PLAY is devoted solely to the exciting and rapidly expanding world of Commodore home computing. It provides valuable information on new products, applications, games, programming techniques, learning-at-home, telecommunications and just about anything else Commodore home computer users need to know to get maximum enjoyment out of their home computing experience. Subscription price: $10.00/year.

The Microcomputer Magazine

Widely read by educators, businessmen, students and home computerists, this bi-monthly publication provides a vehicle for sharing exclusive product information on Commodore systems, programming techniques, hardware interfacing, and applications for the wide range of Commodore's products. Each issue contains features of interest to anyone that uses, or is thinking about purchasing Commodore equipment. Get the most out of your microcomputer with Commodore Magazine. Subscription price: $15.00/year.

FILL OUT AND MAIL TODAY

Name ______________ Phone ______________

Address ______________

City ______________ State ______________ Zip ______________

Computer model: ______________

☐ Address Change. Enter new address above & enclose present mailing label
☐ Renewal subscription
☐ New subscription

GET MORE INFORMATION FOR YOUR MONEY

Please sign me up for:

___year(s) of POWER/PLAY at $10.00/year

___year(s) of COMMODORE at $15.00/year

Canadian and Foreign: POWER/PLAY $15.00/year; COMMODORE $25.00/year

Enclosed is my check or money order for $ ______________

Make check or money order payable to:
COMMODORE BUSINESS MACHINES, INC.
The Meadows, 487 Devon Park Drive, Wayne, PA 19087